MIXERMAN'S

ULTIMATE

GUIDE

TO

PRODUCING

RECORDS, MUSIC & SONGS

THE ANTIDOTE TO MISINFORMATION

EVERYTHING YOU NEED TO KNOW ABOUT
PRODUCING, RECORDING, MIXING & MASTERING
MUSIC AT HOME OR IN THE STUDIO

Published in 2025 by Mixerman Publishes

MIXERMAN
PUBLISHES

An Imprint of Mixerman Multimedia
Asheville, NC
mixerman@mixerman.net

Cover design by Jeff Mutschler

Library of Congress Cataloging-in-Publication Data is available upon request.

ISBN 13: 978-1-955652-03-2

Acknowledgments

Special thanks to my family, friends, and sponsors:

Tanya Rodriguez Sarafin

Maximilian Sarafin

Amanda Vallejo

Mom & Dad

Jeff Mutschler

John Creamer

Dave Rowe

LEWITT

IK Multimedia

FabFilter

PLEASE NOTE – PRODUCT QUALITY & FEEDBACK

This is a print-on-demand product, which can, on rare occasion, print improperly. You are entitled to a quality product.

If you purchased this book on Amazon or Ingram, please contact their customer service directly to request a replacement.

If there's any other problem—please email me directly.

If you find any errors in this book of any kind, I want to hear from you. Whether it's a syntax issue, something I missed, an inaccuracy, or something you think I should address in a future edition—or even if you just want to tell me what you think about the book—please don't hesitate to email me at mixerman@mixerman.net.

I read every message, and your feedback helps shape future editions.

Enjoy,
Mixerman

Contents

Chapter Three
The Home Producer   115

Chapter Four

The Many Roles of the Producer for Hire   301

Chapter Seven
Mixing & Mastering   503

Chapter Eight
The Politics of a Band Entity

Conclusion

Introductions

The Modern Producer

Let's face it. These days, everyone is a producer.

Artists have to be producers, songwriters have to be producers, musicians have to be producers, and most of those producers now have to be recordists, mixers, and mastering engineers too.

Rather than to reject that premise in an attempt to hold on to some archaic elitist notion of the past, I set out to write a modern producing guide that addresses the needs of *everyone*.

Well! That was a monumental task. Nearly 600 pages later, and we have the most comprehensive book I've ever written on the subject of producing recorded music.

Each of the recording disciplines—recording, mixing, mastering, and producing—requires many thousands of hours of practice. The engineering is technical and tedious and takes time and patience to understand. And it can be difficult to get accurate engineering information and strategies online. Misinformation and bad advice run rampant, and strategy is all but ignored. I've seen some highly suspect advice in videos from supposed experts. It's almost as if they seek to confuse people in an effort to keep them coming back for more.

Young producers are sold on all sorts of unnecessarily complicated ways to process their tracks, all so that they can achieve a "great sound." And while music is clearly a sonic medium, sound is really just a means to the end. We can manipulate how someone feels with sound, and we can cause them to react. If we're to place a value judgment on sound quality, it really must exist within the context of how it affects the listener.

Eliciting a reaction is the only goal that concerns me. After all, a hit record is pretty much defined as a widespread reaction to a song, which is surely the desired outcome. To focus on anything else is anathema to me.

That's not to say the engineering and sound design has no importance. It surely does, especially in sound-centric genres like house music. But success in this regard is built from the bottom up and is wholly dependent on the quality of the songs, the performances, and the arrangement. That's what makes up the sound. The engineering allows us to shape and influence tone, design the sound, and control dynamics, but it's the music and the performances that generate the response.

The problem is the engineering can be so obtrusive it can consume your focus. As you build your record, if it fails to meet your vision, the importance of your engineering processes tends to expand—just as your control over sound manipulation starts to diminish. Priorities go awry. Mastering is treated as more important than mixing, mixing as more important than recording and arranging, recording as more important than preproduction or vision—and somehow, the song itself ends up an afterthought.

Every seasoned producer worth their salt will tell you: that's completely backward. The mix is the culmination of your recording and arranging decisions. The master is merely a processed version of the mix so as to meet delivery specs. But if the song doesn't grab people's attention, then the sound is irrelevant. No music fan listens to a crap song only to be drawn in by the sound of it.

The way we produce and reproduce music has changed dramatically since I first began making records in the late '80s. CDs had just overtaken vinyl in terms of overall sales, but most recording studios were still almost completely analog. When I started to work professionally, I was recording to 2-inch tape and mixing to ½-inch tape through an analog console, with a somewhat limited collection of outboard gear. Now, like most of you, I record and mix into a computer, predominantly at home. I have no real limits on my processing choices.

In my earliest years, I only had 24 tracks available for my productions. I didn't have tuning software. I didn't have dynamic EQ. I had a limited number of compressors available—none of them were multiband compressors. I had a limited number of external EQs. Editing was done by cutting tape with a razor blade. There was no time-aligning or tuning things. I didn't even have automation available to me.

Given the inherent limitations in analog recording, every decision required strategy. Now? We have infinite tracks, endless plugins, and unlimited flexibility. You'd think that would make things easier, but in reality, an abundance of choices can be overwhelming, especially to those who are relatively new to producing. Unlimited flexibility, somewhat paradoxically, makes strategy more critical than ever.

An important part of the producer's job was (and still is) to keep the technology out of the way, often by hiring engineers and mixers. This way, the producer could concentrate on the big picture, the artist could focus on being an artist, and the engineer could handle all the technical details—ensuring a quality capture and an effective presentation.

Today you need to learn it all. Which is a little bit of a problem when you consider it took me nearly my whole life (thus far) to learn everything that I share with you in this guide. It takes years of dedicated focus across a varied set of circumstances to master any one discipline. It's absolutely insane to try to master them all at once. But this is now the world that we live in, and the reason for this book.

My Producing Journey

I started piano at the age of 6. I was classically trained, and by the time I was a senior in high school, I was performing Chopin and Rachmaninoff works—which are some of the most challenging piano works to play. I picked up the trumpet at 8, was first chair in my High School Wind Ensemble and lead trumpet for the jazz band.

In 1985 I went to Rutgers University to study jazz piano with Kenny Barron, one of the world's great straight-ahead jazz pianists. I was relatively new to jazz, and it didn't take long to realize I wanted to work in more contemporary music. I also didn't see myself as a professional player. I definitely wanted to be in music. I just didn't really know how yet.

The next year, I transferred to Berklee College of Music in Boston, where I studied Songwriting among other things. I really had no intention of graduating—I didn't need a degree to make my mark in music, had no interest in teaching, and felt back-up plans were prone to back*firing*. So, I changed my major four times just so that I could take specific classes that interested me most.

After my first year at Berklee, I landed at Dimension Sound, a 24-track analog studio in Jamaica Plain, a suburb South of Boston. This was where George Thoroughgood had recorded several of his albums, including his iconic hit "Bad to the Bone."

I lived above the studio and had 24-hour access to the room. I knew almost instantly that was where I belonged. The studio was home to me. I also had mentors to teach me and spent the next four years cutting my teeth as a record maker and engineer, both on my own songs and for outside clients. It took me that long before I was even "good" at any of it.

By the time 1991 rolled around, I made the move to Los Angeles. I wanted to work on big records, and the best way to do that was to live in close proximity to the industry. And although I grew up an hour outside of NYC, I couldn't take the cold any longer. Los Angeles it was.

My first gig upon arriving in Los Angeles was on the Setup staff at Capitol Studios, where I learned how to set up large orchestral sessions. This was largely a glorified runner gig, but there was plenty of setting up and tearing down to do. The biggest acts of the time came through Capitol, and I learned a lot during my six-month stint there.

At the end of 1991, I left Capitol and took a gig as a house engineer at Hollywood Sound. The engineers' room was full of rock guys, and none of them were particularly interested in working on hip-hop. So, I took most of the available hip-hop gigs. Not only did I enjoy hip-hop, but I also much preferred working as a recordist rather than as an assistant.

A month or two in, I was assisting on a session for the Pharcyde, who were having their first single mixed in Studio B. I was in the back of the room with Mike Ross, the President of Delicious Vinyl, as he vented about how much he disliked recording at a studio down the road. I asked why he didn't just record at Hollywood Sound. Apparently, he didn't want to spend $800 a day just to record vocals. This I could understand. I also had a solution.

The owner of Hollywood Sound, Jesse Hodges, had installed a production room upstairs, complete with a Spectral Sonics DAW. Mind you, this was long before DAWs had even begun creeping into studios—very few producers were using them. The industry hadn't even gone through its ADAT phase yet. Jesse wanted $35 an hour for the room and the DAW, the same rate

Mike was paying at the other studio. So, I showed him the room, introduced him to the DAW, and convinced him to record the album there—with me, given my experience as a recordist.

The next evening, I was recording vocals with the Pharcyde. They really only knew me as an assistant, and one of them got the bright idea to hold the Neumann U47—which, for those who don't know, is not designed to be held. It's a large, sensitive mic, usually suspended in a shock mount. Naturally, I told them there would be an inordinate amount of rustling noise, booms and pops, making their vocal recordings largely unusable. I even demonstrated it on playback. Somehow, they didn't seem to mind it. Regardless, I wasn't going to tell them "No." This was a test of my loyalties.

Mike approached me the next evening, as if to relieve me of my duties. Clearly, he'd heard the roughs from the previous night's recordings. Sensing urgency, I quickly explained what had happened.

"They held the 47!"

He was incredulous. "Why would you let them do that!"

"Because if I had stopped them on our very first session to- gether, they wouldn't trust me," I explained. That seemed to satisfy him. He grabbed a scrap of paper, jotted down his car phone number, and then called the group into the room for a meeting.

"No more holding the 47!" he bellowed. Then, as he turned to leave, he overtly handed me his number, looked at the group, and yelled again, "And you need to listen to Eric! He knows what he's doing!"

I spent the next eight months recording *Bizarre Ride II the Pharcyde*, which became my first gold record—and ultimately, one of the quintessential hip-hop albums of all time. Proximity clearly had its benefits, as did practice and preparation. I was paid $120 a day to record that album, which wasn't much even back then. Whatever. Success begets success in this industry, and that album paved the way toward my future.

I parlayed the success of that Pharcyde album into several years of mixing hip-hop, soul, and acid jazz albums—almost exclusively. I went fully independent in 1993 while mixing The Brand New Heavies *Brother Sister* album. In fact, Vicki Giordano, the traffic manager at Hollywood Sound, let me go as staff right in the middle of mixing it. Perhaps as a favor—because on Wednesday, I was making $10 an hour as a staff engineer. On Thursday, I was making $35 an hour, paid directly by the label, for the exact same work.

I loved mixing these genres. They were fresh, and I enjoyed the music. Of course, I didn't have much choice in the matter—those were the gigs that came my way, so those were the gigs I took. Lots of them.

Even so, I had concerns about being pigeonholed as a hip-hop mixer. I wanted to work across a diverse range of musical styles, and becoming too entrenched in one genre had its pitfalls. My ultimate goal was to be a producer, and as much as I liked hip-hop, I was a cultural outsider—I wasn't a beat-maker, nor did I want to be. That put a cap on how far I could advance within the genre, and to me, that was a problem.

Then, as if on cue, opportunity knocked.

In the summer of 1995, I got a call from Andy Factor at Virgin Records to mix Ben Harper. Michael Andrews—the guitarist for The Greyboy Allstars, whom I'd worked with on a Karl Denson album collaboration—had personally recommended me for the gig. Michael is now a somewhat notable film composer.

Andy was calling me about Ben's upcoming sophomore release, *Fight for Your Mind*. Apparently, they had already gone through three mixers, all of them stunningly big names in rock music—all of them summarily dismissed. I literally laughed out loud when he told me the name of the last mixer they'd fired—that's how shocking it was to me.

I was to start right away. I went to the studio that very day.

Ben and his manager, JP Plunier, wanted to make a roots rock record with hip-hop sensibilities, and those famous rock mixers either couldn't—or simply didn't—mix like that. I couldn't understand why the big-name mixers weren't using more low end. We no longer had limitations on bass with CDs, so why was everyone still acting like we did?

Here I was—a child of rock music with three years of mixing hip-hop records under my belt—and these guys wanted to fuse the sound of rock with the low end of modern '90s hip-hop? Yes, please.

Suffice it to say, this gig was right up my alley. Not only did I mix the album with plenty of low end, but I also kept it completely dry. There isn't a single reverb or delay on that entire record, which happened to align with the trends of the time. But I didn't choose that approach because it was trendy—Ben just sounded more intimate and honest without reverb or delay, and that felt like the most effective treatment.

For every track, I was given a pristine, well-comped vocal and a scratch vocal—Ben's live take while tracking the band. JP told me to choose whichever I thought was best. I chose the scratch vocal every time.

They were raw, honest, expressive, and compelling. They also came with a fair share of blatant klunkers and engineering challenges. That didn't matter to me. They made the record like that.

After *Fight for Your Mind* I couldn't get a hip-hop gig to save my life. Once word got out in hip-hop circles that I had mixed a rock record, I was suddenly no longer considered a hip-hop mixer. From that point forward, I was a rock mixer. The shift was immediate.

I had asked for $1,000 per mix on that album, and that became my new rate. I should have priced myself closer to the mixers they'd fired. My $1,000 was surely a bargain. Lesson learned.

In hindsight, I'm actually fortunate I didn't lose the gig for pricing myself too low. People at major labels often view value with suspicion—the more outrageous your price, the more they wanted you. That was the game, though I didn't fully understand it until later.

In 1997, I returned to Capitol Studios—this time as a client—to mix Ben Harper's album *Will to Live*. Two years later, I recorded and mixed *Burn to Shine*, which featured his exceptionally popular "Steal My Kisses." I spent six months with JP, Ben, and all of the Innocent Criminals recording that album. I was paid $500 a day to record and $2,000 per mix.

In the early aughts, manager Gary Waldman approached me about joining his boutique roster of engineers and producers, which included Jim Scott—who was working with some of the biggest rock acts of the time. Gary connected me with Acetone, a beautiful indie band with a cult following, and I produced York Blvd for them. Sadly, it would be their last studio album due to the untimely death of their singer and bassist Richie Lee.

At Gary's urging, I began taking gigs as a dedicated recordist. By this point, I had been mixing almost exclusively for six years. My goal was to produce records, but transitioning from mixer to producer was proving difficult at best. Gary believed that working as a recordist would make that transition easier, so that's what I did. I was probably just as skilled a recordist as I was a mixer, and I was able to command $1,000 a day for the work.

Over the next few years, I recorded Nine Days, Lifehouse, Barenaked Ladies, Days of the New, and a slew of other acts that never quite broke through. One year, I recorded two albums with $500,000 budgets—neither of which ever saw the light of day. One of them was Nine Days' sophomore album.

Once the album was finished, the band was dropped. As one of their label reps allegedly put it, "We don't think we can sell more than 500,000 copies, and we don't want to waste one of our radio spots for that." And just like that, the completed album was shelved.

In 2005, I produced *See the Sun* for Australian phenom Pete Murray. This was his sophomore album, following a six-times-platinum debut. It was my biggest album as a producer, and it did very well for me. I'm not going to tell you what I made on that album, but it was a lot.

In 2009, I returned to Australia to produce *Smash the Piñata* for the hard-rock band Mammal. I brought the tracks home to mix in my house, where I had cobbled together a bunch of acoustic panels, bought an overblown cheese-grater Mac, and set up all my gear in my home office. Unfortunately, the room was far too small for any real acoustic accuracy, and my first round of mixes was completely out of whack. Nothing I did seemed to fix the problem—it only frustrated me more.

So, I called my buddy Wyn Davis and mixed the album at his studio, Total Access, in Redondo Beach. That was an expensive lesson.

In 2011, Wyn had two Foreigner albums to mix but only enough time for one. He asked me to mix the other, but I didn't have a proper room at the time, and renting one wasn't an option given the budget. He suggested I try again to set up a mix room at home—so I did, this time in my garage.

It wasn't perfect, but it was a far cry better than my first attempt. Foreigner was happy with the mixes (as was I), so that's where I mixed for the next few years.

From 2008 to 2015, I was working as both a mixer and a producer-for-hire. I produced a number of Asheville, NC acts out of Echo Mountain, a high-end studio in town. I loved the recording space—it had my favorite Neve console, a ton of great mics, and a collection of high-quality instruments, including some coveted vintage guitars and amplifiers. I could efficiently record everything there.

These were all reasonably well-funded independent albums, which meant I didn't have to deal with labels, and I could bring the tracks home to my garage to mix.

By 2015, I moved my family to Asheville, NC. My mix work was coming in from all over the world, label budgets had bottomed out, and proximity to the industry was no longer an advantage. I certainly had no interest in doing the same work for multi-billion-dollar companies at a quarter of the price. I could no longer justify paying LA prices anymore—not even for the weather.

Since moving to Asheville, I've set up three home mix rooms, each better than the last. I'm certainly no acoustician, but with the wealth of information available online, I was able to create a viable and accurate monitoring space.

It took years of trial and error before I was able to purpose-build my current room, which is so accurate that I now master my own mixes there. I even take the occasional mastering gig when it suits me.

Over the course of my career, I've recorded some of the greatest and most highly regarded players in the world. I've also recorded some of the worst—and everything in between. I've mixed hundreds upon hundreds of songs in some of the best rooms in the world and spent years trying to create a viable mix space at home. I've recorded full productions entirely from my house.

I've made countless records in numerous capacities with budgets ranging from $500,000 to as low as $20,000. I've had complex contracts drawn up by lawyers, and I've written my own that amounted to nothing more than a plain-language email spelling out the terms. I've played on records. Sung background vocals. Written parts. Fully arranged records, including horn and string sections. I know music theory, voice leading, and can identify any musical interval by ear. Over the years, I've even developed nearly perfect pitch.

All of that to say—you're in good hands.

If you want to better understand the full scope of my music career—including the supremely talented musicians, artists, and producers I've worked with—check out my profile on Muso.ai. You'll find me under my given name, Eric Sarafin.

Introducing Mixerman

In 1999, I joined Usenet, which was (and I suppose still is) the unmoderated Wild West of the internet. The level of vitriol was so jarring that I didn't dare post more than a few times under my given name. I made the decision to post anonymously. Mixerman was born.

In 2002, I started writing an online journal about my recording session with a bidding war band and an infamous producer, which I titled *The Daily Adventures of Mixerman*. The whole thing was a ruse—a satire—which I was posting daily as Mixerman on my own Internet audio forum, as if it was all happening in real time. The internet was still relatively new and littered with mundane blogs—a term I refused to even use. This was no blog. It was a somewhat sensational troll, and it seemed the entire industry was all too eager to take the bait.

Every day I would post up a new entry, and the audience would increase in size. I began to get emails from friends—some of them on tour with major acts—recommending I read the entries. Music Industry audio boards were pinging with long discussion threads. Half the participants were shredding me for so brazenly sharing the private details of a session, the other half commended me for it. Self-proclaimed internet sleuths sought to find the session, going so far as to call LA studios and ask for Mixerman. People wanted to know, who was the band?

Who was this producer? Who was Mixerman, and how can he get away with this? It was utter madness.

I went from 200 views per day when I began my story to 150,000 daily views by the time I wrapped it up on the nascent internet. I had become more well-known in the industry as Mixerman than many of my peers with far more impressive discographies at the time. The story was so controversial, it took years before I ever dared to publicly admit I was Mixerman.

In 2008, Hal Leonard published *The Daily Adventures of Mixerman* as a hardcover book under my *nom de plume*. In 2012, I created an audiobook adaptation with my good friend and sidekick, Aardvark. I modeled it after *The Firesign Theatre* works, drawing inspiration from the golden age of radio in the 1930s and 1940s—complete with music, foley, sound effects, and performances by some of the most heralded producers and engineers in the world. More recently, I reworked it into a podcast, now available for free on all the major platforms. If you want an insider's look at just how wacky this business can be—and you like to be entertained—it's well worth a listen.

In 2010 Hal Leonard published my second book *Zen and the Art of MIXING*, which I revised and self-published in 2021. That book is my best-selling work, by far. In 2012 I wrote *Zen and the Art of Producing,* also published by HL. In 2018 I wrote and self-published *Musician's Survival Guide to a Killer Record.*

And Here We Are

This book began as a revision of *Zen and the Art of Producing* (*2012*), which primarily addressed the for-hire producer working out of rented studios. But even I don't make records like that anymore. Sure, I'll book a studio for drums on a band project or to track a horn section, but the majority of my producing work now happens at home. As such, my original producing book seemed more like a throwback to another time. It was also written for what is now an impossibly niche audience. I couldn't revise my way out of this. I had to completely overhaul and expand the work, conceptually and structurally.

Once I'd made the decision to significantly broaden the scope of the book, it was clear I'd need months of intense focus in order to write, revise, and organize it. I would have to greatly limit the number of projects I'd take on as I did. So, I sought sponsorships from companies whose products I use every day in my work—ones that would make any producer's life easier, regardless of skill level. LEWITT, FabFilter, and IK Multimedia all stepped up with sponsorship funding, and I am greatly appreciative for their support.

The organization of this book was the most challenging part. Producing music isn't a linear process, nor is it learned in a linear manner. It's far more circular in nature. Further complicating matters, every one of you reading this, comes with your own unique knowledge base and experience level.

How do you organize interdependent processes—each affecting the other—for an audience with vastly different levels of experience, all in a linear manner? I can answer that. You don't. And you can't. At least I couldn't. What comes out resembles more of a zig zag, where at times, one concept, which may seem completely unrelated, comes out of another. "May seem" being the operative phrase here.

If you've read any of my other books, you'll know that I sometimes enter into massive digressions, to the point that I even call them out as such. I always thought that was just my style—perhaps to some degree it is—but now that I've tried to organize this much information into one exhaustive resource, I now understand the crux of the issue. Everything affects everything else where it comes to producing music, and it all relates to manipulating emotions through sound.

Despite its importance, you won't find a dedicated "Sound Design" section in this book—because everything you do affects the sound. Every decision—your arrangement, your recording choices, the quality of the performances you capture, how you think about space, instrumentation, and musical function, how (and why) you use processors and plugins, how you apply motion and shape distortion, even your approach to artistic refinement—all of that falls under sound design. The sound is so deeply intertwined with the song and the music, that by the time you reach the *Mixing & Mastering* chapter, you'll already have everything you need to set you up for a great mix.

I structured this book in a way that allows producers at nearly any level to follow along, other than the absolute beginner. Even so, you might occasionally come across a term before I've had the chance to fully flesh it out. This was unavoidable. Had I stopped to define every technical term the moment it appeared, this book would be unreadable. So, if you run into an unfamiliar term, *look it up*—factual information in regard to technical terminology is just a quick search away.

Of course, the factual technical information that I offer throughout isn't what sets this book apart. Anyone who has experience engineering music for enough time can relay that to you. My early books barely touched on it. The musical and practical decisions that shape a record are of far more value than understanding the technical ones, and that's what my books have always addressed first and foremost.

In my first version of *Zen and the Art of Mixing*, I don't even talk about how to control a compressor. Which may seem baffling, but learning how to use a compressor really just requires some practice. In the early part of my career, I was mixing records on a daily basis, including gold ones, yet I couldn't have described to you specifically how to control a compressor. I just twisted knobs aggressively until I heard something I liked. And if that didn't work? I'd try a different compressor.

In fact, I wore my lack of technical expertise as a badge of honor. My processing tools were not technical instruments to me, but rather musical ones meant to be pushed well beyond their limits. I wanted to break them in the process. I couldn't care less what those timid engineer-types considered optimal. Frankly, I took offense to being called an engineer. *Mixer!* I would retort.

As far as I was concerned, I was an artist, just like the artists and producers who hired me to shape their sound and maximize their impact. The gear was merely there for me to mangle and control the sound. I made my decisions purely by ear, often relying on hit-or-miss strategies.

Over time, of course, I figured out what all the knobs did and how the controls worked. When I transitioned fully to digital— which is far less forgiving than analog—I was almost forced to learn the technicalities. Writing about it forced that too. And while that knowledge gave me more control and at times made the process more efficient, it certainly didn't make me a better mixer or producer.

Worry not—I can, and do, explain how to control our most important processors, breaking down the technical side in a way that's easy to understand and digest. It's the technical considerations that trip people up, especially in a world where mentoring has gone to die, and bad information is spread around online like the plague. That's why this guide is so comprehensive—because you need reliable, accurate technical knowledge. But make no mistake—the real value lies in the perspective I offer you.

This entire book comes from my unique perspective as a successful professional music-maker with a diverse discography— one that spans decades of changes in technology and musical trends. I don't just explain *how* to produce, but *why* certain decisions matter. And not just why *I* make certain decisions, but why *you* might make certain decisions—whether musical, technical, organizational, monetary, or even political in nature. All of it based on real-world practicalities. That's the good stuff.

There is information and insight in this guide that you just won't find anywhere else.

I will often offer you my preferences to go along with my explanations, all of them based on strategy within the context of musical decisions. There is no strategy that works for all people in all situations. There is only the strategy that best fits the moment, the music, the talent, your goals, and your preferences. Over time you'll develop your own strategies, based on your own experiences and needs. You may even reject my advice at times, which you should. That's one of the more effective ways for you to eventually realize I'm right.

Ahem.

There is no technique in producing music that could be considered invalid. If it works, it works. As such, you'll get my opinions, but you'll find very little dogma on my part. I seek to arm you with strategies to help *you* achieve *your* vision, so that you can create music and songs with intent, exactly as you hear it.

Ultimately, music is meant to evoke feelings from great songs. There is no right or wrong where it comes to the creation of art. There is only your intent, how easily you express that intent, and how you use it to connect with an audience. Nothing else matters.

That's what this book offers you. Whether you're a semi-beginner producing your own songs or even a somewhat seasoned Producer For-Hire. I've discussed everything I could think of in this guide—all of it designed to help you to work in a more effective and creative manner. This is true whether you do everything yourself at home or manage a team in the studio.

Given the broad range of the information, you may come across sections that you feel don't pertain to you. Far be it for me to tell you how to read a book, but I would advise against skipping sections, even if you feel they have little relevance to your circumstance. Even as a self-producer, understanding every role in the process will make you better at producing your own work.

Surely you can jump around and try to derive the information that you feel applies directly to you, but you will surely miss out on countless insights that I weave in throughout the book. Like I said, this is not a linear process, and concepts that can assist you may come from unexpected places.

If you want to be the most effective producer you can be, you need to know everything. That's the point of the book after all. To explain *everything*.

Now that we've gotten the introductions out of the way, let's dive in.

CHAPTER ONE

The Producer

Positioning

"Positioning" is a well-established marketing term. It refers to how you are positioned in the market (go figure). For instance, a Volvo is positioned as a "safe car." A Lexus is positioned as a "luxury car." All successful products have a position in the market, and that position offers appeal in niche markets.

Despite their specific positions, the Volvo and Lexus are both cars and perform the same overall function. Yet, the makers of these cars focus on one specific selling point in order to attract a particular customer. Generally, the position of a product is purposeful. Lexus loads its cars with features that make them luxurious and advertises them as such. Volvo makes sure its cars get high safety ratings, and markets that feature to parents seeking to protect their children. As service providers, we also have a position. We just have limited control over it.

If you want to be a producer, the first thing you need to address is your positioning, both real and perceived. The primary way others judge you is through your record of past work. Further complicating matters is the relatively short shelf life of that work. Yes, the "What have you done lately?" attitude is alive and well in this business—I imagine it always will be.

Your position determines the kinds of records you're most likely to win or lose. If you're known first and foremost as an engineer (based on your discography), you're not likely to produce a singer-songwriter seeking a Songwriter Producer. You could be a fantastic songwriter, but if you're not known as a songwriter, you're positioned as an engineer, whether you like it or not.

Conversely, if you've spent your career writing highly successful vacuous pop songs (I'm not criticizing), then you'll be virtually hog-tied to that kind of record—that is, until you can convince someone you're capable of producing other genres. If you've spent your career producing records that are über-edited and tuned, you'll have a difficult time winning a wholly organic roots record. If you're bristling at the idea of being pigeonholed like this, *good*. Getting past the denial is the first step toward fixing the problem. People will try to pigeonhole you for your entire career and beyond. Understand this.

To change your perceived position is not an easy task. It takes time, and you don't have a tremendous amount of control in the process, although you do have some influence. The first step is to figure out your current market perception. If you feel you have no position at the moment, because you've come to this book as a Self-Producer, that may be true. That doesn't make the information superfluous. You have no idea what twists and turns your career might take, and you should understand the various positions from which producers operate.

Most people don't wake up one day and decide that they want to produce records with absolutely no experience making music in some capacity. Typically, producers transition from some other positions in music. Given enough record-making experience, songwriters, musicians, engineers, artists and studio owners are all in a reasonable position to transition into producing.

There are many different kinds of producers, and we should define them in order to better understand positioning. I'll warn you now: very few people fit neatly into any one of these categories. They are wholly unfair stereotypes, and I promise you that my intent isn't to further propagate pigeonholing in this industry. Unfortunately, we must deal with realities, and you will be spoken of, and about, in these terms as you are considered for projects. Worse yet, most of the time you will not be present to defend yourself or correct the record.

That said, sometimes your position works to your advantage. It's how you attract clients that fit within your current skillsets. But in the long run, as you develop other skillsets, you may want to branch out, which requires confronting your perceived position. The first step is to understand how the market perceives you.

For those of you producing your own records, you aren't positioned as a producer, but rather as an artist. That's the way it works, because to some degree, no matter the situation, you are innately considered a producer of your own work.

The reality is, you won't be known as a producer until you begin to produce others, at which point your position will very much come into play. In order to effectively produce yourself, however, it's helpful to fully understand all of the producer positions, and what a good producer brings to the project.

The Songwriter Producer

When I wrote *Zen & the Art of Producing* back in 2012, the songwriter was one of the weakest positions from which to become a producer. Now it's by far the strongest.

In the olden days, when records were still primarily made in dedicated commercial studios, Songwriter Producers were generally relegated to demos, which they delivered to a publisher to shop. There was a psychology to a good demo, and it usually entailed dumbing-down the product to attract both an artist and a producer. The worst thing a writer could do is turn in a demo so fantastic that no producer dared to touch the track for fear of failing to improve upon it. As such, songwriters often developed all the wrong skills.

The modern DAW has changed all of that. Between perfect recall, and the ability to program and record tracks at home, the songwriter had more time to develop their production skills. The two jobs have become nearly synonymous in the pop production world. If you write in any of the pop music genres, you probably also produce your records, and this is true at the earliest stages of your development.

Songwriter Producers are often directly involved with every facet of the record from inception to completion. They write the song, program the track, record the singer (the artist), record parts, and may even mix the record, regardless of whether they're currently qualified for such tasks. Of course, you become qualified at something by repeatedly doing it.

For many Songwriter Producers, the song and the production are of equal importance. You can't present the song in a compelling manner without the production. They are inexorably attached. Without a production, a song is merely an idea, and to bring that idea to fruition, there must be a production.

Most Songwriter Producers today write and program pop music, which is a genre that all but requires a somewhat fresh production. Please understand, I use the term "pop music" here in a very broad manner. You can classify a genre as anything you like—R&B, electronica, house, hip-hop, reggaeton—if the production is mostly programmed and meant to appeal to a large array of listeners, that's pop music where it comes to production.

Oddly, the best way to achieve a fresh production is to use trendy production techniques, which admittedly may seem somewhat counterintuitive, but consider the alternatives. You can use techniques that are wholly out of fashion which will result in a stale production from an undefinable era. On the other end of the spectrum, you can create something so unique and outside of the mainstream that nobody will even understand it. The goal in producing a popular song isn't to make something wholly new. The goal is to make something that's mostly familiar but comes off fresh.

To be clear, "retro" productions that are meant to remind us of a rather distant era of music are always in fashion to some degree, and can still sound modern, to boot.

Of course, you can make a production sound downright silly if you employ every trendy production technique there is, regardless of whether it fits the song or not. Which is why the Songwriter Producer is such an effective position from which to operate. If you write a somewhat trendy song, then a modern production will often fit perfectly. And since the song and the production tend to be developed simultaneously, the Songwriter Producer can more easily push trends into new territory.

Songwriter Producers, particularly those who have had successful songwriting careers, are exceptionally strong when it comes to working with solo artists lacking material and can be desirable for bands or artists in need of help improving their songs.

It only takes but one hit song to make your entire career. And while nobody wants just one hit, the payoff of a popular record can be so great for the songwriter, that it makes sense to invest time into your craft before a budget ever even exists. As a songwriter, it's critical to develop your arrangement and sound design chops for purposes of producing your songs. Either that, or you need a partner who can cover that side of things.

There is no budget for writing your song, because as a songwriter, you need to write, program and record as many songs as possible. This is how you attract an artist to your song. You must invest time in your "demos" because these will ultimately become the record. As such, the Songwriter Producer is often working in a speculative manner.

If there's any stigma to be had for the modern-day Songwriter Producer, it's that their skill set is often limited to programmed material. That can make you rather one-dimensional, which is always fraught in the music business, because fads, trends, and production styles are guaranteed to change. Meanwhile, you're perceived as outdated.

The Musician Producer

The Musician Producer comes from a musical background. Some musicians migrate to producing because their run of success has either ended or peaked. Some transition to producing because it interests them, or because they're tired of touring. Regardless of the reason, those known as Musician Producers are typically highly proficient at an instrument (maybe several) and are often hired because of this. There is much respect in the music industry for well-regarded musicians and artists who become producers, making this one of the better positions from which to transition.

Musician Producers aren't viewed as having engineering skills, although that's not really an issue since most producers need to perform many of the engineering tasks these days. Musician Producers who are hired largely for their prowess on an instrument may be inclined to perform on the records they make. This can limit you to artists who seek your performances on their album. You may want to be careful about how often you play on records and be very wary of overshadowing your artists as a performer.

The Engineer Producer

In the past, it's been rare for me to use the term "engineer," as I prefer the terms recordist and mixer, but Engineer Producer is an already established category within the industry lexicon— a term I have no control over. So, I relent. Frankly, the pure Engineer Producer is my least favorite kind of producer, perhaps because I am often labeled this way despite my musical background (I told you these aren't always fair classifications). The Engineer Producer is typically categorized as having little musical knowledge and no proficiency on a musical instrument. In many cases, that's actually true.

The Engineer Producer is brought onto projects for their ability to capture great tones. Given these perception issues, the pure Engineer Producer is typically limited to producing bands, or artists who want full control over their musical arrangement decisions. Bands come with songs and even arrangements, and may not feel they need a musical expert, but rather seek someone who can keep the technology out of their way and perhaps act as an arbiter so as to push the record forward.

If you're an engineer wishing to transition into a producing career, and you worry that this perception will limit you (and it will), then the only way to broaden your appeal is to demonstrate your understanding of music. Just for the sake of client perception alone, it's helpful if you're able to converse musically. Otherwise, you'll have no way of overcoming the stigma attached to engineers. I would know. If you look at my discography, it appears that I come from an engineering background. Despite all of my experience in music, I still, at times, come up against the engineering stigma.

Many times, when I first meet with a band in need of a producer, they think they want an Engineer Producer, and that I would operate as such. They are soon disabused of that notion, as I sell them on my vision in which I am intimately involved in every facet of the record production. It's not unusual for a band to go into a meeting with me seeking a glorified engineer and come out excited to have a driving creative force behind their record.

It's always amusing to me when I'm on a session, and the musicians assume I know little about music. They take me far more seriously when I shatter that misconception with a well-timed comment. The best is when I can call out a particular note or interval by ear and then explain why it should or shouldn't be in a particular chord. The change in attitude and respect is immediate. From that moment on, I'm one of them, and I have their full faith and trust. Perception matters.

The Music Fan Producer

While you would think that this is an impossible position from which to become a producer, I happen to personally know some exceptionally talented Music Fan Producers. In fact, I've probably worked with the best there is when it comes to this breed of producer. J. P. Plunier, for one. He produced the first four Ben Harper albums and Jack Johnson's highly successful Freshman effort. JPs only previous musical experience was as a dance club owner in France.

The strength of this position comes from a deep-rooted understanding of music and production history. The Music Fan Producer gains all of their musical knowledge by evaluating records. They are so keenly aware of the production techniques that have been used over the years that they have an invaluable and innate sense of what works, even if they have no idea why. Furthermore, the Music Fan Producer is typically exceptional at combining genres and styles and brings to record-making what an interior decorator brings to a living space—vibe.

The most successful record producer of all time comes from this position. Music Fan Producer can bring a fresh vision to a record through their historical knowledge of music. While it's true that this producer is somewhat limited in the kinds of records they can accept, a team of musicians and engineers can compensate for their shortcomings. Personally, I would much rather be involved with a Music Fan Producer than an Engineer Producer, mostly because the results with the former are far less predictable and therefore less safe. When producing music, we generally want to avoid "safe." At least, I do.

The Default Producer

If you're working for a studio, and you end up as the house engineer on a project without a producer, you become the producer by default—often without credit. If you prove yourself valuable, you can sometimes negotiate a co-producer's credit from this position once the album is done, or just before. If the idea is met with resistance, worry not! You gained valuable experience. Nearly every young studio engineer has acted as Default Producer on numerous occasions, and that includes me. It's part of the learning process.

Just keep in mind that as you work on records, you define your position. If you're credited regularly as an engineer on these records, guess what? You'll be positioned as an Engineer Producer in the future. If you can take steps to broaden your appeal, this is the best time to do it. If you already know music, make sure that you use that knowledge and convert those into credits that work to boost your perceived position (perhaps as a performer or arranger).

The Studio Owner Producer

The Studio Owner Producer has only one qualification for producing—a capital investment in audio gear. Believe it or not, people with absolutely no experience making records or even music, sometimes buy or build a studio. Don't ask me why anyone would do that. It's generally a terrible business model when you don't have a brand as a known engineer or producer. Even in those cases, the move is often met with regret. The only way to really make the business model work is if a Real Estate purchase is involved.

While it's possible to become a successful producer from this position, the amount of learning necessary is monumental. If you're starting out weak in both musical and engineering knowledge, that can prove a difficult position from which to break free.

The Studio Owner Producer's monthly nut alone often forces them to concentrate on filling studio time first and foremost. Typically, this means that the Studio Owner Producer is offering the artist studio time in exchange for experience and the title of producer. That said, it's a completely legitimate place from which to become a producer. Just understand, your improvement and success rate will likely be slow as you must learn every aspect of record-making concurrently and on the job.

I don't care how experienced you are in the studio—producing is a long development process coming from just about any position. But at least with the other positions, one already has a proven skill set useful for record-making. If your only qualification is a collection of gear in a treated recording space, then that makes you more of a studio owner than a *bona fide* Engineer Producer.

Further complicating matters, given the need to meet studio overhead demands, the Studio Owner Producer will often have a long succession of critical failures. These can be difficult to overcome and can greatly minimize one's chances of success. I would imagine that most people who invest their trust fund into a recording studio have also dabbled in record-making to some degree. But if you're a trust-funder looking to overcome your own deficiencies in talent and motivation (don't take offense, that's an expression of envy), then you are far better off learning the engineering side before you define yourself as a producer.

As the engineer, you'll often be put in the position of Default Producer, which will allow you to screw up a great many records without taking the blame for them. If the record turns out great, you'll be able to parlay that engineering credit into more records. In other words, you can take all of the credit and none of the blame early in your career. In the meantime, you're getting much-needed experience under your belt, and over time you'll be able to shift your position to Engineer Producer. At that point, owning a studio puts you in a really great position.

The Gridiron Producer

The Gridiron Producer seeks to make organic recordings of instruments into programmed music. The Gridiron Producer works with acts in excessive need of computer enhancement. There are some genres of music that all but require this kind of producer. Death metal, and most modern hard rock, for example. This is almost a necessity when you have hundreds of KIK drums playing per minute, as is prevalent in the heavier rock genres.

The DAW is the most important instrument for the Gridiron Producer. Drums are sliced and diced, and nearly all parts are aligned to grid.

The Gridiron Producer is beholden to good timing and good tuning over any other production technique. As such, they seek out bands that require technology. Becoming known as a Gridiron Producer is a self-fulfilling prophecy, one that all but guarantees you to be pigeonholed, which can put you in a position where you only get hired for one kind of record. That can make you valuable for a period of time too, so it's not a strategy without merit. The problem is it can be exceptionally difficult to reinvent yourself should that genre or production style go into disfavor.

I can assure you that I have no problem with aggressive editing techniques. They have a sound to them, and can evoke a certain feeling, and as such, all techniques are valid. But if you use the same techniques all the time, then you will surely be stereotyped, and this can be a difficult place from which to extract yourself.

The Hip-Hop Producer

The Hip-Hop Producer is, by default, the person responsible for creating the beat, which is considered half the song. In fact, the producer who makes the beats is also listed as a songwriter, since their role is so crucial to the existence of the work in the first place. It is not unusual for this producer to have stockpiles of beats that they can shop to rap artists. A hip-hop artist's rhymes are often written to existing tracks, and as such, the producer isn't attempting to make an arrangement that works with the lyric and melody, but rather a beat that inspires the artist to flow.

Most rappers spend their time developing their ability to flow in rhyme. The best rappers can rattle off a rhyme on any subject at any moment, and in a compelling manner. Developing this skill is a full-time job in its own right. Given the urban roots of the art form, it allows young artists to be creative with minimal monetary investment. It's a genre that was created on the streets, one in which sonic clarity was often secondary to a powerful beat and rhyme. These days the sound design is typically as dialed in as any of the other popular genres.

If you're not intimately familiar with what it's like to grow up in an urban setting, this can be a difficult genre to excel in. If black urban music is where your interests lie, but you don't have any kind of street cred because you're not part of the culture, you're far better off working on hybrid music, which melds R&B, soul, rock, and/or funk with rap.

I worked on many rap projects in the early '90s and was immersed in the lingo and the culture. Even with that cred, I was still obviously considered an outsider. I never took offense. I mean, I was a young 20-something white dude who came from a middle-class suburban background. I didn't know a single person who spent time in jail, and that alone set me apart from many of the young upcoming hip-hop artists that I worked with. As much as I empathized with the plight of these inner-city rappers, it would be impossible for me to fully relate to their experience. They knew it and I knew it. That made transitioning into producing pure urban hip-hop a nonstarter for me. It would be equally difficult for me to become a country music producer as a cultural outsider. Or reggaeton. Or any other music that is based on a particular cultural identity.

The DJ Producer

For the most part, DJ Producers are just like Songwriter Producers, who seek singers to feature on their productions, it's just that DJ producers perform their songs by spinning them in front of an audience. This makes the DJ Producer both songwriter and artist.

The most common genre for DJs, of course, are electronica, house, and dance. As such, the vocals aren't necessarily the primary feature. That said, there are plenty of DJ produced tracks that have amazing melodies and compelling vocals. I would know, this is the genre that I actually listen to in my free time.

The Absentee Producer

This is the rarest breed of producer in the business, and for good reason. You pretty much can't get away with being an Absentee Producer unless you're so successful that you're literally a mogul in the industry. Yes, the Absentee Producer doesn't even bother to show up to sessions, except occasionally. Rather, they work from their house and hire a highly qualified engineer to act as the Default Producer.

In the original version of this book, I suggested the Absentee Producer wasn't a position for which one should aspire. I've changed my mind on that. This is exactly the role for which one should aspire, since it makes you more successful than the preponderance of all other producers in the world. That said, you really need a string of hit records before you can pull this off.

The Hands-On Producer

The Hands-On Producer is the exact opposite of the Absentee Producer. The Hands-On Producer never wants to leave the room. Ever. For anything. They never want to miss a great moment and are at all times involved in nearly every aspect of the recording and production. Oh sure, they'll delegate certain tasks, but not without taking the time to carefully inspect the work upon its completion. Even on those occasions when the Hands-On Producer temporarily passes their producer's scepter to the recordist or artist, you can usually find them lying on the couch in the back of the room, attentively listening, as they appear to sleep. I'm quite familiar with this type of producer. It describes me.

The Self-Producer

There is nothing wrong with making your own records, especially when you're just starting out. It will provide you with much needed experience finishing records. But if your goal is to become a successful artist, there will come a point when an outside producer can become a necessity.

I would say that there are only a handful of established artists in the world that can effectively produce themselves. For everyone else, this is a very difficult position from which to produce.

If you have no time constraints and no budget, then surely you can Produce your own songs, so long as you have the discipline to finish them. The only pressure that exists is that which you apply to yourself. But once we bring in a deadline and funding, that pressure ratchets up substantially due to the stakes. That is the point in which producing becomes a full-time job, with requirements that can't be properly performed by the artist.

It is nearly impossible to talk yourself down from a metaphorical cliff. There is no instant, trusted, external feedback available. There's no one to take care of all the mundane, but necessary, organizational requirements. There's no one to keep the pulse of the session and make smart, rational decisions on how to change course for the sake of morale. There's no one to offer encouragement. There's no one to propel the vision forward. Once a company invests in you as an artist, then your job is to be an artist. Without a producer there, the process of making your record becomes downright inefficient. This leads to productions that take far longer than they should, often limited in quality by the artist's lack-of-experience.

Only a Super-Artist, with strengths in musicality, songwriting, and engineering, has the requisite skillset to adequately produce themselves at a time when the stakes are high. And let's not kid ourselves. When an artist brings the studio engineer into the fold, they've essentially just hired a Default Producer.

All of that said, if you're new to making your own music, then you really need to discover some things about yourself before you're ready for a producer. Seasoned producers will generally avoid working with an artist or band entity too early, mostly because there is no proof of concept or commitment.

So, if you're an artist, or a would-be artist or band, then you should absolutely produce your own records, music, and songs, and learn all the many lessons that come with the process. The more you understand about the process and about yourself, the more you'll appreciate having someone who can take some of that load off.

The exception to this would be if you're a would-be artist in need of songs (often referred to as a singer), in which case you should find a Songwriter Producer, preferably one with some previous success. The Songwriter Producer will work with you to write songs that fit you, and that may take some experimentation. That said, this is largely limited to the more commercial programmed genres, and as such, Songwriter Producers will either want someone of supreme singing talent, or someone who has a great look and who can dance. Preferably all three.

If you're a singer who aligns more closely as a singer-songwriter, then you're coming from a more honest, intimate, and organic position, so you don't have to be a super model, you don't have to dance (maybe just float around a bit), and you don't even have to be a technically superb singer. You just have to be able to connect with your audience through performance. But if you're missing the songwriting component of the singer-songwriter combination, then you're probably better off looking for a partner. Either another player, or someone who wants to write *with* you. Just make sure you find a Songwriter Producer with the chops to produce organic music.

If you're operating as a band entity, it can become quite problematic to produce yourselves. At the very least, it comes with a number of challenges given the group dynamic. Every band should surely try it, because if you can survive producing your first record, then this bodes well for your longevity. But at some point, a producer will make the process far easier through their leadership and ability to arbitrate disputes that come up along the way. I'll go into great detail as to how a skilled producer deals with band politics, which will demonstrate just how beneficial a producer can be. In the meantime, absolutely, produce your early records.

The Armchair Producer

The Armchair Producer is that person, usually a friend of the artist or the band entity, who thinks that their input into the process as an outsider is just as valuable and appreciated as the input coming from within the team. While it's unlikely that you would buy this book specifically to make the transition to Armchair Producer, it's important to understand how to deal with this breed of producer when they happen to appear on your session.

The Armchair Producer often has the trust of the artist, or Child of Brain in the band (the person whose brainchild it is), which can be a problem and a nuisance. Therefore, you must address the presence of the Armchair Producer early on—otherwise your decisions could be constantly second-guessed.

Given the relationships between everyone involved, castrating the power of a legitimate and trusted Armchair Producer requires a politic approach. Often, the best course of action is to give that person some of your busy work. There's nothing better than translating the enthusiasm and energy of others into a reduced workload for yourself. Editing tracks for timing and tuning can often be left in the hands of the Armchair Producer, as they typically have the chops and will likely work hard to please you. Once you have the Armchair Producer reporting to you, they will relinquish their influence with the artist or band, because they've bought into your leadership. This is good.

The Band Member Producer

The Band Member Producer is similar to the Armchair Producer, only they typically have fewer skills, less understanding of the process, and a big fucking ego. As such, offering a Band Member Producer busy work is often a risky call, unless you want to have to redo it, and then suffer through the ramifications of their bruised ego. Most problematic of all is when you upset the Band Member Producer. If you piss off your Armchair Producer, they'll usually just leave. Problem solved. If you upset the Band Member Producer, you're stuck with them in this state. Either that or they quit the band in a huff. *Uy yuy yuy!* You want to avoid those sorts of scenarios.

You may very well be brought in as the replacement for the failed Band Member Producer, who the group wants to put in check. For some inexplicable reason, even if this producer was enthusiastic about your involvement, they believe part of their role is to run your session. As much as diplomacy is the preferred method of dealing with problems, there is nothing more maddening than to have a member of the team gumming up the general flow of your session. As such, you need to shut this person down with authority.

I promise that you will ignore my advice on this just once in your career. In all likelihood, the rest of the band hired you specifically for the purpose of neutralizing their cancerous band member, even if they didn't tell you as much.

I had a singer from a popular band walk into my session, and the moment he entered the room, he began to dictate what we were recording. If I had allowed his takeover attempts to succeed, I would have completely lost control of the session, and I would have then forced the band to establish who's in charge. They hired *me* for that.

This is not the same as when a singer expresses a desire to sing. When that happens, I'll often drop everything so as to get the singer in front of the mic as quickly as I can. That means they're inspired, and I want to capture that inspiration the moment it strikes. But when a band member starts to arbitrarily attempt to run my session, I tell them straight up: "Only one person runs the session, and at the moment that's me."

As much as record-making is a team effort, there can only be one person running a session at any given time. I even go out of my way to dub members of the band "temporary producers," just so it's crystal clear who's in charge at any given moment. I also reserve the right to revoke that privilege. As long as everyone on the session understands this, I can maintain a somewhat efficient session within the confines of a naturally inefficient creative process.

Sitting down with the band entity to explain how your session will be run is a good start for dealing with any potential Band Member Producers. Unfortunately, this heart-to-heart is rarely enough to prevent uncomfortable situations.

Anyone brash enough to try to take over your session will generally respect your strong rebuke. Therefore, it's best to take a rather unyielding position, stated in uncompromising terms. And while it's totally unnecessary to raise your voice the first time you say, "I'm running the session," I will admit, it's nearly unavoidable the tenth time you have to say it. At least it was for me.

While I would much rather portray myself as someone who has a perfect command over dealing with problematic people, and who can do so in the nicest way possible and avert any confrontation, the reality is there are those in this world who won't allow that, and there are times when you must stand up for yourself and for the job you were hired to do.

The Client Producer

Inevitably, you'll produce an artist who is also the client. They're paying you, and there's no band to supply you with political leverage or backup should there be a disagreement. So, how the hell do you take control of the project, if you're always dealing with the "boss" as it were?

You treat them like any other artist, that's how.

The more seasoned you are as a producer, the easier it is to shut down bullshit from any other position, mostly because you've seen it before, and you understand how detrimental it is to lose control of your session.

I had a Client Producer, with some measure of notoriety, stop everything deep into the overdub process to tell me that he wasn't happy with the temperament of the piano—the featured instrument in all of the productions. This was a piano we had tracked many weeks prior and had listened to repeatedly, and now all of a sudden, the tuning was a problem? Then my client expressed his desire to bring in his expert piano tuning friend to listen and offer his opinion.

I declined.

If you're unfamiliar with piano temperament, the notes that occur between the scale on a piano need to be fudged a little in order to make them fit the scale and sound in tune. This isn't an issue on more expressive instruments because the player can physically pull a note sharp or flat, and to some degree will do so innately. But piano notes are static. They don't bend. So, a piano requires the tuner to temper the scale of the piano so that it sounds in tune.

If there was a problem with the temperament, we would have known it when we were recording it, let alone the other 200 times we'd heard it to that point. There wasn't an issue with the temperament.

So why did I shut my client down rather than to indulge him? Why not simply allow his friend to listen to the piano and offer his opinion?

Suppose this tuning expert had come back to say the temperament was a problem. What's the remedy? We couldn't fix it electronically. Piano samples weren't an option. Were we to go back to the studio, retune the piano, and play it all again? He was willing to incur that expense? I certainly wasn't. I was being paid a set per-track fee for my work, and that would have cost an inordinate amount of time.

An opinion in regard to something that can't be changed is a useless opinion, and where it comes to the making of his record, I'm the person the artist needed to trust. Not someone else with no experience making records, and not his own demons of self-doubt that were manifesting as unfounded tuning concerns.

A crisis was averted, because rather than to please my client by indulging him, rather than to allow them to second-guess my expertise, I shut down the madness before it got out of control. He literally hired me because he knew that he needed someone who could say "no" to him. He'd already scrapped his first attempt at the album because his first producer wasn't in a position to stand up to him. I was doing precisely the job that I was hired to do.

Understand, while he was a known entity, I am also a known entity. It is far more difficult to say "no" when the artist you're producing has more gravitas than you do. It's still a necessary part of the job.

Now, you can say "no" any way that you like in a manner that best fits your personality. You can try to go around in circles in order to avoid saying it, in the hopes that your client will come to their senses. But at some point, you will be forced to set the boundary.

The reality is, no matter how polite you are in the way that you say "no," that doesn't soften the shock of it to the very person who is paying you. This is the generally unavoidable dilemma of producing your client. You need to explain in advance that you run the show, and that's what they're hiring you to do. Otherwise, you will find yourself submitting to endless whims and experimentation, all at the risk of failure.

Now, if you want to work hourly, then surely you should whistle while you work as your client explores endless rabbit holes in the pursuit of producing their own record. But you're certainly not producing it. When you work by the hour you sell your time, not your work, and your time isn't being wasted when you're being paid for it. If you're to be credited as producer, it requires maintaining some control over the process.

As a producer, you're selling your work, and you're judged on the success of your records—largely in terms of sales but also based on the quality of your results. The service that you supply, isn't to facilitate your artist's every whim so as to arrive at their record on their own timeline. It's to leverage your expertise and taste to deliver the record, and to accomplish it within an allotted time and budget, both of which are agreed upon in advance.

For you Self-Producer's out there, if you believe that you would never want to relinquish that kind of control over your record to someone else, I can certainly understand that. But you may change your mind in the future, because it protects you from yourself. And should you ever find yourself involved with a label, relinquishing control becomes part of the deal.

The Hybrid Producer

While it would be nice to categorize people in clean terms, the knowledge base of any given producer is often considerably more complex than the classifications I've laid out above. The problem is that we are at all times dealing with others' perceptions, and while we have some control over those perceptions, that control is akin to pushing a plow through wet clay. It requires a great deal of effort for little relative movement. Still, we must try.

I can assure you, there is nothing more maddening than being pigeonholed. As your name begins to be bandied about, you will often be relegated to a category. If you work in only one genre, it gets even worse. You really only have two viable ways to deal with how you are perceived. Go with it and allow the simplistic perception to define your position and seek records that fall in line with that position so as to make it a strength. Or take active steps to overcome your perceived position by diversifying your discography. In the short run, the easiest solution is to go with the perception. Unfortunately, that can prove problematic in the long run.

If you just want to make a particular kind of record, or work within a single genre, then capitalizing on a stereotypical position based on your past work can yield good results in short order. While such a position can make you highly sought after by certain clients (like major labels), you may find yourself producing rather uninventive and safe projects. These kinds of projects will often yield good, but formulaic, results. The problem—aside from "good" being a rather lame goal—is you put yourself entirely at the mercy of an ever-changing industry. Once your style of production goes out of fashion, you're screwed. All styles and genres go in and out of fashion. As such, it's critical to stay ahead of the trends.

Like basketball, producing at a high level is often a game of runs. Unlike basketball, you might only get one run. Two, if you're lucky. Three, if you become adept at reinventing yourself. But even if you can manage three runs, you will have to survive the painful periods between them. After a while, you might regret the decision to make the same kind of music over and over again, *ad nauseum*. This is particularly true when your run ends, and you discover that not only are you viewed as a one-trick pony, but your trick is no longer desirable. Once this happens, you have limited recourse: you can either retire and do something else or reinvent yourself—a process that can take considerable time and vigilance.

It can take years to overcome the perception issues associated with a discography laden with one style and genre. Not only will it seem as though you're only capable of producing one record, but in a style that is somewhat undesirable. And while one well-timed record can change that stigma, it must be a rather successful one.

The more likely scenario is that you'll have to make several records outside of your predominant musical genre to overcome your established position. Not only will those records be more difficult for you to win, but you'll likely end up having to reduce your rate to secure them. That is why it's so critical for you to continually evaluate the perception of your brand. If you're not vigilant regarding your position, you can literally kill your career, and for good.

Overall talent and a keen ability to sell yourself are important traits that can come in handy. But if you don't get the call in the first place, selling yourself is fairly useless. You can't close a deal that you don't know is on the table. I've caught wind of gigs that I never had the opportunity to pitch. Absent the ability to sell yourself, you are at the mercy of any and all perception issues associated with your name and work. So, discount how you are perceived within the community at your professional peril.

The only way to effectively deal with perception issues is to define yourself through the records you make. The more diverse your discography is, the more difficult it will be to classify you beyond your all-around abilities. And while you will never be considered an "expert" in any particular genre, you may be considered an expert at making great records. That said, you may only be interested in one genre for the now, and you never know what turns your career will take. But it's not a bad idea to be proactive in expanding your wheelhouse over time. Your only control in life lies in preparing yourself for future opportunities.

If you're losing jobs to others because of your weaknesses as a producer—whether perceived or real—then you should work to eradicate those weaknesses. If you don't write music, if you have no arranging skills, or if you don't even play an instrument, you can clearly improve in those areas, which will open you up to a more diverse array of records.

If you're completely unfamiliar with a particular genre, spend some time evaluating it. A good knowledge base in all genres allows you to use cross-genre techniques in your productions. You never know when that knowledge will prove useful.

The Producer For-Hire

Anytime you produce a project with existing songs, you're operating as a Producer For-Hire. Your core job is to deliver the record, but along with that comes quite a bit of responsibility. You fill numerous roles as the Producer For-Hire. You're in charge of the budget, the time, the money, the personnel, the vision, and you lead the entire team to a completed and effective record. We will address all of these roles in detail a bit further along.

Influencing Your Position

Any time the industry is aware of a record you've done that falls outside of your position, you've made inroads toward changing your perceived position. If the record ultimately blows up, you've managed to *redefine* your position. Of course, at that point you're going to be approached with records that fall within the scope of your *new* position. You see why maintaining your position takes vigilance?

It will take a long time before you can rest on the laurels of your discography, and even then, potential artists will want to know what you've done lately. The good news is the more successful and mature your discography, the less likely it is for a stinker to affect your position. Most people only look at your record of success and ignore all the failures. Such is the nature of a discography.

As much as you can take an active role in shaping your perception within the industry, if you're ill equipped to make a record in a particular genre, you're not necessarily doing yourself any favors. How are you supposed to produce a hip-hop album if you never really listen to hip-hop, and if you don't make beats? Granted, making beats isn't all that difficult, but making great beats that aren't dated, or that aren't just a trendy caricature, requires immersion in the genre.

At the very least, working outside of your general knowledge base will increase your costs. If you decide you want to get some bands on your discography, and you have no skills as an engineer, you should probably hire a recordist, and then ultimately a mixer.

Much of what you learn about producing you'll learn as you produce. "Earn while you learn" is alive and well in this industry. That doesn't mean you shouldn't take steps to learn more, particularly if you wish to expand the kinds of records you can make.

There is so much to know when it comes to producing, that even if you plan on hiring other people to fill in where you're deficient (which you should, and will, do), you ultimately need a working knowledge of everything that goes into making a record. This takes time, but it also takes perseverance on your part. The good news is, no matter how deficient you are in certain seemingly important areas, you can still produce great records. I'll bet you're happy to read that!

CHAPTER TWO

Songwriting & Arranging

The reality is, I can't teach you how to write a great song. Nobody can. You do that by listening, evaluating, and mimicking great songs.

You can evaluate the harmonic structure, melodic structure, rhyme structure, rhythmic structure, and contrast (which we'll discuss shortly), whether it's part of the song or the production. If you take some time to figure out the structure of highly effective hit songs, this will illuminate all sorts of useful techniques that you can use as both a songwriter and a producer.

The best way that I know to appreciate just how important the song is to a successful production, is to produce a cover. This allows you to experience what it feels like to work on a hit.

The most enjoyable projects I ever mixed were Foreigner's early 2010's *Feels Like the First Time* and *Acoustique: The Classics Unplugged* albums. The songs were all proven hits. They were also songs from my childhood, which only magnified my enjoyment. When you work on a hit, the song can no longer be the weak link, and this provides excellent opportunities for learning.

While it's true that I can't teach you how to write a great song, I can certainly bring to light some of the techniques and strategies that go into a great song, production and arrangement, and many of them have to do with effectively propelling the listener forward so as to maximize payoff.

Whether you're a Songwriter Producer, A Home Producer, or a Producer For-Hire, the principles in this chapter are far more critical to your success than any of the engineering.

Forward Motion

Forward motion is the underlying principle of success for all art forms that reveal themselves over time. Movies, TV shows, plays, and songs are all art forms in which you must keep your audience engaged over time. Once you bore the listener (or viewer), they'll move on, which makes this one of the most critical concepts in both writing and producing successful works.

Well-written songs have forward motion built into them. As producers, we want to accentuate that forward motion with our arranging decisions, which will also make the payoff more effective.

The payoff is the release, which offers us the opportunity to push the listener forward, but all the sections of the song work towards this end. Intros can be used to tip off and set up the payoff down the line. Verses lyrically set up the concept of the song, which push us towards the payoff. Pre-choruses often operate as an acceleration point to hurl us towards the payoff. The bridge offers us a new musical theme and operates as a payoff of its own since it often delivers the overall meaning of the song. Breakdowns offer us a respite from the full production and buy us more time to push the listener once again. All of your decisions in regard to your song and arrangement should promote forward motion.

Promoting Forward Motion

There's no doubt about it, the most effective forward motion is derived from the song itself, and there are specific techniques that songwriters employ to accomplish this goal. That said, a songwriter could use every technique I'm about to share and still write a terrible song. They're merely tools and many songwriters use them innately. Some don't use them at all. But on those occasions when you discover issues with forward motion, these techniques can help you identify the problem and devise a possible solution.

Reserve the Tonic

The tonic is the central, foundational pitch of a musical key, serving as the note to which melodies and harmonies naturally resolve. To the listener, the tonic signifies "home." As such, it's often the final melodic note of a song because the tonic has the power to end all forward motion. Given this, songwriters will sometimes avoid the tonic (both melodically and harmonically) until the payoff.

As a Songwriter Producer, you might try writing your top lines (the melody) such that you avoid the tonic entirely until the payoff, if only as an exercise. It's not critical that you never hit the tonic until the chorus. What's more important is that you avoid halting forward motion with the tonic before you even reach the payoff.

It can also be highly impactful to reserve your highest melodic note(s) for the chorus. Higher notes generate more energy and excitement, and implementing this technique can also increase the payoff.

Accelerate Rhyme Structure

Many songs have a B-section (prechorus) which is a musical way to transition us from the verse to the chorus. Oftentimes, there is some sort of acceleration that occurs in the B-section, which can come from the production, the song, or both.

As an example, it's not uncommon for the rhyme vowel to change to something new in the B-section. If the rhymes are "ohs" in the verse, then a good songwriter might switch to "ay" rhymes in the B-section and the "ee" rhymes in the chorus. Billy Joel routinely reserved certain vowel rhymes for the choruses (and bridges) of his songs.

Another common strategy is to accelerate the rhyme structure. For example, if the verse follows an AxxA rhyme—where the first phrase rhymes with the last—it might shift to an ABAB rhyme in the B-section. Coupled with quicker, shorter melodic phrasing, this creates excitement and propels the listener toward the chorus for a satisfying payoff. Additionally, the rhythmic and chordal structures may also intensify so as to enhance the effect.

Forced Harmonic Resolution

Where it comes to music theory, there are certain chords within the structure of the song that call for resolution. In straight ahead blues, after we hear the V chord, we expect the I chord, which brings us "home." The same is true for the I vi ii V I progression, which is a staple of classic R&B music. That V chord basically forces us to the I.

The sus-IV chord, in which the third note of the chord is replaced with the fourth note of the chord, all but forces resolution back to the third. Even if you've never studied any music theory, you will recognize a forced resolution, because you'll feel compelled to sing it.

Sometimes, you may choose to avoid a resolution for purposes of tension. This typically happens at the end of the song, where the goal is to rob the listener of that resolution so as to promote a feeling of unease.

Song Form

There's an old adage in the music business: "Don't bore us. Get to the chorus." You should live by this credo, and there's a very good reason for it. The chorus is the payoff. It's the place where we most commonly derive lift, and it's the part of every popular song that people remember. And while it's true you want to create some tension ahead the payoff, most listeners only have so much patience. You need to get to that payoff before you lose them.

Each section in the song form (verse, chorus, bridge) has a specific role, but it's how these sections work together that promotes forward motion. The most effective songs provide several payoffs along the way. The chorus payoff alone, along with its natural release acts as a fulcrum to push the listener forward through the song.

Most popular songs hit the chorus in under 40 seconds, which seems to preclude such things as two-minute intros. Of course, like anything in music, there are exceptions to every rule.

Take The Rolling Stones' "You Can't Always Get What You Want." That song has an exceptionally long intro, which functions as an operatic interpretation of the chorus. I remember the first time I heard the full production of the song (some ten years after it had been released). Even as a lad I was absolutely mesmerized by the operatic opener. And I wasn't even a Stones fan. The lone guitar and the soulful vocal that followed came out of that perfectly. What a setup! That intro draws you in as a listener and pushes you to the verse. All of that said, radio station DJs routinely queued up that song at the first verse. Streaming services don't have DJs.

In reality, there's no set time to get to the chorus, and if you can keep the listener's attention for two minutes, that's a fine length for the intro. Whatever works. All that matters is that the song and production keep pushing the listener forward.

The difficult part about evaluating a song, its form, and its overall effectiveness is the subjective nature of the task. I would argue that it's not nearly as subjective as you might think. If you produce a song, play it for a focus group, and 75 out of 100 people shut the song off before the intro is over, guess what? The intro is undoubtedly too long.

Since you probably don't have access to 100-person focus groups, your only reasonable measure is to put yourself in the place of the listener—the first-time listener in particular. If you were hearing this song for the first time, would it draw you in and hold your attention? If not, where does it lose your attention? Do you find yourself skipping ahead to work on the track? When you make your evaluation in this manner, it becomes quite easy to cut the fat from an intro or even an exceptionally long verse. Of course, the verse has lyrics, so trimming the verses can be tricky, since this can alter the perceived meaning of the song.

If you find that it's taking too much time to get to the chorus, then you might consider starting the song off with it. This way, they experience the payoff immediately. There are countless examples of songs that start with the chorus.

Lyrics

Lyrics are part of the song's forward motion. It's not just the music. Hip-hop songs can have long, drawn-out raps with very little musical deviation and no true melody; that doesn't mean there's a lack of forward motion. A compelling rap or lyric can certainly hold the attention of the listener and push them forward, especially when combined with accelerated rhymes. Essentially, the lyric is operating as the story, and a good story will keep us engaged.

The whole operating principle of hip-hop music is the use of flow, rhyme, and content to carry the listener forward to the payoff. That's why you can have an effective rap production with nothing more than a static beat. In those situations, the lyrical content promotes all of the forward motion necessary. The same is true for songs that are sung, of course.

Should you find a lull somewhere along the way, or if things seem a tad too repetitive, you can always change the arrangement up slightly, or you can drop the beat out momentarily in order to buy more time, in which case, the arrangement is helping to promote the forward motion. Gang vocals which emphasize certain words and phrases are also designed to promote forward push through the song.

Drops

A drop is basically a mute, typically of everything other than one part that carries through. Sometimes there's more than one part that carries through the drop.

A drop can do a number of things. In hip-hop, drops are used routinely to highlight a vocal line and to provide a momentary break in the repetitiveness. A well-timed drop right before the chorus can be used to accentuate the payoff, given that it provides exceptional contrast.

Bass drops, which were all the rage in recent years, plunge the arrangement into a downward-sweeping sub-frequency. They're exciting and undeniably effective—but probably dated by now, given how often they show up in TV productions. That's the death knell for any production trend.

Drops are by no means relegated to just hip-hop and EDM productions. I use them all the time in pop and rock productions as a mixer because they're so effective.

Drops programmed at mix time on organic band productions aren't always all that natural (especially if the cymbals are dissipating at the drop point). I don't typically care all that much about a natural presentation so long as the drop doesn't distract the listener, and so long as the drop buys me more forward push.

Drops on more organic music can be a tad shocking when you first program them. It's possible that the drop could use some of love, or it might just be new. I'll often program a drop and then live with it for a spell as I continue to mix. If the drop remains awkward as I work, then I'll either adjust it or abandon it.

This is where taste comes in. You can put many, many drops in a hip-hop production that carries a super repetitive beat. But rock productions can seem a bit tricked-out if you treat them like a hip-hop production. Besides, a looped beat is relentless and unchanging. A band is dynamic, and capable of performing their own drops, and if you want drops to sound completely natural on organic band productions, this is best worked out in pre-production.

You should reserve drops purely to assist with lacking forward motion. In other words, don't add drops just to add them. It's a tool that you can use effectively with impunity on one production, and not at all on another.

Phrasing

If you've ever listened to your average middle school concert band, then you're probably familiar with bad phrasing. It sounds something like this: BLAT, BLAT, BLAT, BLAT, BLAT! Which is probably why my Jr. High school trumpet teacher hammered into my head: SHORT! Dit! Dit! Dit! Dit! Dit!

It can be difficult for inexperienced players to fully control their instrument, and so every note tends to come out at the same length and volume as the previous note. Short notes are too long. Long notes aren't long enough. They're all just long, loud, and not especially musical. Anyone who learned an expressive instrument went through this stage in their musical development.

Phrasing is how players, songwriters, and producers make a part musical and singable, which often mirrors how we generally talk. We don't speak in an even meter, devoid of dynamic. When we combine words, we make phrases in which some syllables are short, some are long, and others are accented. That's phrasing, and whether you're singing words, or playing notes on an instrument, it's probably one of the more important concepts for you to understand as a producer. Great phrasing is what often separates great singers and players from mediocre ones. Let's start with vocal phrasing.

Vocal Phrasing

The words, of course, have a big influence on how one might sing them. More often than not, we want our melodic lines to match rhythmically with the natural way that we would accent syllables in a word or a phrase.

All multi-syllabic words contain an accented syllable, and certain words within a phrase or sentence will have accents too. Take the word elegant. It's not pronounced *EL· E·GANT*, with each syllable receiving equal weight. It's pronounced *EL·ə·gant*, with the first syllable carrying the accent. That's the most natural way to sing it as well, especially since the final vowel doesn't sustain well when held.

There will certainly be times when a singer will purposely place the accent on the wrong syllable or the wrong word in a sentence. I suppose it's always done on purpose to some degree, but sometimes a mis-accented syllable is done with a wink and a nod from the performer. It can be amusing and effective to put the accent in the wrong place of a word or phrase. You hear it all the time. But when phrase after phrase employs the accent in the wrong place, you risk the vocal coming off comical. Just consider some really amateurish rapping. It sounds kind of silly to have words accenting in the wrong places.

The more honesty or authenticity that you wish to pull from your singer, the more important it is for them to sing it in a manner similar to how they might say it. This is especially true for singer-songwriters who seek a personal connection with their audience. If you listen to Willie Nelson's "On the Road Again," he sings the phrases exactly as he might speak them.

A single syllable vowel treated like multi-syllabic words can also sound somewhat amateurish. We'll exclude runs from this, because a run is more of an embellishment than a bad habit. Great singers capable of impressive and precise runs also understand how to use their vowels to make the run smooth and natural.

Suppose we have a lyric that ends on the word "day." When a singer holds out the vowel along with melodic note movement, this can become super awkward. For starters, when you hold the vowel on "day" a proper singer will hold the open "eh" sound, rather than the closed "ee" sound.

The "y" from the word "day" isn't generally heard until the singer finishes the word. So "day" across multiple notes comes off as Deh-eh-eh-eh-ee. Terrible. It's stupidly unnatural, and when people hear the word sung like that, they'll laugh. It's even worse if the singer goes to the "ee" vowel early and holds there. Dah-eeeeeeeeeeeeeee. The "ee" vowel is an undesirable vowel to hold, unless you seek a back woods country kind of feeling. Even then, it's not great.

Of course, every good practice has its exceptions. In the chorus of One Direction's "End of the Day," Harry Styles stretches the word times into "tie-ee-eye-ee-eye-ee-imes" over an up-ward-moving melodic scale. He alternates between the "eye" and "ee" vowels—both of which sing well—creating a kind of vocal melodic turnaround. The elongation also adds contrast to the rest of the phrasing, which is far more straightforward. And really, what better word to take your time singing than *time?* We call that prosody—but more on that later in the chapter.

In the song "Yesterday" Paul McCartney holds out the word "day" and all the subsequent "ay" rhymes for two beats each. And while he could sing all of those words with a short "ay" (as many others have done since), the melody is arguably more compelling when it's held out a bit. That said, had Paul held all of those "ay" rhymes for 4 beats instead of 2, it would get a little weird. Awkward, even. Try it yourself.

Where it comes to vocal phrasing, there's more to consider than just the phrasing, especially in pop music where the melody is of equal importance to the lyric. If it works for the singer to elongate a word across melodic notes, then it works. You can't take the art out of this. Use this information to help you identify a problem. When something that's sung sounds bad, or wrong, or amateurishly awkward, that's when you should address the phrasing.

Singer's Vowels

Singer's vowels are the intentional shaping of vowel sounds to enhance tone, resonance, and clarity in a singer's perfor-mance. Unlike spoken vowels, which can be relaxed or muddled depending on accents or casual speech, singer's vowels are open, rounded, and sustained. This precise shaping allows the voice to project more effectively, stay in tune, and blend seamlessly with the music. For instance, a singer might adjust the word "love" to a slightly more open "lahv" to create a warmer tone or to improve resonance on a high note. These subtle modifications don't change the meaning of the word but help the singer maintain vocal control and balance across their range.

Mastering singer's vowels can dramatically improve a singer's performance. They help reduce strain—especially on high notes—by allowing the vocalist to stay relaxed and resonant. Singer's vowels also ensure that the lyrics are clear and intelligible, drawing the audience into the emotional core of the song. They're also easier to sing in tune. If your singer is struggling, consider adjusting the vowels they hold.

Instrumental Phrasing

Now, where it comes to instruments, they too speak, it's just that they don't employ words in the process. But make no mistake, instrumentalists play phrases. Just as we intertwine long and short note durations and then accent syllables with our words, we do that with our instruments too.

Then of course there's motion, which for an instrumentalist is expression. Notes can be played blandly and evenly, or they can implement bends, vibrato, growls . . . really, any sound that an instrument makes is fair game to be worthy of our musical productions and performances.

Many times, I'll ask band guitar players to play certain chord staccato, or very short. *Dit!* Less proficient players can have a difficult time with that. If a player doesn't ever use super short notes, then they're not using accents, and they're losing contrast between the short and long notes, which comes off weak.

Let's take Peter Gabriel's song "Sledgehammer." That song starts first with some flutes, followed by a synth line, which is performed and phrased as a horn line:

Bah dah doo dit! Doo dah—

The fourth note in the line, the "dit!" is short. Now imagine if that dit! was held. Bah duh doo dah—doo dah. It's not as crisp or compelling that way and doesn't have nearly the forward push. So, keep your phrasing in mind, and if you want to have a better understanding of it, listen to songs with great horn sections. Salsa and big band jazz horn sections are excellent places to start.

Effective Songwriting

Now that we've discussed forward motion and its role in songwriting and arranging, let's evaluate Billy Joel's "Pressure." I encourage you to load up the song in your preferred streaming app so you can follow along.

The song opens with a subdued short instrumental intro, setting up the iconic chorus synth part.

The first verse begins with short melodic phrases, each followed by Billy Joel's vocal response: "Pressure!" This call-and-response structure happens twice over a G-to-D chord progression. But on the third line, he shifts to G minor—a bold harmonic change that, paired with the melody, creates forward motion all on its own.

At first, the beat stays consistent with a "four to the floor" pattern—a steady KIK drum on every beat—while the snare lands on the third beat of each measure, creating a half-time feel. A measure after the G minor arrives, the snare switches to the 2 and 4, pulling us out of half time and accelerating the song's momentum. Combined with the elongated melodic phrases, this rhythmic shift propels us through the B-section straight into the chorus.

Billy Joel's melodic choices also contribute to this motion. He avoids the tonic entirely in the verse, keeping the listener in suspense. When the B-section arrives, he hits the tonic, but the melody continues to push forward. Finally, at the start of the chorus, he lands triumphantly on the tonic D, singing "Pressure!" over a D minor chord. Even here, the momentum doesn't stop because the lyric passes the baton to the instrumental which carries us forward once again. Billy continues his calls of "pressure," driving the refrain home.

This song is a masterclass in how songwriting and production can work together to push the listener forward. Producer Phil Ramone mirrored the natural propulsion of the song with brilliant arrangement decisions, from rhythmic shifts to the interplay of melody and harmony.

Billy Joel is a craftsman where it comes to writing songs. He routinely reserves the tonic until the payoff. He routinely accelerates his rhyme structure as he heads to the chorus. And he reserves certain vowels for the chorus where it comes to his rhymes.

While modern songwriting tends to rely more on production than on these structural songwriting techniques, the lesson remains the same: forward motion is essential to a song. Whether it comes from the lyrics, the melody, or the arrangement choices, every element must work to pull the listener toward the payoff.

A great production can elevate even a simple song, and a great song can last forever. After all, Beyoncé didn't rewrite *Blackbird*—she used Paul McCartney's original guitar track, complete with his foot tapping. And yet, it was a hit song once again.

Arranging

Although producing requires you to wear many hats, arranging is arguably one of your most important roles. The better you are at it, the more seamlessly your production will come together for the mix.

Six Musical Functions in an Arrangement

There are six basic functions in any given arrangement: melody, harmony, rhythm, response, countermelody, and bass.

Melody

The melody is not only the most important function in the song but also defines the song itself (in conjunction with any lyrics). This is true whether the melody is performed by a vocalist or instrumentalist. Given its overall importance, it's our goal to focus the listener's attention on the melody. This can be achieved by placing the melody prominently in the production and consciously designing the arrangement in such a way that it supports the melody at all times.

Harmony

Harmony is basically the chord changes. Polyphonic instruments like guitar and keyboard—often referred to as rhythm instruments—can provide the entire harmonic structure of a song. Monophonic instruments like horns and strings must be performed as a group in order to offer full harmonic support. Harmony is not copyrightable, which is why you will often hear the exact same chord progressions in other songs.

Rhythm

Rhythm is the structure in which the melody operates. A rubato (or free form) melody is neither satisfying nor readily repeatable. Modern music is often based on a strong rhythmic component. This is what makes us move. While drums and percussion are the most obvious rhythmic element in a production, rhythm can be derived from nearly any instrument or part, even if it serves another function in the arrangement. The bass, for instance, often supplies both the harmonic support and the rhythmic foundation of a track.

Any music with a defined pulse has accents. Given the most common four beats-per-measure treatment, pop and rock tracks tend to accent the two and the four while hip-hop tracks often accent the one and the three. In the case of a waltz—which has three beats per measure—the accent is on the one. These days, it's common to accent all four beats.

Working around the accents are the internal rhythms. These are the rhythms that weave around the main pulse, and they help to influence how the listener moves. Within a drum pattern, the internal rhythm is typically provided by the hi-hat, ride, and sometimes even snare ghosting. Percussion, guitar, and keyboards are also good candidates for providing the internal rhythms.

Response

Response, as in call-and-response, is an important part of Western music. It is most prominent in gospel music. The preacher sounds the call, and the "chorus" behind them offers the response.

The Who's "My Generation" is a great example of this technique. Roger Daltrey sounds the call: "People try to put us d-down," and the band sings the response: "Talkin' 'bout my generation."

Response isn't limited to a chorus of singers. In Led Zeppelin's "Black Dog," Robert Plant sounds the call, which is followed by the band playing an infectious riff. This kind of musical response is designed to momentarily grab the listener's focus and pass it right back to the vocal.

Countermelody

A countermelody is a distinct melody that plays alongside the vocal (or primary melody). A great countermelody can stand on its own, but by design, it remains subordinate—and I mean that literally. When the melody moves, the countermelody typically holds (or moves harmonically with the progression), and when the melody holds, the counter usually moves. It weaves around the vocal to avoid stealing focus. That said, you don't want to be too rigid in your counter movements. Think of it this way: the more effective a countermelody, the louder you can place it in the production without distracting from the main melody

Bass

Bass is the foundation of a record. It serves as the glue between rhythm and harmony, grounding the progression while driving the groove forward. Unlike melody—which typically operates in the mid-to-high frequencies—bass resides in the lower register, giving it a unique role in shaping the feel of a track.

A bass line can be rhythmically intricate or melodically expressive without competing with the vocal, simply because of where it sits in the frequency spectrum. It can be used purely to provide weight by following the tonic movement of the harmony—an approach commonly heard in '80s productions. Or it can be far more musical and rhythmically dynamic, adding movement, energy, and even a call-and-response interplay with other instruments.

A well-crafted bass part enhances a production in ways that go beyond just filling out the low end (otherwise known as taking up space)—it can define the groove, reinforce the harmonic structure, and introduce melodic or counter-melodic hooks that make the record more compelling.

Multi-Functions

A part can serve more than one function in an arrangement and not all functions are required at any given moment. Many productions don't include a countermelody, for instance. A guitar part can serve as both rhythm and harmony. A clever tom-beat could even serve as both rhythm and countermelody. A tuned 808 KIK drum can serve a rhythmic and bass function.

As you produce your arrangement, it's important to understand what functions any given part is serving, and to evaluate what's missing from your production that might help you with forward motion. If your prechorus isn't hurling the listener into the chorus as it should, then one possible solution is to bring in a countermelody to create tension for purposes of release at the chorus. Or you could add a rhythmic part for purposes of acceleration.

Mixerman's Five Planes of Space

It may seem strange that I talk about space in terms of your arrangement, but that's precisely what we're dealing with here. Think about it. We can absolutely consume a production with low-end frequency information. That would be space. Our panning is limited to the width of our monitors. Also space. We balance our parts in the production, and whatever is placed loudest will appear closest and most up front. Space. Reflectivity, which is achieved through the addition of spatial information (reverbs and delays), creates the illusion of distance and depth. Space. And finally, we use the contrast between sparse and dense sections to create a contrast dynamic that reveals itself over time. Space!

Of course, where it comes to space and time, we do have limitations because it's contained. We work within a defined range of audible frequencies. The width of our production is limited to the extent of our sides. Our balances require some measure of proportionality in order to maintain the illusion of depth. And you can only cram so many things into a dense production before you lose all contrast and find yourself unable to decipher all of the information.

Given that we are operating on what amounts to a sonic canvas, we must be mindful of our space and how we use it. And so, I have defined the following as my Five Planes of Space.

In a stereo image there are five planes of space that we use to create a four-dimensional image (the fourth dimension being time): panning—left to right; frequency—up to down; balance—front to back; reflectivity—far to near; and contrast (dynamics)—sparse to dense, bright to dark, asymmetrical to symmetrical.

Panning—Left to Right

The strongest stereo image is derived from two wholly independent mono sources panned hard left and hard right. In the case of guitar (for instance), the strongest image will come from two unique players on their own instruments performing their own unique parts. This is a stronger image than one produced by one player performing a true double with the same guitar.

Why is that?

Musicians who have reached at least a modicum of proficiency on their instruments tend to play with some consistency, which creates a subtle sonic fingerprint. If I have the same player on the same guitar perform a true double, panned hard, there will be enough timing differentials to produce a strong stereo image. There will also be subtle timing and tonal similarities. As such, the guitars will not appear quite as wide as they might were we to switch some things up. Changing out the guitar on the double will serve to slightly widen the image.

The weakest stereo image (aside from most keyboard patches) occurs when you employ stereo miking techniques, mostly because you're collecting both side and center information. It's still a stereo image, but the two sides are not wholly independent, as such, they form an image that spreads across the entirety of the field, including the middle.

I routinely pan stereo organic drum overheads hard left and hard right because the stereo image isn't all that wide to begin with. Meanwhile, others on the Internet proudly proclaim that they toe their overheads in, meaning they soft pan them. But all that does is cram even more sonic information in the middle, which both reduces the apparent size of the kit, and increases the competition for space in the center of your production.

When you pan two independent parts such that one sounds only through the left monitor and the other only through the right, you have defined the edges of your width plane. Make no mistake, you will make your life easier if you use the full width of your stereo field. Why? Because when you muck up the middle you eat valuable space.

When you toe in your two guitars to internal pan positions rather than to pan them hard, and when you bring in your drum overheads rather than to pan them hard, you are purposely choosing to reduce the space within which you have to operate. This would be like moving all of your living room furniture off the wall by two feet. You've accomplished nothing other than to reduce your usable space.

From the perspective of the listener, it makes no difference where you pan anything. None at all. For starters, Music Fan really doesn't care. You will never hear a punter complain about where things are panned within a production. They might muse about it on rare occasion (usually positively), but your panning decisions won't ever cause someone to shut off your record.

The fact of the matter is, unless the listener is wearing head-phones, they are usually located outside of the stereo image. We can't even really consider headphones in terms of imaging, be-cause the closed ear nature of them prevents the two sides from interacting, which is a skewed and unnatural image that doesn't align with the three dimensional manner in which we actually hear. When you play music through monitors the music inter-acts within a space. Not so with headphones.

I'm not suggesting that headphones should be ignored, or that they're bad, or that no one should ever listen in headphones. There's nothing quite like the solitude of great music in headphones. That doesn't change the fact that the imaging is unnatural and skewed. So, when you listen in headphones and freak out about the unnatural sound of a hard panned guitar— that can be chalked up to the nature of headphones. It's not strange to hard pan a guitar. That technique is used every day and has been since stereo was introduced. It's the headphones that make it sound strange. And for whatever reason, you'll only notice it on your own productions.

There is no compromise available for dealing with how a track is heard on headphones as compared to how it's heard through monitors. If wide imaging in headphones weirds you out, then you shouldn't ever listen to music in them, because it's a common treatment.

All of this might make you wonder, if it doesn't matter to the listener where anything is panned, then why does it matter if you soft pan your sides? You can pan your parts anyway that you like in terms of your art, of course. But if you avoid hard panning, it will make your job more difficult. This is purely about real estate, which, in terms of a record production, amounts to space. And the more space with which you have to operate, the easier it will be to balance your arrangement.

Not to overstate the obvious, but if the punter doesn't care about the panning, but hard panning will make your life easier, then it makes no sense whatsoever to avoid the full width of your stereo image. I can assure you, there is more precedent for hard panning in a hit production than there is for soft panning, and with almost no regard to symmetry.

Asymmetry isn't something to be afraid of either. It should be cherished. Seriously, why would we want everything symmetrical all the time? That would be boring and lack contrast. You do yourself no favors operating in fear of contrast, which is arguably one of your more critical production tools in modern music. Make no mistake about it, asymmetry is the contrast for symmetry. One doesn't exist without the other. You want to summarily reject one of your most effective tools for producing dynamic and contrast?

If you find yourself uncomfortable with asymmetry—if you can't fathom the idea of having one electric guitar panned hard or having a tambourine all the way to one side without anything on the other side to counterbalance it—then you are operating out of an irrational fear.

You significantly reduce your contrast when you require symmetry at all times throughout your production. Meanwhile, I will do everything I can to get lift out of a chorus, even one that has its own natural payoff. It's a powerful dynamic to go from the asymmetry of a single guitar on the left, to two guitars panned hard left and hard right.

It's surprising how many people listen to music their whole lives without realizing that hard panning and asymmetry have been staples of modern music production—"modern" meaning any music produced since the early '70s. But in a way, that just proves the point. As a music fan, you likely never noticed the panning because it was working as intended. It wasn't until you started working on your own music that panning ever became an issue.

In general, I pan hard or don't pan at all in my productions. I will certainly use internal pan positions on occasion, particularly on dense productions. But I've gone through periods of my career where it was downright rare for me to use an internal pan position other than the center.

You will see discussions online about LCR mixing (Left, Center, Right), which isn't a system or a method, but rather a contrived exercise in which you implement the specific limit of three pan positions, regardless of circumstance. This is a reasonable exercise to establish the discipline, but there is nothing in music production that should be done "regardless of circum-stance."

That said, if you frequently choose to pan hard, you will re-move a major impediment from your balance decisions. And that extra space will have an enormous impact on the quality of your productions.

Frequency—Up to Down

The illusion of height in a production is created through fre-quency. If you close your eyes, and you sit within the stereo field of your monitors, you will notice that the frequencies stack neatly from low to high.

The reason for this is simple. The higher the frequency, the more directional it is. Low-end information tends to crawl along floors. High-end information will arrive to your ears like a laser. This is an important concept, because if you can visualize how the frequencies appear, then you can construct your arrange-ment as if you're erecting a building.

Consider the spray head on a garden hose for a moment. When set to "jet," the stream from the hose is focused and highly directional in nature. Very little water goes to the left or the right. When that jet stream hits a hard object, it immediately reflects. When it hits a soft object, like a towel, it's absorbed. This is precisely how high-frequency waves react.

When we adjust our hose to a gentler, wider setting, the spray goes everywhere. It's not directional in nature, and it doesn't reflect all that much. It generally gets everything in the area wet. This is precisely how low-frequency sound waves re-act. Whereas the low end goes everywhere, you need to be in the line of fire of the tweeters or horns in order to get their full bril-liance.

The power that frequency has over the listener should not be underestimated. How you balance frequency information in an arrangement can have a direct bearing on how the listener feels.

Really, the way that your parts fill the frequency spectrum in an arrangement is equally important to their musical function. Frequencies are the building blocks of music, and as such, we'll spend quite a bit of time on the subject. In the meantime, there are more planes of space to discuss.

Contrast—Perceived Dynamics

Whereas we can listen to a mix and immediately hear frequency, panning, and balance decisions, we discover contrast over the course of the record—that is to say–time.

Contrast is used to create the illusion of dynamics in modern music. Dynamics, by definition, is: a variation in force or intensity, especially in musical sound. Unfortunately, dynamics in music have been greatly reduced over the years. Generally speaking, we've completely eradicated tempo fluctuations from modern music, (which affects intensity), and many records use very little of the available dynamic range from the loudest to the quietest parts of a mix (which we call loudness).

That said, we do often listen to music in noisy environments, and too much dynamic range can be a problem if you ever hope to hear your record well in the car, or while the dishwasher runs, or the vacuum, or any external noise within your vicinity. This means we need to create the illusion of a dynamic in other ways, and we accomplish that with contrast.

When I mixed Ben Harper's "Roses From My Friends" (from his third album, *Will to Live*), I originally sculpted an enormous dynamic range for that mix. The chorus was quite exciting given how much louder it was than the verses. Unfortunately, once I got the mix into my car, I found myself tuning out until the chorus kicked in. And if I started the record at a level such that I couldn't ignore the verse, then the chorus tore my head off. What was an exceptionally effective payoff in the sound–isolated confines of the studio, was too dynamic for a proper payoff in the real-world environment of a car. Given this, we brought the verses up in level in relation to the choruses.

Now, while we had to reduce the overall dynamic range of that mix in order for it to work in the outside world, we still had contrast in our favor. The verse is sparse and sweet, while the chorus is dense and aggressive, so we get the illusion of more dynamic range than actually exists. Not only do dynamics offer contrast, but contrast offers us the perception of a dynamic in its own right, which can increase payoff.

Then there's symmetrical contrast. We already touched upon this, but a single guitar in the verse panned hard will contrast nicely with double guitars panned hard in the chorus. If we add a Rhodes in its lower register and place it in the verse opposite the guitar, we will now have stereo symmetry in the verse, which will greatly minimize the symmetrical contrast we had earlier. Where we've lost, we've also gained. There is now a contrast in frequency that occurs between the dark Rhodes in the verse and the presumably bright, gritty electric guitars that take over in the chorus. It doesn't matter from where you derive your contrast, so long as it exists.

That said, contrast, while a definitive plane of space, is nothing more than a tool. Just as you can mix a song in mono, and thereby reject all that great stereo width, you can choose to use little to no contrast within your arrangement. Songs can have their own natural contrast, which you can choose to mirror, or allow to stand on its own.

Reflectivity—Far to Near

Reflectivity is the illusion of space. Whereas we accomplish the three-dimensional illusion of width, height, and depth through panning, frequency, and balance respectively, we accomplish the illusion of reflectivity within all three dimensions plus the fourth—time.

Sound exists within the context of its surroundings. We don't just hear a direct sound source unless the source happens to be right next to our ear; we hear sound within a certain space. A drum struck in a small room takes on a tight, controlled character, while the same drum in a hall resonates with openness—and neither sounds anything like a drum played at the edge of a vast cavern, where the sound expands into the abyss. We perceive the sound based on our proximity to the source, and we perceive the space by how the sound waves travel and reflect over time. The amount of time it takes for a sound to fully dissipate in any given space is called the decay time. A large hall will have a much longer decay time than a small room, but in either case those reflections occur over time.

The decay time of any given room is determined by its overall size and shape, along with the nature of the materials contained within that space. A large hall will have a considerably longer decay time if it's empty than it will when it's filled with people. That's because people absorb sound, and the more absorptive materials that are present, the shorter the decay time.

Reflections will appear to us as reverb in enclosed spaces, and as delay in open spaces, particularly where there are large obstacles nearby. While reverberation is the quick, successive bouncing of sound waves off reflective surfaces, delay is a distinct repeat caused by a sound traveling for a significant distance, hitting an object, and returning to us.

We've all experienced this kind of delay in real life; whether yodeling across a ravine (who among us can resist this?) or calling out to a friend near a large building, we perceive a one-time direct reflection from a distant object as delay, although that reflection often includes some measure of reverberation, as well. And depending on the environment, there could be considerably more than one repeat.

In order to effectively create the illusion of great distance, we must also take into account the frequency response of the source. The further away the sound source is from our position, the less high frequencies we hear. That's because much of those frequencies got sucked up along the way.

If you want a trumpet to appear as though it's way in the distance within a production, you would place it low in the overall balance, roll off some of the high end, and send that signal to a reverb unit too. Placing the trumpet low in the mix makes it appear in the back of the sound field. The reverberation in conjunction with the high frequency roll-off provides the illusion of distance. You can create the sense of even more distance by introducing a delay, also with a high-frequency roll-off.

Sometimes reflectivity is contained within a recording. Sometimes reflectivity is added into the mix after the fact to create the illusion of space that didn't exist at the time of the recording. Unfortunately, our control over reflectivity in a production only works well in one direction.

Whereas reflectivity can easily be added, it can't be taken away so easily. There are transient shaping and "de-verb" plugins that can remove space, which can be effective on short percussive parts, but often produce obvious unflattering artifacts on parts with any kind of sustain.

We can also use gates and mutes to cut off the decay the moment a part goes tacit, but that doesn't remove overtly audible reflectivity from the part itself, which becomes rather obvious once it's cut off. So, while there may be tools that we can use to deal with an overly reverberant capture in a pinch, the illusion that we seek could very well be shattered, regardless of our processing efforts.

A part with no reflectivity feels intimate to the listener. A part with significant reflectivity can feel larger than life. When we lose control over our reflectivity, we lose control over the feelings we seek to evoke in the listener through the illusion of our space.

This is why so many recordists employ close-miking techniques. When you consider the possible ramifications of your final balances, it's often better to err on the side of too little space in your capture, than too much.

In general, drums and percussion react well to reflective treatment, since short, percussive bursts don't lose much clarity from the acoustic slap of the space. Electric crunch guitars, on the other hand, lose all clarity within an overly reflective room. There may be a time that's the desired effect, but usually not, because that space softens the tone of the crunch guitars, which is typically counter to the feeling we seek to create with our aggressive guitars.

Violins, on the other hand, often get treated with copious amounts of space, usually a large hall because the tail from the reverb can be dramatic, which falls in line with how violins are often used in an arrangement.

If the violins sustain in a large hall, we don't really perceive the space until the violins stop, at which point we hear the tail of the reverberation. The space also softens their tone, which can be desirable, because stringed instruments can be somewhat grating, especially violins given their higher register in the frequency spectrum.

Reverb in general softens tone because it acts like an airbrush, which is why so many people try to use reverb to hide the flaws of their performance. Unfortunately, reverb is not especially effective for disguising a poor performance. In fact, it can make the performance issues more glaringly obvious and problematic, particularly if you seek a feeling of intimacy or edge.

When you put a long, sweet reverb on a hard rock vocal, you instantly soften both the vocal and the production. Yes, hair-metal bands from the '80s often used reverb, but hair bands didn't generally perform hard rock; they performed pop rock in the guise of hard rock. The whole point of reverb on a hair band was to soften the tone in order to appeal to a wider audience.

The reverb also helped the singer and the band to appear larger-than-life. When applying reverb, you should consider exactly how that reflectivity affects the overall feeling derived from the production.

It's not uncommon to mix and match acoustic spaces in a production. The drums can sound like they're in a large, reflective room, and the guitars can sound like they're in an anechoic chamber, with no ill-effects to the listener. In fact, this is often the preferred treatment as it allows us to create the illusion of a rock band in a large room while maintaining immediacy from our guitars.

How you deal with the spatial reflectivity on your record can completely make or break a production. Too often, reverb is employed out of some misplaced reflex rather than as a tool for manipulating how the listener feels. Think of reflectivity as a way to create a spatial illusion appropriate to the production.

Balance—Front to Back, Large to Small

Balance is a game of relativity and is the holy grail of the five spatial planes. I've left balance for last since it has a direct relationship with the other four planes of space in the arrangement.

Fundamentally, the balance of a part has to do with how loud it is in relation to all the other parts that are playing at any given moment. A loud vocal doesn't exist in a vacuum. We deem it's loud in the relative terms of everything else in the production. In fact, all internal balances are merely an exercise in relativity. As such, balance is our most effective tool for directing the listener's focus. Whatever you place loudest gets the attention. We have no control over free will, of course. One can focus on the hi hat if they like. But that's not how most people listen to music.

RELATIVITY IN BALANCE

Balance has much to do with the mixing process, as that is the time that we finalize those decisions. It's good to think of balance in terms of your arrangement too, because that's how we manipulate the listener's focus, and it has everything to do with how the listener reacts. You mix the drums in a dance track loud because you want to compel the listener to dance. You place a vocal loud so as to compel the listener to sing.

It's important to think of balance in purely relative terms. If you bring up the drums, you've also essentially brought down all the other parts. If you bring up every part but the vocals, you've pretty much brought down the vocal.

Relativity also exists between sections. Whatever happens now in a production, serves to set up what happens next. Balance is the fulcrum you use to push the listener forward. If you boost a simple snare fill before a chorus to generate some excitement, you've effectively provided some added forward push for the listener. But if you bring that snare roll up too much, you can actually weaken the entrance of the chorus by making it seem small in comparison.

You should give as much weight to how a balance decision affects the current section as you do to how it affects the next one, and this is best considered as you build your track. Two electric guitars blaring from top to bottom of a production offers little to enhance contrast. To bring down the relative level of the guitars in the verse would be a reasonable solution to the problem. Unfortunately, the timbre remains the same, which limits the effectiveness of the balance adjustment. Normally, when you play softer, the timbre softens, as does the level and nature of the distortion. As such, a pure level ride isn't always sufficient. Muting one of the guitars in the verse would offer considerably more contrast and help to promote a payoff.

Relativity affects everything in a production. If you bring up the low end on the bass, the KIK could sound small. If you place a big, broad, full-spectrum acoustic guitar on top of a gritty rock track, you could very well dwarf the drums. If you pack a production with parts in the upper midrange, you'll probably be forced to place the vocal exceptionally forward so as to compensate for all that midrange competition.

Each and every balance decision causes an equal and opposite balance reaction, both in real time and in what lies ahead. If you think along these lines as you build your arrangement, you will improve your results significantly.

The Interdependence of Space

Where it comes to creating the illusion of our space, it's important to keep in mind that all of our planes are interdependent. Let us review.

We have five planes of space that fit neatly within the four dimensions of width, height, depth, and time. Panning is balance across the monitors in order to provide us the illusion of width; Frequency is balance across the spectrum to supply us with the illusion of height; Contrast is balance relative to the next event in time, which provides us with both real dynamics and the illusion of dynamics; Reflectivity creates the perception of space based on how it's balanced within all four dimensions of the mix. And balance in conjunction with the other four planes provides us with the perception of depth, making balance the driving force behind all five planes.

Frequency Deep Dive

Given that music directly relates to frequency, it would be a good idea if we spent some time on the subject. As you will likely recall from Physical Science class, frequency is produced through vibration. Pluck a string and it vibrates. Hit a drum, it vibrates. The faster the vibration, the higher the frequency, the higher the note.

Now, we measure frequency in cycles per second, which we represent as Hertz, named after Heinrich Hertz, who proved the existence of electromagnetic waves. We write the expression as

Hz, and for multiples of 1000 we use the term kHz, or kilohertz. Sometimes we get lazy and write the letter K to indicate kHz. I'll stick to the proper terminology for the purposes of this guide.

The human range of hearing extends from 20 Hz to 20 kHz, but if you're an adult, good luck hearing anything over 18 kHz. And if you're old, you're lucky if you can hear over 16 kHz. That doesn't mean there isn't useful information extending well above our range of hearing; we just can't actually hear it directly.

The low E string on a bass guitar sounds at 41 Hz, which means the vibration of that string cycles 41 times every second. The A above middle C on a piano cycles 440 times every second for 440 Hz. And the top note on a violin, which is E7, cycles 2637 times per second, which would be expressed as 2.6 kHz (with rounding). That's right, the top note on a violin is 2.6 kHz. No wonder it's so annoying. That note lives in the most present range of our hearing, which also happens to be the fundamental frequency of a crying baby. Go figure.

An octave above any note is twice its frequency. So, an octave above A4 at 440 Hz is A5 at 880 Hz. An octave above that is A6 at 1760 Hz. All the notes and thereby frequencies in between the octaves define the scale by dividing the octave into relatively equal parts. I say relatively, because we need to compromise a little on certain notes in the scale for purposes of tuning. We use 12 steps in the modern Western scale.

All instruments have a fundamental frequency range, and anyone who composes for an orchestra is acutely aware of these ranges, particularly in terms of notes. For instance, a cello has a four octave range that extends from C2 to C6. In terms of frequency, that would translate as a range of 65 Hz to 1 kHz. And while the overtones will extend far above 1 kHz, and the grate of the bow on the string will emit a rather high frequency, 1kHz is the frequency that we will perceive the loudest when C6 is bowed.

Some instruments like pianos and keyboards, acoustic guitars, and even drums, fill an enormous swath of the frequency range. As such, they tend to occupy considerable space in a production.

Masking

You can only get away with so many parts living in the same frequency range before you get masking, which is exactly as it sounds. You're masking certain frequencies of one part with the common frequencies of another part, but the relative level of the parts is what determines how much masking there is. In other words, you can combat some masking issues partly with how you balance the parts.

The further away in frequency range two instruments are, the less masking will be an issue. An egg shaker is never going to mask a clean 808 KIK drum or vice versa because their frequencies don't cross. The 808 KIK lives down around 60 Hz, and an egg shaker's fundamental lives at about 6 kHz. That's approaching a 7 octave differential.

Where the problems arise is when you combine parts that predominantly occupy the same ranges. The most common example of this would be the KIK and the bass. Those two instruments require some attention in order to derive clarity between them. And if you combine a sub-frequency synth bass with that 808 KIK drum? Not only will you get masking, you'll likely get beating too.

Beating occurs when two held notes are ever so slightly out of tune with each other. If you've ever tuned a guitar then you're familiar with the sound. That's how you know two strings are in tune with each other. The beating stops. The lower the frequency, the slower and more violent the beating. So, if the 808's low-end bloom occurs at an ever-so-slightly lower frequency to a synth bass, you could very well get some obvious beating artifacts, to the point that it could get almost violent in terms of how your woofers react. This is a tuning issue. Not an EQ issue.

As much as it's good to avoid too much masking, you can't avoid it entirely nor would you want to. You risk too much clarity, and that can actually make us feel uncomfortable. Parts will generally cross frequencies in all but the simplest of arrangements. But the more information that you cram into the same frequency range, the more difficulty you'll have with clarity, and the more EQ you'll require to aggressively carve out and shape the parts such that they can all be heard.

Just to be clear, I have no issue with aggressive use of EQ. But if you consider frequency as you arrange your record, you will have less instances in which you need it. Which means there will be fewer times in which you are dealing with sound rather than the music.

Note duration makes a big difference where masking is concerned. The KIK drum and a bass cross frequencies, but the KIK has a short duration, which provides us the space that we need to derive some clarity between the two parts. This is true even if the bass is playing whole notes. But if that KIK sustained for a few seconds, (like a long 808 KIK), combining that with whole notes from the bass could be considerably more challenging.

A great arranger will consider how a part fits within the frequency makeup of the production as readily as they will the rhythmic, melodic, or harmonic functions. We don't seek to fill the full frequency range at all times. There would be no contrast if we did.

I mean, if you want a heavy feeling of foreboding, one way to do it is to drop your arrangement down to just your low-end instruments. If you want a lighter feeling, dump the low-end instruments and add some lilting flutes in the upper midrange. We can directly affect how the listener feels by how we employ frequency in our production.

We choose our instrumentation for many reasons, including availability and musical function, but it's critical to also take frequency into account. A tambourine doesn't seem the best candidate for a hard rock track with a wash of aggressive cymbals and shredding guitars. You need more high-end information, why? It would make far more sense to place your rhythmic overdub in a frequency range with more available space.

Instruments like the B3 organ can take up an enormous amount of space, or just a little. You don't have to have an organ with all stops at full, nor do you have to use both hands. And if your track has a dip in the lower midrange, then you would do well to voice your chords to fill that range in your production. This is why it's so important to view frequency as space. Because it is.

You can't get nearly the low end out of a dense track as you can a sparse one. In fact, if you put too much low end on a dense track, it will sound like pure mud. Conversely, it's far more difficult to overshoot the low end on a sparse track. Frankly, you'd be downright foolish not to exploit that.

Harmonic Series

Everything in a recording interacts, and this includes frequencies. When you bow a violin or strike a piano key, we don't just hear the fundamental frequency that defines the note, we also hear a whole series of mathematically related frequencies above that note. We call these frequencies overtones. Were it not for the interaction of the fundamental frequency with these overtones there would be no timbre. A piano would sound just like a violin which would sound just like the sine wave produced by a test tone. The fundamental in combination with the overtones makes up the mathematical ratios that define the Harmonic Series.

The first harmonic of any given note is defined as the fundamental. This is the frequency that sounds the loudest by far and which we perceive as the note. The second harmonic, which would be the first overtone, is twice the frequency of the fundamental, which means it sounds an octave above it. In other words, if we play a low E which sounds at 41 Hz, the second harmonic sounds faintly at 82 Hz.

To determine the third harmonic, we multiply the fundamental frequency by 3, the fourth by 4, the fifth by 5, and so on forever, well beyond our range of hearing. The Harmonics in technical terms are a multiple of the fundamental, but frequencies also appear as notes, and so in practical terms they create an interval. It's a little easier to understand with a chart.

THE HARMONIC SERIES

Harmonic	Frequency	Note	Interval
1	41 Hz	E1	Fundamental
2	82 Hz	E2	1 octave
3	123 Hz	B2	Perfect 5th
4	164 Hz	E3	2 octaves
5	205 Hz	G#3	Major 3rd
6	246 Hz	B3	Perfect 5th
7	287 Hz	C#—D	Subminor 3rd
8	328 Hz	E4	3 octaves

You'll notice that the further up the Harmonic Series we go, the closer the intervals become. By the time we get to the 7th Harmonic, the interval between it and the 6th Harmonic falls between notes and is defined as a sub-minor 3rd. That is called a "blues" note, which offers ambiguity between the major and the minor nature of the music.

You'll also notice how the 2nd, 4th, and 8th Harmonics are all octaves from the fundamental. That will prove useful when we get into tone shaping with EQ, and when applying distortion, because you can bring out the notes of a part by boosting those even octave harmonics.

Frequency Range of Instruments

The following is a chart of some common instruments, along with their note and frequency ranges.

FREQUENCY AND NOTE RANGES

Instrument	Note Range	Frequency Range
KIK		60 Hz - 100 Hz
Snare		150 Hz - 250 Hz
Toms		60 Hz - 250 Hz
Cymbals		3kHz - 5 kHz
Bass	E1 - C4	41 Hz - 262 Hz
Piano	A0 - C8	27 Hz - 4186 Hz
Guitar	E2 - F6	82 Hz - 1397 Hz
Violin	G3-G7	196 Hz - 3136 Hz
Cello	C2 - B5	315 Hz - 1175 Hz
Tenor Sax	G#2 - E5	104 Hz - 659 Hz
Alto Sax	F#3 - D6	185 Hz - 1175 Hz
Trumpet	F#3 - D6	185 Hz - 1175 Hz
Voice	E2 - A5	82 Hz - 880 Hz

Composers deal with notes. Engineers deal with frequency. Producers deal with notes and frequency. But they really are all one and the same.

The note ranges of all instruments are readily available on the Internet, but where it comes to frequency, you really don't need a chart, you'll use your ears.

Notice how the highest fundamental frequency produced by a piano is 4 kHz, which is higher than the top note of a violin which sounds at just at 2.6 kHz. That means the tiger's share of all harmonic information above 4 kHz are overtones. Which is why when you view a balanced mix on a spectrum analyzer, it's not flat across all frequencies. If it were, it would be unlistenable.

You'll also notice that the drums have very low fundamental frequencies, but we know that they also tend to have an attack at a much higher frequency, the fundamental of which tends to fall between 1 kHz and 3 kHz. The attack is very short in duration and therefore takes up minimal space.

We really don't tend to think about frequency in relation to notes as we make music, but it should be one of your main considerations where it comes to your production. It's not just level that you have to balance, but frequency too, because a good balance of frequency within your arrangement provides your production with clarity. Conversely, too many frequencies in the same range at the same level will lead to problematic masking, and a total lack of clarity.

Even with a well-balanced recording, you'll likely want to manipulate and shape frequencies within your production. For that, we use an equalizer, or EQ, which is ubiquitous at this point. You use it in your car, you use it on your amplifier, and you most certainly use it in your DAW.

Frequency Tonality

We can break down frequency into four basic ranges: Low end, Lower midrange, Upper Midrange, and High end (oftentimes called top end). While some instruments fit neatly into these ranges, others span multiple octaves, covering a large swath of the spectrum. This is where EQ comes into play, allowing us to shape and refine a sound's tonal balance—something we'll dive into in the next chapter. First, it's important to understand these fundamental frequency ranges and how they behave.

LOW END

20–30 Hz: This is mostly rumble and subs and is generally not boosted, but rather attenuated. Some people choose to filter these frequencies as a matter of course, but I don't recommend that unless there's a specific problem that you wish to filter out such as air conditioner rumble or trucks driving by.

30–60 Hz: These frequencies are quite low and "boomy" in nature and will not replicate in most small speakers. While this frequency range is particularly useful in making a production sound big, it can easily overpower everything else if too abundant. The energy down here often needs to be contained and shaped through compression.

100 Hz: This frequency is low but is easily replicated in a six-inch speaker. It's a far more focused low frequency than the subs, although it's still not all that directional in nature.

LOWER MIDRANGE

200–250 Hz: This is the start of the lower midrange, and where directionality of frequency generally begins. It can be described as "woofy," as it's not a very clean low end. Too much of this range can cause a mix to sound thick, dark, and muddy. Too little and your mix will sound scooped out and lacking in power. This frequency replicates well in a two- to four-inch speaker and can be quite useful for making the bass audible in small stereo systems, phones, and laptop computers.

500 Hz: This frequency is the middle of the lower midrange. It is often accused of sounding "boxy," and for good reason—it sounds boxy! You are far more likely to cut this frequency from a signal than to add it. However, there are times that it's a useful frequency to boost for purposes of tone-shaping, as it has some presence attributes to it. It can be used as a thickening agent for tambourines. Or as a presence agent for a vocal. And even as a presence agent for KIK drums that sound scooped. Sometimes you need a little boxiness in your life.

750 Hz: This is getting toward the upper end of the lower midrange. This frequency is also boxy in tone and tends to reduce clarity in a mix when too abundant; however, it can also add presence to a part in the right situation. I use this frequency in a similar manner to 500 Hz, although it's considerably more present in nature. When you cut presence, you begin to reduce clarity. Of course, you can also reduce clarity by boosting this frequency too aggressively. I'm far more likely to cut boxy frequencies than I am to boost them.

UPPER MIDRANGE

1 kHz: This is the beginning of the upper midrange. It's an exceptionally "present" frequency as it approaches the peak of our hearing. This can be a very handy frequency for pulling clarity but can also sound boxy if used too liberally.

2 kHz: This happens to be the basic frequency of a crying baby, which might explain why it's our most easily heard frequency as humans. Too much of this frequency and "harsh" will be an adjective you'll hear when someone describes your mix. I often refer to 2 kHz as "strident," but that certainly doesn't make it a frequency to avoid. When a part doesn't seem to pop out of your arrangement, you can use 2 kHz to help with that. Both electric and acoustic guitars love this frequency as it lives in the heart of their string rake. It's also a really good frequency to attenuate when a vocal is too strident.

3–4 kHz: This frequency range, much like 2 kHz, is helpful in adding or removing bite from a recording.

6–9 kHz: This is the tail end of the upper midrange. This is where we exit the "bite" range and enter into dentist drill territory. This range of frequencies can give you a nasty headache, and quick. Percussion, esses, and cymbals live in this range.

That said, it can be a useful frequency range to open up a sound for purposes of clarity.

HIGH END

10–12 kHz: This is the lower end of the high-end frequencies (say that three times fast). The addition of this frequency range can be helpful in opening up a sound and/or offsetting the coloration of a microphone or processing.

12–16 kHz: This is extreme high end, and this range of frequencies will often bring out unintended distortion artifacts as quickly as it will open up a sound, but it can still be quite useful, depending on the overall quality of the EQ. If you were to boost this frequency across your whole production, you would bring up mostly percussion parts. You'll also bring out the overtones.

18–20 kHz: This range is beyond most of our hearing, and while there is definitely information up there, bringing it up with EQ only adds audible spitting and noise. Even if you can hear frequencies this high, you don't generally want to aggressively boost this information.

The Record's in the Midrange

It's important to understand just where the meat of your production lies, and that's in the midrange. If you were to take your favorite record (any record) and filter out the frequencies from 4 kHz up along with the frequencies from 200 Hz down, all of your harmonic and melodic information will remain audible. I demonstrated this principle in a YouTube video titled "The Record is in the Midrange."

Mariah Carey's highest whistle note on her song "Emotions" clocks in at 3263 Hz. Even a piccolo tops out at 4698 Hz. This means all of your melodic and harmonic musical information generally sits below 4 kHz. Everything above that frequency are harmonic overtones, cymbals, percussion, and noise. Everything below 200 Hz are sub frequencies. And while there are certainly fundamental bass notes below 200 Hz, those don't reproduce in a lot of consumer systems. It's the octave overtones that reproduce as audible bass notes on smaller systems. All of this adds up to one thing. Your record lives in the midrange.

Of course, you wouldn't want to deliver a record without subs and without top end. The subs give the production weight and allows the record to sound big. The top end is useful for clarity and excitement. But make no mistake, the most important information lives in the midrange.

To gut your midrange is to gut the power of your production. Many new producers emphasize the low and high end to make their record big, often at the expense of the midrange. This is a mistake for a couple of reasons. For starters, many, if not most, larger consumer systems already have a hyped up low and top end, which is what we call a smiley curve. It's best to counter that curve with a solid midrange, rather than to exacerbate it by applying your own smiley EQ curve.

There's also *apparent* loudness, which lives in the heart of our hearing. Loudness has to do with the dynamic range of your record, which is measured in LUFS (Loudness Units Full Scale). We will discuss loudness at length further along, but a production exhibiting a prominent midrange will sound louder than a production featuring a smiley EQ curve, even if their LUFS measure identically, and even after level matching. Consider this when you EQ your parts. Rather than to boost top end for purposes of clarity, consider addressing frequencies in the upper midrange instead. It can make a world of difference in your results.

Instrumentation

Instrumentation is at the very least influenced, if not somewhat dictated, by genre. A typical rock production will include bass, drums, guitars, and vocals. A hip-hop track could be nothing more than a beat, some harmonic samples, a rap, and some ad libs. EDM might include loops, programmed drums, and keyboards. R&B often calls for plenty of KIK and bass with some keyboards, perhaps a guitar, along with stacks of vocals.

Even taking genre into account, there is a ton of wiggle room where instrumentation is concerned, and you are by no means locked into the usual. That said, one instrument can absolutely define a genre—like the buzzy and aggressive bass treatment you'll hear in Dubstep productions. If you produce a Dubstep song without the signature bass, you might be the only person who calls it Dubstep.

Of course, genre is just one consideration. But if you know what you're making, then it does tend to point you in the right direction in terms of your instrumentation. That is, unless you're producing world music, at which point you have a vast array of supremely grating instruments available to you. Should I ever hear another Erhu again, it will be too soon.

If you're in a band, then your instrumentation is nearly built in. You write your songs based on your personnel, and you operate together to create an arrangement. Those of you who program your tracks may feel unencumbered by genre, which opens up a vast array of instruments. Regardless of your situation, my advice is the same. As you build your track—as you consider your instrumentation—take frequency range into account.

Clearly, the instrument and the player are the first consideration. It's all well and good to decide you need a super-expressive violin part to pump up the sadness factor, but if you don't have a player who can pull it off, the part could sound nothing short of whiny.

Once you've determined the feeling you want a part to evoke, and in what frequency range you need the part to live, you have contained your options significantly. A piccolo flute would certainly use a similar frequency range as a violin–but will that produce the feeling of sadness you seek? Tenor saxophone can express a feeling of melancholy, as can trombone, but they both sit in a lower frequency range from the violin or the flute, which could disqualify them if your production calls for the part to live in a higher register.

Instruments have certain traits that make them good candidates to produce certain feelings within your production, and a good player understands how to pull those feelings from their instrument. A great fiddle player can express melancholy just as readily as elation, so long as the tempo is in agreeance. Really, you can probably evoke any feeling from just about any instrument under the right circumstances, but there are more usual choices for a reason.

The player, the instrument, and the nature of the part will have the greatest influence on how it makes you feel. But that doesn't mean you should ignore frequency and balance in the decision-making process. I mean, if all you have is a tenor saxophone available for this sad part that you have in mind, then it may make sense to put your harmonic chordal voicings either in a higher register or a lower one, so as to make room for that saxophone. The lower register would seem more likely to reinforce a feeling of melancholy.

Of course, you may recall that masking can be combated with balance. Should you place the saxophone forward in the balance, it will not be subject to significant masking. Which is all well and good if it's a solo. But if the sax is playing a countermelody or some other part subservient to the vocal, you will be forced to balance it lower in the production. At that point masking can be an issue, and register should be considered.

In order to determine the best register for a part all you need do is attempt to balance it. If you find that you're almost forced to place the part louder than you imagine it, then you have a masking issue that you might want to address. Oftentimes, the easiest way to deal with the masking is to put the parts in their own general register.

Chord voicings are also important as your inversions can be the difference between masking and clarity. There are also musical reasons to consider your voicings. Both the internal and the top note movement of chords will have a significant effect on the musical strength of a section. The top notes of a chord provide a melodic musical sub-theme that you can lean on in your production. Your voicings can also be used to create excitement within the production, particularly if you walk them up the register for purposes of climax and payoff.

Simple Arrangements

A simple production keeps the focus on the song. The song is the art here. The production is just a vehicle for the song, and the only time that you should need to make the production more important than the song is when the song falls short. If it's your own song, and you find that you must lean heavily on production techniques, then it's time to admit the song isn't strong enough to stand up on its own.

Many producers try to cram too many parts into their productions. That isn't defined by how many tracks you use. I've mixed productions with over 80 tracks that were masterpieces in which everything went together perfectly. Many producers, including myself, will often split guitar parts by section (i.e. intro guitar, verse guitar, chorus guitar), or use layers to create a more complex tone for a single part, so track count doesn't necessarily indicate complexity of the arrangement. But if you're having a difficult time with your record; if you find that you can't seem to balance everything without the record sounding small; if you find that your dynamics are completely lacking because you've filled every bit of space in all five planes—you probably have too many parts.

It takes tremendous skill to mix a production that's packed with instrumentation in a particular frequency range (usually the midrange). It took me years to develop that particular ability. If you find yourself indiscriminately plugging in part after superfluous part and it seems increasingly difficult to balance your record while maintaining clarity and punch, or if you feel that your record sounds small, this would be about the time to consider putting your arrangement choices under some extra scrutiny.

I balance my production before every session. I balance after every session too, because it tells me where I'm at in the production. Every time I introduce new parts, I experiment with my balances. Parts will sometimes interact in unintended ways, and I often seek almost random discoveries as I build my production. The goal is to get the production in a place where my singer is inspired. If you're the singer, then you'll need to inspire yourself. The best way to do that is to make sure that everything in your arrangement serves a purpose and means something, otherwise you'll have to deal with the arrangement later.

Hey, some of my favorite mixes have come from completely confused arrangements in desperate need of underdubbing techniques and mangling. But I was always coming in fresh as a third-party specialist with license to do whatever I thought was right. Who's your specialist? And even if you have one, you're leaving much up to chance when you don't strategically construct your arrangements.

As a producer, I rarely record a vocal before I have my arrangement fully worked out. It happens. There can be scheduling logistics that force such a decision. Sometimes the singer is inspired before the arrangement is fully ironed out, at which point I capitulate. Setting aside instrumental tracks, the whole purpose of your production is to act as a vehicle for the vocal performance. The vocalist is the direct connection to the audience. It's the vocal that sells the song. And if the production is unfocused, or too dense, and lacks any kind of forward push, then it will be difficult to perform. And yes, this is true even if you're the vocalist.

The main advantage to a simple arrangement is space. When you have space, your parts mean more, they go together well, and your vocalist has the room to fill that space with a compelling performance. Oh, and you can get away with more low end too. Low end makes your record big. It makes your record warm. And it is the foundation upon which you build your production.

There's no doubt, some artists and producers gravitate towards dense productions, and not every arrangement in the world should be simple or sparse. There's certainly room in music for diversity of style. But if you struggle to put it all together, if you can't seem to make your record big, the issue likely stems from too many parts.

Writing Parts

As important as it is to implement techniques that promote forward motion, the parts themselves need to be compelling, if not interesting. Regardless of your role as producer the writing of parts is fully within your domain.

A bass player pedaling eighths on the tonic at all times is a boring part. It's still a part. And it could even be the best available part for a production. Not every part can be the star. Sometimes a super simple part does exactly what it should for a production because it stays out of the way. But in the case of pedaled eighths on the bass part? Those are really just taking up space.

If you're the songwriter or the cowriter, then you have full control over all of your parts. It's the band entity that typically needs the most help with this.

Many band players seem to muddle their way through a song, rather than to come up with repeatable phrases that people can sing. It's the repeatable nature of the parts that makes a song and production accessible, so to play something nebulous and unsingable is counter to the goal. One possible reason for this common malady is the constant need for bands to fill time. A band with barely a set of material is hired for three sets, which prompts them to extend their songs live. What may have started out as a tight song becomes a jam, and repeatable parts are somehow abandoned in the process.

I certainly understand muddling through parts in order to find them. I do it myself, as it's super effective. But the moment I play something that I like, or that I find interesting, even if it's just a phrase, then I'm on my way to making the part, because I want to use repetition to my advantage.

If a Side-Player or a band member doesn't come up with a repeatable part, then I'll listen carefully to what they play, and highlight the phrases that I think are most compelling. Then we begin to lock those phrases in as we work out the rest of the part. This can be a tedious and somewhat time-consuming process because you're writing a part as the player is learning it. Some players can learn parts faster than others.

Once a part has been worked out and structured, we may have the opposite problem—an overly-simplified part. A lack of variance can be just as uninteresting as a lack of repeatability— it's boring.

There's no doubt that some parts should be simple and are designed to repeat in a precise manner. This is especially true in pop music. But if you're working with a band entity, precise programming can be counter to an effective record. We want the parts to contain repeatable themes, but we often want some slight variations to those themes so as to retain the human element. Essentially, we want the part performed. Parts that naturally become increasingly more complex over the course of the production also push the listener forward.

Whether you choose to create a part that appears programmed or performed depends on the part itself, the production, and your own personal preferences. But even tightly programmed parts do well with some built-in variation—as if they were performed.

Prosody

Prosody is the consistency between lyrics and music. For the songwriter, prosody is an important tool. A song like "Wind Beneath My Wings" has a melody and a lyric that are both meant to be inspirational in nature (to someone other than myself, I'm sure). The emotional impact of the music will generally match the lyric, and this is the most basic form of prosody. Most good songwriters use prosody innately, but there are also more literal examples.

In the Supremes' "Stop! in the Name of Love," the melody does precisely what the lyric says. The word "stop" is sung, and the melody stops on that word. That's prosody. A melody moving up on the word "up" or down on the word "down" is another great example of prosody in songwriting.

Good prosody isn't always quite so obvious. In Johnny Cash's song "Ring of Fire," the melody in the chorus actually moves up as he sings the word "down" three times. He sings: "I went down, down, down, and the flames went higher." While at first blush, the lyric seems to literally contradict the melody. In reality, Cash is exposing the inherent contradiction between falling in love as opposed to love being an uplifting experience. This idea is represented brilliantly by the imagery of the lyric and specifically how it works counter to the melody, thereby illustrating musically the contradiction. There's no doubt that this was a conscious decision by a great songwriter.

Stephen Stills' famous song "For What It's Worth," which was first recorded by Buffalo Springfield in the sixties, is an excellent example of how prosody was enhanced by the production. If the song doesn't immediately come to mind, you'll probably recognize the chorus lyric, "Stop children, what's that sound, everybody look what's going down." In the last chorus of that song, the entire production comes to a halt on the word "stop."

Another example of prosody from a production standpoint would be the Genesis song "Just a Job to Do," in which Phil Collins sings "bang, bang, bang" in quick succession followed by two reverberant snare hits and the lyric "down they go." In this case, the snare hits act as gunshots within the production. This is not only effective, it's smart.

Don't go nuts with this. If you add reverb to the snare every time you hear a word like "shoot" or "bang" you risk turning a good tool into an overused joke. The literal translation of a lyric into a production technique is powerful when used judiciously, particularly if the prosody accentuates something important within the context of the song. But as with everything, good taste comes into play.

Paradoxical Prosody

Sometimes artists choose to create a feeling with their song that is completely out of alignment with the lyrical content. The Police's iconic "Every Breath You Take" would be a good example of this, seeing as it's a stalker's anthem. But the music is so powerfully positive, that it's commonly played at wedding receptions. This demonstrates just how powerful the music can be in relation to the lyrics.

Of course, from the perspective of the stalker, which is the main character in the song, this is a wholly positive song. An argument could be made that the musical feeling is actually in alignment with the lyrical content.

Motion

Motion is used for three purposes. To make a production (or part) more interesting, to hide performance flaws, and to provide a contrast dynamic for purposes of forward push.

Motion is a staple in music. Tremolos, phasers, flangers, delays and taps, Leslie cabinets, choruses, ring shifters, filters, and even uber aggressive compression will produce motion, which is an important part of production. It's one of the primary ways that EDM music propels the listener forward. When the bottom end is filtered out of the production for an entire section of the song, that is done specifically for purposes of forward push.

We will discuss motion effects further in the *Mixing & Mastering* section, but it can be such an important contrast dynamic, I felt I should discuss it with you in terms of your arrangement decisions.

I'll warn you now, motion can get messy if you apply too much of it. So, taste is important in this regard. If everything in your production has motion slathered all over it, your production will end up a big mess (which is also true with reverbs and delays). You want your motion to mean something.

Electric pianos and lead synth parts really love delay and distortion too. Synths without any distortion or delay are typically bland and uninteresting. Just about every keyboard player I've ever met prefers a bit of delay on their keyboards, mostly because the delay will hide minor flaws in their playing, but partly because it's more interesting that way.

Guitar players will often employ whammy bars, tremolos, and wah-wah pedals, all for the purpose of motion, so as to make their part more interesting. They'll even physically create motion by bending the strings or the neck of the guitar.

Risers and sound effects used to whip us into a new section offer motion to a production. Brass and strings are super expressive instruments that can offer us loads of motion, including vibrato. Autotune certainly offers us motion in the form of arti-facts.

You know what offers no motion? A sine wave. Which is what a test tone is. Those certainly aren't fun to listen to. So, as you arrange, you should consider how you use motion to your bene-fit.

Motion is often shaped through our processing tools, mark-ing the shift from arrangement into the engineering side of production. Nearly everything we've discussed in this chapter revolves around music and its presentation through arrange-ment—the core elements of a compelling song and production. When you think in musical terms, the engineering becomes less of an obstacle and more of a tool. The key is to get engineering out of your way. The first step is to shift your mindset. *Check.* The second step is to understand the technical considerations and how to apply them effectively—which is exactly what we'll tackle next.

CHAPTER THREE

The Home Producer

These days, most of us fall under the category of Home Producer. Songwriter Producers and Self-Producers tend to fit this description, as do many Producers For-Hire.

This chapter is designed to help all of you Home Producers who must also engineer your own records. If we can get the frustrating technical hurdles out of your way, you can place your focus where it belongs—on the music itself.

I have no interest in bogging you down with unnecessary technical details, but rather to convert technical concepts into practical strategies. As such, I break everything down to its core. Even with that approach, it may take a few reads and quite a bit of practice before it all clicks. Once it does, recording, mixing and mastering will become more enjoyable and less stressful processes, because they become integrated into all of your musical decisions.

Where it comes to plugins, these are tools we generally use for sound design and manipulation within a mix. Most Home Producers are only working with 2 channels of conversion, which means the plugins that you apply in your DAW don't affect the raw recorded tracks on the way in. This essentially designates your plugins as strictly mixing tools.

Since the mix is the culmination of all your decisions, much of what we discuss regarding internal processing tools is framed in relation to the mix, that is to say, the end game. You'll achieve better results by considering how your production functions in that context, rather than treating mixing as a completely separate process.

The same applies to much of the information from the previous chapter. Your arranging decisions—how you think about space, frequency, balance, and musical function— have a direct impact on the final production, and therefore the final mastered mix. If you're in charge of all of these processes, there is no distinguishing between them. They become part of a single continuous workflow. Your mix is your production, and your production is your mastered mix.

Even your capture—that is to say, any part recorded with a mic—directly affects your mix, and that includes the quality of the performances. This is especially true if the recording is compromised in some way. Let's say you want an intimate, present, in-your-face vocal, but your vocal capture is slathered in room tone. That issue will negatively impact your mix because you can't present the production as you intended.

At that point, you have two choices: compromise your vision to accommodate the sound or compromise the performance to accommodate your vision.

If you refuse to compromise your sonic vision, then your only real option is to re-record the vocal in a more appropriate space. But what if the original, sonically compromised vocal performance shits all over the new one? Now you're stuck choosing between performance and sound. Neither choice matches your vision. This puts you in a nasty position, one you would do well to avoid. And while sometimes errors can miraculously work out in your favor, that is not something to rely upon.

As such, it becomes important to capture the sound the way you envision it the first time, so that you don't have to make uncomfortable decisions or compromises down the line.

If you want to maintain control over your mix and production, then you need to engage in some measure of strategy so that you can work assiduously towards your end vision. At all times, you are making your evaluations and decisions based on how your production mixes together. Therefore, viewing all of the processes as interconnected rather than as isolated steps can lead to more cohesive and intentional results.

Before we get too deep into the weeds, let's take a step back—because nobody starts out thinking about mix integration, sonic vision, or plugin workflows. It all begins with making music.

The Beginning

Most of us start out by producing our own songs. It's the gateway to producing.

You might use a program like Garageband or Ableton lite, or any of the numerous entry level DAW programs. These sorts of programs—which often come with large loop libraries—allow for satisfying results with minimal knowledge and abilities.

Then you want more. A vocal, perhaps.

A USB mic works for that. You likely already have one of those, and it's really easy to hook up. Just plug it into your computer. How hard could producing songs really be?

After a while your little computer speakers seem inadequate, so you decide to hook up your Bluetooth speaker, only to discover there's a delay. What the hell? Then you try your Bluetooth headphones. The delay is still there. Then you spend half your day trying to figure out why this delay exists, because how could anyone work like that!

The answer is nobody can work like that.

You spend hours scouring the internet for what could cause this problem. You don't even really know how to ask the question because you don't know any of the terminology, which can make the search for answers seem impossible. Then you finally—and very much accidentally—stumble upon the answer. There is a delay that occurs when sending music through the air to your Bluetooth device, and it's called latency.

Motherfucker! Latency? Why on earth would they call it *that?* It's a fucking delay!

Now you plug your wired earbuds into your computer's output. No delay . . . erm, latency. You're back on track, and now you can finish this amazing song.

Some of you, who play piano (or who have perhaps tinkered with it), might find the loops a bit limiting. You want to add your own part. And although your entry level DAW offers you a way to program MIDI without an external device, you would prefer to play the part. Go figure. Unfortunately, that requires a piano-like keyboard of some sort. So, you go online and research keyboards, and after going down the rabbit hole of dedicated synthesizers, you come across "MIDI controllers." They cost hundreds of dollars!

Fortunately, you have some of your birthday money saved up, and you find a MIDI keyboard for under $100. It's small, like 30 keys, but hey, it's better than trying to enter one note at a time. So, you click to make the purchase. A day or two later, your MIDI keyboard arrives, you plug in your USB cable. You load up the software sampler in your DAW and you can hear sound! How easy was that? After some time with the manual, you figure out you can record your part as you play it, and you happily perform your first MIDI part. Then you play it back. You're horrified. Confused even.

I didn't play that!

Yes you did.

The track is speeding up and slowing down!

No it isn't.

Miracle of miracles, after countless attempts to play the part, (otherwise known as practice), you see a video about quantization on YouTube.

Oh my god! I can put the notes on the beat!

Unfortunately, the stupid thing puts some of your notes on the wrong beat. In fact, it's worse than it was before. A little more research reveals it's because you were actually that far off. How could this be? You are the star—the darling of your piano teacher. Yet you can't play a part close enough in time such that the notes snap to the right place? Apparently not.

Then, you decide to look at your DAW manual, which uses all sorts of terms that make absolutely no sense to you. Still, you muddle your way through the MIDI section as best you can, and there it is. You can actually move the MIDI notes around after you play them and even after you quantize them. And so you do. You spend hours moving little graphic bars around and placing them all perfectly on the beat. Then you notice that some of the notes sound way louder than others. Which is a problem. Back to the manual.

Aha! You can adjust the velocity of the MIDI notes and make them more even! You spend another few hours adjusting your 4-bar keyboard part.

You're now a month in and you still don't have a usable song because you still haven't recorded a vocal since getting sidetracked by the Bluetooth debacle, and then the whole MIDI programming tedium. To make matters worse, you really want to play your masterpiece for your friends (you don't even care that it's not done), but that would require inviting them over to hear it for themselves because you have no idea how to export it from your DAW. Instead, you call them up and play it over the phone, only for them to tell you it sounds bad, which kind of hurts your feelings.

Fuck them.

Once you realize you don't actually have to play the part again, you can actually copy and paste your 4-bar keyboard part, you have your verse! You can't even fathom making a new section at this point (that was exhausting), so you perform your first verse vocals against what you have. Genius! This is going to be a hit!

You're so excited with your progress, you just have to share, which requires you to figure out how to finally export the damn thing. That takes you three days, and then another day to understand how to put it on your device so that you can finally play it for your friends in its full fidelity.

You go to your friend's house, and after 30 minutes of trying to pair to their Bluetooth speaker to your phone, you're finally able to play them your song. It sounds like a complete garbled mess. The low end is overbearing. The vocals are unclear and too loud in some sections and too soft in others. And there's this nasty distortion that happens every now and then. Nothing sounds like it did at your house. You try the car. Same issue, only worse. And you have to turn the volume all the way up even to hear it, and there's all this noise. How embarrassing!

Your friends trash your effort, and so you are determined to make it better. You decide that you really don't like the sound of the piano sample, and after exhausting all of the possibilities in your DAW, you go back online and discover that people actually purchase sample packages for better samples. Unfortunately, these packages won't work with your DAW lite (which you didn't discover until you'd already downloaded the demo). You need to purchase the full DAW, which is kind of expensive. The sample library is even more expensive.

All you want to do is to make a song, and all you seem to come across are technological hurdles that make the process nothing short of difficult, time consuming, and expensive. Even after you get past the initial hurdles, there's an endless parade of more hurdles. All of which require more money that you don't have.

As if that's not bad enough, every time you make a purchase to overcome one problem, you've managed to introduce a whole host of new problems, all of which require more purchases. Your DAW lite is too limiting, so you buy the full version, which is certainly more powerful, but also ten times more complicated to use. More hurdles. More frustration. Then, according to lots of random strangers online, the plugins in your DAW aren't adequate. You need to buy expensive third-party packages even before you've learned how to use the plugins you have. You don't even know what a compressor does—but apparently you already need a better one.

Then you find out the USB mic you're using is for total amateurs, so you purchase a mic (which was the least expensive of the mics you found recommended online), only to realize you need an interface too. Then, after you figure out how to set up your interface, you realize you need studio monitors.

So, now you have a brand new interface, brand new monitors and a professional condenser mic, which sounds terrible. Like it's in an echo chamber. What kind of awful mic comes with reverb? After more research, you discover that you need to treat your room acoustically. That's not cheap either.

Rather than to treat your bedroom—you can hear birds on your recordings anyway—you convert your closet into a vocal booth. You cover the walls and ceiling of the closet with packing blankets, only to discover the vocals you record in there sound boxy. The compressor makes the boxiness worse and the EQ guts the sound of your boxy vocal, all of which is how it works, but you don't know that, so you seek a new compressor and a new EQ—perhaps even of the analog variety.

Then one day you read that interfaces have converters, and if you want good sound, you need better converters. Then your preamps are the problem. Then you discover the mic you bought is shit, the compressor you bought is shit, the EQ you bought is shit, your monitors are shit, and even your room is total shit. Which is distressing since you sleep in that room.

All of it shit, shit, and more shit. Which is exactly how you would describe what it sounds like every time you play your newest effort outside of your room.

I could go on and on and on, because it's endless. And perhaps this story doesn't align perfectly with yours, but you surely went through enormous frustration, and I would imagine you've wondered more than once—*what kind of money pit hell have I gotten myself into?*

You want to record your song, or you want to program your song, and the technology is constantly in the way, and buying things never seems to alleviate the problem.

Not only do you need to learn all the tools and all the engineering, but your true goal is to write great songs, and that takes a lot of practice too. As does arranging. As does performing. All of it requires practice. Lots and lots of practice.

Producing music also requires a monetary investment. There was a time where recording really required a proper studio. In some instances, a studio is still a necessity. A good studio provides a dedicated acoustical space, sound isolation, and lots of equipment to meet your recording needs. But if you're not recording a band of players—if you're programming much of your music and perhaps recording no more than one or two mics at a time—then you can largely bypass the studio. And when you first start writing songs, you should. There's still an investment to be made. It's a mere fraction of the required investment when I was starting out.

Picture this. It's 1985, and I have a six-year-old Apple II+ ($1,500, complete with a monochrome green screen). It had a whopping 64 KB of RAM and two floppy disk drives. That's 64 kilobytes. There are a million kilobytes in a gigabyte. So, if you have a computer today with 64 GB of RAM, you have a million times more memory than I did back then.

I bought a third party sound card (for $300) and that allowed me to plug in a MIDI cable, I bought software for recording, programming, and reproducing MIDI, thinking I could use it to reproduce an entire symphony out of my Yamaha DX7 ($1600). I was so excited! After programming the first part, I come to find out I could only play one part out of any given keyboard.

Oh. My. God!

My first synth—the Roland Juno-60—was of no help. It didn't have MIDI ports. So, I sold the Juno-60 and bought the MIDI-ready Juno 106 ($1600). Of course, I took a $400 loss in that exchange, but at least now I could play two MIDI parts at a time. Then I got an Ensoniq keyboard module ($1200), now I could program three MIDI parts at any given time. That still wasn't enough, so I got a 4-track Fostex cassette recorder ($600). Then there was my Electro-Voice PA speaker (I had one), and my TOA mixer (let's add another $2000 for those). And don't even get me started on cables!

So, here I am, with basically 7 tracks of recording and programming capability, mono monitoring out of a PA system, and I've spent $6500 (not counting the computer). I was making $3.25 an hour at my fast food job, and about $40 a week delivering newspapers.

I'm not trying to go all Boomer on you here—I couldn't if I wanted to since I'm a Gen X-er—but I had to flip burgers for 2,000 hours to pay for all of that.

Consider that I didn't have compressors. I didn't have EQ. I didn't have effects. I had no processing whatsoever. And I had a disgustingly atrocious $100 Audio-Technica dynamic mic. Is it any wonder that I ended up in a studio by the time I was 20?

As I attended school at Berklee in Boston it became quite apparent: the only way I could possibly record and produce my songs was to get myself into a commercial studio. I wasn't interested in owning a studio, and it would have taken forever, anyway. I just wanted to record my songs. I didn't even know I wanted to be a producer yet.

So, now let's take a look at your buy-in today, compared with what you get. Your computer will cost the same as mine did $1500, but most of you likely already have that available, as did I, so I'm not counting that in the initial price of entry.

You need a DAW. It's $200 for Apple's Logic. You need an entry level interface for $300 (mic preamps included). A pair of monitors for $400 (I mixed my best known and successful works on $300 Yamaha NS10s). A condenser mic for $100 (you can get a LEWITT 240 for that price, which is actually a really great sounding mic). A decent sized MIDI Keyboard for $300. Speaker stands, cables, and various accoutrements for $300. And let's add in a few acoustic panels for $400. We get to a grand total of $2000 initial buy-in for a bare minimum system to adequately record your songs.

My buy-in was $6500, which is the equivalent to $18,000 today. Your buy-in is $2000, and you have proper monitoring, processing tools, and no limitations on how many MIDI tracks you can record. You even have a mic that I could record anyone on. You have everything that you would need to program and record your songs for a mere fraction of the cost, and you make way more money than I did, even at minimum wage.

The point of all this is, you can have enormous power to create with what is actually a minimal investment, especially when viewed within the historical context. That doesn't make the investment any less painful, I understand. And your costs will only increase over time. You'll want more acoustic treatment. Better monitors and headphones. A better interface. A better MIDI controller. Analog preamps, analog compressors. Third-party plugin packages. Third-party Amp Sims. And all of that costs money. All of it requires a massive investment in time to set up and use, which brings with it lots of frustration too.

Just understand, where it comes to technology getting in the way of producing commercially available music and records, that's always been the case.

The good news is, time and effort and learning can all help you to get the technology out of your way, and that's what we're here to do. Let's begin with our most basic and necessary tools.

THE GEAR

The DAW

There are about 20 DAWs on the market. Some are Mac-exclusive (like Logic Pro), while others run only on Windows. Most, however, are cross-platform. The computer and DAW you choose have little to no impact on sound quality, as DAWs don't inherently have a "sound"—except perhaps Harrison Mixbus, which models the harmonic characteristics of classic Harrison mixing desks from the '80s.

Your choice of technology should always be based on what makes your life easier. Some DAWs are better suited for recording and engineering, while others excel at writing and arranging. However, they all function in similar ways, and as time progresses, DAW companies inevitably copy each other's platform features.

I've personally operated two DAWs—that's one more DAW than most people have operated, and there's a reason for that—DAWs are complicated and take a long time to master. Given how few I've used and the fact that each has its own set of strengths and weaknesses, I can't definitively tell you which DAW is best for you. In all likelihood, the best DAW for you is the one you're already using. If it no longer meets your needs, then it might be time to switch—but be warned, transitioning to a new DAW is a painful and time-consuming process. I always recommend purchasing a tutorial video when learning a complex DAW.

I use Logic, but I also buy Macs—which is why Logic is priced at $200 and hasn't required a paid update since 2013. Apple wants me to buy more Macs, and I happily do for various reasons. I'm not here to sell you on a Mac or my choice of DAW, but it's worth considering that the cost of a computer is only part of the equation.

Plugins

All DAWs come with plugins that handle a variety of audio processing tasks. Some of these plugins are staples that will appear on many of your channels—like EQ and compressors. Others serve more specialized purposes and might only be used occasionally.

The stock plugins that come with your DAW are typically good enough to get you started. I regularly use stock plugins in Logic, so there is nothing inherently inferior about them. If we devised a somewhat ridiculous exercise in which I had to mix a record using only stock plugins, this wouldn't be a problem.

That's not to say I don't use third-party plugins—I have plenty. But I also have decades of experience and a vast basis of comparison, so I'm in a good position to judge whether they're actually worth it. If a stock plugin gets the job done with the least resistance, that's the one I'll use.

When DAWs first hit studios in the late '90s, the stock plugins bundled with Digidesign's Pro Tools were—to put it kindly—atrocious. Third-party plugin suites at the time were really only slightly less atrocious—we'll call them mediocre. But better is better, and professional engineers were willing to pay thousands of dollars for plugin packages that replaced the atrocious with the mediocre.

There are companies, still to this day, who sell the exact same wholly mediocre plugins they were pushing over two decades ago. Sure, there have been updates to them over the years, but the functionality and the GUIs of some of these dinosaur packages aren't even worth the pennies-on-the-dollar prices they offer.

The takeaway? You can spend good money on third-party plugins that are actually worse than your DAW's stock plugins—and if you haven't spent enough time learning what you already have, you won't even know it.

If you rush out and load your DAW with third-party plugins you don't know how to use, you'll just end up overwhelmed. I see it all the time—someone buys multiple plugin bundles and then has no clue where to begin. That's what happens when you try to bypass the learning process. Don't do that.

We'll go into various plugin types in detail later, including some specific third-party recommendations so you know where to start. For now, let's continue to discuss the most basic requirements for producing your music.

The Interface/Converters

Your interface is how you get audio in and out of your computer, and it houses both your A/D (Analog-to-Digital) and D/A (Digital-to-Analog) converters. The A/D converters transform analog signals into digital, while the D/A converters do the reverse. Since D/A conversion directly affects what you're hearing, it's part of your monitoring chain.

These days, you're unlikely to find subpar converters in anything but consumer devices. The converters in your computer's headphone output are typically dreadful (even on Macs), severely skewing what you hear which will affect your decision-making. Some lower-end interfaces have questionable headphone outputs as well, though this has improved significantly in recent years. Generally, most interfaces now include converters that are more than adequate, even at the headphone output. Conversion quality simply isn't the issue it once was—even as recently as the early '10s.

Most Home Producers only need two D/A converters for stereo playback. How many A/D converters you need depends on how many channels you plan to record at once. If you never record more than two channels at home, then a two-channel interface will suffice. If you're tracking multiple channels at once, you'll need a multi-converter unit.

You'll often hear people online insist that you need ultra-expensive converters for mixing and mastering. I won't tell you converters don't matter, but the actual benefit of top-tier conversion is marginal compared to the increase in price. If you're making serious money from your music—or you're independently wealthy—then sure, go ahead and invest in high-end converters. But for most people, your interface's built-in converters won't hold you back.

For the majority of us, D/A conversion is only used for monitoring. The converter's sound isn't imprinted on your mix when you bounce it internally—just your decisions. The only time the converter's sound gets captured is if you print your mix back into your DAW, which really only happens when running through an analog chain. That would require a multi-converter unit. For everyone else—including me—the converters are simply part of the monitoring chain.

Monitoring has three key components: the converters, the monitors themselves, and the room. If you're working with budget monitors in an acoustically flawed room, then I promise you won't notice much difference between expensive and affordable converters. On top of that, hearing the subtle nuances between converters requires ear training, which develops naturally over time. So, before even thinking about upgrading converters, you're far better off addressing your room acoustics first, followed by your monitors. Once those are dialed in—and once your production business is thriving—then, and only then, does it make sense to consider higher-end converters. Until that point, your converters won't be what's holding you back. Most consumers' converters will be far less detailed than the converters in your interface.

Converters, like monitors, are highly personal. You could ask five top-level engineers what they think the best converters are, and they could easily give you five different answers, all of which will likely offer superior conversion. So, in the upper echelons of converter units, it really comes down to taste and features. There's no gold standard, just personal preference.

For most Home Producers—and certainly most mixers—a simple 2-channel AD/DA interface is all you need. These range in price from a few hundred dollars to several thousand, but at the lower end, differences in conversion quality are relatively minor. You're far better off choosing an interface based on its features rather than obsessing over how it "sounds." They pretty much all use the same chips anyway. Most interfaces include built-in preamps, which, while not as desirable as high-end analog preamps, are perfectly usable.

Interfaces typically come with a software control panel for routing, input/output metering, and monitoring adjustments. The routing panel allows you to monitor directly off the input, which will eradicate latency—the bane of our existence in the studio.

Latency

Audio conversion takes time. Not a lot of time, but enough to matter. For a player, the difference between being on top of the beat and behind it can be as little as 3 milliseconds (ms). Your conversion can easily introduce more latency than that. While hearing even 5 ms of latency isn't the end of the world, it's far from ideal, and some will find it downright intolerable.

You can reduce latency by adjusting the buffer size in your DAW. The buffer gives your computer time to process audio. The larger the buffer, the greater the latency, which makes recording increasingly difficult. A buffer size of 1024 samples can generate as much as 60 ms of delay—fine for mixing, since that delay only affects what you see on the screen, but impossible for recording.

As tempting as it is to set your buffer to the lowest possible setting at all times, doing so puts a significant strain on your computer. This can lead to digital pops in your recordings, or worse, can cause your system to crash entirely. If a buffer size of 32 samples is causing issues, try 64. If that's still a problem, go to 128. The higher you go, the more noticeable the latency becomes. You can get away with far more latency on a vocal than you can on something percussive in nature.

The more RAM your system has, the lower you'll be able to set your buffer. While 16 GB may seem sufficient at first, it won't take long before you wish you had significantly more. RAM is not the place to skimp when buying a computer for audio production. Get as much as you can afford so your system can handle large sessions without stuttering or crashing. This is especially important for Mac users since Apple doesn't allow RAM upgrades after purchase. Insufficient RAM can cost you in terms of both time and sanity—and that's a price you don't want to pay.

If your interface allows for direct monitoring through its control panel, you can bring latency down to zero. In this setup, you monitor the music from your DAW while hearing your live mic input directly from the interface, bypassing the conversion process entirely. The trade-off? You can't monitor your input with plugins—that is unless your interface includes DSP (Digital Signal Processing).

For vocals, this usually isn't an issue. You don't typically need to hear plugin processing in real time while tracking a vocal. But if you're recording guitar through an amp sim, direct monitoring isn't a viable option. The control panel only gives you the dry signal—not the amp sim—making for an uninspiring playing experience. A guitarist needs to hear the tone (and sustain) of the instrument to perform their best.

Most DAWs have a low-latency mode that temporarily disables plugins causing delay. Unfortunately, if the plugins you've inserted on the source channel introduce latency, then they will be disabled when you engage this mode. Which means you won't be able to monitor through those plugins as you record. At which point, you'll either need to choose less taxing plugins for monitoring or perform without. This is one reason why analog compressors still have value today.

The Stereo Output

As we've established, there are really only two D/A converters in play when monitoring your production through an interface, and they are located in your DAW at the Stereo Output—the final point where all audio from your session is summed into two channels: left and right.

DAWs and interfaces may refer to this channel by various names, including the 2-bus, the Mix Bus, the Master Bus, or the 1-2. All of these terms refer to the same fundamental signal path: the last stop in your DAW before the audio reaches your interface and is sent to your monitors.

For consistency, I will primarily refer to this as the Stereo Output, though I may occasionally use the other terms interchangeably. Regardless of what your DAW calls it, this is the most critical place to manage your gain staging, which we will discuss further along.

Monitors

There are two kinds of professional monitors—passive and active.

Passive monitors require an external amplifier, which needs to be carefully matched to the speaker. The power of your amplifier is probably the most important factor, as improper power can cause your monitors to operate inefficiently—or worse, distort or underperform when pushed.

Active monitors, on the other hand, have built-in amplifiers, which offers a number of advantages. For starters, the amp is specifically matched to the speaker. If you don't like the amplifier-speaker pairing of an active monitor, then you don't like the monitor—simple as that. Active monitors also travel well, although they can be absurdly heavy. Still, if you find yourself working in a different room, active monitors eliminate a major variable from the equation.

Monitor Types and Tweeter Designs

Beyond the choice between passive and active, monitors also come in different types based on their placement and room size.

Nearfield monitors are designed for close listening, typically placed within a few feet of your position to minimize room reflections.

Midfield monitors are meant for larger spaces and positioned farther away, requiring a more treated environment to perform optimally.

Soffit-mounted monitors (also called flush-mounted monitors) are built directly into the walls, usually in high-end control rooms. This placement minimizes phase cancellation and low-end buildup caused by reflections off nearby surfaces, creating a more controlled listening environment. However, soffit mounting requires careful acoustic design to avoid resonance issues.

Some monitors also use concentric tweeter designs, where the tweeter is positioned in the center of the woofer. The idea behind this is time-alignment—ensuring that both the high and low frequencies emanate from the same focal point, improving phase coherence and imaging.

Another variation is ribbon tweeters, which can soften the high end and reduce ear fatigue over long sessions. Whether this is beneficial depends entirely on your preference and how the monitors translate outside of your room.

Choosing the Right Monitors

Professional monitors range anywhere from $300 to $15,000, with high-end models incorporating adaptive cardioid designs that adapt to the room. That said, your first set of monitors doesn't need to be expensive. As you advance in your producing journey, you may want a higher-end pair, but it's important to remember that your room is as much a part of the sound as the monitors themselves. We'll dive deeper into that later.

Microphones

When it comes to microphones, it's more important to understand how and where they shine. The brand of mic is of far less consequence than the design type. Therefore, you need to understand certain aspects of mic design, because they relate directly to your decision-making process.

One of the most common questions that I see online is, "What vocal mic should I buy?" The answer to that depends on your recording reality. Typically, commenters just blurt out answers—usually the only mic that they own. But to adequately answer this question depends on many other queries. Where are you recording? Is there any acoustical treatment? Is the space reverberant or compromised in some way? Is there good isolation? Are you the only person singing into the mic? Are you recording various people over time?

The space in which you're recording is half of your capture. Sound doesn't occur in a vacuum. Sound interacts within the space, and that interaction is picked up by the mic. If your vocal sounds like a reverberant mess in your room, it will sound that way on the mic. That said, some mic designs will pick up more ambient room information than others.

One solution to this problem is to use a dynamic mic (like the popular Shure SM7b). You may also place an acoustic shield in front of the mic, which helps to block out the returning sound of the room. There's a reason why so many Songwriter Producers use a dynamic mic, and it's not because it's the best mic for vocals. Occasionally it is, but usually not. Their popularity has much to do with how well dynamic mics reject off-axis information, which can make them a better choice than condensers in a compromised space.

In most cases, the better mic design for vocals is a large diaphragm condenser mic (LDC), but it will pick up far more of the space around it than a dynamic mic, so the space will affect the quality of the recording. If the space is relatively neutral, then this could prove the ideal mic choice.

As you can already see, there is strategy involved when selecting a mic, and if you only have one or two mics in your arsenal, that strategy becomes even more critical to the quality of your results.

If you're not familiar with these mic designs, then that was probably all a bit confusing, which only emphasizes my point. It's to your advantage as a producer to have an understanding of basic mic designs (and their available settings) when choosing a mic for a particular application. Although much of the information is technical in nature, the purpose is to help you make good practical strategic decisions so that you're able to choose the right tool for the job.

Some of these mic designs may have no relevance to you at this stage. And in some cases, I will talk about how they are used in the studio (like on drums) so as to better illustrate mic selection strategies. Even if you can't fathom recording drums today, you never know what tomorrow brings, so this kind of information will only make you stronger. Think of it like eating your vegetables.

The Capsule

Microphones have a capsule, which is simply a membrane suspended in a housing. Basically, that round thing inside the microphone grate reacts to the sound waves, which are then converted into an electrical signal, and cause your speakers to react in a similar manner the other way.

Suffice to say, the capsule picks up the sound. That's about as technical as we need to get for the purposes of this guide.

Pick-Up Patterns

Every capsule has a pick-up pattern, which describes the overall manner in which a mic collects and rejects sonic information. What the hell does that mean? Well, sometimes you want a mic to pick up lots of information around the mic. And sometimes you want a mic to pick up just the sonic information directly in front of it. The pick-up pattern is what determines this. On some mics the pick-up pattern is selectable. On other mics the capsules are modular and can be swapped out by the end user. That said, most mics have only one available pattern, which is usually all you'll need. They call it cardioid, and it's the most common pick-up pattern around.

Cardioid

Cardioid really just means heart-shaped, referring to the microphone's polar pattern, which picks up sound primarily from the front while rejecting much of the sound from the rear. The shape isn't a perfect heart but rather a rounded pattern that bulges at the front and tapers at the sides, resembling an up-side-down anatomical heart. This design helps focus capture on the intended source while minimizing background noise and room reflections.

Cardioid patterns are also subject to something we call "proximity effect." When you place a cardioid microphone in close proximity to a source—like a singer—you will get a boost in low-end information. You may also get some measure of distortion, but that's not always a bad thing. In fact, you can use proximity effect to your advantage. If you want more low end out of your capture, just move the mic closer to it. If you want less, just pull the mic back.

For the most part, the mics that you have will employ a cardioid pick-up pattern. But there are other patterns available. There's hyper-cardioid and super-cardioid, which are even tighter patterns that are more directional in nature. These tight patterns don't typically have a lot of relevance for the Home Producer, or even in the studio for that matter. They're often used by nature recordists to focus on a specific sound source. It allows the recordist to pick up more of the loon in the distance and less of the crickets in their immediate vicinity.

That said, a hyper-cardioid mic can be incredibly useful in certain recording scenarios. If I were recording a drummer who sings while playing, a hyper-cardioid mic would be my first choice because it rejects more of the drum bleed than any other mic.

Omnidirectional

Basically, when a capsule is set to omnidirectional, it picks up sonic information in all directions evenly around the microphone. This is particularly useful for "gang vocals" as your crew can surround the microphone, which will then pick them up evenly around the mic.

Given the 360 degree pickup pattern, you'll collect considerably more room information than with the more directional cardioid patterns. For most home recording applications, omni is not a desirable pattern because they lack proximity effect. But it can be an exceptionally useful pattern when you want to surround the mic with performers, or if you seek some level of ambient information from your capture.

Figure-8

A figure-8 pattern primarily picks up information from the front and the rear of the capsule and rejects the side information. This can be useful for recording two performers facing each other. Both the front and the back of the capsule go to just one preamp, so you need to get the blend between your performers right at the mic, which you achieve by adjusting how loud they sing along with their physical distances from the mic.

Nearly all ribbon microphones are figure-8 by design. Some condenser microphones allow you to switch between the cardioid and figure-8 patterns.

Powered Microphones

Many microphones require a power source as part of their design. Most powered mics accept 48 volts of phantom power, which you can typically send to the mic from the preamp (this includes interface preamps). The power function is usually labeled as "48V" with an indicator to let you know when it's activated. There are two very good reasons for that indicator. A mic that requires power won't reproduce sound without it. And you can fry many ribbon microphones with 48 volts of power. Really, it's not advisable to plug any mic into 48 volts hot, as it will cause your monitors to pop violently.

The inclusion of a powered transformer in a microphone has to do with design considerations and should have no bearing on mic selection. If it needs phantom power, send it power. If it doesn't—don't.

Tube Microphones

Some condenser microphones incorporate a vacuum tube for purposes of amplification and derive voltage from their own dedicated power supply. The mic won't sound without it, nor will it operate on phantom power. In general, tubes offer a warmer tone than solid state microphones, which can be beneficial for strident instruments.

Plugging a tube mic into a live power supply is a great way to give yourself a nasty shock that could kill you instantly.

I kid! It's unlikely to kill you—I just want you to remember this advice, and humorous hyperbole is effective for that purpose.

Do yourself a favor and make sure the power supply is off for at least 30 seconds before connecting or disconnecting your tube mic to it. You've been warned.

Microphone Types

Now that we understand the pick-up patterns, let's talk about the types of microphones. There are five types of mics that you will come across: small diaphragm condensers (SDC), large diaphragm condensers (LDC), ribbons, dynamics, and speaker mics.

Condenser Microphones

Condensers have a fast transient response, full frequency range, and robust gain, all of which is just a fancy way to say they're sensitive to sound. That means condensers don't require an especially loud sound source to excite the capsule. There are two basic kinds of studio condenser mics—small diaphragm and large.

SMALL DIAPHRAGM CONDENSER (SDC)

Small diaphragm condensers tend to have a wide cardioid pickup pattern, which means they excel at capturing off-axis information, and can offer a detailed sonic image when used in pairs for stereo miking. If you want to get a nice aggregate stereo image (like from a drum kit), a pair of SDCs overhead can be an excellent choice. But then, so are LDCs and ribbons.

LARGE DIAPHRAGM CONDENSER (LDC)

The large diaphragm condenser is probably the most widely used studio mic there is. The LDC capsule is larger than that of the small condenser, which seems to make a whole lot of sense given the definitions of large and small.

LDCs, like SDCs, are sensitive microphones, but aren't quite as good at picking up off-axis information as their smaller counterparts. That isn't a negative or a positive characteristic trait. It's just information that you use to your advantage. The size of the capsule leads many to believe that LDCs have a more extended low end, which is a myth. Generally speaking, you will get a full frequency response from any studio condenser.

LDCs are often the first choice for vocals, drum overheads, room mics, stringed instruments, et cetera.

PAD AND ROLL-OFF

Some condenser microphones include a pad (often as a switch), which reduces the microphone's output before the signal reaches the preamp. When placing a mic in front of an outrageously loud guitar cabinet, the signal can be so hot that even at the preamp's lowest gain setting, it still produces unwanted distortion. Engaging the mic's pad helps reduce the signal level before it hits the preamp. Many preamps also include their own pad, which functions similarly by reducing input gain.

Essentially, if you're experiencing distortion even at the lowest gain setting, engage the pad. If not, leave it off—because using a pad unnecessarily lowers the mic's sensitivity, forcing the preamp to work harder and potentially introducing unwanted noise or subtle tonal shifts.

A roll-off switch engages a selectable low-frequency filter, used to reduce excess low end caused by proximity effect or to tame a source that's naturally bass-heavy. I rarely use the roll-off since I can achieve the same result with mic placement or EQ, but it can come in handy in certain situations.

Dynamic Microphones

A dynamic microphone diaphragm operates similarly to the woofer in your monitors in that the diaphragm is connected to an induction coil and magnets. That's about as technical as we need to get.

These are workhorse microphones that are less susceptible to damage from abuse and moisture, which is why they are so commonly used for live sound reinforcement. Dynamic mics can take downright oppressive sound pressure levels without ill effects.

Dynamics also exhibit excellent rejection properties, which means they don't pick up information on the sides all that well. This can be an important consideration when choosing a mic. It makes them a good choice for recording snare drums, because they better reject the hi hat, which many drummers tend to hit too hard.

Dynamic mics don't have the full transient response of condensers and, therefore, aren't used for purposes of fidelity to the source. If you want to capture a tom drum tone accurately, you would be better off with a condenser placed a foot or more off the head. Unfortunately, this kind of placement is impossible on a full drum kit complete with cymbals. Even if you place condensers in close proximity to the toms, you'll still pick up a ton of cymbal information. Dynamics in close proximity will pick up more low-end information from the tom than top-end information from the cymbals, often making them the best choice.

In general, we use the close dynamic mics on a drum kit to fill in missing information. For instance, if you place a pair of SDCs in a stereo configuration over the drums, they will pick up a rather accurate image of the drums in that space. But because the SDCs are several feet from the skinned components (toms, snare, KIK), there is no proximity effect. As a result, there can be a definitive lack of low end. We can fill in that low-end information by placing dynamic mics in close proximity to the toms and snare and then blending them in with the overhead image.

While it's true that dynamic mics aren't as sensitive to sound pressure levels as condensers, they are way more sensitive to placement. The dynamic mics' general lack of sensitivity and capsule speed virtually requires proximity to the source. There-fore, the tiniest movement in any direction of a dynamic mic can, and will, result in a notable differential in tone. This is im-portant to understand, because a dynamic mic can make you work harder than you should. There are many engineers who enjoy dicking around with dynamic mics in front of a guitar cab-inet. Personally, I prefer the far more forgiving ribbon or condenser for that application.

Since dynamic mics lack sensitivity, they aren't the greatest choice for miking from distance. A dynamic over the drums will sound quite trashy, which could be great if you're making a punk record, or if you want lo-fi drums. But in general, your dynamic mics work better in close proximity to the source.

There are times that a dynamic is the optimal vocal mic. That said, they can be a major pain in the ass for this application be-cause of their sensitivity to position and the general mobility of singers. Given this, dynamic mics are often preferable on sta-tionary sound sources, but this is by no means a rule. It's more of an observation.

Ribbons

The capsule from a ribbon mic is made from an extremely thin strip of corrugated aluminum suspended in a strong mag-netic field. Ribbon mics are technically dynamics because they employ an induction coil, but we don't ever refer to them that way because they have such unique capture properties. As such, ribbon mics get their own classification–quite simply, ribbons.

Due to a generally steep rolloff above 16 kHz, ribbons have a rather smooth top end and can often be perceived as dark in na-ture. They also have a rather slow response to transients, which can have the effect of rounding off those transients. Given this, ribbon mics are used to great effect as drum overheads, and to capture guitars, and even vocals, although most people would probably find them intolerably dark for a modern vocal capture.

Myself included. There is nothing quite like a good ribbon for capturing your more strident brass instruments, and they are almost always my choice of overheads for drums these days.

Many vintage ribbons can't take an excessively loud source. An aggressively played KIK drum can disintegrate a ribbon membrane in an instant, so be mindful of where you place them. That said, some of the relatively newer lines of ribbon microphones (like the Royer line) can handle just about any source at any level, including a blaring guitar amp. In other words, if you have a ribbon mic, make sure you understand its design tolerances before placing it in front of excessively loud sound sources.

The large preponderance of ribbon mics are bi-directional, which means they have a figure-8 pattern—the rear pattern often brighter than the front. And although a surge of 48 volts can disintegrate the ribbon membrane under the right circumstances, there are some ribbons that require phantom power.

Ribbons may have a steep roll-off on the top end, but that just means you can brighten the shit out of them without bringing up annoying sizzle distortion that some cheap condenser mics introduce.

As you'll soon discover, I'm a big proponent of distortion for purposes of sound design, but top-end sizzle is particularly exhausting, and is something I prefer to avoid.

If you're a musician recording at home, in all likelihood you don't have a ribbon mic available to you. I've recorded all sorts of records without a single ribbon, so they are by no means a requirement. They are, however, a great addition to your arsenal over time.

Speaker Mics

Okay, now it's time to blow some minds. Remember how I told you that the woofer of your monitors operates just like the diaphragm in a dynamic mic? That's because a speaker is basically the opposite of a mic. What goes into the mic comes out the speaker, right? So, it makes sense that—if you were so inclined—you could use a speaker as a microphone. And you can. You just need to attach a connector to the wires to do it.

Essentially, a speaker placed in front of a sound source will act like a massively large dynamic microphone. It doesn't really matter if the speaker is still housed in its cabinet complete with the crossover, or if it's a single woofer outside of the cab, either way, they can be a bit unruly as microphones.

The bigger the speaker, the more low-end information it will pick up. A 15-inch woofer will pretty much only capture the subs, but when combined with a condenser mic on a KIK drum (you don't need a lot of that sub information), this can provide desirable results.

Speakers are not efficient as microphones given the size of the diaphragm, which is referred to as a cone when used as a monitor. They are, however, great at supplementing the sub-frequency information in your capture. Speaker mics can also produce interesting results on their own, particularly when they're smaller in size, and especially when they're still in their housing complete with crossover and tweeter. A small speaker cabinet placed in front of an amplifier can produce some rather interesting guitar tones.

I often use speaker mics to supplement the sub-frequency information from bass cabs and KIK drums. Keep in mind, a 15-inch woofer may be a great way to extend the sub-frequency blossom of a KIK drum, but you need to be careful with frequencies that low. It's really easy to blow out your monitors if you're not prudent with how you introduce the speaker mic into the blend. The tiniest amount of that sub-frequency goes a long way, and a sudden burst of subs could send your cones flying across the room. I'm once again being hyperbolic, of course. But you can certainly blow a woofer this way.

Headphones can be used as microphones too. And they're stereo, to boot! I can't say I've ever used headphones this way in the studio. They are, however, a great way to record a rehearsal.

Stereo Mics

A stereo mic has two capsules mounted one above the other. Some stereo mics allow you to rotate the top capsule 45 degrees for purposes of tightening the width of the image.

Stereo mics are typically condensers, (although Royer makes a stereo ribbon mic) and can be extremely handy as the capsules are phase-coherent within the housing, meaning it makes it difficult to fuck things up. Unfortunately, you won't come across many of these unless you visit a commercial facility. They are generally unnecessary for most home producers. This is a mic that can be most useful in a large studio.

The beauty of a stereo mic is that you don't have to use both capsules. That means a stereo mic isn't a wasted investment— you can rely on it for more than just stereo capture. If you're someone who loves recording in stereo and you find yourself regularly setting up stereo pairs, then a stereo mic might be a worthwhile addition to your arsenal.

USB Mics

USB mics aren't a type of mic at all. They're just mics that connect to your USB port on your computer rather than directly into a mic preamp. Most USB mics are likely condensers and can be useful for podcasts and the like. Generally speaking, these are not high-quality microphones.

Direct Box / Direct Injection

A direct box, while certainly not a microphone, is used to plug an unbalanced line level signal into a balanced microphone input. A balanced signal requires three wires, which is why a mic has a three-pronged XLR output. An unbalanced input comes from two wires, which attaches to the tip and the sleeve of a ¼-inch guitar cable. A stereo cable has a ring for the third wire and is therefore a balanced cable. Fun stuff!

A direct box is often referred to as a DI, which stands for "Direct Injection." Guitars, basses, and keyboards—anything with a 1/4-inch unbalanced jack to be recorded directly without an amplifier—is most accurately captured through a DI.

A DI often has a thru-port, which allows you to daisy chain the signal to an amplifier—meaning you send the same signal to multiple destinations in sequence. This way, you can record both a direct and amplified signal at the same time, if you so desire.

When recording guitars through an analog amplifier, you may choose to record the DI signal too. The point of that isn't to use the DI signal in conjunction with the amplified guitar, (although you wouldn't be the first, and that can even be a cool trick on occasion). You generally record the DI as backup. If your amp tone doesn't work out, then you can use the DI to send to another analog amp to re-record. Or you can bag the amp and use an amp sim exclusively. And while backups are good, it's not something to rely upon. It's always best if you can get the right guitar tone before moving forward. Otherwise, all of your subsequent decisions are dubious at best.

A microphone requires far more amplification than a line-level instrument. So, if you were to put an XLR adapter on your ¼-inch jack and plug a line-level instrument directly into your analog preamp's mic input, the signal would be excessively hot, overloading the preamp and introducing copious amounts of distortion. Which might be kinda cool every now and then. But in general? You want to properly match the impedance and level by using a direct box, which steps down the instrument's level to mic level before sending it to the preamp's mic input.

That said, many mic preamps and audio interfaces include a line-level input, often integrated into the center of a combo XLR jack. If your interface allows you to plug in a ¼-inch jack directly, it likely has a dedicated instrument or line-level input, negating the need for a DI box. In fact, most of you just starting out will record your direct signal this way. That said, if you wish to send the signal to an amplifier too, then a Direct Box is the way to go.

Now that we've gone through all of the basic microphone types, including the patterns and controls, let me offer you this dandy little cheat sheet for quick reference.

Microphone Attributes Cheat Sheet

DYNAMIC MICS

- Don't require power.
- Tend to be relatively small.
- Work best in close proximity to the source.
- Have good rejection properties.
- Great for skinned percussion instruments (toms, snares), some vocalists, and electric guitar amps.

LARGE-DIAPHRAGM CONDENSER (LDC) MICS

- Require power.
- Have fast transient response.
- Tend to be bulky and may need extra space for placement.
- Sensitive—often require a shock mount.
- Work well both up close and at a distance.
- Strong proximity effect in cardioid mode.
- Often feature selectable polar patterns (omni, figure-8).
- Not great at rejecting off-axis sound but also not ideal for capturing it.
- Typically, the first choice for vocals, even when other options may be better.

Small-Diaphragm Condenser (SDC) Mics

- Require power.
- Have fast transient response.
- Small and narrow—fits easily in tight spaces.
- Sensitive, works well at various distances.
- Have proximity effect in cardioid mode.
- Often have selectable polar patterns (omni, figure-8).
- Superior off-axis sound collection—great for stereo miking.
- Common applications: drum overheads, acoustic guitar, vocals, percussion, room tone, hi-hats, snare drums (in isolation).

Ribbon Mics

- Generally, don't require power, but some do.
- Almost always figure-8 polar pattern.
- Noticeable high-frequency roll-off above 16 kHz.
- Decent side rejection but no rejection at the rear.
- Perform best with a robustly powered mic preamp.
- Good for recording almost anything, offering smooth, natural tones.

Speaker Mics

- Work like a giant dynamic microphone.
- Excellent for capturing sub-frequency information.
- If a crossover and tweeter are present, they can yield interesting capture results.

The Home Producer's Vocal Mic(s)

Many producers—and this is especially true of today's Songwriter Producers—really only have one mic available to them, and it's often a dynamic mic. The current darling dynamic mic being the Shure SM7B, which costs around $400.

Most singers sound their best on large diaphragm condensers. While SDCs can also prove a good choice for vocals, they aren't nearly as popular for the job. I personally never use an SDC for vocals. So, there you go.

Not all vocalists sound best on condensers. I've recorded more than a few singers with a dynamic mic, because that proved to capture the singer most flatteringly. In some instances, a dynamic is the best mic for the production due to their more pronounced midrange. In other instances, it's the best mic logistically, like on those occasions when the singer is playing acoustic guitar. So, there are certainly times to use a dynamic mic on a singer, just not all the time.

So, why would so many home producers choose a dynamic mic like the SM7B to record vocals if condensers are often the better choice?

There are a number of reasons, starting with the fact that it's one of the most popular vocal mics around. And when something is popular, it often becomes the default choice—especially for home producers who lack experience. If everyone is using an SM7B to cut vocals, then the mic itself can't possibly be the weak link in your production, right?

It's a logical safety net. When you have limited experience and no real basis for comparison, the safest bet is to follow what's already working for others. And in many cases, the SM7B is a practical choice—it's forgiving, it handles untreated rooms better than condensers, and it doesn't pick up every tiny noise in your space. But that doesn't mean it's always the best mic for the job.

Frankly, the SM7B is a reasonable choice for newer home producers and artists recording in less-than-ideal rooms. While rejection properties aren't a major concern in a quiet, neutral recording space, they become critical in an acoustically compromised room full of early reflections.

Many producers use a Cloudlifter with their SM7B, though it's probably unnecessary with an analog preamp. A Cloudlifter takes phantom power (48V) from your preamp and converts it into an additional 25 dB of clean gain, which is significant. Ribbon mics can also benefit from a Cloudlifter, especially when using lower-gain interface preamps.

Whether an SM7B needs a Cloudlifter depends on your source volume and preamp. If you're using an interface preamp and struggling to get enough signal, a Cloudlifter can help. Otherwise, you may just be solving a problem that doesn't exist.

It's also common for producers to place an isolation shield in front of the mic to help with problematic rooms. Nearly every audio company that makes a compact front-mic baffle has its own proprietary name for this device—Reflection Filter, Isolation Shield, or Portable Vocal Booth. Designs vary, with some featuring a full foam housing for the mic, but most are simply curved screens covered with foam that sit directly in front of the singer and mic. The foam helps reduce the reflections returning to the mic.

That said, reflection filters don't address reflections occurring between the floor and ceiling. They aren't a substitute for proper acoustic treatment. In some cases, they can negatively affect the sound, introducing comb filtering and unnatural tonal shifts when the singer moves. It's not necessarily a tool that will improve your results—it might even create more problems than it solves.

In general, we want minimal room reflectivity reaching the mic capsule. A direct vocal capture provides clarity and a sense of intimacy, allowing us to use effects like reverb and delay to expand the space and reduce that intimacy when desired. Things can get messy when a vocal already has noticeable room tone, and then you try to add even more space artificially.

A little room tone is fine—if the space is too dead, you lose high-end detail—but the dry signal should almost always be far more apparent than the reflections on a vocal capture.

Room tone and early reflections schmear the sound, making it harder to distinguish words. The rejection properties of the

SM7B, along with the absorption of a reflection baffle, can help mitigate a problematic recording space, though neither is a complete fix.

Then, of course, there's the current trend of treating vocals like bullhorns. Steep filtering below 200 Hz, coupled with an aggressive midrange boost allows you to place your vocal lower in the overall balance of a track featuring a robust low end. Dynamics are generally the better choice for this kind of treatment, as they naturally emphasize the midrange.

The good news is, if this describes your vocal chain and overall approach, you're probably in decent shape for most popular genres—which, I suppose, is a win for the Hive Mind. The reality is that most people sound okay on an SM7B, even if few sound great.

Is it ideal? If you're able to work uninterrupted and get your song across with minimal sonic issues, then sure, that's ideal— I suppose. The problem is, you haven't actually solved your biggest issue: your room's acoustic makeup, which is preventing you from using a condenser mic in the first place.

So no, this is not an endorsement of the SM7B. It's simply an acknowledgment of why so many people choose it—because they can't or won't deal with their room issues.

If your room is relatively neutral in tone, or if you've put in the effort to make it acoustically palatable, you're almost always better off recording vocals with a large-diaphragm condenser. At the very least, you want to have that as an option.

LDCs for Vocals

There's a great deal of variance in the quality of large-diaphragm condensers, and like wine, price isn't always an accurate indicator of quality. Some microphone brands rely heavily on name recognition and price their products accordingly. Meanwhile, some vintage mics could be described as "corked." The older a mic is, the more likely it needs maintenance—if not a full overhaul—due to years of wear and tear.

I would never buy a vintage mic from an unknown source without hearing it first. After decades of exposure to different environments and varying levels of care, no two vintage mics will sound exactly the same, and some could be in rough sonic shape. Counterfeits are also rampant, with some rather convincing fakes, that is, until you open them up. The vintage mic market is full of scams and disappointment.

These days, I wouldn't bother with a high-profile vintage mic, because I know I'd be paying far too much. People buy those mics for perception, not necessarily for sound quality. Frankly, there are too many modern options available for a fraction of the cost that outperform them. If your goal is to impress people with an expensive vintage German microphone, it's not a bad investment—you'll likely be able to resell it for more than you paid. But if you're after great recording quality, there are far better choices.

Then there are certain new stock condenser mic lines that have become enormously popular, which frankly leaves me a bit bewildered. One mic in particular introduces an excessive amount of unpleasant top-end distortion, yet it's routinely recommended as an all-around great vocal mic.

I don't like to bash a product or a company—it tends to upset those convinced they made a great purchase. Instead of pointing out where you may have gone wrong, I'd rather focus on helping you make things right.

Where it comes to mics, there is one line that stands out as a clear winner, and I say this as someone who has used just about every mic line out there. There are plenty of boutique manufacturers making great condenser mics, but they can also be quite pricey. So, if you want a mic that sounds great on most people without breaking the bank, you'd do well to get yourself a LEWITT mic—just about any LEWITT mic.

I couldn't tell you exactly what LEWITT does to make their mics so universally great, but they are the most natural-sounding mics I've ever used. For years, I relied on the LEWITT LCT 940 for every vocalist who came through my room. Its variable electronics, which allow you to blend between tube and solid-state FET, offer a range of tonal options that can be tailored to the performer. Every singer I recorded with this mic sounded great, which is a rare quality in a mic.

I picked up the LEWITT LCT 1040 the moment it was released, which is currently their top-of-the-line microphone. It comes with a whole slew of tonal options, and now I use the 1040 on every vocalist who walks through the door. If you're going to invest in a high-quality, top-tier LDC, these are the two models I recommend over anything else.

Even their inexpensive mics sound great. If you're looking for an entry-level mic that won't cost you a fortune, there's the LCT 240, which employs a slightly smaller capsule and costs under $100. The 240 does not sound like a $100 mic—it sounds better than some mics that fetch considerably more. You can go up a level and get the 440 PURE, which has a full-sized 1-inch capsule and is priced under $300. Both the 440 and the 240 offer the best bang for your buck when you're just starting out, and they will remain useful even as you upgrade your arsenal. They are the ideal entry-level mics.

You choose your LEWITT mics based on the features they offer. For instance, the LCT 441 is similar to the 440 PURE but includes multiple polar patterns. If you want to record in stereo, you can get the LCT 640, which captures both the front and back of the capsule simultaneously. This allows you to change the recording pattern post-recording using their plugin, or you can use it for a straight stereo capture.

The LCT 840 is their dedicated tube mic, which I haven't used but is on my to-buy list. The LCT 540 features onboard controls like a pad and a roll-off and is a clear sonic upgrade from the LCT 440. So, if you can swing the extra bread, it's probably worth it. The thing about good mics is that they generally retain their value, making the purchase a minimal risk.

I picked up the LEWITT RAY recently, which features some really cool tech that maintains a focused proximity even as you move away from the mic. This can be especially useful for dynamic singers who pull back on big notes, as it helps retain proximity without the usual loss of body and presence. Some singers (and podcasters) also struggle to stay consistently on the mic, and the RAY is clearly useful for that as well.

Just so you understand, I reached out to LEWITT and specifically asked them to sponsor this book because I genuinely love their entire line of mics. If I'm going to write a book about producing that speaks to everyone, it would be a huge disservice to leave you all floundering.

Rather than going online and asking random people with no apparent *bona fides* what the best vocal mic is or which mic line to trust, you can listen to me—with my vast basis of comparison—and make a purchase with confidence. Consider my recommendation your protection. A mic this highly recommended will never be the problem. Then you can get the microphone out of your way and focus on what actually matters—the performance.

Their entire line of mics is great. I haven't heard a LEWITT mic I don't like, and there isn't a single LEWITT mic I wouldn't recommend. That includes their drum mic kits, their dynamic mics—all of them. And when you get your first LEWITT mic, you'll probably have the same reaction I did.

Holy crap, what mic is that? That sounds amazing!

And then we buy more.

The Art in the Technicalities

Understanding Phase Relationships

Things get complicated when multiple microphones are placed in close proximity to one another, primarily because they will interact. These interactions become even more pronounced on shifting sources, like an acoustic guitar, but they can also affect stationary instruments, such as drums or an electric guitar amp.

Whether you're recording in stereo or using multiple mics on a single source, you need to understand how these microphones interact and what those interactions sound like. These phase relationships dictate how signals combine, and if not managed properly, they can weaken or even cancel out important frequencies.

In the next section, we'll go through some listening exercises that require you to sit in front of your DAW. You'll also need a polarity inversion plugin (sometimes called phase reverse). If you're unsure how to reverse the phase on a channel in your DAW, ask your favorite AI for help. They all have a way to reverse phase, because that's a critical function to have available.

Polarity

Before we get fully into microphone interaction, you first need to understand what it means to invert polarity—and more importantly, what inverted polarity sounds like. This requires sitting in front of your monitors, positioned directly in the middle of the stereo field. If your monitors aren't set up so that they are perfectly equidistant from your seated position, that must be corrected first. These exercises rely on your ability to hear imaging clearly.

Additionally, daisy-chained computer monitors, where the left speaker receives input and then sends the signal to the right, will not provide sufficient stereo width. If headphones are the only viable option, then you should use those.

Open a clean session and bring in a mono KIK drum on a mono-designated channel. For this exercise, the KIK must remain purely mono, meaning it should sound squarely in the center with no side information whatsoever.

Now, go to your Stereo Output channel and insert a stereo plugin that inverts polarity (sometimes incorrectly referred to as a phase reverse switch). Once the plugin is inserted, click on the ø symbol on the left side. This will invert the polarity of that side. Listen to your KIK drum.

Weird, huh? Notice how the KIK is no longer in the center but instead shifts to the sides? Do you hear how the low end has been significantly attenuated? That's no bueno.

If you look at a graphical representation of a waveform, you'll see a horizontal line bisecting it—this is the zero line (or null line). It represents the moment in the waveform's oscillation where there is no sound.

Simply put: When the waveform moves above the null line, your woofers push out. When the waveform moves below the null line, your woofers pull in.

When your mono KIK drum is centered, it sends the exact same signal at the exact same level to both the left and right monitors. This keeps the KIK drum perfectly centered in the stereo field.

But when you invert polarity on the left side, you flip the waveform so that it moves in the exact opposite direction of the right channel. Now, as the left woofer pulls in, the right woofer pushes out, canceling out some of the low end and eliminating the strong center image. Since the woofers are no longer working in tandem to reproduce the KIK in the middle, the sound shifts outward and loses impact.

A/B this a few times to hear the difference, then bypass the plugin for the next exercise.

Now let's import a stereo audio file into your DAW. It can be anything—your favorite record, your latest production. We call this program material. Play it. Sounds nice, huh? Now engage that left ø button on the stereo output channel again.

Whoa! Can you locate the center of the image? Did you notice the obvious dip in low-end response? Can you feel the music almost wrapping around your head? Now disengage the left ø button. Once again, you have a defined center image, and your low end has returned. We like that. Now click the right ø button. It's the same issue—you now have an undefined center that seemingly wraps around your head. But it's not quite as obvious as it was with the KIK drum, is it?

Before I explain why that is, we need to perform another exercise.

Reset the polarity to normal on your stereo bus, then open two audio channels and import (or record) two unique guitar parts (or keyboard parts), preferably ones that work musically together. Pan one hard left and the other hard right. The musical nature of the parts can be identical, but the recordings must be unique so they can be heard distinctly from the left and right.

Now reverse polarity on the left side. Put it back. Reverse polarity on the right side. Put it back.

There's no obvious difference, is there? That's because those hard-panned parts are completely independent of one another. Inverting polarity on the left guitar causes the left woofer to pull first rather than push. But because it's wholly independent of the right guitar, it doesn't interact with the audio on the other side. They have no relationship beyond a musical one.

Let's mute those guitars and return to our stereo program material. Invert one side and listen again. When we invert program material, the pure side information isn't affected by the inversion, which is why the effect isn't as obvious as it was on a mono KIK drum. The low-end attenuation could be significant, or it could be subtle. But that skewed center image? You want to become allergic to this sound.

I'd recommend performing this A/B test in headphones as well. It's not as easy to pick out in headphones, is it? The interaction is reduced considerably because the left and right sides are isolated from each other. We combine the signals in our head, which minimizes the obvious interaction. The center image still skews, but it no longer wraps around your head.

Believe it or not, for anyone unfamiliar with this sound, the skewed center image from the program material, along with the attenuated low-end frequency response, can actually be easy to miss. In fact, many of us had to sit down and have someone demonstrate this repeatedly until we could hear it for ourselves—and you need to do the same. I'd recommend returning to your stereo program material and A/B testing until you can instantly recognize the inverted signal. You should even listen to what that skewed signal sounds like as you get up and walk around your room.

This doesn't need to be performed blind. You don't have to worry about expectation bias. Once you can hear it, you can hear it.

This is the same interaction that occurs when you reverse the wires on one stereo speaker. In fact, once you become attuned to it, you'll start noticing that some of your friends have their stereo speakers wired out of polarity, and it will drive you crazy to hear the audio shift as you walk through their living room. You'll probably even fix the problem for them. All it takes is flipping the wires at the terminal of one speaker to bring them back into polarity.

You'll often hear people refer to polarity as phase. But there are 360 degrees of phase. When we invert polarity, we are inverting phase by 180 degrees—the exact midpoint of 360 degrees. Polarity is binary; it's either normal or inverted by 180 degrees. One or the other. That's why a simple button press can fix the problem or break it again.

It's when we introduce a time differential that we start dealing with degrees of phase, and that's when things get considerably more complicated.

Time Differential

In order to create a stereo image from an identical signal, there must be a time differential. Let's load a mono guitar track into your DAW and make a duplicate of the guitar and its channel. Pan the two identical guitar signals hard left and hard right. As long as the faders are at unity, you will hear only one guitar—the same guitar—appearing in the middle. It won't sound like it's coming from the left and right speakers independently. This is the same as placing the guitar on a single channel with the pan knob in the center. Either way, the identical signal is pushing the cones in perfect sync, which causes it to appear in the middle. To make it sound like two separate guitars spread across the stereo field, we need a time differential.

Let's insert a sample delay plugin onto the duplicate guitar channel. If you don't have a sample delay, any standard delay will work, but it must be mono, and all parameters must be reset. There should be no filters, no feedback, no LFO, no delay time, no level boost—nothing. Even with the delay plugin engaged, your guitar and its duplicate should still appear solidly in the center before moving forward. Got it? Good. Now set the delay to 23 ms, then listen. *Voila!* The guitars now appear from the sides rather than in the center.

That might seem like a clever little trick to make a mono guitar sound stereo, but it's really just *faux stereo,* and we call it the Haas effect—named after Helmut Haas, the researcher who first documented the phenomenon in the 1940s. While the 23 ms time differential is enough to push the identical signals to the sides, it's not enough to prevent some degree of cancellation when heard in mono. This can be problematic.

This is where the arguments get fierce online, because many young record-makers wonder why the hell they should care about mono. I wondered the same thing several decades ago. By the mid-'80s, stereo was the norm, so why would mono matter?

For starters, anytime you're well outside the stereo image, you're essentially hearing an acoustically mono signal, which means some degree of cancellation can occur between those two guitar parts as they reach your position. This can manifest as a dip in overall level, and that dip can shift as you move around the room.

But does cancellation really matter? As with anything in this craft, it depends. Total cancellation surely does.

Why Mono Matters

For our next exercise, bypass the sample delay on the duplicate guitar to remove the time differential entirely, but keep both guitar channels panned hard to the sides. Now, we need to invert the polarity of the duplicate guitar channel, but this time, it must be done directly on the channel itself. First, remove the polarity inversion plugin from the stereo bus entirely, then insert a polarity inversion plugin on the duplicate guitar channel and invert it. Listen.

Much like the mono KIK drum we started with, your guitar image will now appear skewed, and the low end will be somewhat attenuated. Now pan both guitar channels to the center and listen again. You will hear absolutely nothing. Gone. Nada.

Where'd they go?

When we invert a guitar against a duplicate of itself, the original guitar is the exact opposite of the duplicate, which causes the signals to cancel completely.

This is called null. And like polarity, it's binary. Either the two files null, proving they are identical, or they don't, proving they aren't. Two files that are close but not exact, when inverted and summed, will produce a smattering of sound. That smattering tells you only one thing—the files are not identical.

Incidentally, this is called a null test, and we use it to confirm whether two files are truly identical, removing confirmation bias from the equation.

Okay, with our guitars still canceling completely, raise the level of your original guitar fader ever so slightly, then continue to raise it. You'll notice the guitar reappear, and as you increase the level, the guitar will continually emit more sound. The moment the two guitars have a volume differential, the sound becomes audible again. The cancellation is still occurring, but now one of the files is slightly louder, so what we're hearing is the difference in level between them.

Now, bring the guitars back to unity (0) so that they cancel completely again, and then pan them hard to the sides. Once again, we have a skewed image and attenuated low-end response because of the polarity inversion on one of the guitars. Guess what happens when we hear that in a mono playback situation? They'll cancel completely, just as they did when summed to the center.

While you could argue that a little cancellation might not matter much—especially on a relatively unimportant part—total cancellation in mono absolutely does.

I once requested a rough mix from a band and was told the mono roughs hadn't been made yet.

Mono roughs?

Naturally, I asked why on earth I'd need a mono rough. The answer? Because the guitars disappeared when played from their phone. That I needed to hear for myself.

Apparently, the guitar player couldn't handle an asymmetrical image and didn't want to perform his part twice. His solution was to copy the guitar track, pan the duplicates to opposite sides, and reverse the polarity on one of them—just as we did a moment ago.

Whereas in my room, I could clearly hear the skewed center image, it was when I played the stereo rough from my phone that the guitars disappeared completely. Why? Because the speakers on my iPhone are so close together that the two guitars canceled each other in the air before they could even be heard. This total cancellation would likely occur on a small Bluetooth device too.

So, when you hear the argument that mono doesn't matter, know that it *can* matter.

Where it comes to producing music, I can't and don't consider every fucked-up listening situation. I certainly don't worry about people who choose to use just one earbud. If I did, I'd mix everything in mono. I don't concern myself with people who have their speakers wired out of polarity. And I can't do anything about those who place their left and right speakers right next to each other—effectively creating an acoustic mono signal. And then there's the phone.

What I *can* do is protect my balances from shifting in those moments when the music does collapse to mono, whether that's due to acoustics or playback limitations. In this case, the guitars canceled completely when reproduced from speakers in close proximity to one another. If that's not a problem, I don't know what is.

Now, had there been a 23 ms time delay on one side, the guitars wouldn't have canceled out entirely because the time differential would have prevented it. Make no mistake—there would still be some degree of cancellation, just not total cancellation. Does it really matter?

Probably not.

That said, I find it perplexing that so many people would go to such great lengths to avoid recording a second take. A performed double will always produce a strong, stable stereo image, and in most cases, it will take less time than duplicating and delaying. Even if you're "mixing" and realize you need a double, you might as well just record it right then and there.

Then, of course, there are stereoizer plugins, which people use to help them attain more width. These plugins create *faux* width by introducing phase manipulation, delays, and EQ differentials between the left and right channels. While they can be useful for certain effects, they're ultimately an illusion—one that comes with trade-offs. The moment you sum that widened track to mono, the trick collapses, sometimes taking entire frequency ranges with it. Worse, stereoizers can introduce unnatural movement or instability in a mix, especially when multiple elements rely on them. If you need width, your best bet is to achieve it naturally—through arrangement, panning, and true doubling—rather than relying on phase manipulation to fake it.

Where it comes to cancellation caused by phase trickery, you're giving up some control over how your balances will translate in different environments. We already lose some control simply because every playback system sounds different. But there's a big difference between a system naturally degrading your track's sound (which happens relative to all tracks) and your balances shifting due to a technical phase issue that you introduced yourself. Personally, I avoid anything that puts my balances at risk in outside environments.

Everyone stumbles upon the Haas effect. But I have to tell you, 23 ms is an enormous time differential when it comes to musical timing, and that's a real problem for rhythmic parts.

It's also kind of a problem on vocals. Beyond that, sure—use the Haas effect if you like.

Thing is, now that you know what it sounds like, you probably won't.

Phase Coherency

At this point, you may be wondering—what does any of this polarity crap have to do with microphones? Well, remember that skewed stereo image from your program material? The one I told you to become allergic to? Your microphones can—and will—interact in a similar way, creating what we call a phase coherency issue. Unfortunately, your polarity inversion button won't always fix it. That's because phase isn't just a binary flip; it exists in degrees.

The good news? You now know what a 180-degree phase issue sounds like and how to fix it—just invert the polarity of one signal. But phase problems aren't always that simple. To deal with lesser degrees of phase coherency, we need to talk about sound, time, and how they relate to microphones.

As you may recall from physics class, sound travels relatively slowly—especially compared to light. This is most obvious over large distances, like in a storm, where thunder arrives several seconds after the lightning flash. You can even estimate the lightning's distance by counting the delay: every 5 seconds between the flash and the clap equals about a mile.

Fortunately, in the studio, we deal with much shorter distances. Setting aside variances in temperature and humidity, sound travels at roughly one foot per millisecond. One millisecond is just 1/1000th of a second—a tiny unit of time, but when it comes to microphone interaction, even small differences can create big problems.

To illustrate this, let's use drum miking as an example. Most home producers don't have the space or gear to record live drums, but since a drum kit is typically recorded with multiple mics, it's the perfect way to demonstrate the complexities of mic interaction and phase coherency.

Imagine you position two identical microphones two feet (about 61 cm) above a crash cymbal—one a foot (30 cm) to the right and the other a foot to the left. When you strike the cymbal, both mics capture nearly identical information. Assuming they're truly equidistant and you have adequate space, there's no time differential between them. The left mic picks up the sound at the exact same moment as the right. If the levels are perfectly even and the channels are panned hard left and right, that crash cymbal will appear dead center in the stereo image, with some slight ambient information filling out the sides.

Of course, a cymbal moves when struck, which can introduce subtle variations in how each mic picks up the sound over time. But for the sake of understanding phase coherence, we're focusing on its initial impact and overall wash.

Now, let's say you raise the right microphone by six inches (about 15 cm)—just half a foot. That slight change means the cymbal crash will now reach the right mic about half a millisecond later than the left. This tiny delay causes phase interaction between the two signals throughout the duration of the washing cymbal, creating an effect where the sound seems to wrap around your head.

Why? Because that small increase in distance introduces a time differential, throwing the two mics out of alignment. As a result, they're no longer phase coherent.

Once microphones are spaced more than a few feet apart, phase coherency is no longer a concern. With enough time separation, they start to behave more independently. While three feet (about 91 cm) is typically enough to minimize problematic phase interactions, certain frequencies may still interact, and some situations may require more distance—or allow for less. The best way to determine the right spacing is by ear.

For example, if you place two microphones three feet apart—one positioned as an overhead on the snare side and the other on the floor tom side—they're likely far enough apart to capture sufficiently independent direct signals. The left mic hears the direct strike of the snare, while the right mic picks up a more ambient version of that same hit 3 milliseconds later. Likewise, the right mic hears the direct strike of the floor tom, while the left mic picks up a more ambient version of it 3 milliseconds later.

This extra bit of spacing gives you a better shot at phase coherency because the time differential helps create a proper stereo image. Notice, I said *better shot*.

This setup is known as the Spaced Pair technique. The challenge with spaced pairs on drums is that you can't always position the mics more than three feet (about 91 cm) apart, and sometimes that's not enough distance to fully avoid phase interactions. As a result, fine-tuning is often necessary to minimize phase coherency problems between the two mics.

The most effective way to check for phase coherency between your spaced pair is to engage a polarity inversion on one of them. Do you remember what the program material sounded like when it wrapped around your head? That's exactly what you're listening for.

If you hit the left ø button and the center image of the cymbals suddenly skews while the low end attenuates, your mics were already phase coherent. If, instead, the center image tightens and you *gain* low end when flipping the polarity, then you had a phase coherency issue—and you just fixed it.

But what if neither setting sounds quite right? If flipping polarity gives you two different but equally problematic sounds, then your mics are only slightly out of phase. In that case, they need to be time-aligned.

This is really the crux of phase coherency—time. The best way to correct timing issues between microphones is by adjusting their distance from the source until they're in alignment—a process that ultimately has to be done by ear.

You can position the mics to look perfectly symmetrical, but that means nothing if they don't sound right together.

But what if you've already recorded your mics? Or what if someone else recorded them? Fortunately, timing can be adjusted in a DAW just as easily as with mic placement. To bring two microphones into phase coherency, all you need to do is slide one of the audio files ever so slightly in time. And I do mean *ever so slightly*. We're talking about adjustments in samples.

You can even fix the issue by eye. Just zoom way in on the waveforms and nudge one until they move above and below the null line in tandem. This isn't perfectly precise since the waveforms aren't identical, but they're similar enough that a visual alignment will get you close. From there, fine-tune by ear.

If that sounds like a pain in the ass—well, I suppose it is.

Fortunately, there are time alignment plugins that automatically analyze the two signals, measure the time differential, and delay one side accordingly to bring them into phase coherence. Pretty slick, huh?

Maybe. Maybe not.

This is where things get tricky. Those two overhead mics don't just interact with each other—they interact with every mic on the kit, including the KIK mics, snare mics, tom mics, hi-hat mic, and possibly even the room mics. No matter how many mics you have on a drum kit, they all need to work together and remain phase coherent. And that will be next to impossible using time alignment tools.

As soon as you fix one phase relationship, you've likely thrown three others out of whack. That's why, when recording a multi-mic drum setup, phase coherency has to be addressed *at the source*—through mic placement and careful adjustments. Every mic affects the others, and the only way to get them

working together sonically is to consider their interactions before you hit record.

Phase coherency isn't just a concern with stereo miking—it
can also be an issue when using multiple mics on a single mono
source. Take a KIK drum, for example. Let's say you place a dynamic mic inside the drum and a speaker mic outside. The
internal mic captures the attack and body of the drum, while the
speaker mic picks up the subs. With only about a foot (30 cm)
between them, these two mics will interact, and the nature of
that interaction largely depends on their relative levels.

Remember when we caused two identical guitar signals to
cancel out completely, only for the sound to return as we increased the level of one? Relative levels change the phase
interaction between two signals. With the guitars, the signals
were identical, so the cancellation changed in a linear fashion.
But with microphones, the signals aren't identical, meaning the
frequency cancellation becomes dynamic.

Because of this, simply inverting polarity on one mic won't
always fix the issue. As you adjust levels, you're not just changing volume—you're also altering the nature of the cancellation
itself. That's why time alignment can sometimes be a better solution than polarity reversal.

That said, I qualified that last statement for a reason—just
because cancellation is happening doesn't necessarily mean it's
a problem. You might actually *like* the way the two mics interact.
Back when I was mixing on analog consoles, I didn't even have
the option to time-align microphones. My only real tool was the
phase reversal button, combined with how I balanced the signals.

You may even prefer your KIK drum with one of those mics
inverted. This will usually manifest as a change in low-end response—one inversion will make the KIK feel like it sits above
the bass (in terms of frequency), while the other places it below
the bass. You can shape that low end and control the degree of

cancellation simply by adjusting the relative balance between the two mics.

Things get even more problematic with a shifting source like an acoustic guitar. It's a compact instrument that isn't perfectly stationary, yet people still insist on recording it with two mics. The problem? You can't position two close mics on a guitar and keep them three feet (about 91 cm) apart.

Not only will phase coherency issues cause those mic signals to wrap around your head when panned hard, but as the player moves—even slightly—the interaction between the mics will shift as well. And time alignment can't fix shifting time.

This is why I never record an acoustic guitar with more than one mic—unless the second mic is a room mic, placed far enough away from the close mic to avoid phase issues. I don't want to hear them, and I sure as hell don't want to deal with them.

That doesn't mean you *can't* record an acoustic guitar in stereo. The challenge is that the player has to remain as stationary as possible, and that can force engineering considerations to take priority over performance—something I never like to do. Performance should always come first.

For that reason, I prefer to record a solo acoustic guitar in mono and create the stereo image with space—either by using a stereo pair of mics placed at a distance or by adding depth with reverb.

If you'd like to place two mics in close proximity to one another, it's not the worst idea to invest in an auto-align tool. I've already taught you what to listen for, and that's the important part. All time alignment does is apply a delay—essentially the same as manually nudging the audio—and it'll get you very close in short order.

If you're only dealing with two mics, there's nothing wrong with using time alignment as a fix. But if you're working with more than two mics in proximity, no plugin will save you from phase issues across an entire setup. The only way to truly avoid those headaches is to get it right at the time of recording.

Stereo Miking Techniques

Proper stereo miking with two independent mics all but requires using mics with similar design properties. This doesn't mean they have to be a perfectly matched pair, but they should have comparable design and pickup characteristics to capture a solid stereo image. A dynamic mic on the left—designed for close-miking with strong off-axis rejection—paired with an SDC on the right—which has no proximity effect and excels at capturing off-axis information—won't produce a natural or useful stereo image.

We've just discussed the spaced pair technique, which is often preferred for LDCs due to their size and bulk. Now, let's talk about the X-Y technique.

X-Y

The next simplest way to record in stereo with two mics is an X-Y configuration, where the capsules are placed adjacent to each other. This setup works best with small-diaphragm condensers (SDCs), which are typically slim, pencil-like mics rather than bulky anvils. This is what an SDC X-Y configuration looks like.

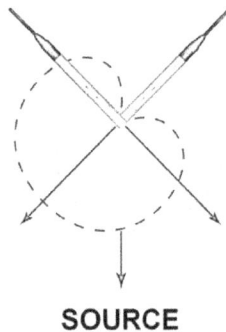

SOURCE

The two capsules can either face each other at a 90° angle or cross as pictured. Either way, in an X-Y configuration, the capsules are positioned so they are the exact same distance from the source, ensuring phase coherence. The two heart-shaped patterns represent the cardioid pickup pattern for each mic, capturing a balanced stereo image while minimizing phase issues.

You can use the X-Y technique with a pair of LDCs or ribbons, but you'll need some additional equipment. First, you'll need a microphone bar to spread the mics apart. Two LDCs can get quite heavy, so you'll also need a sturdy mic stand with a counterweight to keep the entire setup balanced. The bulkier the mics, the trickier they are to mount—even with a microphone spreader.

There are other stereo miking configurations—Blumlein, mid-side, and ORTF—but I rarely used any of them, even as a dedicated recordist, so I can promise you they aren't essential techniques as a producer. If stereo miking is something that interests you, or if you'd like to explore these methods further, I encourage you to do a little outside research.

The Source

While microphone selection plays a role in achieving a good capture, the quality of a recording ultimately comes down to the source. And the source has three key components: the performer, the instrument, and the room.

If all three are great, recording is easy. But if there's an issue with any one of them, recording becomes a challenge. The best way to simplify the entire process is to address the source first and foremost.

Source Performer

If the performer is atrocious, the greatest recording chain ever curated will only reveal their atrociousness with perfect clarity. If the performer is jaw-droppingly amazing, their performance will transcend even the most compromised recording chain. I say this as someone who has recorded hundreds of performers—ranging from brilliant to unbearable—on the best equipment in some of the most iconic recording rooms.

You can accept this now, or you can spend years metaphorically banging your head against the wall before finally realizing that you're largely at the mercy of the talent. Sure, there are ways to extract something usable—or even interesting—from a problematic performer, but that requires adjusting the part to fit their abilities, which ultimately means fixing the problem *at the source.*

No matter how you slice it, sonic issues are *source* issues, and sonics only become a concern when the source itself is compromised. You can't listen to someone performing badly on the mic and think, *well, at least it sounds amazing!* No, it doesn't. That doesn't exist. If the performer is making you cringe, it's the sound they're making that's causing you to cringe. There's no comfort in the quality of the capture when you're stuck wondering how you got yourself into this mess.

Source Instrument

If an instrument is compromised in some way, that flaw will be captured in the recording. If a singer has a cold and sounds congested, there's no plugin that can fix it. No tool can remove the sound of congestion or compensate for the lackluster performance of someone who isn't feeling their best.

A guitar with intonation issues or a drum kit with an audible rattle is best addressed at the source. Sure, there are repair plugins that might remove the rattle and polyphonic tuning software that can adjust individual notes within a chord, but those fixes come at a cost, often introducing their own distracting artifacts. Repair tools are useful when you have no control over the capture and no other available options, but they're not a plan to rely on when you have the ability to fix the source directly.

With that in mind, it's always best to work with performers whose instruments are up to the task. Fortunately, great performers tend to choose instruments that allow them to deliver great performances.

Source Room

As I've already pointed out, the source room is half the capture and is often the most problematic part of the source for home producers. The sound that emanates from the performer exists within a space, and the sound waves interact with that space based on its size, shape, and material makeup. While the mic primarily picks up what's in its immediate proximity, the character of the room can influence the overall tone of the recording. If the room is too present in the capture, it can negatively impact the quality of the recording.

If you're working in a compromised room—one that's overly reverberant, boxy, or plagued by delay slaps and rattles—then your source is compromised too. If what you're hearing in the room doesn't sound good, the recording won't sound good either. You can't separate the room from the source unless the source is so quiet that it doesn't excite the space at all, in which case the room's ambient noise floor might actually be louder than the source itself.

Many producers try to use their recording tools to compensate for a compromised source. While that's certainly an option, it's rarely the most effective one. The better approach is to address the room itself. And if you're monitoring in the same compromised room where you're recording, treating the space becomes even more critical.

A problematic room is easily the most common and pervasive issue for home producers. Audio groups are filled with frustrated producers acting as their own recordists, struggling to understand why their vocal recordings sound so awful or why they can't achieve a professional sound. More often than not, it turns out they're recording in a closet or some other obviously compromised space. At least, it's obvious to me once they finally post a picture of their setup.

The same goes for their mixes. They struggle endlessly, frustrated that the sound seems to change every time they take a break—a telltale sign of monitoring issues—or that no matter what they do, their mix falls apart when they play it in the car.

When producers ask how to fix their room, the advice they get is often completely misguided or outright wrong. No amount of optimism (or delusion, as it were) can overcome a critically compromised space. I dealt with the same issue myself. After mixing in well-designed commercial studios for 20 years, I had to figure out how to make a home studio work for both mixing and recording, and it was a long and painful process. Fixing a room acoustically requires an investment of both time and money. And with all the bad information floating around, it often ends up costing more time than money.

You'll come across plenty of producers who swear by cheap, DIY solutions to fix their room issues. Egg crates. Foam on the walls. Adhesive sound panels. The manufacturers of these products never provide specifications on how they perform or what frequencies they absorb—because they're not particularly effective for the task. And why would they reveal that?

People will talk about using mattresses as bass traps. Couches as bass traps. All of which completely ignores sound absorption coefficients and the geometry of the room. I'll admit, I've tried some of these solutions myself over the years.

What's the big deal? I have skills! I can compensate for bad acoustics.

Sadly, no.

Here I was—an expert at mixing, recording, and producing—yet my skill set was all but eradicated by the acoustic realities of the room I was working in. Turns out, there's a reason those expensive studios invested so heavily in acousticians, designers, and proper buildouts.

Acoustics

The first step to fixing a problem is acceptance. As long as you convince yourself that you can simply compensate for a problem room, you will struggle.

Let me preface this section with this: My purpose isn't to dissuade you from working with what you have or to suggest that you have no shot at becoming a professional just because you're learning your craft in a compromised space. You *can* make great music regardless of your acoustic environment. Great music has been made on the streets with nothing more than a mic and a boombox. The classic Motown records from the '60s were recorded in a house with almost primitive acoustic treatment. Don't think for a moment that compromised acoustics will prevent you from achieving musical greatness—or even success, for that matter.

If you write and produce an amazing song, and a major-label artist wants to sing it, you'll be placed in a commercial studio with highly skilled professionals to bring your vision to life. Your musical skills matter far more than the engineering. Successful songwriters can make millions from just *one* song. Successful engineers get paid by the hour. So, you tell me which has more value.

That said, I can certainly understand your quest for a professional sounding product and the desire to work in monitors rather than headphones. If you find yourself constantly frustrated because your sonic vision never seems to match the results, and if you struggle to capture your source the way you hear it in your head, or if your mixes never translate as expected outside your space, then the only way to fix those issues is to deal with the acoustics.

If you know exactly how you want your record to sound, only for it to sound completely different outside your room, that's an acoustics issue. If your balances, EQ curve, and spatial presentation are all out of whack, then the sonic decisions you're making in your room are flawed. What you're hearing from your monitors is a distortion of reality. It's a lie.

You can't just reference your way past a lie—because the reference is a lie too. And sometimes, it's a lie of omission, like when an entire low-end frequency band disappears due to standing waves.

If you don't fix your room—and every room that isn't purpose-built for mixing and recording needs some level of fixing—you'll have a monumentally difficult time delivering tracks the way you sonically envision them.

The Challenge

I suppose this would be about the point that I should reveal to you exactly how to make your room perfect. Unfortunately, that entirely depends on the specific realities of your space. Every room presents its own challenges, and some spaces are nearly impossible to make acoustically accurate for proper translation in the outside world.

Small rooms with relatively low ceilings are an absolute acoustical nightmare. Low ceilings, in general, create severe acoustic problems, and even 8-foot (about 2.4-meter) ceilings—which are fairly common—are considered low when it comes to both monitoring and recording.

As long as those issues exist, you'll have to take your production outside of your room to find its flaws, and that's an exceptionally inefficient way to work.

I've seen people ask for help treating all kinds of problematic rooms—L-shaped spaces, long narrow rooms that resemble hallways, square rooms, bedrooms where they sleep, rooms with closet cutouts, ceilings under seven feet high, even spaces with chandeliers or ceiling fans creating unpredictable reflections. Of course, ceiling fans can be easily removed, but solutions for some of those other problems can be challenging at best.

These frustrated producers genuinely believe they can fix fatal acoustical flaws—often for little-to-no money—or that they can simply learn their space over time and compensate for its deficiencies. Nothing could be further from the truth.

Of course, I'm telling you all this as someone who is not an acoustician. I have no formal credentials in that regard. Everything I know comes from experience, backed by practical knowledge. It's the result of a long and difficult transition from highly regarded, outrageously expensive mix rooms, to a converted room in my house—several rooms, actually.

I've had to muddle through these issues just like everyone else. I too firmly believed I could make any old space work, that I could reference my way to an understanding, and that my skills would overcome even the most fatally flawed acoustics.

Then I tried it.

Fail. Not once. Multiple times.

What's particularly baffling—as you dig deeper into the rabbit hole of acoustic treatment—is the wildly conflicting opinions between acousticians. Which is strange, considering this stuff is supposed to be based on math. It really makes me wonder how anyone is supposed to figure this shit out when even self-proclaimed experts can't seem to agree. Of course, here I am—a total hack when it comes to acoustics (at least I know it)—giving you advice on how to fix your situation in the abstract.

What could possibly go wrong?

And while I've spent countless hours learning what I can about acoustic practicalities, offering advice on the subject is nothing short of fraught. My failures have been limited to my own rooms, which gives me an inadequate knowledge base to claim any expertise. So I won't stray too far out of my lane in this regard.

What I *can* offer is concrete information on curating a more accurate monitoring environment. Some of it comes from extensive reading on studio acoustics, and some of it comes from firsthand experience correcting my own rooms over time. Take what I provide here and supplement it with guidance from reputable sources.

Positioning

First, if your room is rectangular, it's recommended to position your monitors along the short wall. This allows for the greatest possible distance behind your listening position, which helps with more accurate low-end response. Even in relatively narrow rooms, this orientation is usually the best approach.

It's commonly recommended that you place yourself at 38% of the room's length and your monitors so they form an equilateral triangle with your listening position. If you end up sitting at 50% of the room's length, you're right in the middle of a major problem—standing waves. This can cause certain low-end frequencies to cancel out while boosting others, making it impossible to get an accurate read on your mix.

Don't get mad at my use of the word *impossible* here. It's not pessimism—it's just reality. It's also impossible for a human to jump 100 feet (about 30 meters) in the air on Earth, yet nobody would take issue with that statement. Optimism and encouragement won't change the laws of physics. They'll only cause you to believe something that isn't true.

The size of your monitors matters in relation to how far away you place them from your listening position. Small bookshelf monitors should be positioned closer to you, which introduces other acoustic challenges—especially if you're using a desk of any kind. A desk acts as a reflective surface, creating a schmear in the sound. You can learn to live with the schmear. I know I did. But I wouldn't want to live with it again. These days, there is nothing between my seated position and my monitors.

You want the tweeters of your monitors to be level with your ears. Most monitors are designed to be placed vertically, with the tweeter positioned above the woofer. It's best to follow the manufacturer's recommendations for orientation, as improper placement can disrupt the alignment between the tweeter and woofer, affecting clarity and balance. So, make sure your monitors are set up as intended, with the tweeters aimed directly at your ears.

Acoustic Treatment

Once your monitors are placed, you need to address reflection points on the walls (and possibly the ceiling), which will require acoustic panels. You can have a mate move a tall mirror along the side wall until you can see the front of your monitor in the mirror from your listening position. That is the first reflection point. The mid-to-high frequencies will hit those spots and reflect, and so they are a good place to put acoustic panels.

Foam panels can certainly knock down high frequencies, but there are far better options if you're able to spend a little more. Ideally, you want panels made from Rockwool or Owens Corning 703—both materials used by highly regarded acoustic panel manufacturers. These are the most effective, and there's published data on the frequencies they absorb.

Panel thickness affects the frequency range they address. Thinner 2-inch (5 cm) panels are broadband absorbers designed to handle reflections in the mid and upper frequencies. Thicker 4-inch to 8-inch (10 cm to 20 cm) panels are more effective at trapping low end. Leaving an air gap between the panel and the wall increases their effectiveness even further.

You can buy packs of Rockwool or Owens Corning 703 and build your own panels, but it's a time-consuming process that requires research, tools, and some skill working with wood and fabric. That said, you're not limited to plain burlap—I glued handmade Indian scarves onto my 703 panels, and they worked just fine. The key is that the fabric needs to be breathable.

If you'd rather avoid the DIY route, you can buy fully built acoustic panels and bass traps from a number of companies. Just make sure their panels are made from proper acoustic materials with published acoustic absorption coefficients that match your needs. This is by far the most expensive solution, but it saves time and offers you a professional build.

If your ceiling is 8 feet or lower (2.44 meters), you'll want acoustic panels above your listening position as well, ideally with an air gap. This setup is called a cloud, and it helps reduce vertical reflections that occur between a parallel floor and ceiling. Controlling these reflections can improve stereo imaging and overall clarity at your listening position. Even with higher ceilings, a cloud may still be beneficial, depending on the room's overall acoustics.

Rockwool is messier to work with than 703, but it comes in thicker panels, making it the preferred material for bass traps.

If you place enough 2-inch (5 cm) broadband panels throughout your room, you can significantly reduce reflections and overall reverberation in the mid-to-upper frequencies. Modular baffles that stand on the floor can also help create a more controlled space for vocal recording. This will greatly improve the acoustics for recording vocals, but it won't do much for the low-end issues that affect your monitoring.

Dealing with Low End Issues

Bass traps that extend from floor to ceiling straddling the corners are the most commonly recommended solution for managing low-frequency buildup. Placing bass traps on the back wall can also be effective.

While full-height traps are ideal, there are more portable solutions available, and even partial trapping in the corners can still provide some benefit. However, the effectiveness of these alternatives will depend on the specific room, as well as the type and thickness of the materials used.

Bass traps are large and bulky because absorbing low frequencies requires mass—and not just any mass. Your mattress is *not* a bass trap. Proper low-end control requires thick acoustic panels, ideally made from acoustically tested materials like Rockwool.

The smaller the room, the more bass trapping you'll need, which means sacrificing valuable space in the process. In some cases, a small room might mathematically require more trapping than there's space to place it, which is one of the reasons small rooms can be so problematic.

Windows can pose a problem because they reflect high frequencies. In my mix room, I covered the windows with acoustic panels to prevent them from acting as reflection points. I don't really need to see outside while I'm working, and they're positioned to the side of me anyway.

Windows also let outside sound leak in, so it's a good idea to seal any gaps as best you can to improve isolation from the outside world. The same goes for doors, though clearly, you can't hermetically seal yourself inside if you ever plan to leave. Perhaps you don't. It's still inadvisable.

Heavy curtains can help block sound, but keep in mind that fabric primarily absorbs high frequencies, which can introduce other acoustic issues. That said, every inch of my room is covered with tapestries, and I have two sets of heavy curtains—completely against the "rules." I also have two large hand-knotted rugs on the floor, which goes against acoustic convention as well.

I used to completely cover expensive control rooms with tapestries, and none of my records suffered for it. If I want a more live space for recording, I have other rooms available. And for anything that requires more space and more microphones, I rent a studio.

How reflective or dead you want your room to be is ultimately a matter of preference—there's a range of what's considered acceptable. There's certainly some wiggle room for form over function. How much? I can't quantify that for you. All that really matters is how the sound you hear in your room translates outside of it.

Of course, this just further illustrates how complex acoustics can be and how some choices come down to your needs along with personal preference. I don't need a live room for recording, and I don't like live rooms for mixing—I've always preferred somewhat dead rooms.

Just because I break some rules doesn't mean I break all the rules, nor does it mean all rules *can* be broken. I also have a lot working in my favor.

I have floor-to-ceiling bass trapping in all the corners of my room. I have numerous acoustic panels made from 703 and Rockwool. And I have a rather large room with dimensions that follow the golden ratio—where the width is 1.6 times the ceiling height, and the length is 2.56 times the ceiling height. In my case, the ceiling is 9.5 feet (about 2.9 meters), the length is about 25 feet (7.6 meters), and the width is about 15 feet (4.6 meters).

The golden ratio helps minimize standing waves, and the 25-foot run from the front to the back of the room alleviates many low-end acoustic issues. A 60 Hz sound wave takes 18.7

feet (5.7 meters) to fully develop. When your low end has the space to unfold naturally, it becomes less of a problem. That said, bass trapping is still a necessity.

It's important to note that not all acousticians consider the golden ratio a definitive solution for every room. Some advocate for alternative ratios or approaches depending on the intended purpose of the space, specific use cases, and practical constraints.

The reality is most of you aren't building a room from scratch just yet—you have to work with what you've got. But it's important to understand that the most effective acoustic treatment strategies often begin with purposeful room design.

BOUNDARY EFFECT

Placing you monitors too close to your back or side walls can lead to acoustic issues known as the boundary effect, where certain frequencies interact in ways that can distort your perception of the mix.

Boundary effect issues arise when sound waves from your monitors reflect off nearby walls and interact with the direct sound at your listening position. This interaction creates boundary interference, which can result in comb filtering—a phenomenon where certain frequencies are either amplified or canceled out due to phase interactions. This interference is particularly problematic in the low-end, leading to an uneven bass response that makes accurate mixing nearly impossible.

While it's often recommended to place monitors 2–3 feet (about 60–90 cm) from the back wall, that isn't always practical. In many home studios, that distance could place you at the halfway point of the room, which is undesirable. The ideal monitor placement also depends on speaker design. Front-ported monitors are less sensitive to wall proximity, while rear-ported monitors may require more space.

THE CARDIOID SOLUTION

Cardioid monitors, like the Dutch & Dutch 8c, are specifically designed to eliminate boundary effects, which is why I installed those monitors in my own room. They're also stupidly expensive, but I make most of my income mixing and producing records, and it costs more for me to work inefficiently. At the very least, it's good for you to be aware of the technology.

Cardioid monitors employ a boundary-coupling design. They are specifically engineered to work in close proximity to walls, treating the boundary not as a problem to be avoided but as an integral part of their acoustic design. The added rear-facing woofers emit low-frequency energy toward the wall, which reflects back and is subsequently canceled out at the front of the monitors via a time aligned and phase-reversed signal. This approach neutralizes the problematic reflections and creates a more consistent and accurate low-frequency response in the listening environment.

In effect, the cardioid monitors transform the wall into an asset rather than a liability, allowing you to achieve low-end clarity without requiring an acoustically perfect room or excessive bass trapping. Frankly, once I fully installed the 8C monitors, all of my translation issues went away.

The hardest part of transitioning from mixing on large desks in acoustically designed rooms to mixing at home was adapting to the monitoring. For years, I battled with it, and my mixes often took twice as long as they should have. I can promise you, I wrestled with more mixes than I care to admit—all because my mix room wasn't acoustically accurate enough.

It wasn't until a friend introduced me to the Dutch & Dutch 8cs, which he helped install in my room. Those monitors were the missing piece to the puzzle—the thing that finally made my home mix room accurate.

When I read posts on acoustic forums from people desperately trying to make their rooms accurate, I see their frequency measurements, then the actual spaces they're working in—and I can *feel* their pain. I just want to reach through the screen, shake them, maybe even slap them and throw some cold water in their face.

You're never gonna make that room accurate with acoustic treatment alone, I want to say to them. *Your only real shot is to invest in cardioid monitors that adapt to the room.*

If you're still in the early stages of learning then, of course, cardioid monitors aren't a reasonable expense. I certainly wouldn't have bought them if I hadn't heard for myself what they did. But if producing music is how you make your living—if your time has real value—and you're spending much of your day battling the frustration of an inaccurate monitoring environment, then this is actually a cost-effective solution with minimal risk. My 8cs have only gone up in value since I bought them.

While I'm sure many of you would like me to offer a recommendation for monitors in a more reasonable price range, the reality is, if your room is accurate, you could probably learn to mix on just about any set of professional monitors, regardless of what I thought of them.

I mean, I mixed my biggest records almost exclusively on Yamaha NS-10s, which are bookshelf monitors with a pronounced midrange. I judged the low end based on how the woofers moved. But I was also mixing in some rather accurate rooms, which were purpose-built and designed by top acousticians. And while there were always large soffit-mounted monitors available to check the low end (the bigs), I honestly didn't need them and rarely switched to them.

The reality is, monitor choice is completely personal—it's how your room affects your monitors that matters. If I were to make any recommendation, it would be to get powered monitors at a comfortable price point from a company that specializes in speaker design. Beyond that? Invest your money in your treatments.

All of that said, if you don't have the ability or the budget to facilitate an accurate monitoring space, worry not. There are other viable workarounds, such as high-quality open-back headphones paired with crossfeed plugins. We'll discuss headphones in more depth shortly.

Diffusors

You'll often see recommendations to install diffusors, but if you just throw a couple of diffusor panels on the back wall without proper planning, you could do more harm than good. It's crucial to understand how diffusors interact with your room and to ensure you're using products designed around established mathematical principles, like Quadratic Residue Diffusor (QRD) panels. Not everything labeled as a diffusor is built to proper QRD specifications. Buyer beware.

Fixing problem acoustics is not as simple as buying some acoustic panels or diffusors and randomly placing them on the walls. When positioned correctly, modular acoustic treatments can effectively control early reflections and tame the more directional upper frequencies in your room. Positioned improperly, they can actually make matters worse.

That said, diffusors won't fix low-end nodes—frequencies that disappear due to cancellation. Nodes can wreak havoc on your monitoring accuracy. If a critical frequency is missing in your listening position, you might unknowingly boost it in your mix, only to find it overpowering on other systems. You can't compensate for what you can't hear, and diffusors won't change that.

Room Compensation Software

There are room EQ compensation tools like REW that can help. REW allows you to accurately measure your room's frequency response using a $100 calibrated MiniDSP Umik-1 mic, and it even calibrates to your converters. This donation-based software can apply EQ filters to your monitors to help smooth out low-end inconsistencies.

The problem is, if a frequency is completely canceled out due to room acoustics, no amount of corrective EQ can bring it back. Even with partial cancellation, there are limits to how effective EQ correction can be. Tools like REW are meant to address minor issues, not fix fundamental acoustic problems. If you aggressively boost a missing frequency to balance things at your listening position, it could end up being overpowering in other areas of the room.

If you really want to understand your acoustic reality, get yourself a calibrated measuring mic, download REW, and follow the measurement procedures carefully. That way, at the very least, you'll know what you're dealing with.

The Problem with "Learning the Room"

People get so confused as to how it's possible that you can listen to a record in your room, and it sounds great, but you can't seem to mix your own record in that same room. Somehow the low end never translates predictably outside of your room. That's because you're not actually hearing everything.

Let's say you've measured a huge dip from 100 to 150 Hz because a standing wave has caused a node that largely cancels that frequency at your listening position. This is actually a very common issue. The missing range of low frequencies won't necessarily cause a well-balanced record to sound bad in your room, but if you have an excess of 100–150 Hz in your mix, you won't even know it as you mix there. And if you constantly reference other records, you are referencing them with that void of 100 Hz, which then starts to sound normal.

To make matters worse, low end problems are rarely so straightforward as just a cancellation of one frequency. You could also have a 5 dB boost in how you hear 60 Hz, among other wild variations in low end reproduction. You could listen to your favorite record in your room, and not even notice the low end issues. Yet, if you try to mix in an environment where certain low end frequencies are largely inaudible, you have absolutely no idea how much of that frequency exists in your mix. You literally can't hear it. Then when you get it to your car, it's blowing up your speakers, and you're totally confused.

So, you can't compensate for the low end issues caused by nodes because you're operating somewhat blind until you fix it with the many acoustical strategies I've laid out for you. And don't even ask me to explain modes, they are far more complex than nodes. Suffice to say they are just more standing waves that will make it difficult to know what you're hearing across the frequency spectrum.

Then there's our brains, which maddeningly adapt to the room. You will get used to an acoustically compromised room in only a few minutes time. There you are, happily mixing away. Everything sounds great. Then you take a break, which allows your brain to reset. When you return, the mix sounds nothing like it did. If you were heavy handed on the low end, the mix now sounds muddy and dark. If you were light on the low end, the mix is strident and unpleasing. Then you fix it. Take another break. And now you have the opposite problem. I've experienced all of this as a fully accomplished mixer. It's like you're losing your mind. No matter what you do you can't seem to get the low end right because you're shooting at a moving target as your brain constantly adjusts to the room.

If you want to render a talented mix engineer absolutely use-less, just have them mix in an inaccurate room. Think about that. If you can render a talented third-party mixer useless in a room, then how are you supposed to overcome the issue as a producer with limited mixing experience?

You fix it, dear Henry, dear Henry. You fix it.

Headphones for Mixing

Monitoring in headphones presents its own set of chal-lenges, but in some situations, it can be a viable alternative to working in a compromised room. While most professional engi-neers prefer mixing on monitors in a well-treated space, that's not always possible. If your room is highly inaccurate and you can't improve it with treatment or better monitors, mixing in headphones may be the best option for you.

Not all headphones are created equal, and the vast majority aren't accurate enough for critical listening. Consumer head-phones are typically designed for enjoyment rather than accuracy, often featuring hyped bass, scooped mids, or exagger-ated highs. Even many studio headphones, while perfectly acceptable for monitoring while tracking, don't provide the flat, honest response needed for mixing.

I tend to avoid recommending gear I haven't personally used, so while plenty of lists claim to name the "best" mixing headphones, I'll focus on models I've worked with firsthand. That said, if you're looking for alternatives, I suggest checking user experiences from engineers who mix professionally in headphones.

Open-back headphones, like the Audeze line (among oth-ers), are widely preferred for mixing because they provide a more natural and open soundstage compared to closed-back de-signs. Closed-back models tend to introduce more internal resonances that color the sound, while the open-back construction allows air and sound waves to pass through the ear cups, reducing internal reflections. This generally results in a flatter frequency response and a more accurate stereo image, making open-back headphones ideal for critical listening and mix decisions.

That said, open-back headphones have their drawbacks since they allow sound to pass through freely. They offer zero isolation. If you're working in a noisy environment or need to prevent bleed while recording, open-back headphones may not be practical.

Additionally, bass response in open-back designs can feel less pronounced because they don't contain low frequencies the way closed-back headphones do. However, this can actually work in your favor for mixing, as it forces more balanced low-end decisions that translate better to speakers.

If you're using open-back headphones for mixing, pairing them with a high-quality headphone amplifier is crucial. A good amp ensures you're getting the most accurate response by providing sufficient power. Equally important is your digital-to-analog converter (DAC)—a subpar converter can introduce unwanted coloration, distortion, or loss of detail in your monitoring chain. Many audio interfaces include built-in headphone amps and converters, but not all are created equal. If your interface's headphone output lacks clarity or struggles to drive high-impedance headphones, an external DAC and headphone amp combo may improve accuracy.

One of the major downsides of mixing in headphones is the skewed and unnatural stereo field. Unlike speakers—where sound from the left speaker reaches both ears (and vice versa)—headphones isolate each ear completely. This creates an exaggerated stereo spread, making panning decisions unreliable and causing phantom center elements—like vocals and KIK drums—to feel unnaturally detached.

To counter this, crossfeed plugins blend a small amount of each channel into the opposite ear, mimicking real-world speaker listening. Crossfeed plugins help reduce ear fatigue and make stereo imaging decisions feel more natural. Some well-regarded options include Goodhertz, CanOpener, and Waves NX, which offer adjustable crossfeed settings to simulate speaker-like listening. I haven't personally used any of these, but they're widely recommended and could be worth exploring if you struggle with stereo imaging in headphones.

Some modern headphone systems build crossfeed directly into their design, offering even more advanced spatial emulation. The Steven Slate Audio VSX system is a prime example of this technology.

The VSX headphone system goes beyond simple crossfeed, using impulse responses and spatial modeling to replicate the sound of well-known mix rooms, mastering studios, and even consumer environments like car speakers and club systems. Instead of merely simulating stereo bleed between ears, VSX emulates what it feels like when you're sitting in front of real monitors in a treated space.

Many engineers rave about this system. I don't mix on headphones, but I did pick up a pair of VSX, mostly for monitoring while recording vocals in my room (the closed-back design makes them especially useful for recording applications). At first, I found them a little weird, but that's probably a good thing, considering how inaccurate most headphones are for mixing. Over time, I noticed that when I got things sounding great in the VSX, it translated almost perfectly to other environments. They made me work a little harder, but once I got it right, my mixes held up everywhere.

Mixing in headphones all the time can be challenging, and prolonged use isn't great for your hearing. Comfort is also a factor—some headphones become physically fatiguing after long sessions, especially if they have a high clamping force or heavy ear cups. If you plan to work extensively in headphones, both comfort and accuracy are worthwhile considerations.

That said, not all of your work requires perfectly accurate monitoring. No matter how inaccurate your room, it won't prevent you from writing a great song or arranging a compelling production. It won't stop you from compiling a vocal from multiple takes. It only limits your ability to make a mix that translates beyond your environment. If you're in a space that can't realistically be made accurate, apply enough acoustic treatment for an accurate recording capture, and rely on high-quality headphones for accurate mixing.

At the end of the day, great music is about performance and arrangement, not just the mix. You can produce an incredible song in headphones, even without an ideal monitoring setup. But when finalizing a mix, a second reference—whether a treated room, trusted monitors, or even checking on consumer playback systems—can assist in achieving your goals.

If headphones are your primary mixing environment, investing in a quality reference pair and using crossfeed or virtual monitoring tools will go a long way toward making your mixes translate better.

Distortion

Before we discuss our various recording and mixing processing tools, I'd like to take a moment to address distortion. Throughout this book, I'll frequently reference distortion—its properties and how it factors into sound design—so I want to make sure I don't give you the wrong impression or promote misunderstandings as we progress.

First, distortion does not necessarily mean aggressive, overt, or obviously degraded sound. At its core, distortion simply means to alter or change something, ostensibly in an "unflattering" way. But in music and art, unflattering is often what makes something compelling. Picasso's paintings wouldn't be valuable if they weren't distorted representations of reality. We love distortion because it adds character, which makes things more interesting, textured, and emotionally engaging.

Really, the question isn't whether you *should* distort. Distortion is a critical component to record production. The question is really a matter of *how much* distortion and on what, and that's not an arbitrary decision. You can distort overtly such that everyone would recognize it as distortion, and you can distort subtly such that you would need to compare to the original in order to recognize the distortion. But make no mistake, distortion is your friend.

As I discuss strategies for setting levels on analog mic preamps and compressors, you might begin to wonder whether I distort everything all the time. Which I don't. Certainly not in an audible manner. But it's an important consideration, and it's beneficial to understand how to use distortion to your advantage.

When I worked in the all analog domain, low distortion specs were touted, because you wanted to keep your distortion in control. These days, many Home Producers are using virtual interface preamps, which often lack in useful distortion properties. This makes externally derived distortion an important part of your sound design. If you're not deriving your distortion at the time of recording, then you need to shape your distortion profile using plugins. Whereas we once worked to minimize distortion, now we have to be deliberate in how we apply it—because a production without the right kind of distortion can sound sterile and lifeless.

Distortion Purposes

Distortion does not always present itself as breakup. Distortion can merely be a slight thickening of the tone that occurs from an analog preamp or compressor. Aggressive overcompression is essentially a type of distortion. How else would you describe heavy pumping effects, or the sound of harmonics that resonate as you put a part into a steady state?

There are specific reasons to strategically introduce distortion to your parts and production. Those being: agitation, edge, thickening, resonance, sustain, obfuscation, or clarity.

Agitation

If you want to agitate the listener, overt, aggressive distortion is a great way to do it. This kind of distortion is a staple of industrial and punk music, especially on '80s punk records. Personally, I don't use distortion to agitate—I don't make records for that purpose. I generally want my records to wrap around the listener like a big hug.

That said, agitation is a perfectly legitimate reason to apply copious amounts of irritating distortion.

Edge

There are plenty of reasons to give your record some edge, but mostly it's to introduce some measure of toughness. Distortion that provides edge could possibly cause agitation too, especially if you're liberal with it. You judge that by how irritating you find it. I personally prefer to use distortion for purposes of edge to help toughen up a record that's coming off too sweet.

Sustain

Aggressive distortion can cause a part to sustain, which can be useful on KIKs, snares, toms, bass, and of course, guitars. We love sustain on guitars—it's one of the most desired byproducts of high-gain distortion.

When you push a guitar into excessive distortion, you're technically over-compressing it, which is part of what creates that sustain. Guitar players often use a compressor in their chain to maximize the level going into the amp, which then compresses it even further.

You can also derive sustain through aggressive over-compression alone, which can make the overtones of a part as loud as the fundamental. And make no mistake—aggressive over-compression is absolutely a form of distortion.

Resonance

Resonance is a more aggressive, less stable form of sustain—similar to guitar feedback. It causes a specific frequency in a sustained part to "sing" and can be a powerful effect when used intentionally. That said, excessive resonance can easily overtake a mix, especially on outside playback systems. So, be mindful.

Obfuscation

It's completely legitimate to use distortion to obfuscate a sound or a part. Not everything in a production needs to be recognizable, clearly heard, or defined with sharp transients. Sometimes, we want to create an ambiance, evoke a feeling, or add depth—and obfuscation through distortion can help achieve that.

Clarity

Just as distortion can be used to obfuscate, it can also be used to enhance clarity—especially for low-end instruments. Distortion brings the overtones forward. Low-end information is felt more than it's heard, and distortion emphasizes the harmonic octaves, bringing the part into a more audible range.

This is exactly why 808 KIK drums functioning as bass parts are often hit with copious amounts of distortion—to improve clarity. Not only does this make low-end parts more defined in full-range consumer systems, but it also helps them translate on smaller playback systems that can't reproduce deep sub frequencies.

Exciters are a prime example of this—they introduce distortion specifically to enhance clarity, adding presence and definition to otherwise buried elements.

Thickening

The thickening of tone that occurs with subtle distortion can help an otherwise anemic part stand out, making it easier to place in a production. Thickening can also be more overt, at which point we start getting into sustain and resonance as well. Aggressive compression tends to thicken parts too.

My biggest advancement in production and sound design came when I began to understand the importance of distortion and implemented it as part of my process. Without it, my productions felt thin, uninteresting, and lacked overall toughness. If you listen to productions from the last 30 years, distortion is practically a feature.

Even if you're making generally clean music, you'll still want some measure of distortion in your productions—it just won't necessarily be overt. Think of distortion like seasoning in food. A production devoid of distortion is like food without seasoning. Both are critical components to something tasty.

Distortion Flavors

There are many varieties of distortion—breakup, crunch, spit, buzz, sizzle. There's low-end distortion, which can have a woolly character. There's bit distortion, and there's clipping. Each of these flavors has its own unique qualities, and when you have control over the types of distortion you introduce, you gain greater control over the presentation of your track.

First, let's define some flavors of distortion and understand where they shine.

Clipping

In most cases, we aim to avoid clipping in hardware, as it tends to manifest in an unpleasant, jarring way—often making the listener instinctively recoil. That said, controlled clipping distortion can sometimes be desirable, especially when used to bring transients into almost comically militant compliance. But the moment clipping becomes too overt, it can cause the listener some serious agita.

You should never allow your stereo output converters—the converters you're using to monitor your production—to clip. Clipping at this stage is completely out of your control and puts you outside the delivery specs for all distribution formats, including CDs, streaming, and vinyl, which could result in your master being rejected.

If you want to introduce clipping artistically, use dedicated plugins designed for that purpose. These allow you to shape clipping distortion without compromising playback consistency across different systems.

Clipping distortion is commonly used in hard rock, death metal, and industrial music. But there are far more genres where you'd never want any kind of audible clipping. Used overtly, its purpose is purely agitation. But when applied subtly, it can serve as a tool for balance control.

Bitcrusher

Bitcrusher distortion is an exceptionally abrasive form of distortion that works by downsampling the audio, reducing its bit-depth to produce a lo-fi tone with digital artifacts. The lower the bit rate, the more pronounced these artifacts become, particularly in the form of aliased high-end frequencies—which manifest as spitting, noise, and an almost hollowed-out sound.

Aliasing occurs when audio is sampled at a rate too low to accurately capture its full frequency spectrum. Instead of reproducing the original frequencies, the system misinterprets them, generating unintended, often harsh artifacts—particularly in the high end. This is why aliased distortion can sound brittle or unpleasant.

A bitcrusher can produce a very cool effect, adding a raw, degraded quality to a sound. However, it can also be exhausting to the listener if used excessively. Even if your goal is agitation, it's worth demonstrating some restraint with how much bitcrushing you apply.

Total Harmonic Distortion (THD)

Total Harmonic Distortion, or THD, is a measurement that manufacturers often highlight to sell analog gear. While once a critical spec in the analog era, it's not particularly meaningful in today's predominantly digital workflows.

Back when every piece of gear introduced some level of distortion, THD was a real concern—as unintended distortion could compound across multiple stages of the signal chain, potentially degrading the sound of a production. But these days, you're far more likely to intentionally introduce distortion than to go out of your way to avoid it.

Overdrive

Overdrive is probably the most useful and common form of distortion, as it adds warmth and harmonic richness without being inherently aggressive. Unlike harsher distortion types, overdrive preserves more of the dynamic range within a part, allowing for a more natural, musical saturation.

Surely, you can obliterate the signal as you break it up with overdrive distortion, but at some point, we wouldn't describe the distortion as overdrive any longer. There's a line. Overdrive can bring some modicum of edge and clarity to electric guitars and bass but can also be useful for obfuscation and thickening.

Crunch

Crunch distortion is commonly associated with high-gain electric guitars, often used for power chords that require sustain. This type of distortion is typically derived from an amplifier or pedals—virtual or otherwise—and sits prominently in the upper midrange, where it adds bite and presence without fully saturating into heavier distortion. The rock, metal, and pop genres often call for crunch guitar.

Buzz

Buzz distortion acts like a separate layer over the source. As such, it typically only affects a somewhat narrow frequency band. Its resonance puts a definitive edge on anything that sustains. Buzz distortion is especially useful for offering clarity on low-end instruments like a clean synth bass, or even an electric bass part. The buzz brings out the upper octave harmonics, which help the notes remain audible even as the arrangement gets more dense.

Fuzz

Fuzz distortion affects the full range of frequencies, which makes it somewhat more complex in nature. Unlike buzz, the delineation between the tone and the dirt is not so evident. Whereas buzz offers clarity, fuzz can offer either clarity or obfuscation, since it distorts the entire signal. When it comes to bass, you can add copious levels of fuzz distortion for purposes of edge and clarity. Fuzz distortion introduced in a subtle way can appear woolly in nature.

Wooly

Distortion of the low frequencies often comes off woolly. Used aggressively, it can start to sound unstable, as the low-end energy causes an especially dirty breakup. Used judiciously, woolly distortion can be relatively inaudible beyond a slight bit of breakup in the low end, which is often masked within the context of the production. Rock bass guitars love woolly distortion, although they can consume your entire mix when used too overtly. KIK drums react well to woolly distortion too. While it's true that woolly distortion can add clarity for transient instruments, it can also obfuscate instruments that sustain.

Saturation

Saturation distortion occurs when an audio signal exceeds the maximum level that a device (like a tape recorder, amplifier, or effects pedal) can handle. Saturation adds both odd and even harmonics to the signal and rounds off the peaks due to the compression that occurs. This can result in warmth, a richness in tone, and dynamic control.

Now, while it's true that saturation distortion will reduce the dynamic range of a part, it's not really the purpose of the distortion so much as a byproduct of it. If you merely want to reduce dynamic range, a compressor is the better tool for that.

Saturation is the most versatile form of distortion, as it can be used for nearly any purpose. Applied aggressively, it can agitate and add edge. It can enhance clarity in low-end instruments, create sustain, thicken a sound, introduce resonance, or even obfuscate.

Saturation plugins are a staple in modern music production. As with all distortion, judiciousness and taste come into play, even if your primary goal is to agitate. If you use too much saturation distortion, your production could lack clarity, punch, and contrast.

There are many excellent saturation plugins available today, each with their own unique character. Over time, it's worth building a collection of different flavors. If you're looking for a great all-around saturation plugin, FabFilter's Saturn 2 is a great choice—available as a standalone plugin or as part of Fab-Filter's broader suite.

Tape Saturation

Tape saturation distortion supposedly models odd harmonic distortion which is, indeed, the kind of distortion you can expect from a tape machine. While tape saturation affects all harmonics, it emphasizes the odd harmonics—the ones that occur between octave harmonics.

Some people claim to put tape saturation plugins on nearly everything, and that's a great way to turn your production into a schmeary mess. If you like what modeled tape saturation brings, then by all means use it. Just don't buy into the idea that these plugins accurately replicate the sound of analog tape—they really don't.

Most engineers sought fidelity from tape, not overt saturation. Saturation could be useful as an effect, especially in rock music, and there were times when you might deliberately push it for character. You could even make the case for slathering it thick on a particular record—but not on all records, all the time. Aggressive tape saturation tends to lop off transients, which softens the overall sound through obfuscation.

People who've never used tape tend to believe printing to tape made things warm or even dark. When I printed a mix to tape, the mix opened up and became wider and the low end deeper. The medium benefitted the sound. It didn't darken it or alter it in a negative way. Frankly, modern complex intelligent clarifiers like Soundtheory Gullfoss produce a sound far more reminiscent of tape than any tape machine plugin I've ever used.

Spitting

Spitting distortion can occur across any frequency range and creates a sense of instability, as the breakup feels almost random. This type of distortion can sometimes resemble digital pops mixed with other forms of breakup, making it unpredictable and erratic. When used intentionally, spitting distortion can add texture and character to a part.

Tube Distortion

Tubes, sometimes called valves, introduce even-order distortion, which is supposed to be less musical than odd, but I'm not even sure I know what that means anymore as I personally find tube distortion to be rather pleasing in nature.

The beauty of tubes is they can absolutely sing if given enough level, making them excellent for purposes of sustain and resonance. Valve distortion is often described as "warm," as it resonates most apparently in the lower midrange, and therefore, acts as a thickening agent. It's particularly effective at providing sustain, without overt top-end distortion, although you can certainly get a tube to buzz if you desire.

Tube Screamer

Tube screamer distortion is an emulation of valve distortion and is derived from a pedal. They are often used to inject more gain to an amplifier for purposes of sustain. Tube screamers tend to filter out the top and bottom end, placing them squarely in the midrange. As a result, they can make power chords sound downright small, but they can be quite useful for apparent midrange.

Breakup

Breakup is a mild form of distortion that introduces grit without significantly affecting sustain or resonance. It allows for some audible distortion while preserving the overall dynamics of the instrument or performance.

Breakup is effective on virtually any instrument, including vocals. Electric guitars that sound too clean often benefit from a touch of breakup—it's still a clean guitar, but with just enough texture to make it pop in the mix.

Breakup can be achieved through a guitar amp, a preamp, or even a saturation or overdrive plugin, making it a versatile tool for adding subtle character to a sound.

Applying Distortion

Now that we've established the importance and diversity of distortion properties, we should talk about the practical application of distortion. How much distortion is too much?

It depends on the production, of course. Some productions call for distortion on virtually everything. Others call for very little overtly audible distortion. But you always want to introduce some measure of distortion.

So, where's the line? You can make the track pure white noise if you think it's going to sell records. Excess distortion is a matter of taste and would fall under artistic license. Too little distortion on the other hand is a technical issue. Just as you wouldn't want to eat a meal with no seasoning, you wouldn't want to listen to a record completely devoid of distortion.

That said, too much of anything is rarely a good thing. Developing taste and restraint is critical. If you want to overtly distort a part, then you should be bold about it. But if you want that bold part to really stand out, then consider leaving other parts clean for purposes of contrast. If everything is boldly distorting, then none of it will stand out.

It's the same with effects. If you slather your entire production with reverbs, then there will be little-to-no clarity, which reduces contrast. If you put reverb on some parts and leave other parts dry, then you provide yourself much needed contrast.

For much of recording history, capturing audio too cleanly wasn't really an option. You would need preamps with exceptionally low distortion specs, which you would gain super conservatively. You had to avoid many EQs which could introduce annoying high end distortion. You had to choose compressors that had super low THD specs. Of course, none of that changed the fact that you introduced distortion when you went to tape. Then, on the consumer side, the turntable stylus would add yet another layer of distortion.

For the first half of my career, it was actually difficult to avoid distortion. But with the advent and popularity of distortion-less interface mic pres, it's now actually possible to make a record with too little distortion.

Distortion can be used to agitate, and this usually comes down to the balance of top-end information. Pleasing distortion tends to roll off at the very top frequencies, while distortion in the upper harmonics enhances clarity. But when distortion contains copious levels of upper midrange and top-end content, the result is almost always agitation.

KIK drums are routinely distorted in my productions, and you might not ever even notice. That's the thing about low-end distortion. It's not necessarily audible in context and often acts more like a thickening agent. Sometimes I want to hear the distortion on the KIK drum in context, but then that's typically for purposes of edge. I'll also use distortion in conjunction with compression to assist with punch.

I suppose the big takeaway is this: If your recording equipment isn't introducing enough distortion, and your production sounds anemic, lacks edge, punch, or clarity, then you can use distortion to help with any—or all—of those maladies. But then too much distortion can cause those problems too. This is where practice comes into play.

Mic Preamps

Now that I've explained distortion and how you use it to your advantage, let's talk about some of the tools that can be used to help you derive that distortion, starting with mic preamps.

As I've mentioned, interface preamps don't distort. These preamps are fine when you're just starting out, but as you progress in your production journey—especially if you're building a business—you'll do well to invest in external analog preamps. Once you do, you should know how to get the most out of them.

Analog mic preamps can range from a few hundred dollars to several thousand, especially for highly coveted vintage models like the Neve 1073

You judge an analog preamp by how it distorts, and there is no preamp that distorts quite as beautifully as a 1073. This is true whether you push the gain all the way up or set the gain to just before obvious distortion occurs. Driven hard, it can sing with resonant saturation distortion. Used subtly, it thickens a sound beautifully. That said, I'd never pay thousands of dollars for one—even as someone who acknowledges that it's the best preamp ever made.

The reality is a preamp won't fix a bad song. It won't fix a lackluster performance. And digital distortion algorithms are now so convincing—pleasing even—that it makes little sense to spend excessive money on a preamp unless you happen to have stupid money. When you have stupid money, you can spend it stupidly, because it doesn't matter. For everyone else, there are better places to allocate your resources, like on the acoustic treatment of your room, for instance.

You can find plenty of great analog preamps in the $600 to $1000 range. My favorite new-stock mic preamp right now is the A-Designs Pacifica, which costs just over $1000 per channel. That's not cheap, but it's the price of quality.

All preamps distort in their own unique way. Some analog preamps are designed to produce very subtle distortion, like the Millenia line, which is the darling of classical music recorders, and for good reason. They have the sound of a quality analog preamp without the overt distortion.

When recording highly dynamic music, you want a preamp with plenty of headroom before audible distortion kicks in. For modern genres, you might choose a preamp that distorts more readily. Some preamps thicken a signal as they distort. Others get beefier. Some simply break up. But make no mistake—all analog preamps distort when pushed hard enough. The key is using their distortion properties to your advantage.

Preamps react best just before the point of overt distortion. So, it's a good practice to push your preamp into distortion, then back off the gain until it sounds optimal—this is something you judge by ear. If you don't bring the preamp into distortion, you won't know where the line is, and you're likely underutilizing the preamp's character. Even if your goal is a clean capture, you should push it into distortion and back down—that's how you find the sweet spot.

If, along the way, you decide you like the overt distortion, then leave the gain there. But if you never bring the preamp to distortion, then you could very well be missing out.

Frankly, mic preamps are the most overrated part of your signal chain. There are tons of preamps on the market, each with its own subtle tonal signature, and professionals will have their favorites, perhaps even lots of favorites. Really, you just need preamps that will stay out of your way. That's a rather low bar.

I've gone deep into the world of mic preamps. When I recorded Ben Harper's *Burn to Shine* in 1999, I had access to a ridiculous variety of mic preamps—including all sorts of rare gear that producer JP Plunier and I were buying from auction sites. At one point, we even repurposed old Ampex tape electronics as preamps. It was stupid.

We also had a massive mic collection and let me tell you—it's easy to waste time and money obsessing over mic-to-pre-amp pairings for every instrument on every song. I swear, we tried every possible combination.

I'll never do that again. What a wank.

Looking back, I can say with certainty that all that experimentation gave us zero benefit. I was being paid as a for-hire, dedicated recordist and I had lots of time to experiment without bogging down the session. But as a producer, you have bigger concerns. You want the engineering to stay out of your way as much as possible.

You can record an entire record with just one variety of preamp. I've done it many times, using only the preamps from a console. Don't buy into the hype. If you can get an analog preamp that adds some flavor—particularly in how it distorts—then go for it. Otherwise, use your interface's preamps and apply your distortion attributes with plugins.

PROCESSORS AND PLUGINS

Equalizers (EQ)

Our most powerful tool for shaping frequencies in a production is EQ. An EQ allows us to boost or cut frequencies within a part—or even across the entire mix—to shape the overall tone.

There are many types of EQ, but the only one we really need to focus on is the parametric EQ—the most commonly used EQ in record production.

Bell Curve

There are two types of EQ adjustments on a parametric EQ: bell curve and shelf. A bell curve EQ places the selected fundamental frequency at the center of a specified range of frequencies, which taper off to form the curve.

The width of the bell curve is determined by the Q factor. The higher the Q, the narrower the affected range; the lower the Q, the wider the range. This range of affected frequencies is called the bandwidth. The center frequency is the most prominent point in the curve, with the surrounding frequencies gradually tapering off in amplitude.

The figure below illustrates a two-octave bell curve. Here, the fundamental frequency is set at 1 kHz, with the curve extending down to 500 Hz and up to 2 kHz. The peak of the curve represents an amplitude of +3 dB, while the base on either side represents 0 dB.

Every doubling of frequency represents one octave, so in this case, the affected frequencies span one octave below and one octave above the center frequency, resulting in a two-octave bandwidth. From a purely technical perspective, Q-based octave range isn't measured this way—it's far more convoluted. But since we're working with music, two octaves should actually cover two octaves.

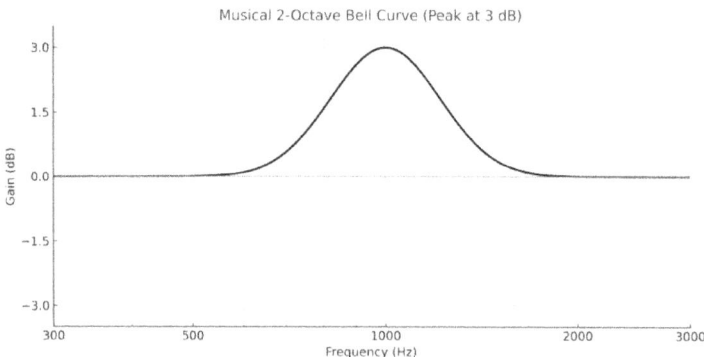

Musical 2-Octave Bell Curve (Peak at 3 dB)

Shelf

Shelving EQ comes in only two types—high shelf and low shelf. Like a bell curve, a shelf affects a range of frequencies, but instead of centering on a selected frequency, the chosen frequency acts as the starting point.

For example, a high-frequency shelf set to 5 kHz will affect all frequencies above 5 kHz, whether you're applying a cut or a boost. Conversely, a low-frequency shelf set to 100 Hz will affect all frequencies below 100 Hz.

A shelf looks like this:

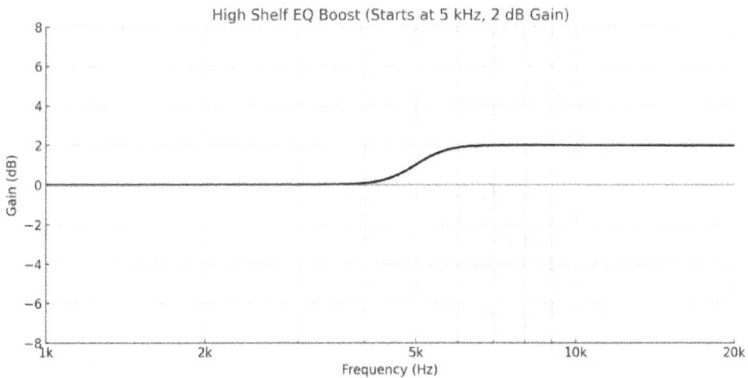

This probably has you wondering when to use a shelf and when to use a bell curve. If you want to bring out or cut a specific range of frequencies, use a bell curve. If you want to adjust the overall balance of the top or bottom end of a sound, use a shelf.

That said, there's no right or wrong way to EQ. All that matters is what you hear. If it sounds right, it is right.

Filters

There are two types of filters on a parametric EQ: the high-pass filter (HPF) and the low-pass filter (LPF).

A high-pass filter allows high frequencies to pass through unaffected while removing low frequencies. A low-pass filter does the opposite, allowing low frequencies to pass while filtering out the high end. That's right—a high-pass filter removes low frequencies, and a low-pass filter removes high frequencies. That's not confusing at all!

For example, a high-pass filter set to 100 Hz will remove frequencies below 100 Hz, while a low-pass filter set to 10 kHz will remove frequencies above 10 kHz.

Most plugin filters allow you to adjust the slope of the curve, which determines how aggressively the filtered frequencies are rolled off. A steep slope of 48dB results in a sharp cutoff, while a more gradual 12dB slope creates a smoother transition.

I've seen some engineers, particularly outside of the United States, apply high-pass filters to every channel as a standard practice. This is often done at the mic preamp stage, meaning the low-end is removed before the signal is even recorded. The problem with this approach is that once you eliminate frequencies at the capture stage, there's no getting them back.

Unless you're dealing with unwanted low-end artifacts from the room that need to be removed, I generally recommend against high-passing everything on the way in. You can't accurately determine how much low end a part should have until you hear it in the context of the full arrangement.

Over the course of my career, I've used high-pass filters far more often than low-pass filters. However, in recent years, I find myself using low-pass filters more frequently than ever before. Why is that? I'm not exactly sure. But I don't think it's that I've changed—I think more people tend to record with overly bright microphones.

A low-pass filter can really dull a sound, and it's not usually the best way to shape the top end of a part. If I apply a low-pass filter to a guitar, it's usually to tame the sizzle on the top end, which in turn makes the upper midrange more apparent. This can actually help electric guitars cut through a mix while also reducing masking from cymbals.

If a low-pass filter feels too aggressive—and they often do—try a high shelf cut set above 16 kHz instead. This allows you to attenuate the top end without completely eliminating it.

High-pass filters can be useful for shaping the bottom end, especially if you need to control the subs in a bass or KIK for clarity. But if you use a high-pass filter to completely remove sub-frequencies from your low-end instruments, you could be stripping away valuable information. Some overlap in frequency between instruments is natural. The goal is never to eradicate masking—it's to control it through tone shaping and level adjustments.

If you're going for the currently trendy bullhorn vocal effect, setting a high-pass filter as high as 200 Hz can help. This allows the vocal to sit deeper in the mix while still cutting through. That said, the slope that you set makes a big difference in how much low-end frequencies you're removing.

Keep in mind, sub-frequency information is what helps a track feel big. You want to shape your low end so that everything works together in balance, but you don't want to kill your subs in the process. As tricky as it is to balance a powerful low end, it can actually be even harder to mix a record without it.

The Q Factor

The Q factor determines the range of frequencies affected by an EQ adjustment, allowing you to narrow or broaden the bandwidth significantly. As a general rule, overly broad bandwidths affect too many frequencies to be useful, while overly narrow bandwidths isolate too few.

According to Wikipedia, the Q factor is "a parameter that describes the resonance behavior of an underdamped harmonic oscillator." That's all well and good—and perhaps even interesting to someone—but in practical terms, Q values typically range from about 0.1 (very broad) to 10 or more (very narrow), depending on the EQ. A broad Q setting can affect nearly the entire spectrum, while a narrow Q can create a sharp, resonant whistle when boosted.

Not all EQs interpret Q the same way. One plugin's "2.0" might look totally different in another. Some EQs limit how wide or narrow you can go, while others—like FabFilter—let you sharpen the Q into a sonic scalpel. So, you can't match curves between EQs based on Q values.

As much as I hate assigning fixed values (since people tend to take them as gospel), a Q that covers anywhere from two to four octaves provides a gentle, musical curve that works well as a starting point. By default, I set my bell curve EQ bands to span two octaves and adjust from there as needed.

The narrower the bandwidth, the more surgical your EQ becomes. Extremely narrow curves are known as notch EQ—typically used to remove resonant problem frequencies. A notch EQ carves out a very specific frequency with minimal impact on everything around it.

Aggressive EQ techniques—such as extreme boosts or deep notches—are used to fix or mangle sounds, while subtle to moderate EQ is used for tone shaping. The more control you have over your recording and production, the less you should need aggressive EQ techniques. If you're hearing a problem while tracking, that's the best time to address it, rather than relying on EQ to fix it later.

Q also plays a role in shelving EQ and filters, though it functions a little differently than it does with a bell curve.

A higher Q setting on a shelf creates a resonant bump at the cutoff frequency before rolling off, while a lower Q produces a smoother, more gradual transition.

With filters the Q affects how steeply the filter rolls off frequencies. A higher Q filter can introduce resonance at the cutoff frequency, emphasizing it before attenuation kicks in. This can be useful for adding presence or character but can also create unwanted ringing if overdone. A lower Q filter results in a more natural, gradual roll-off, which is often preferable for transparent filtering.

Many EQ plugins allow Q adjustments for shelves and filters, which can be helpful for fine-tuning how aggressive or natural the frequency transition sounds.

Tilt

Some EQs include a tilt function, a handy feature that will likely become more common in plugins over time. Visually, a tilt EQ resembles a seesaw balanced on a frequency fulcrum in the middle of the bandwidth.

Tilt the seesaw to the left, and you attenuate the low end while boosting the top end. Tilt it to the right, and you attenuate the top end while boosting the low end.

If all you need is a subtle way to open up a tone, the tilt function is an excellent tool for the job.

Frequency Analyzers

Most DAW EQs provide a visual representation of frequency manipulation, allowing you to see the range of frequencies you're affecting. While this visual modeling is useless for making actual EQ decisions—those should be made purely by ear— it can be incredibly helpful in accelerating your understanding of frequency balance and EQ in general.

That said, analyzers can be deceiving. Your tracks won't appear perfectly flat, nor should they. Even a well-balanced mix won't look flat, and you might find yourself tempted to boost excessive amounts of top end just to make the analyzer look "right." Don't do that. This is an auditory medium.

An analyzer shows the general frequency makeup of a sound, including any buildup in certain areas. But a buildup doesn't automatically indicate a problem. You'd expect a bass guitar or KIK drum to have an excess of low-end energy, for example. If your goal is to make the frequency response of every track look flat, you're working against the very nature of sound—that would be a very bad goal indeed.

It's best to use the analyzer to confirm what you're hearing, not to define it. A visual bump at 750 Hz on an acoustic guitar might stand out on the display, but that doesn't necessarily mean it needs to be cut. That same 750 Hz bump, which often contributes to a boxy tone, might actually help the guitar sit well in the full production. While you'll cut 750 Hz far more often than you'll boost it, if the overall mix benefits from that frequency presence, it makes sense to leave it—even if it appears out of balance on the analyzer.

The most effective way to find offensive frequencies by ear is to boost and sweep. Don't be shy. Boost by 4-6 dB, or even more if necessary. This is a fact-finding mission. You want to exaggerate the frequency response, making problem areas obvious, and then sweep across the spectrum until you find the most obnoxious spot. Once you've identified it, cut it.

How much you cut should be determined by ear. Keep in mind that after exposing yourself to an exaggerated frequency boost, your perception might take a moment to reset. You may need to revisit your adjustment to refine the cut.

If you notice multiple problematic frequencies close together, widen the Q to create a more natural cut. If you find issues in different areas of the spectrum, open up another EQ band and address those separately. You can even run multiple EQ modules in series if that makes things easier.

That said, overusing notch EQs can create strange holes in the sound. Notches should be reserved for overt problems and should be somewhat rare in implementation. If you find yourself notching routinely, chances are you have acoustic issues that need to be addressed.

EQ Strategies & Myths

Many of you have probably read claims online that it's better to cut with EQ than to boost. There's some truth to this when it comes to notch EQ (a very narrow EQ band), but some take it to the extreme, suggesting that a professional mixer would never apply an EQ boost. I can assure you, I'm just as likely to boost as I am to cut.

In terms of technique, I give no thought whatsoever to whether I'm cutting or boosting. That decision is made based on the realities at hand. While there are plenty of general rules worth following in record-making, others are so outdated they may as well be myths. This is one of them.

This idea stems from the days of tape, which introduced hiss. Boosting the top end off tape meant boosting the hiss along with it. If you were to add top-end EQ on playback across multiple channels of an analog 24-track recording, the accumulated noise could become unbearable.

Beyond that, many analog EQs introduce top-end distortion, which can be fatiguing for the listener. Engineers working in the analog domain avoided excessive top-end EQ boosts whenever possible to minimize the buildup of hiss and distortion. That doesn't mean they never boosted—it was sometimes the best solution—but there was always a strategic approach to it, based on limitations that largely no longer exist.

So, it wasn't completely bad advice to avoid EQ boosts given the artifacts of analog tape. But now? It makes no sense, particularly since DAW EQs generally don't model the distortion properties of their analog counterparts. This means you can boost and cut EQ with relative impunity.

Some argue that boosting can introduce audible phase shifts, causing subtle smearing. While this is technically true, it's rarely an issue in practice. Aggressive boosts of 6 dB or more, combined with narrow Q settings, can make phase shifts more noticeable, in which case a cut may be the better approach. Phase shift can also cause comb filtering when applied in parallel to an unaffected signal. But for most shaping EQ, natural phase shift isn't something to worry about. As always, let your ears be your guide.

Many of your EQ decisions will involve frequency swapping—rebalancing one frequency range to make room for another. For instance, when working with a KIK drum and bass, you want one to occupy a lower frequency range than the other. If your KIK drum is blooming at 50 Hz, and your bass is also living in that range, clarity between the two can be difficult to achieve. The mix will often sit better if each instrument has its own fundamental low-end territory.

In this example, you could bring the KIK drum's fundamental frequency up an octave by cutting 50 Hz and boosting in the 100-200 Hz range, creating more space for the bass to dominate the sub frequencies. Sometimes, you'll want the opposite approach—allowing the KIK to live under the bass by boosting its subs and keeping the bass more prominent in the upper low end. It all depends on the arrangement. For reference, the fundamental frequency of the low B on a five-string bass is around 30 Hz, while the low E sits at approximately 41 Hz.

I always encourage aggressiveness in recording and production, because timidity is a terrible mindset for creating art. If a part requires an extreme EQ curve to work, there's no reason to hesitate. That said, many parts may only need subtle EQ shaping—or none at all—especially if you're mindful of how frequencies stack up as you build your arrangement.

EQ in Solo

Another one of my favorite myths is the idea that you should never EQ in solo. Or better yet, the claim that a professional would *never* EQ in solo. Laughable.

I'll grant you this—if you solo every instrument and EQ each one in isolation with no regard for how they interact, you're in for a rough time. EQ decisions should always be based on how a part functions within the context of the production, not in isolation. But when it comes to *implementing* those decisions, there's no reason to avoid soloing. It lets you hear how a part sounds on its own compared to how it sits in the mix. Both pieces of information are valuable.

Solo exists so you can isolate a signal, magnify problems, and remove distractions. Want to find that annoying midrange honk in a snare? Solo it. Trying to pinpoint a nasal quality in a vocal that only appears in certain phrases? Solo it. Working on de-essing a vocal and want to know exactly how much sibilance you're pulling out? Good luck doing that without solo. EQing a bass guitar and trying to figure out which frequencies are clashing with the KIK? Solo them one at a time. You'll find the problem faster, then un-solo and hear how your fix translates.

The point is, solo isn't the problem. The issue is ignoring the *interdependency* of your decisions while working in isolation. It's not like you won't hear your adjustments once you go back to full mix playback. So really, there is no argument for avoiding solo.

Solo deniers insist that EQ should only be applied in the context of the full mix. If that works for you, great—that's a valid approach. Personally, I find that an exceptionally difficult way to work. So don't believe for a second that you should avoid solo as a tool for applying processing.

Solo all you like. I do.

Exciters

Exciters boost the upper harmonics from a selected frequency point, making them particularly useful for enhancing audibility. Since they also introduce some distortion, they're often used to improve clarity—especially on elements like bass.

One of the most important decisions when using an exciter is where to set the frequency point. Exciters work by generating or emphasizing harmonic content from that point upward. A lower frequency setting (around 1–3 kHz) can result in a warmer, fuller enhancement and is generally smoother on the ears. A higher setting (6–10 kHz) will emphasize air and brilliance but can quickly introduce harshness, sibilance, or brittle-sounding distortion—especially on vocals or cymbals. Choosing the right starting point is key, and your ears will always be the final judge.

For example, when working with bass, I often set the frequency point as low as 200 Hz to accent the fourth octave and help the part cut through more clearly—especially on smaller playback systems.

That said, exciters should be used sparingly. It's uncommon to need more than one or two in a production, so don't go overboard. As much as I'm a proponent of distortion, top-end distortion is exhausting to the listener and far more likely to result in agitation than clarity.

Frankly, it's exceptionally rare for me to use an exciter on a vocal. While they can add a sense of presence and air, they also tend to introduce harshness and an unnatural top end that becomes fatiguing over time. If your exciter is introducing high-end sizzle to the vocal, it's going to be far less inviting—and you'll have gained nothing in terms of clarity. If you do use an exciter on a vocal, keep it subtle and always check it in the context of the full mix.

You really only want to apply processors that address a specific problem or need, whether that's technical or creative. If you're struggling to get a part to sit right with EQ, that's the time to try inserting an exciter and see if it helps. Sometimes, a little extra harmonic content is all you need—but too much can quickly become a problem.

Sub-Frequency Generators

Sub-frequency generators can be useful, but adding subs should be approached with some measure of caution. If low frequencies have been somehow eradicated from a part—like a KIK drum with no real sub content—or a loop in desperate need of low-end reinforcement, a sub-frequency generator can help. That said, they often sound artificial.

I'm not exactly sure how the hell they work, but in practical terms, they analyze the existing fundamental and generate an undertone—usually an octave below it. If your KIK drum drops off sharply below 100 Hz, a sub-frequency plugin can synthesize that missing low-end content and add weight where there was none.

That said, it's incredibly easy to add stupid amounts of sub, which can throw your entire low-end balance out of whack. Use sub-frequency generators judiciously, or you'll end up with a mix that feels bloated, undefined, or completely overpowered in the subs—especially once it's reproduced on a consumer system, which tends to accentuate those frequencies.

Compressors

Compressors are used to reduce dynamic range, shape tone, boost output, and control low end. They are powerful and versatile tools—arguably the most important in your arsenal.

Analog compressors, which most plugin compressors are modeled after, vary widely in both tone and response. Understanding how different designs react can help you choose the right one for the job.

When pushed to their extremes, compressors can create bold, even dramatic effects. Used more subtly, they reduce your workload by helping a part sit more consistently in the mix, preventing it from getting lost due to masking or excessive dynamics.

Make no mistake—compression is critical to modern production and mixing. If you're too timid with it, you'll likely wonder why your mix sounds flat or lifeless. Compressors make a mix pop, whether applied to individual tracks or across the entire mix bus. The most accomplished mixers use copious amounts of compression, especially when working with organically recorded music, which starts out far more dynamic than your typical programmed production. After all, a KIK and snare sample that never changes in level doesn't need dynamic control. Your average band drummer does.

Before getting into the mechanics of how to use a compressor, it's important to first understand the different analog designs and how they react. Just as microphone types have distinct attributes that influence your choices, so do compressors.

Yes, it's time to take our vegetables again.

VCA Compressors

Solid-state VCA (Voltage Controlled Amplifier) compressors impart minimal color to the tone and have fast, responsive attack and release times, making them ideal for controlling transients and peaks. They excel on snare, percussion, and room mics, for fast dynamics control with minimal tonal coloration.

While generally considered clean compressors, VCA designs can be used to introduce distortion when pushed to their fastest attack settings. Notable examples of VCA compressors include the dbx 160, SSL G384 Bus Comp, Focusrite Red 3, and API 2500.

FET Compressors

FET (Field Effect Transistor) compressors are highly colored and serve both dynamic control and tone shaping. They have fast response times and tend to sound aggressive, thanks to the harmonic distortion they introduce—arguably their most appealing characteristic.

Because of their speed and tonal impact, FET compressors are incredibly versatile, often adding punch, presence, and energy to a part. They are particularly effective on vocals, drums, and bass, but they also shine on electric guitars, drum room mics, synth leads, and even rap vocals, where a bit of bite and growl helps the part cut through the mix.

The 1176 is by far the most common and widely used FET compressor, known for its fast attack, aggressive compression, and distinct tone.

Valve or Tube Compressors

Valve, or tube, compressors impart noticeable color and pleasant harmonic distortion, adding richness and warmth to the tone. They typically have slower attack and release times compared to solid-state VCA compressors, making them less effective for controlling fast transients, such as those produced by drums.

Instead, tube compressors excel at smoothing out dynamic material in a musical and forgiving way, making them a favorite for vocals, bass, and other sustained instruments like strings, horn sections, pads, and acoustic guitars. A good tube compressor can add polish to instruments that benefit from a warmer, more organic tone.

The Teletronix LA-2A is one of the most well-known tube compressors. It also happens to be an optical compressor.

Optical Compressors

Optical, or opto, compressors use a light source and sensor to control compression. Their relatively slow attack times and smooth, automatic release curves make them ideal for bass and vocals, where they can enhance sustain without introducing harsh compression artifacts.

They also work well on acoustic guitar, cello, ballad piano, and synth pads. Optical compressors often introduce a degree of harmonic distortion, adding subtle warmth and character. Some models also function as leveling amplifiers, providing consistent dynamic control with minimal pumping or unnatural artifacts.

Notable examples include the Teletronix LA-2A, the Tube-Tech CL 1B, and the Manley ELOP.

Leveling Amplifiers

Leveling amplifiers are designed to provide smooth, automatic gain control, reacting gradually to the input signal. They typically feature a slow, natural attack and release, making them ideal for vocals, bass, and other sources where maintaining a steady output is desired.

They're also great for background vocals, acoustic guitar, solo instruments like violin or saxophone, and even spoken word or podcast narration. Because they respond smoothly and naturally, leveling amplifiers are a go-to choice for keeping performances consistent and well-balanced in a mix without sounding overly compressed.

Many optical compressors also function as leveling amplifiers—most notably the Teletronix LA-2A and the Tube-Tech CL 1B. But vari-mu compressors like the Gates STA-Level and the Manley Vari-Mu also behave like leveling amps.

Vari-Mu Compressors

All vari-mu compressors use tubes, but not all tube compressors are vari-mu. What sets vari-mu designs apart is how they respond to signal level—the more signal you feed them, the more they compress. This creates a smooth, natural gain control that's musical and forgiving, especially on vocals and mix bus processing.

Vari-mu compressors tend to have slower attack times and smooth release curves, making them well-suited for vocals, mix bus compression, and mastering. They also do particularly well on acoustic ensembles, piano, string sections, and vocal stacks—anywhere you need cohesion and warmth without obvious compression artifacts.

They add warmth, depth, and a sense of "glue" to a mix. While not as aggressive or fast as FET or VCA designs, they excel at transparent leveling and subtle dynamic control. They also tend to impart a rather obvious tonal color, which isn't always a net positive—it depends on the material and your personal taste. Frankly, I find the coloration from some analog vari-mu compressors to be a bit overbearing, but I'm not so sure that translates as readily to plugin models. Notable examples include the Fairchild 660 and 670, and the Manley Vari-Mu.

From Design to Decision

Now that I've described all the basic analog compressor designs, you may have noticed the biggest difference between them are their time constants and their coloration. There are really just fast and slow compressors and highly colored and more transparent compressors. Really, it comes down to fast vs. slow compressors, and highly colored vs. more transparent ones. And while those traits can guide your choices, you can use any type of compressor on just about any source. It all depends on how it reacts in the context of your production—which is something you determine purely by ear.

At all times, my initial choice in compressor is merely a guess. While I'm more likely to reach for a VCA or a FET style compressor on organic drums, I could just as easily choose a slower tube-style design for the job. It depends on the sound I seek—and often, I won't know what that sound is until I hear what doesn't work. So, there is some hit-or-miss to the selection process. If your first choice isn't grabbing you, then try something else. Over time, you'll develop preferences, but it's always good to experiment outside of them.

The most important decision point when it comes to compression isn't which design you choose—it's *audibility*. Do you want to hear the compression working? Or do you want it to remain invisible?

There are really only two ways to use a compressor: audibly or inaudibly. Whether you choose an aggressive, obvious compression sound or aim for something transparent and subtle, that's an artistic decision—not a technical one. When used aggressively, compression can cause heavy breathing and introduce distortion artifacts, which most certainly has artistic merit. You can think of overt over-compression as a kind of distortion for purposes of flavor.

The decision to use audible compression should make sense within the overall vision and context of the production. There are a number of ways in which to make compression more apparent:

- Lopping off the initial transient to soften the attack
- Holding a part in a steady state with no dynamics
- Increasing the apparent size of the recording room
- Creating obvious breathing artifacts
- Inducing a sudden dynamic drop (fortepiano or *fp*)
- Introducing breakup distortion
- Enhancing punch through parallel compression

The compressor you choose will naturally affect how audible your compression is. Some are designed to be remarkably transparent—like the PSP Flare—though you can drive them into audibility. Others, like the Kush Audio UBK-1, are built for overt character. And some are exceptionally versatile in their audibility, like the FabFilter C2.

Compressor Control

The best way to figure out where a compressor shines is to push it to its limits. This is true of all compressors, virtual or analog. That said, it's a lot easier to compress with intent if you understand how all the controls work.

Gain Reduction

Gain reduction is the mechanism that controls dynamics by reducing the level of a signal once it crosses the threshold.

Before we get into it, it's important to understand that gain reduction isn't a setting—it's the result of how your compressor is set. The threshold, ratio, attack, and release all work together to determine how much gain reduction occurs. The compressor applies this reduction only when the signal exceeds the threshold, and how it responds depends on the rest of the settings.

Essentially, the more you compress, the more gain reduction you apply to the signal, and the meter ostensibly shows how much of that reduction is occurring. But that value is only marginally useful, because every other control on the compressor affects that reading—and so does the source material.

The reality is, some compressors need only a slight nudge to hit the sweet spot, while others can handle slamming the meter without crumbling. Your time constants—attack and release— play a huge role in this. You can get away with considerably more gain reduction when the attack and release are fast, and a lot less when they're slow.

So, if you're staring at your gain reduction meter, timidly chasing a specific number, you're making decisions based on a somewhat meaningless target. Until you really understand what you're hearing, the meter won't tell you much. And it certainly won't tell you if it *sounds good.*

Input

The input control determines how much signal is fed into the compressor. Some compressors don't have a dedicated input knob, in which case you'll need to adjust the level of your source—either using clip gain to modify the level of the audio file itself or by adjusting the send level from a previous processing stage.

Most of the major DAWs offer easy access "clip gain," which is a quick and simple way to adjust the levels of the audio files themselves. Unlike at the fader, where you lower the level of the audio after the plugin processing, clip gain brings down the level before the processing occurs. If you're using a model and it's distorting in an unflattering way, clip gain is the most effective way to reduce the input to the device.

To be clear, the word "clip" here refers to a specific portion of audio, as in a clip of audio. Don't confuse it with digital clipping distortion, which is something else entirely. Clip gain is a non-destructive way to reduce the level of your audio file. It's just an unfortunate and confusing use of the word clip.

Threshold

The threshold sets the point at which compression kicks in. Any signal that exceeds the threshold triggers gain reduction, while anything below it passes through unabated.

If your compressor has both an input gain control and a threshold control, the two work together. Increasing the input signal pushes the signal closer to the threshold, making it easier to trigger compression.

I'd love to give you a magic number for setting the threshold, but there isn't one. It all depends on the level of the incoming signal—and how the rest of your compressor settings are dialed in. That said, if the compression feels too obvious or heavy-handed, adjusting the threshold is a good place to start.

Ratio

Most compressors have selectable ratio settings. The higher the ratio, the more aggressively the compressor reduces the signal once it crosses the threshold. A ratio of 4:1, for example, means that for every 4 dB the input exceeds the threshold, only 1 dB gets through. *Yawn.*

Here's the bottom line: a ratio of 2:1 is mild compression, 4:1 is medium, 8:1 is heavy, and anything at 10:1 or above means the compressor is functioning as a limiter—essentially crushing the dynamic range.

The best ratio depends on the material and the compressor itself. Higher ratios tend to be more audible, while lower ratios allow for more invisible control. If you're just looking to tame dynamics, 4:1 is typically a good place to start. If that's not enough, you can either increase the ratio—which will make the compression more obvious—or stack multiple compressors in series to achieve a more transparent result.

To achieve invisible vocal compression, for example, I'll often use several compressors in series. Many plugin compressors that model analog gear tend to introduce artifacts too early, so it's often more effective to use multiple layers of mild compression than to rely on a single, aggressive setting. The key is to avoid overloading any one compressor, which makes the compression easier to hear.

That said, if you *want* the compression to be audible, then by all means—be more aggressive and use fewer compressors.

The Knee

Some compressors include a knee control, which determines how abruptly the compression engages once the signal exceeds the threshold. A hard knee applies compression more immediately and aggressively, making it more audible, while a soft knee gradually eases into compression for a smoother, less noticeable effect. If your compressor feels too grabby and that's not what you're going for, try a softer knee. If you want the compression to be more pronounced, a harder knee is appropriate.

Attack and Release Times

The most significant tonal settings on a compressor come from the attack and release times. Some compressors have fixed reaction times that aren't adjustable by the end user.

The attack time controls how quickly the compressor reduces the level of the signal once it crosses the threshold. A faster attack setting clamps down quickly and is more likely to tame transients, while a slower attack allows more of the transient to pass through before compression fully engages.

An attack time of 0 ms—essentially immediate—doesn't just tame transients; it can introduce noticeable distortion and breakup artifacts. Even when aiming for audible compression, this isn't a setting you'll typically want to use. A small increase to 1 ms can make a dramatic difference, opening up the tone significantly. As you adjust the attack, listen to how the compressor affects the initial entry of the sound.

The release time determines how quickly the compressor resets after engaging. A super-fast release allows the signal to recover almost immediately, while a slow release keeps the signal compressed for longer.

A slower release results in a more even dynamic and can make compression less obvious by creating a smooth leveling effect. However, sudden transients can still create dramatic effects—especially if paired with a semi-fast attack and an extremely slow release. Given enough level above the threshold, the compressor can clamp down aggressively, almost muting the signal before slowly ramping back up. This can be particularly interesting on cymbal crashes due to their hard initial attack and long sustain. You can literally carve a hole in the sound using a compressor like this. If the cymbal's natural sustain isn't long enough, you may need to shorten the release time for the effect to work. Or you could compress it twice, once to extend the sustain of the cymbal, and then to create the effect. As always, everything is source-dependent.

You can also use release time to control resonance. If a KIK drum has a problematic sub-frequency bloom or an excessive ring, a slower release can help suppress these issues. The compressor clamps down and holds just long enough to tame the low-end resonance. But you'll want the release fast enough to reset before the next KIK—otherwise, it'll carry over and suppress the next hit, robbing it of punch.

On the other hand, if you only want to control the initial attack of the KIK without overly suppressing the low end, a fast attack and fast release is the better approach.

There's no universal setting for attack and release times because there are too many variables. These settings must be dialed in by ear. Learning to hear how different attack and release times shape a sound is an essential part of developing your skills with compressors.

Auto Release

Most plugin compressors include an Auto Release function, which allows the compressor to adapt its release time dynamically based on the incoming signal.

When Auto is engaged, the compressor applies a fast initial release to preserve loudness, followed by a slower taper to smooth out the transition. In effect, it combines both fast and slow release behavior in one, making it exceptionally useful for inaudible compression. The gradual ramp in release time helps minimize pumping and breathing artifacts.

When your goal is transparency, Auto is often the safest setting. That doesn't necessarily make it the most optimal—but it's rarely a bad place to start when you're aiming for invisible compression. Auto allows you to be more aggressive with gain reduction while reducing the risk of unwanted artifacts. And if the material calls for a more deliberate or exaggerated release shape, just switch it off.

I almost always have Auto enabled on my Mix Bus compressor, where transparency is critical. But when I'm compressing individual parts, I generally prefer to set the release manually.

The Mix Knob

Most plugins come with a mix knob, which lets you adjust the ratio of processed (wet) to unprocessed (dry) signal. This is essentially a built-in form of parallel compression—a technique we'll cover more in-depth later.

The mix knob can be especially useful when using an aggressive compressor that you want to tame by blending it with the original signal. You can crush the sound to get all the tone and movement you want, then back off the mix knob to restore some of the original dynamics. This gives you the best of both worlds: impact and energy without sacrificing natural feel. It also allows you to more easily control the overall audibility of the compression.

This method is especially effective on organic drums. But it's also a great way to shape the tone of drum samples, which often don't need dynamic control so much as tonal shaping. This is an effective way to add a super hard attack to your KIK drum sample, without killing your low end in the process.

That said, while there are times when blending in some dry signal makes sense, your attack and release settings are usually enough to shape the tone. The mix knob is just another option—it's there if you need it, but it's not essential. After all, analog compressors don't have mix knobs.

Sidechain High-Pass Filters

Compressors tend to react to low-end energy first. Low frequencies carry more energy and are usually the first to cross the threshold, triggering gain reduction. As a result, the compressor attenuates the low end as it compresses, which is part of how it shapes tone.

Some compressors include a sidechain high-pass filter (HPF), which rolls off low frequencies in the signal the compressor is *listening* to—not the signal you hear, but the one used to trigger compression. This can be useful when you want the compressor to respond less aggressively to low-frequency energy and react more to the mids and highs.

Personally, I don't use sidechain high-pass filters all that often, because more often than not I *want* my compressor to control and attenuate the low end. That's what makes a mix pop. I'll use EQ to shape how much low-end content hits the compressor in the first place and then follow the compressor with another EQ to enhance the now fully controlled low end. The sidechain function reacts very similarly to the mix knob—both offer a way to dial back how hard the compressor reacts to transient-heavy low-end material.

Audible Compression Settings

If the goal is to make compression an obvious part of the sound, attack and release settings become your primary tools. A fast attack and fast release, combined with an aggressive threshold, can dramatically shape a signal. This approach works exceptionally well on stereo drum room captures, where compression can emphasize the size and sustain of the space. By clamping down on the initial transient while allowing the ambient information to pass freely (which creates sustain), the room appears larger than it actually is. Setting the attack to 0 ms will also introduce distortion, which may or may not be desirable depending on the production.

This technique is particularly effective on organic drum room mics, as it enhances the apparent room size while introducing harmonic saturation. However, it's not a great approach in a poor-sounding room, as it will only amplify undesirable reflections and resonances. In such cases, a slower release time can help suppress the room's trashier qualities.

A snare drum compressor with an aggressively fast attack can lop off the transient, which is somehow the championed snare tone of Indie rock bands the world over. It's a very particular sound, and whether or not it suits your production depends entirely on context.

On the other end of the spectrum, the long attack and release times of a tube compressor can be used creatively as well. When applied aggressively to a piano, for instance, tube compression can significantly enhance the overtones, resulting in a rich, steady-state tone. Don't be afraid to push the threshold and ratio when going for this effect.

Choosing the Right Compressor

I've used hundreds of analog 1176s and LA-2As throughout my career, and I've yet to hear a modeled plugin that actually sounds or reacts like the real thing. Rather than frustrating myself by pulling up a compressor that does one thing—and not particularly well as far as I'm concerned—I prefer a more versatile tool that gives me broad control over tone and behavior.

The FabFilter Pro-C2 is my current go-to compressor for this reason. It includes a variety of compressor "styles"—Clean, Classic, Opto, Vocal, Mastering, Bus, Punch, and Pumping. These aren't direct emulations of specific hardware, but rather modeled behaviors that reflect the general characteristics of different compressor types. The Clean setting reacts like a VCA compressor. Classic mimics a FET compressor. Opto behaves like an LA-2A-style optical compressor. The Bus setting provides the kind of glue you'd expect from an SSL-style VCA compressor, making it a good choice for drums or mix bus processing. The Punch setting enhances transients, similar to what an 1176 does, while Pumping is more exaggerated and useful for creative, audible compression effects.

If you're newer to compression or unsure what approach to take, presets offer a great way to sample tones. The FabFilter C2 includes instrument-specific presets, which are useful for quickly getting to an appropriate starting point. I use them—not because I rely on presets, but because they help streamline my workflow. They allow me to focus on how the compression makes me feel, rather than getting bogged down in technical decisions.

Of course, I don't just pick a preset and leave it as is. Attack and release settings, in particular, affect how the compressor reacts, and I always tweak them to suit the material. But using presets to get me close speeds up the process exponentially.

If you want to simplify your life when it comes to compression, and if you would rather not think about them in terms of technical design, then I highly recommend picking up a FabFilter C2. It covers nearly every compression need in one unit, with a large and easy-to-navigate GUI—something all the FabFilter products are known for.

That's not to say I don't use other stand-alone compressors. I surely do. I want a wide variety of compressor tones available to me for speed and creative flexibility. Some plugin compressors do one specific thing especially well, and they absolutely earn their place in my arsenal. But if I could only have one compressor plugin, the FabFilter C2 would be my choice—because it covers so many tonal options so well in a single, well-designed unit.

Applying Compression Intelligently

Pardon my repeating myself, but this honestly can't be said enough—and repetition is how we learn. Compression should always be applied and adjusted based on what you *hear*. Every combination of attack, release, ratio, and threshold settings has its place, and there's no such thing as a universally "correct" setting—it all depends on the material and your vision.

For example, a vocalist singing long, drawn-out notes with extended sustain will require a far longer release time than an MC performing a more percussive rap. So, your attack and release times are often best set based on the nature of the part.

Further complicating matters, if you're applying aggressive compression on a vocal with a fast release, the tails of phrases could actually come up in level as the compressor resets. Conversely, a slow attack time on a vocal can cause the first word of every phrase to pop out. You *can* deal with both of these issues using automation, but wouldn't it make more sense to adjust the attack and release times?

Controlling your compressors requires critical thinking. Every adjustment affects the others, and settings should always be tailored to the specific part, instrument, and mix. The best way to improve your compression skills is to experiment, listen, and adjust based on feel. While a compressor is certainly a technical tool, it's also an artistic one—and should be treated as such.

Compression in Series

If you want the effect of aggressive compression without it appearing obvious, one way to achieve that is by stacking compressors in series—using multiple compressors one after another. Layered compression allows you to control dynamics more transparently, reducing the risk of noticeable artifacts.

That said, in my productions, only certain elements tend to get compression in series—primarily the parts that sit in the middle of the sound field: KIK, snare, bass, and vocal.

The KIK and bass form the foundation of the track and keeping them rock solid is essential. If the KIK is programmed and already lacks dynamic variation, there's little point in compressing it beyond possible tone-shaping, which is best handled with EQ or parallel compression. An organically recorded KIK, on the other hand, may require heavy compression to keep the low end rock solid. If one compressor isn't enough, stack another.

We tend to put a beautifully robust low end on our records these days—which is how it should be—but keeping that low end in control is critical to a balanced mix and often requires layers of compression. One effective approach is to push the low end into the compressor, let it attenuate, and then add the low end back in on the other side. If that's not enough, adding another EQ and compressor can help maintain control. I can assure you, if you get the low end dynamically contained, the rest of the record will fall into place.

Oftentimes, compression is applied in series at different stages, especially on organically recorded material which is naturally more dynamic than programmed material. We'll discuss busses in-depth shortly, but all of my drums go to a DRUMS bus, which allows me to process them as one part. This means the organic KIK gets compressed at the channel, and then again at the DRUMS bus. I might even have a compressor on the mix bus, which will affect the KIK once again—since the compressor reacts to low end first.

Of course, the vocal is the main focal point of the production, and an overly dynamic vocal can be a major problem. You certainly don't want one phrase dipping out of audibility while the next one tears your head off. And while we don't necessarily want to put the vocal in a steady state (which is exhausting to the listener), that's likely better than an overly dynamic vocal, and that's saying something.

Typically, I have an EQ inserted both before and after every compressor in my vocal chain. I also tend to use different attack and release times for each compressor in series. How I set each one is entirely program dependent, but I often use the varying time constants to my advantage—maybe a fast release on the first to catch spikes, and a slower release on the second for a more natural sustain.

To make your compressors work less aggressively—and to use fewer of them—pre-automation can be extremely helpful. If I'm given an overly dynamic vocal to mix, I'll go in, cut the vocal into regions, and even out the level using clip gain. I usually raise quieter phrases and lower louder ones, and I mostly do this visually—because the compressor will handle the finer shaping. This makes for a smoother, more controlled vocal without it sounding obviously compressed. If the vocal was already heavily compressed during recording with analog gear, it will likely have a fairly contained dynamic range, making additional pre-adjustments unnecessary.

EQ Between Compressors

Inserting EQ between compressors can be incredibly useful for tone-shaping. For example, if a vocal is strident, I can either attenuate the harsh 2 kHz frequencies before the first compressor or boost somewhere between 100 Hz and 200 Hz before compression. Boosting the low end and pairing it with a slow release time can cause the compressor to naturally smooth out the harshness.

In general, it's a good practice to use surgical EQ before compression and broader tone-shaping EQ after. However, as I've already pointed out, release time settings can be just as effective for taming problem frequencies as EQ.

Multiband Compressor

A multiband compressor allows you to compress multiple frequency ranges independently. It divides the spectrum into a set number of bands covering 20 Hz to 20 kHz. The number of bands can vary, and the width of each band is adjustable. Any change to one band affects the others to maintain full-range coverage.

Not only can you apply different compression settings to each band, but you can also boost or cut frequencies before compression and adjust attack and release settings for each range. This level of control might sound enticing, and in some cases, it can be incredibly useful. But as powerful as multiband compressors are, they are aggressive tools—often best reserved for problem-solving rather than everyday compression.

Some mastering engineers use multiband compression to muscle the balances of a finished mix so as to reshape the overall EQ curve. As a mixer, I rarely use them, mostly because I have full control over my tonal balances. This makes them better as a tool for fixing a problem when you have limited control, than as an everyday tool to be used for tonal shaping.

New producers often gravitate toward multiband compressors, only to find them frustrating and confusing. That's because they are somewhat confusing—and, more often than not, more trouble than they're worth. I'm all for being aggressive with your tools, but hyper-aggressive tools themselves can complicate the process. If you struggle to make a multiband compressor work for you, don't feel like you're missing out. Anything you can do with a multiband compressor can be accomplished with regular compression and EQ, often with greater precision and control.

Frankly, the better tool for compressing specific frequency ranges is the dynamic EQ, which is very similar to multiband compression. It's a tool that is useful for solving issues that might call for a multiband compressor, but without the complexity.

Dynamic EQ

A dynamic EQ functions like a standard EQ but adds the option to engage dynamic behavior—meaning it can react to the incoming signal based on threshold settings. Unlike a static EQ, which applies a fixed boost or cut at all times, a dynamic EQ can be set to apply gain changes only when a specific frequency exceeds (or falls below) a threshold. This makes it an incredibly precise tool for managing frequencies that are only problematic in certain moments, rather than throughout the entire performance.

For example, if a vocal becomes strident in certain spots but not others, a standard EQ cut at 2 kHz won't work—it would dull the vocal when that frequency isn't an issue. In the past, before dynamic EQ was available, I would split the vocal onto separate channels, applying the cut only to the problematic sections and switching between them as needed. A more efficient approach is to use a dynamic EQ at 2 kHz, which will only reduce that frequency when it becomes excessive while leaving the rest of the performance untouched.

Dynamic EQs are problem-solving tools rather than everyday mix tools, but when you need one, they can be invaluable. The most ubiquitous dynamic EQ is FabFilter's Pro-Q3, which has become an industry standard for good reason. While I often reach for the stock EQ in Logic for quick adjustments, I'm finding more and more instances of Pro-Q3—if for no other reason than its superior and large graphical interface.

As for EQ plugins in general, there isn't much difference in sound from one to another—at least not in the way there is with analog hardware. Some will argue otherwise, but I've always been able to hear clear differences between various analog EQs, which is largely due to their distortion characteristics. Digital EQs don't naturally introduce distortion, which is why they tend to sound the same. Recognizing this, FabFilter recently released Pro-Q4, which now includes selectable distortion properties, which introduces tonal diversity that doesn't exist in many plugin EQs.

Dynamic Resonant Suppressor

A dynamic resonant suppressor is a useful tool for fixing frequency buildup issues without requiring much technical know-how. It functions similarly to a dynamic EQ but uses intelligent detection to automatically identify and attenuate resonant peaks that contribute to harshness or muddiness—without requiring you to manually sweep for problem areas. The most well-known example is Oeksound's Soothe 2, though there are several others on the market.

These suppressors can be particularly effective on problematic vocals, cymbals, and overheads, though they can be useful in other applications as well. Sometimes I'll put Soothe 2 on a vocal and find that it actually sounds better without it, as it can smooth things out too much. While the suppression controls allow you to dial in how aggressively it targets resonances, they can sometimes introduce a sort of veil to the sound that isn't always a net positive.

Where these tools really shine is on drum overheads. A harsh set of cymbals can be softened to the point of sounding as if they were recorded with ribbon microphones, making it possible to bring them up in the mix without introducing listener fatigue.

A resonant suppressor is not generally a tool to apply to an entire mix. It's usually far better to deal with harshness at the individual track or bus level, where you have more control.

If you add a dynamic resonant suppressor to your toolkit, start by exploring the presets—many of them are pre-programmed by professional engineers and can serve as a great starting point. These plugins aren't always easy to dial in from scratch, and presets can save time while helping you understand how the controls affect the sound.

As with any powerful tool, it's easy to overdo it. While dynamic resonant suppressors can solve problems, they can also strip out the energy and character of a sound if used too aggressively. In other words, it's easy to do more harm than good. So be judicious with them and keep them in your back pocket to fix problems when they arise.

De-Essers

A de-esser is a type of compressor that targets a specific frequency range, typically between 2 kHz and 16 kHz, where sibilance occurs. It works by dynamically reducing these frequencies when they become excessive, preventing harsh or distracting esses.

Most de-essers include a "listen" function, which allows you to solo the affected frequency range and sweep through it to pinpoint the most problematic high frequency bursts. Once identified, you can apply attenuation to that narrow band, reducing the level of the esses without necessarily dulling the vocal. In some cases, adding a slight high-shelf boost after the de-esser can help restore balance if the vocal starts to sound too dark.

The best way to minimize excessive esses is through mic placement, but that isn't always enough. Some singers naturally produce sharp sibilance, certain microphones emphasize it, and compression often exaggerates the problem by bringing esses forward.

I tend to be aggressive with de-essing because I find excessive sibilance incredibly distracting. Some people don't mind a bit of essiness, and as with anything, how much you suppress it is a matter of taste. That said, leaving esses completely unchecked can pull focus from the performance, so some level of control is often necessary.

Overly aggressive de-essing can introduce a lisp or even remove esses entirely, neither of which sounds particularly natural. That said, I find excessive sibilance so irritating that I'd rather hear the occasional de-esser artifact than be overwhelmed by a thousand sharp esses. Fortunately, the current production trend leans toward more aggressive de-essing, which I'm all for.

Background vocals can typically handle much heavier de-essing. I often ask background singers to avoid pronouncing esses at the beginning and end of phrases, as those tend to flam when stacked. Flamming esses are nothing short of sloppy, and if I can limit their occurrence at the recording stage, my background vocals de-esser becomes far more effective.

As a mixer I don't have control over the recording process, so I often remove esses from stacked vocals at the beginning and end of phrases by applying aggressive fades. Esses that occur within the phrasing tend to be more in time, so they can often be controlled with a de-esser applied to all the background vocals at once (on a bus), rather than processing each track individually. Most plugin de-essers include a "background vocal" setting, which helps smooth out multiple voices in a more natural way.

De-essers can be frustrating to dial in, and like any tool, some are better than others. Even the best de-esser takes time to set up properly. Generally, you want it to be as transparent as possible, but sometimes compromises are necessary. If the esses are particularly aggressive, using two de-essers in series can be an effective solution.

Esses react well to reverb as the percussive nature of them results in a splash of space. This tends to soften the esses somewhat, but that doesn't necessarily supplant the need for a de-esser. Even with the splash of verb, I can't stand esses. As with everything, this all comes down to taste.

As you get familiar with your de-esser, don't be afraid to push it to its limits. There's no point in being timid with esses. Those sharp bursts of high-frequency distortion can cut through a mix from the next room and quickly become fatiguing to the listener.

I have quite a few de-essers in my arsenal, which shouldn't be surprising given how much I loathe excessive sibilance. My go-to is the FabFilter D2 because it's highly effective without being overly complicated to dial in. For particularly harsh esses, I'll use the D2 in conjunction with the Eiosis de-esser, as the combination provides even more control when needed.

Stereo Compressors

Obviously, stereo compressors are useful for compressing stereo sources. When using stereo miking techniques—whether for drum overheads, piano, or a full mix—it's best to use a stereo compressor to ensure both sides are processed evenly. This prevents the left and right channels from reacting differently, which could cause an unbalanced or shifting stereo image.

In the analog world, stereo compressors require specific design characteristics to ensure matched gain reduction across both channels. If the left and right signals were compressed independently, you'd get unpredictable stereo movement, which is almost never desirable. Some analog compressors achieve this through a linked control circuit, while others are true dual-mono designs, where each channel operates separately, which can sometimes be useful for widening effects.

In a DAW, mono compressors automatically function as stereo compressors when placed on a stereo track or bus. They apply identical compression to both channels, effectively mimicking the behavior of a linked stereo compressor.

For most mixing applications, keeping stereo compression linked ensures a stable and balanced sound. But if you're after creative effects, unlinking the channels can introduce movement and depth that can be used as an effect of sorts.

Analog Compressors

I use plenty of analog compression when recording, but none when mixing. I want perfect, instant recall of my mixes, and the only way to achieve that is to stay completely in the box. This lets me jump between projects seamlessly and makes revisions a far smoother process. But when it comes to recording, analog compressors absolutely make life easier—especially down the line.

When I receive tracks for mixing where the vocal hasn't been compressed through an analog unit, it inevitably adds significant time to the mix process. For whatever reason, analog compressors just seem to handle dynamic control more effectively than their plugin counterparts. Applying compression at the recording stage helps shape the dynamics early, making the mix process smoother and more efficient.

Compression is a fundamental part of modern production, and the best and most successful producers, mixers, and recordists use plenty. In fact, they're often aggressive with their compressors, and you shouldn't be afraid to do the same. If you're concerned that you'll over-compress something—you very well might. That's a natural part of the learning process. You will never learn how a compressor best reacts if you don't ever push it.

When I compress with an LA-2A or 1176, the VU needle moves freely, and my parts don't sound overcompressed unless that's the tone I'm after. More often than not, I prioritize invisible compression over audible compression, which is why I want to compress in stages throughout the production process.

When working fully in analog, it was standard practice to compress vocals in multiple stages—on the way in, while compiling takes, and again in the mix. This approach helps the vocal sit properly and makes the mix process far easier. The same applies to any other recorded parts in need of dynamic control.

If you're producing a super dynamic record that can only be properly admired in a listening room or a studio, you may not need much compression at all. But if you're working in modern commercial genres, compression—especially analog compression at the recording stage—is one of your most beneficial tools.

Is an analog compressor absolutely necessary? No. But if you struggle to get vocals to sit properly, a good analog compressor can go a long way towards alleviating that problem.

Limiters

Limiters are essentially high-ratio compressors that prevent audio from exceeding a set threshold. But when we talk about limiters, we're really referring to more than one kind.

Some compressors include a peak limiter mode, which changes the compressor's output control into an input control for the peak limiter. When engaged, the limiter reacts to transients by knocking them down. To trigger the limiting, you increase the output, then adjust the balance accordingly. This process often introduces some measure of distortion.

In general, what defines limiting is the ratio. A compressor set above 10:1 is technically limiting, while anything below that is still considered compression. There's no magical threshold where compression suddenly becomes limiting—it's just that higher ratios result in far more aggressive dynamic control.

The simplest way to think about the difference is this: compression reacts to the bottom of the mix by pushing it up, while limiting reacts to the top of the mix by pushing it down. That's surely a gross oversimplification, but practically speaking, it helps frame when to use one over the other.

Aggressive tools have their place, but they require judicious use. If you routinely rely on extreme processing, you'll create more problems than solutions. What kind of problems? That depends on the tool and the material. But if you lean on naturally aggressive dynamics processors as your default approach, you'll likely place more of your focus on the engineering than the music.

Limiters, in particular, are too aggressive for most mixing applications—unless you want to hear artifacts. If you're after a bit of edge, a limiter can be a great choice, but that's an artistic decision, not a technical one.

You could apply some modicum of compression to every single part in a production and deliver an amazing track that does everything it should. But if you take that same approach with limiters, you risk a production that sounds small.

I rarely use high ratio limiting. And when I do, it's to introduce audible compression rather than to merely control dynamics. Limiters have their place, but they aren't the right tool for everything, all the time.

Limiters should not be confused with brickwall limiters, which are considerably more aggressive and have a more specific purpose.

Brickwall Limiters

A brickwall limiter is a specialized limiter that operates at a ratio of infinity to one. No matter how much level you send to it, the audio will not exceed the set output ceiling.

The purpose of a brickwall limiter is twofold. First, it prevents your production from peaking over 0 dBFS, which will introduce clipping. Second, it controls dynamic range for the sake of loudness. It's a tool primarily used in the final stage of processing to prepare a record for delivery. Ideally, you shouldn't use a brickwall limiter for anything other than achieving competitive loudness for a mix or a reference.

Surely you won't die if you insert brickwall limiters throughout your production. You will, however, likely fuck up your record, and maybe the record after that, and perhaps even the record after that—until you finally realize they're far too aggressive for processing individual elements. The problem is, they force parts into a steady state, which can feel instantly gratifying, as if you've unlocked some magic formula for mixing. Then months later, you listen back and wonder why your record sounds so small.

I remember when I first started working in Logic, I discovered the adlimiter, which is a type of brickwall limiter. I didn't know what the hell it was at the time—I just tried it. And oh my, didn't that just make everything I put it on sound nice? I threw it on all sorts of channels and busses. I went nuts.

Well, when I came back the next day, my mix felt small. As I started bypassing each instance of adlimiter one by one, the mix opened up, sounded bigger, and felt far more compelling.

Can you believe I did that several more times before I finally swore the thing off?

Unlike compressors, brickwall limiters don't layer well. They rely on lookahead processing and extreme gain reduction to prevent peaks from exceeding the set threshold.

Each limiter introduces non-linear artifacts—like pumping, smearing, or aliasing—which accumulate and become more pronounced with each stage. They also introduce intermodulation distortion, which makes the harmonic content harsher and more fatiguing.

A single brickwall limiter already significantly reduces dynamic range. Stacking them will only result in a lifeless, overly proportional, and irritating mix.

You also don't want to work while monitoring through a brickwall limiter. It's exhausting. You'll find yourself needing more frequent breaks, and those breaks will become less effective over time. If you're working in a relatively quiet studio environment, brickwall limiting offers no real advantage—it's just making your job harder. Brickwall limiters offer no value added in terms of your mix. They merely allow for your mix to translate better in noisier environments.

Maximizers

A maximizer, like the one in the Izotope Ozone package, is another type of dynamics processor designed to increase the perceived loudness of your track while maintaining as much transparency as possible. It typically achieves this by applying a combination of limiting, compression, and soft clipping, pushing the audio closer to its peak level without introducing excessive distortion. Like a brickwall limiter, it prevents peaks from exceeding a set ceiling, but it also applies adaptive gain to boost quieter parts more smoothly.

Personally, I prefer a brickwall limiter—specifically the Fab-Filter L2—because I already apply my own compression at various stages, and I have a solid command over my dynamics, which just comes with practice and experience. As a result, the distinctions between a maximizer and a brickwall limiter become somewhat negligible. If your mix is overly dynamic, you might find the auto-gain compensation in a maximizer useful, but it's always best to address excessive dynamics in the mix itself rather than relying on a final-stage processor to smooth it out.

So, yes, there are technical differences between a maximizer and a brickwall limiter, but they serve the same purpose—to maximize loudness and reduce the dynamic presentation of a mix.

THE STRUCTURAL DYNAMICS OF FLOW

Basic Signal Flow

Before we get into gain staging—the bane of the modern producer's existence (although it needn't be)—we should discuss signal flow. If you understand how audio moves through your system, gain staging becomes far easier to understand.

Signal flow is simply the path audio takes to go from point A to point B. And as with everything in music production—and life itself—what happens now affects what happens down the line.

Once audio is inside your DAW, signal flow becomes more complex, especially since different DAWs handle routing in their own ways. Some even let you customize how the signal flows, which is powerful but potentially confusing. While you'll get a feel for the quirks of your own system over time, it's important to understand how signal flow generally works.

In most DAWs, recorded audio on a channel flows through the inserts first, then to the fader, and finally to the pan knob, before reaching the output. This setup ensures that any processing—such as compression, distortion, or EQ—is applied *before* you adjust the channel's level.

That's important, because if the fader came before the inserts, any volume changes would affect the signal level going into your processors—and that would alter how they behave.

For example, if the fader came before the compressor, lowering it would result in less compression, thereby changing the dynamics of the track. The same principle would apply to distortion, saturation, and gating. If your fader were shifting the tone or impact of your plugin chain, you would constantly be chasing your tail.

That said, there *are* times when it's useful to control the signal level before it hits your processors, and this is where busses can come into play.

Busses

A bus is simply a way to route audio. By default, DAW channels output directly to the stereo output, but you can reassign a channel's output to a bus instead. When you do this—let's say we assign a track to bus 1—that audio is now routed through bus 1's return channel before reaching the stereo output. Some DAWs automatically create a bus return when you assign a track to a bus. Others make you set it up manually—which, frankly, is just maddeningly unnecessary work.

Once audio is routed through a bus, you now have two faders controlling the signal: the original track's fader and the bus return's fader. The key difference is that the original track's fader lives *before* any processing on the bus, which means it affects the input level going into any processors located on the bus inserts. This allows for greater flexibility in how you process and control the signal.

That said, you don't generally need two separate processing chains to control a single signal. The main purpose of busses is to combine signals to a single channel.

For example, if a KIK drum is recorded with two microphones—one inside and one outside—I'll route both tracks to a KIK DRUM bus. This allows me to control the entire KIK sound with one fader. Once I've established the right balance between the two mics, I can process them together on the bus.

I avoid compressing the mics individually because each compressor would react differently, leading to shifts in tone and other undesirable artifacts. I want to treat the KIK drum as a single entity, keeping the mic balance static.

Busses are powerful routing tools, and understanding how they function will make your workflow far more efficient. We'll go through more detailed bussing strategies shortly.

Aux Sends

Aux sends are technically busses, but they differ in that they allow you to send audio down a parallel path—sometimes multiple parallel paths—which can make things a bit more complicated.

So far, I've described a linear signal flow: audio moves from point A and ultimately arrives at point B. An aux send allows you to simultaneously send the audio to point C for parallel processing. Some DAWs refer to them as "*fx* sends," which is perfectly fine by me, since their primary purpose is to route a signal to an effects unit from multiple channels while maintaining full control over the dry signal.

Every channel in your DAW includes aux sends with rotary knobs that control how much of the audio is sent down that path. Some DAWs treat aux sends as assignable busses, while others treat them as separate entities—conceptually simpler, but functionally the same. Some automatically generate a return when you activate an aux send, while others require an extra step.

Let's say we have a guitar track routed to the stereo output, with the fader set to unity and no inserts. If we activate an aux send on that channel, the DAW will generate an aux return. Once we set the rotary knob on the send to unity, we're now sending a full copy of the guitar signal down the aux path. At this point, the guitar is following two parallel signal paths:

The direct signal flows from the guitar channel to the stereo output.

A second signal flows from the aux send to the aux return—and then to the stereo output.

At this stage, we've effectively doubled the guitar's output level, since it now exists on two separate paths feeding the same mix. This is where parallel processing comes into play. The goal of an aux send isn't to duplicate volume—it's to apply processing separately on the aux return.

For example, if we insert a reverb unit on the aux return and set it to 100% wet, we now have a dry signal from the main guitar channel and a reverberant signal from the aux return. The aux send knob controls how much of the guitar is being sent into the reverb, while the return fader lets us balance the wet-to-dry ratio in the mix.

Pre-Fader vs. Post-Fader Sends

By default, most aux sends are post-fader, meaning their level follows any fader adjustments on the original channel. This ensures that if you lower the level of a vocal, for instance, the reverb level follows proportionally. You don't want to bring the lead vocal down and have it swimming in reverb—it should maintain the same wet-to-dry balance.

Sometimes, though, you want an aux send to behave independently of the fader. That's where pre-fader sends come into play. When set to pre-fader, the aux send level stays constant, regardless of fader movements.

Why is this useful? Suppose you want to fade the vocal out into reverb at the end of a song. A pre-fader send lets you lower the dry vocal while the reverberation stays intact.

There's also post-pan, which allows the aux send to follow the pan position of the dry signal. This is useful when you want an effect—like delay—to stay locked to the source's location in the stereo field. If you hard-pan a guitar left and send it post-pan to a delay, the delay follows the pan instead of sitting dead center.

If you're only applying reverb or delay to a single instrument, it's often easier to just insert the effect directly on the channel. But when multiple tracks need the same effect, aux sends are far more efficient.

Suppose you have 20 vocal tracks. Do you really want to insert a separate reverb on each one and adjust them individually? Even if you copy the same plugin, it's inefficient—and a waste of CPU. Instead, send all 20 vocals to a shared reverb via an aux send. Now, if you want to tweak the effect, you only have to do it once.

Aux sends also give you precise control over balances. If high harmonies are exciting the reverb too much compared to low harmonies, just lower the aux send level on those channels. This keeps your dry vocal blend intact while refining what's feeding the effect. Sure, you could EQ the reverb return—but adjusting the sends is often faster.

Using Aux Sends on Busses

Aux sends aren't limited to individual channels—you can also send audio from busses. For example, if you've routed 20 harmony vocals to a vocal harmony bus, you could apply an aux send from the bus instead of from each individual vocal track. This keeps things clean and saves time.

That said, using a bus send means all the vocals will share the same wet/dry balance. If you later decide that a few of those vocals need less reverb, you'd have to compensate by adding individual sends to all the *other* tracks. At that point, it might have been easier to just send from each vocal channel in the first place.

Another thing to consider: a bus send is essentially pre-fader relative to its individual channel sends. Suppose you're sending reverb from the individual tracks of 20 harmony vocals. If you then lower the harmony vocal bus fader, the dry vocal level decreases—but the reverb level stays the same. This alters the wet/dry balance.

One way to maintain consistency is to route the reverb return through the same bus as the vocals. That way, when you lower the vocal bus fader, both the dry and wet signals drop together, preserving the ratio.

Creative Routing

Aux sends open up a world of creative possibilities. You can use them to create stereo width by sending a mono signal to a stereo delay. You can use separate sends for different effects, such as one to reverb and another for delay. You can even route effects returns into other effects, like sending a delay return into a reverb for a more natural effect.

Ultimately, aux sends provide incredible flexibility for routing effects, managing CPU load, and refining balances across multiple parts. Once you understand their place in signal flow, you'll find them indispensable. Whether it's adding depth with reverbs and delays, experimenting with parallel processing, or creating spatial movement, aux sends allow for greater control and efficiency in your mix.

Processing Order

The order in which you place your processing is a fundamental part of signal flow. Each plugin directly affects the next one in the chain, shaping how the sound evolves at every stage. While there are strategic approaches to organizing your chain, the final decision always comes down to what you hear.

A common question is whether EQ should go before or after compression. The answer? It depends. We touched on this earlier, but in the context of plugin order, it's worth revisiting.

An EQ before a compressor will shape how the compressor reacts to the signal, while an EQ after the compressor adjusts the overall tone of an already-compressed signal. Both approaches are useful, and in many cases, you may even want EQ both before and after. There's no sonic penalty for multiple instances of digital EQ, so don't be afraid to experiment.

For instance, boosting low end before a compressor can influence how it responds to a vocal. If a vocal becomes strident in the upper register, a low-end boost ahead of the compressor will cause it to react to that energy first, which can help tame some of the harshness. That EQ boost might also cause other parts of the vocal to feel too woofy, at which point you can use an EQ after the compressor to reshape the overall tone.

Effects placement also matters. If you place a delay at the first insert on a guitar track, any compression that follows will affect both the dry signal and the delay together, making the delay more apparent. You'll have more control if your compressor is first in the chain, because you're compressing the dry signal—and the delay is reacting to the processed signal.

Typically, it's best to place effects like delay and reverb at the end of the chain, which gives you the same signal flow you'd get from an aux send. Of course, if the delay was captured at the amp—meaning it's already printed into the tone—then that decision and blend already exist. This may limit how aggressive you can be with compression on that part.

Saturation distortion also interacts dynamically with EQ and compression. Boosting low end into a saturator can produce a more pleasing distortion, while EQ after the distortion lets you refine the overall tone. Placing a compressor ahead of distortion smooths out the signal before it's saturated, resulting in a more even distortion tone. Compression after distortion allows for more dynamic and unpredictable saturation. The best approach depends on the sound you're after—try both and choose what works best for the production at hand.

De-esser placement is another point of debate. Some prefer de-essing first to tame harsh frequencies before further processing. I prefer it last, ensuring that compression or saturation doesn't bring back those problematic esses. That said, there are times I'll put a de-esser first, and I might even place a second one at the end. These decisions are entirely dependent on what best controls the esses in that particular vocal.

As you can see, there's no single correct order for processing any part in any instance. The only thing that matters is how your chain reacts to the material. That said, if a change in processing order produces a negligible difference, don't overthink it—just move forward. If it sounds good, it *is* good. Live by that mantra.

Sample Rate and Bit Depth

This may seem like a digression from the subject at hand, but sample rate has some bearing on how you might gain stage, especially as we all transition to 32 bit recording, so it's something we must discuss.

The sample rate describes the number of samples in a second. In the case of a CD that's 44,100 samples every second. And yes, I realize CDs are becoming less common—I don't even have a CD player anymore—but they are still the format of choice for many independent artists and bands, and for a very good reason. They can be sold. Besides, the only consumer delivery format that is of a higher sample rate than CDs is . . . well, none. But if you read engineering forums, you'd think we all listen to music at 96 kHz or higher.

By definition, the highest frequency a digital system can reproduce is half its sample rate. So, for a CD at 44.1 kHz, that's just above 22 kHz—about 2 kHz outside the range of practical human hearing. Some argue that extending the range up to 48 kHz (as with a 96 kHz sample rate) improves fidelity, though this remains hotly debated.

A sample rate of 96 kHz will reproduce frequencies up to 48 kHz, well beyond our range of hearing, and many argue this sounds better. I don't find the sonic differences of much consequence, particularly when you consider that most music is still streamed as MP3s, and I don't see that changing any time soon.

A more practical reason for working at higher sample rates is that they allow for more effective anti-aliasing filters, reducing artifacts during extreme pitch-shifting or time-stretching. Another argument is that some plugins perform better at 96 kHz, though in my experience, I haven't noticed much difference—maybe that's more relevant for certain modeled gear. But even if true, it's not going to make or break your production, and there are far more compelling reasons to work at 48 kHz.

Of course, 96 kHz files are also twice the size of 48 kHz files. Not only does that double your necessary available drive space significantly, it also more readily taxes your computer resources. If your computer is long in the tooth, or if you're light on RAM, then you may not even be able to operate efficiently at that sample rate. As a third-party mixer, I still receive the majority of sessions at 48 kHz or lower.

There are arguments for every sample rate, some more valid than others, and some depend on how aggressively you process your audio. But here's the bottom line: no one listening to your record will ever care what sample rate you used. It won't affect whether they like your song, stream it, or buy it.

Then there's bit-depth, which defines the resolution of your capture and determines the available dynamic range. CDs are 16-bit, but since the early aughts, we've all recorded at 24-bit, which offers more dynamic range with less noise.

At 16-bit, you get a theoretical dynamic range of 96 dB from ceiling to noise floor. At 24-bit, that range jumps to 144 dB. Since every 6 dB is roughly double the volume, 144 dB is a massive range—far beyond what you'll ever need. And given that modern music production is largely about making records louder, a vast dynamic range is often irrelevant. Even in classical recordings, your actual dynamic range is never anywhere close to the theoretical limit.

Then there's 32-bit floating point, which expands the dynamic range to around 152 dB. This makes it virtually impossible to clip permanently—if you record too hot, you can just gain the signal down later. Unlike 24-bit fixed-point audio, where exceeding 0 dBFS results in clipping, 32-bit float retains all information even above 0 dBFS, so you can recover peaks after-the-fact. As of this writing, not many interfaces or converters operate at 32-bit, and only some DAWs support it. But that's likely to change quickly. When it does, it will simplify gain staging significantly.

While it's very easy to record something too hot, it's actually quite difficult to record something so low that it becomes unusable. Oh, you can do it if you're super stoned, I suppose, but as long as your signal generally sits above -18 dBFS, you'll maintain strong signal integrity without risk of clipping. In a fixed-point system, extremely low levels can theoretically reduce resolution, but with 24-bit recording, this is rarely an issue in practice.

And no, you don't need to be living in the yellow part of your meters at all times. The goal isn't to get as close to zero as possible—it's to record a magical take that isn't compromised by harsh clipping distortion. So, give yourself some headroom when recording. If your performer gets a little too excited, you'll be glad you did.

Gain Staging

Gain staging is a common topic in mixing and mastering circles, and unfortunately, there's a lot of confusion and bad advice floating around—especially when it comes to DAWs. Gain staging is simply level management across different stages of your signal chain—hence the term "staging." It's a topic that frustrates a lot of people, so I'll really get into the weeds here. If anything is unclear, don't hesitate to consult your favorite AI assistant for clarification.

In the digital domain, there is a hard ceiling at 0 dBFS (Decibels Relative to Full Scale). This is the maximum level you can send to your converters before clipping occurs. Any signal that exceeds 0 dBFS at the converter will result in harsh, uncontrollable clipping distortion. While distortion can be useful when applied intentionally with plugins, digital clipping at the converter level needs to be avoided.

Your converter meters show the true level hitting them, while your DAW meters may or may not—depending on whether they're set to pre-fader (before processing and fader adjustments) or post-fader (after processing and fader adjustments). If you're recording, set your meters to pre-fader to monitor what's actually hitting your converters. If you're mixing, post-fader metering is more useful, as it reflects the true output level of your processing. When in doubt, check the meters on your interface or its software panel.

Since digital meters measure in negative values below 0 dBFS, every 6 dB reduction halves the signal level. For example, -6 dBFS is half the volume of 0 dBFS. However, this has no bearing on how loud you *hear* the audio—that's determined by your monitoring level. The goal isn't to get signals as close to zero as possible, but to maintain headroom and avoid clipping.

-18 dBFS is a level of some significance, because it aligns with analog zero. Analog doesn't have a hard ceiling—in fact, we often push analog gear well past zero because electronics can respond favorably to excess level. This is not true with digital zero. Converters react badly when you exceed 0 dBFS, which is why -18 dBFS is commonly used to match analog zero. It gives you the headroom necessary to push analog gear beyond reason—without exceeding digital zero in the process.

Gain Stage One

Stage one of gain staging begins at the source, which is then picked up by the mic (or DI input), which goes to the preamp, then to your interface, and finally through the A/D conversion process. At 24 bit, if your signal exceeds 0 dBFS at the converter, it will clip, and that distortion will be permanently recorded. To prevent this, you need to leave enough headroom so that the loudest moments of a performance never exceed 0 dBFS at the converter.

That said, if you accidentally record something hotter than intended, don't panic. Even if a few transient peaks clip, it's not the end of the world. Are you really going to re-record the best take your drummer has ever laid down because a couple of snare hits clipped? Probably not. You could replace the clipped snares with clean ones from elsewhere or even ignore the clipping altogether if it's not audibly offensive.

If a signal is recorded too hot, you can clip-gain it down later, but this won't remove the clipping itself—unless you're working in 32-bit floating point. If clipping occurred on the way in, that distortion is baked in for good.

If you're looking for a target range, a peak level between -18 dBFS and -6 dBFS is a safe, practical zone. These are guidelines, not rules. The only real rule is to avoid exceeding 0 dBFS while also ensuring your signal isn't so low that it disappears into noise. And with today's 24-bit recording, even low-level captures aren't much of an issue unless they're absurdly quiet. We used to deal with far worse hiss when recording to tape, so don't stress if your levels dip below -18 dBFS occasionally.

This is another reason why analog compressors can be helpful. Beyond their tonal benefits, they act as a safeguard against overs by taming peaks before they hit the converter. With an analog compressor in the chain, you're far less likely to clip your input signal—making it easier to maintain a controlled, balanced level on the way in.

Gain Stage Two

The next gain stage has to do with your processing. As long as there's no converter on the channel, you can absolutely hammer it with level, and it won't distort. I'm not saying you should crush your channels with level—you'd really have to go out of your way to do that anyway, and it would be somewhat pointless. But there will be no sonic degradation when you do.

That said, you *can* cause some plugins to distort—and in some cases, to clip—and this tends to confuse people. It brings in all sorts of consternation and freak-outs, followed by insanely over-complicated and unnecessary solutions to combat something that isn't even a problem.

It's by design.

If you hit a modeled compressor with too much level, it very well could distort. That's no longer a gain staging *problem*—it's a gain staging *decision*. Frankly, if you don't like the flavor of the distortion (and I wouldn't blame you), and if you find yourself spending time devising strategies to avoid it, then you probably shouldn't be using that model of compressor.

Whenever you hear distortion coming from a plugin, your reaction shouldn't be, *"Oh no! It's distorting! My production will be ruined!"* Rather, it should be *"Cool! Distortion! Let me see how I can use that to my advantage."*

Evaluating this is really simple. If the distortion sounds good, explore it—dial it in until you find the sweet spot. You might even push it further and make it more overt. If the distortion sounds bad, just bring down the level of your audio file using clip gain until it doesn't.

This isn't something to be timid about. Adjust the level at the file—or at the compressor's input—until it sounds right and move on. If that doesn't work, change plugins. There's plenty of them.

Gain Stage Three

Now, most of you—myself included—aren't using multi-track converters. And if you are, then you need to be mindful of how much level is hitting each individual converter on each channel.

Most of us are only using two channels of conversion, located at the Stereo Output. This is where all the audio from every track is summed down to two channels—left and right—and it's the only place where D-to-A conversion actually occurs. That makes the Stereo Output the most important place to manage your gain staging.

You will often see people online suggest leaving 6 dB of "headroom" for mastering. This comes from the idea that a mastering engineer needs space to process the mix without clipping. While avoiding clipping is obviously important, the idea that you must always peak at -6 dBFS is a complete misunderstanding of how digital audio works. There is no sonic penalty or advantage to peaking at -6 dBFS versus -3 dBFS or even -1 dBFS. If I bounce the same mix at -1 dBFS and another at -6 dBFS, and then gain-match them, they will sound identical. I've even made a video proving this. The only real rule here is: don't clip.

This whole 6 dB rule originated when a mastering engineer wanted to help people avoid clipping their mixes. The recommendation was an oversimplified way to keep levels in check. Unfortunately, this advice has only managed to convince people that headroom offers some sort of sonic advantage—which it doesn't. As if a mastering engineer somehow doesn't have clip gain to set the level where they want it.

Spending time and effort to keep your mix below -6 dBFS is misguided and defies logic. 0 dBFS is the ceiling—not -6. Nearly every track you hear on streaming services or CDs peaks just below digital zero. So, why then would you want to avoid that level, when it's going to end up there anyway? I'll answer that: *you wouldn't!*

There are all sorts of complicated strategies that have been devised to keep your output level at the Stereo Output below 0 dBFS. Some people suggest you set your KIK drum so that it hits -18 dBFS at the Stereo Output and then mix from there. It's not the worst strategy in the world, but it's not going to help the sound in any way. That's a myth.

And since faders often have a tendency to creep up over time—especially as you mix—it's possible that your level will go over 0 dBFS at some point. So, it's important to understand how to deal with this occurrence, rather than rely on a strategy that could just as easily fail to do what it was meant to do.

There are many solutions bandied about for keeping your level below 0 dBFS as you work, and most of them could make your life more complicated. For instance, you could bring down all of your faders when you find yourself going over 0 dBFS at the Stereo Output, but if you're using busses with processing, that could completely throw your mix out of whack.

Automation can also complicate this solution, since automation overrides manual fader moves. You can use trim functions to lower levels of automated channels, but that requires you to find the automated channels and make calculations—which is inefficient and prone to error. We want to avoid that.

You could, of course, just bring the Stereo Output (or Master) fader down—but many DAWs place the inserts before the fader at the Stereo Output. Should you decide to apply a mastering chain later on, you'll want that Stereo Output fader at unity so it doesn't affect the output level of your inserts. As an example: if you set the output level of your brickwall limiter to -1 dBFS, but your fader is 2 dB above unity, your output level will now be 1 dB over 0, which will clip. So, you'll essentially be working against yourself.

The simplest method is to place a gain plugin at the first insert point of your Stereo Output channel. This is an effective way to deal with the natural upward creep of the faders. At any point that you find yourself going over 0 dBFS, just bring down the overall level with the gain plugin. Once you're ready to apply processing on the Stereo Output, you can simply start on the second insert.

Personally, I prefer to use my bussing to control my levels to the Stereo Output, and I do that through an All BUS.

The ALL BUS

In my mix sessions, everything—and I mean everything—goes to a bus. While this might seem like it would complicate matters, it actually simplifies gain staging issues and offers considerably more control over both your processing and balance.

Like many mixers, I organize my sessions by grouping similar instruments together. All the drums are in one section, as are the guitars, synths, horns, and vocals. These groups are then routed to their respective busses, often layered in a nested structure, like Russian dolls.

We've already discussed the idea of combining two mics from a KIK drum—one inside and one outside—into a bus. The same approach applies to a snare drum (top and bottom mics), electric guitars recorded with two mics, stereo pianos (MIDI or organic), bass DI and cabinet mic, overhead drums with the hi-hat mic, and room mics.

MIDI drums may be bused slightly differently. I might have multiple sets of MIDI drums in a production, and I'm more likely to keep each set intact in its own bussing. But if I have several MIDI KIK drums playing the same pattern, I'll bus those together as one single KIK. If I want to process parts together, I combine them on a bus. If I want to process them independently, they go to their own busses.

Once I've combined mics and parts into busses, I set up busses for my busses. For example, verse guitars might get their own bus. If each verse guitar consists of two mics bused together, then those busses feed into a larger VERSE GTRS bus.

If several keyboard parts come in during the bridge, I'll route them to a BRDGE SYNTHS bus. This way, I can easily adjust the level of those bridge synths without affecting keyboard parts from other sections. Lead vocals go to a bus. Harmony vocals go to a bus. I might even create multiple harmony vocal busses for independent processing of verse harms and chorus harms.

Then I send all of those busses to even more busses. The KIK bus, SNARE bus, TOMS bus, OHs bus, and ROOMS bus all feed into an ALL DRUMS bus. Electric guitar sectional busses go to an E GTRS bus, acoustic guitars go to an AC GTRS bus, and all of those are routed to an ALL GTRS bus. All lead and harmony vocal busses go to an ALL VOX BUS. I even have an *fx* bus that contains most of my effects returns.

Every session is slightly different in terms of how I specifically set up my bussing, but everything gets routed to a bus, and all of those busses ultimately feed into an ALL BUS—the only channel in my session assigned to the Stereo Output.

In other words, by the time my session is set up for mixing, I have a single fader controlling everything that reaches the Stereo Output. The ALL BUS fader determines the level sent to that final channel.

So, why do I stack my busses like this?

For starters, Logic makes this very easy by allowing for nesting, which provides a clear visual representation of how the busses flow. Secondly, there are no negative consequences to routing audio through a bus in a DAW. It makes mixing more efficient by giving me broader control over levels and processing.

Adjusting multiple elements at once is often much faster than tweaking individual channels.

For example, if I have a solid drum balance but want to bring the drums up in the mix, I don't want to adjust each individual drum channel or bus. That's time-consuming, requires multiple fader moves, and can get complicated by automation. Since I can predict that I'll need this kind of control, it makes sense to set up these busses in advance.

This layered approach also allows for multiple stages of compression. I can apply compression to my KIK at the KIK bus, which is then affected by compression on the ALL DRUMS bus, which in turn is shaped by any compression applied at the ALL BUS (the whole mix).

While multiple layers of processing can be useful, the ALL BUS primarily allows me to control the overall output level without ever touching my Stereo Output fader. If my levels start creeping up and I find myself exceeding 0 dBFS at the converters, I can simply pull down the ALL BUS fader to bring my output level into compliance.

It's worth noting that some DAWs have inserts routed pre-fader, meaning the Stereo Output fader functions just like my ALL BUS fader since it's ahead of any processing on the Stereo Output channel. Personally, I would still set up an ALL BUS and keep my Stereo Output at unity, because the fader would otherwise affect any compression applied on that channel.

Of course, you don't have to adopt this level of bussing beyond combining mics. I set my sessions up like this mostly for the speed and flexibility it offers while mixing. And since so many people seem to struggle with gain staging and signal flow, I offer this approach as a solution—with added benefits. It not only helps maintain proper levels, but it also streamlines mixing, making broad adjustments easier and more efficient.

You might be wondering—what's the difference between bussing and grouping? A group locks audio together for editing purposes and links the faders so that moving one moves them all. But a group doesn't actually combine the signals; each channel still has its own output, meaning there's no way to process the group as a single entity.

Groups can be useful—sometimes necessary—when editing parts that need to stay locked together. But when it comes to processing multiple signals as one for purposes of the mix, bussing offers far more flexibility.

Sidechain

Many processors include a sidechain function, which allows you to compress a signal based on the input of another signal.

Radio stations use sidechaining as an easy way to automatically attenuate the music when the DJ speaks. A compressor is inserted on the music channel, and the mic is routed to the sidechain input of that compressor. When the DJ talks, the compressor reacts to the mic signal and reduces the level of the music. Attack and release times determine the fades—typically set fairly quick for both. So, when the DJ speaks, the music immediately drops. When the DJ stops, the music ramps back up to full volume.

A sidechain can also be used to make a synth pad pulse rhythmically by running a hi-hat signal into the sidechain of a compressor on the synth channel. The compressor reacts to the hat, which causes the synth to compress in time with it. For a more aggressive pulse, you can use the sidechain on a gate instead, set to close momentarily based on the input from the hat. This technique works well for any sustained part—including a vocal.

Some producers like to send their KIK drum to the sidechain of the bass compressor to attenuate the bass every time the KIK hits. If your goal is to generate an audible pumping effect, this is a perfectly reasonable way to do it. Motion is a great way to make a track more compelling, and sidechaining your KIK to your bass is one way to achieve that. LFO tools are another option for adding rhythmic motion to a track—and one I much prefer for this kind of effect, since they offer more precise control. You'll often hear this type of pumping on electronic dance records.

If you read online forums, you might get the impression that producers routinely sidechain the bass to the KIK drum as a standard practice to improve separation. I've managed an entire career without ever sidechaining my KIK to my bass for that purpose—and I think if you listen to my records, you'll find I have a pretty good command of KIK and bass relationships. If sidechaining like this makes your life easier or helps you get the sound you want, by all means, use it. But it's not the required practice it's often made out to be—and if the parts are too dynamic, it can cause more problems than it solves.

There's no doubt that balancing the KIK and bass can be one of the more challenging aspects of mixing. Many producers look for complex processing solutions instead of addressing the core issue: low-end translation problems caused by their room. Even in an acoustically accurate space, getting the KIK and bass to play nice can be tricky—so I certainly understand the frustration. But there's no magic bullet or shortcut to learning how to get those relationships right. It just takes time, experience, and practice. Same as everything else.

Parallel Compression

Parallel compression is achieved by blending an uncompressed signal with a heavily compressed version of the same signal. Why would you want to do that? Because aggressive compression tends to attenuate low-end information, which can be problematic for certain elements like a KIK drum. By combining an over-compressed signal with the dry signal, you retain the full depth of the low-end bloom while adding the punch of a hyper-compressed transient. This technique is especially useful for hip-hop KIKs, where getting a massive low end while maintaining attack and punch can be a challenge.

I recommend using an aux send for this setup. The idea is to crush the KIK drum with a compressor on an aux return and blend it back into the mix to enhance the attack. You can push the compression so hard that the signal is reduced to nothing but a tiny, sharp pop—and you'd be surprised how little of that pop is needed to alter the tone. Applying EQ to the parallel signal can further shape the attack: boost the presence range (750 Hz to 3 kHz) going into the compressor to enhance articulation, or push around 200 Hz to add weight and punch. This is all a matter of taste and experimentation.

Distortion is another powerful tool for shaping punch, and it pairs well with parallel compression. If you place a distortion plugin ahead of the compressor on the aux return, the distortion will react to the low end, which the compressor will then tame. Again, a little goes a long way.

As we discussed earlier, many plugin compressors now include a "mix" knob, which essentially gives you parallel compression directly inside the plugin by blending the dry and compressed signals. While this is convenient, I still prefer the aux send method—it allows for more extreme signal manipulation and lets me blend from the mixer itself. That flexibility can speed up the workflow, especially if I want to introduce additional processing to shape the attack further.

Some rock mixers are known for using heavy parallel compression across their entire drum kit—some even claim to use it on nearly everything. Personally, I don't use parallel compression routinely. KIK drums? Absolutely. Possibly even snare and toms. But I rarely apply it to a full drum kit. That's just a matter of preference.

Parallel compression is a useful and sometimes powerful tool, but it's often presented online as some kind of essential, routine technique. Like if you're not using it all the time, you're doing something wrong. In reality, it's just another option. Try it out so you understand what it does and use it when it makes sense for your mix or to solve a problem. If it works for you, great—use it. But don't think for a second that parallel compression is required for achieving professional results. It's just one more tool in the toolbox.

VU Meter

There's a whole slew of YouTube producers and engineers who suggest using a VU meter in your DAW to set levels before hitting a modeled plugin. The idea behind this advice is to prevent unwanted distortion—often described as "optimal"—while completely ignoring the fact that the distortion is part of the model's design. Besides, "optimal" is an entirely subjective construct.

It makes absolutely no sense for someone with no experience in the analog domain to use a VU meter in a DAW. It offers you no real advantage. In the analog world, you've got a lot more wiggle room when it comes to level, and a VU meter provides an average reading, not a precise peak. That makes sense to use in a domain that lacks a hard ceiling. But for digital? You're better off with the precision of digital meters.

When I was mixing on Neve 8068 consoles, I'd often slam the VU meters from the moment I hit play. I was pushing maximum level into the desk because it made the console sing. The electronics in vintage Neve consoles responded positively to high levels, adding a sound I could use to my advantage. But not all consoles reacted the same way—SSLs, for example, would crumble under that kind of gain. I knew I could only push a little over zero on the VU before things started falling apart. Just as my headroom wasn't exact, neither was the meter. But in the digital world, everything is precise—including the ceiling.

The moment you go over zero on the mix bus in a DAW, you're clipping. So, using a VU meter in that context makes no sense whatsoever. The advice to use a VU meter before hitting modeled gear is meant to mimic how we judged levels in the analog domain, but in practice, it's only served to confuse the living shit out of thousands of Home Producers who've never touched actual analog gear.

And frankly, the confusion generated by more complex techniques can be good for business. The more confused people are, the more likely they are to keep coming back for more advice. Always be wary of the advice you're getting on mediums that rely on return visits.

In the digital world, anything a VU meter tells you about level, a digital meter will tell you too—only with more precision. So put away the VU meter and set your levels by ear. If your modeled compressor starts distorting in a way you don't like, bring down the input level. You don't need a VU meter to tell you that you're sending too much level. What you do need is to train your ears—and the only way to do that is to stop staring at meters and start listening.

Troubleshooting

Before we close on the structural dynamics of flow, I'd like to address troubleshooting, which has somehow become a lost art.

Troubleshooting is how you find and fix signal flow issues. That may seem somewhat basic but based on the posts that I read every day, it's clear that troubleshooting is a process that eludes many young producers. We need to fix that.

Start Simple

When chasing down problems you should always start with the simplest solution and work your way logically and methodically through a series of possibilities. There's a reason why tech support always starts by asking if the power is on—it's the simplest possible solution.

At its core, troubleshooting is a process of elimination, and we want to remove the most likely culprits. After that, we want to isolate the issue so that we can figure out precisely where in the signal flow the problem occurs.

Let's say you have a modeled 1176 compressor on your vocal channel, and your vocal sounds distorted. This could be caused by any number of problems.

- The compressor could be bringing out existing distortion on the capture.
- The modeled compressor could be introducing the distortion.
- The distortion could be coming from a modeled plugin further down the chain.
- It could be coming from the Stereo Output channel.

At the moment, all we know is we hear distortion—and either we don't like it, or we want to control it. In either case, we have to isolate the problem and recognize there could be more than one cause. While that's not typical, it's always a possibility worth keeping in mind.

The most logical first step would be to take a quick gander at the Stereo Output channel to make sure you're not going over 0 dBFS. If you have plugins on that channel, they will affect the level, so you always want your meters set to Post Fader when mixing. Let's say the output level at the mix bus is in safe territory.

The next simplest solution is to bypass the 1176 on the first insert. If the distortion goes away you've isolated it to that plugin. To fix the distortion you need to adjust just the level going to the 1176, either using the input knob or by clip gaining the audio file down.

Now, if you have a plugin chain—including multiple modeled compressors—you can't assume the first one is the culprit. In more complex chains, you'll need to bypass all the plugins, then reintroduce them one at a time to isolate the issue.

Let's say you have two compressors with an EQ between them. You bring compressor 1 back in, and the distortion returns—now you know you're hitting it too hard. Too easy. But if the signal stays clean through compressor 1 and the EQ, and the distortion doesn't reappear until you enable compressor 2, then the issue is the level feeding into that second compressor, and that's where we want to address the problem. Fix it by lowering the output of the first compressor or adjusting the input on the second.

Either way, the distortion should go away.

Escalation

Some issues can be far more complex and require progressively more drastic solutions in an attempt to isolate the problem.

There was one time that I had a full second of latency between the mic and what I heard. I brought my buffer all the way down to 32 samples. That didn't fix it. I already had Logic's "low latency mode" on, which automatically bypasses plugins that would introduce latency. Since that wasn't working as expected, I systematically powered down every plugin in the chain—starting at the channel, then the busses, and finally at the Stereo Output. The latency was still there. Now I had to try more drastic solutions.

I closed my session and created a new one. Once I opened up the channel, the latency was gone. This isolated the latency issue to the session itself. I reopened my session, and the latency returned. This was baffling.

The next logical step was to reboot Logic and then the computer itself. When that didn't clear the issue, I decided to remove all of the plugins from the chain, one at a time, including at the Stereo Bus. *Bam!* The latency went away.

Apparently, even a powered-down "mastering" plugin on the 2-bus can introduce latency into the system. It made no sense—but it was happening. Rather than unravel my active mix session trying to figure it out, I bounced the mix as-is and imported the file into a new session for overdubs. That workaround became my standard practice for overdub sessions. More on that later.

Test Tools

Some issues can be tricky to chase down because they occur on channels with intermittent signals—like tom strikes. Rather than waiting for the next hit, or looping a short tom clip, drop an oscillator on the channel. Every DAW includes a test tone plugin you can use to trace problems. I use it whenever there's uncertainty about how my signal is flowing. A steady tone is easy to follow across busses and channels, and it also makes level discrepancies instantly obvious.

Meters are another essential troubleshooting tool. Say I've plugged my mic into Input 1 of my interface but hear nothing. If I see no signal on the DAW channel meter, that tells me the mic signal isn't making it to the track. The issue could be the mic, the cable, the interface, or a DAW setting—but instead of starting with the mic (the least likely and most time-consuming fix), I begin inside the DAW and work backward.

First, is the track assigned to Input 1? Check. Is it in Input or Record Ready mode? Check. If everything looks right in the DAW, then I move upstream—starting with the interface.

I open the interface control panel and check the meters. No signal there either? Then the problem is before the software: possibly the mic preamp, a cable, or the mic itself. Am I using a condenser? Is phantom power on? Is the preamp getting level? Does swapping the cable help? Is the mic actually working?

Let's say the interface *is* showing signal from Input 1. That means the issue lies inside the DAW—either a missed setting or something totally bizarre, maybe even "impossible."

This is a hypothetical and unlikely scenario, but I want to take it to the extreme just the same. Let's say everything is set exactly as it should be—I've checked my routing, rebooted the computer, opened a clean session—and I'm still getting no signal at the channel.

Next step? I plug the mic into Input 2 instead. And bam—there's the signal! But it's showing up on Input 1.

If I close the session and open a new one, and Input 2 maps correctly to Input 2, then I've isolated the issue to the session settings. But if Input 2 still goes to Input 1, then it's a global DAW setting. Let's say it's the latter.

First, I'd check the internal routing. If that looks right, then it's time for a reboot—Logic first, then the whole machine. If that doesn't fix it, I'd revert to an earlier version of Logic. (I always keep archived versions on an external drive in case of a catastrophic bug.)

That's Impossible

Now, the odds of this particular issue happening are low—especially since I'm the only one who uses my room, and I'd *never* change my routing like that (*and if I did, I'd remember!*). But

I bring it up because it's exactly the kind of problem I'd call "impossible."

Over the years, I've encountered plenty of "impossible" problems. But if it's happening, then by definition—it's possible. And the only way to solve it is by applying solid troubleshooting techniques.

Like anything, troubleshooting takes practice. The more you do it, the better you get. Here's a checklist to help guide you when things go sideways.

Troubleshooting Checklist

1. **Diagnose the problem**. What are the most likely causes? Is it hardware, software, routing, or user error?

2. **Try the simplest solutions**. Before you start unraveling everything, rule out the obvious stuff first. Start with what's easy. Is something muted? Is a solo button killing your signal somewhere upstream? Use your meters to quickly point you in the right direction.

3. **Isolate the problem**. Trace your signal flow and pinpoint where in the chain the problem is occurring.

4. **Bypass suspect elements**. Disable plugins, gear, or routing blocks one at a time. If the problem disappears, you've found your culprit.

5. **Swap components**. Try a different mic, cable, channel, plugin, or track. If the problem persists, you've eliminated that element from suspicion.

6. **Use a test signal**. It gives you a static signal that's easy to follow and helps reveal level or routing issues.

7. **Try a new session or project**. Open a fresh project and rebuild the essentials. If the problem disappears, there's

something wrong in the session itself—either a setting or a corrupted element.

8. **Check your global system settings**. Sample rate mismatches, buffer sizes, or incorrect I/O assignments can create head-scratchers that persist across sessions.

9. **Restart everything**. Quit the DAW, reboot your interface, and restart the machine. It's often the last thing we try—but when something's behaving abnormally, rebooting becomes the most likely solution.

If you're relatively new to troubleshooting, this checklist should help you get through it. There's no perfect order to follow—that'll depend on the issue at hand. Just stay logical and strategic to keep the process efficient. Over time, troubleshooting becomes second nature.

PROGRAMMING TOOLS

These days, many productions are built entirely through programming, using MIDI, loops, and samples that allow a producer to create an entire track without recording a single note with a microphone. While these tools can unlock flexible, efficient workflows, if you're not careful, they can also get you in trouble. In this section, I'll walk through the programming methods we rely on most, how to use them effectively, and how to avoid the common pitfalls that come with them.

Samples

Producers have been sampling recognizable parts of hit songs since digital technology became widely available in the early '80s. Over the years, countless hits have leveraged the sound of identifiable tracks from the past. Vanilla Ice famously sampled the bass line from "Under Pressure" for "Ice Ice Baby." Kanye West's 2005 hit "Gold Digger" featured a sample from "I Got a Woman" by Ray Charles. Kanye's 2007 track "Stronger" sampled Daft Punk's "Harder, Better, Faster, Stronger," which helped spark a major resurgence in Daft Punk's popularity in the U.S. for years afterward.

Not all samples come from iconic songs. Some are more obscure and may not be instantly recognizable. Beyoncé's "Freedom," for example, includes samples from Kaleidoscope's 1969 record "Let Me Try" and features a freedom song sourced from Alan Lomax's collection of 20th-century prison work songs.

Sampling involves using a direct recording from an existing track, and if you want to do that legally, you must obtain permission from two separate rights holders: The owner of the master recording (usually the record label). The songwriters and publishers who control the composition itself.

The cost of clearing a sample depends on two major factors: the recognizability of the sample and the popularity of the artist who seeks to use it. A relatively unknown producer may pay more than a superstar like Beyoncé, who has more negotiating power due to her brand and earning potential.

The going rate for a sample is often half of the new song's publishing royalties—but everything is negotiable. The owners of an obscure track may settle for less, while the owners of an iconic hit may demand a higher percentage. They could also just say no. They control the rights.

If you want to sample a record, the first step is identifying the rights holders. Start by finding the record label that released the track, which will point you to the master owner. Then use ASCAP, BMI, or SESAC to identify the publisher and songwriter(s). Once you have that information, you'll need to negotiate two separate agreements—one with the label for the master rights and one with the publisher for the composition.

Both may charge an upfront fee, in addition to a percentage of future royalties.

If this all sounds overwhelming, you're not alone. It's a time-consuming and tedious process to navigate—which is why there are now sample clearance agencies like DMG Clearances or Tracklib that can handle the negotiations and paperwork on your behalf.

A common myth is that using a short snippet—such as a second or two—qualifies as fair use and doesn't require clearance. That's false. In commercial music, any recognizable sample must be cleared, regardless of length. There's no legal "safe zone." Whether it's a few seconds or a full chorus, if the original owners discover it, they can block your release or sue for infringement.

Some producers try to sidestep clearance by manipulating a sample—pitching it, reversing it, chopping it beyond recognition—hoping it no longer resembles the original. While this can sometimes make negotiation easier, it doesn't exempt you from seeking permission. If the rights holders can still identify the source, they can take legal action or demand compensation.

That said, heavily reworked samples can give you better negotiating leverage—especially if the rights holders feel the new version no longer directly competes with the original.

Another approach is interpolation, which involves re-recording a part of a song instead of using the original audio. This allows you to bypass the need to license the master recording (owned by the label), though you still need permission from the songwriters and publishers. Interpolation is often used to modernize a sound or to sidestep high clearance fees. Examples include Mariah Carey's "Fantasy," which interpolates Tom Tom Club's "Genius of Love," and Olivia Rodrigo's "Good 4 U," which interpolates Paramore's "Misery Business."

If you want to avoid clearance headaches altogether, platforms like Tracklib offer pre-cleared samples from real recordings. You can license them upfront for a small fee and a predetermined royalty split, which saves you from direct negotiations. You can also use royalty-free sample libraries from places like Splice, Loopmasters, or Cymatics. That said, I've not personally used any of these services, so due diligence is strongly advised.

Of course, the point of using a sample is often to take advantage of its familiarity—which is exactly why those kinds of samples command a high price. Make no mistake, half your publishing is a very high price indeed.

Keep in mind: just because you're willing to pay the price of admission doesn't mean you'll get permission. Labels and publishers aren't obligated to say yes. Some artists and estates— like Prince's or The Beatles'—are notoriously protective. Others, like James Brown's estate, are more open but may demand steep fees.

Sampling is a powerful creative tool, but it comes with legal and financial strings. Some producers sample freely and deal with clearance only if a song blows up—which is exceptionally risky. Others avoid it altogether to sidestep that risk. If you plan to sample, do your research, budget accordingly, and either negotiate up front or stick to pre-cleared alternatives.

Sampling is an art form—but getting it wrong can cost you a lot more than just a few royalties. Even if your song doesn't earn a dime, you can still be sued for statutory damages—up to $150,000 per infringement—plus the other side's legal fees. This is not a risk worth taking.

Loops

Loops are how many of us make our first productions. They're easy to use and can provide instant, positive results— but they also come with some serious drawbacks.

Most DAWs come with large loop libraries that automatically conform to your session's tempo, and which also results in a change of pitch. These loops are generally license-free, meaning you can use them in your productions without clearing or paying for them. That's great—until you realize they're license-free for everyone. If someone else owns the same DAW or subscribes to the same loop platform, they have the same rights to that loop you do. You might hear your loop in someone else's song—and you can't do a thing about it.

Here's the real problem: if you use a license-free loop and your track becomes a hit, other producers can reuse that same loop in their own music without crediting or compensating you. You've just given away a piece of your hit for free. Granted, that's a big "if," but you only get so many shots at a hit record, and if your track takes off, you want to own the copyright to every element in it. Total control means fewer headaches later.

That doesn't mean loops should be avoided. Far from it. They're incredibly useful and often a great way to generate ideas. This is especially true for drum loops and percussion loops, which are less likely to be identifiable—even when they're widely used. When I was mixing hip-hop in the early '90s, there were maybe ten drum loops everyone used. On their own, they were instantly recognizable, but once fully arranged, they often disappeared into the track.

Melodic loops are another story. A catchy loop that can be hummed is far riskier—those get noticed, and not just by listeners.

There's also a legal distinction to understand.

License-free loops, such as those included with GarageBand, Logic, or Ableton, can be used freely in your work. You can copyright your finished track, but you can't copyright the loop itself or prevent others from using it.

Royalty-free loops, like those from Splice, Loopmasters, or Cymatics, are generally sold with usage rights exclusive to the purchaser. These are much safer in terms of originality and ownership—but even royalty-free loops may come with restrictions, so always read the licensing terms carefully.

One major risk of using widely available loops—license-free or otherwise—is being flagged by content ID systems or streaming platforms. YouTube, Spotify, and Apple Music use automated algorithms to detect duplicates. If another artist releases a track using the same loop before you, your song may be mistakenly blocked, demonetized, or even removed—regardless of whether you used the loop legally.

You might even find yourself in "copyright jail," and forced to take a class on copyright, which is insulting and obnoxious when you were clearly operating within your rights. You're not the one who needs the class. They are. To add insult to injury, reaching these companies to make your arguments can be maddeningly difficult, which is by design. So, yeah, save yourself the headache.

If you like using loops but want to minimize the risks, consider manipulating them beyond recognition:

- Pitch-shifting and time-stretching
- Reversing
- Chopping and re-sequencing
- Layering multiple loops together
- Adding effects like saturation, filters, or reverb

These techniques won't give you legal ownership, but they can make your track feel more original and reduce the risk of it being flagged or duplicated.

Another option is recreating the loop from scratch. If a loop inspires you, use it as a reference and rebuild it using your own instruments, sounds, or samples. You still won't prevent others from using the original, but you'll own your version entirely.

It's also helpful to understand the difference between loops and one-shots. Loops are pre-recorded repeating patterns—musical phrases, beats, riffs. One-shots are individual sounds like drum hits, synth stabs, or vocal chops. One-shots offer more flexibility and are far less risky because they don't usually form an identifiable melodic or harmonic sequence.

Many producers start with loops to sketch out ideas, then replace them as the production evolves. This can be a great workflow: use loops to move fast, then build something original.

Even if you copycat a melodic loop and re-record it yourself, that won't stop others from using the original. You'll own your version—but you'll still be competing with anyone who uses the same loop you started from.

I use loops all the time because they give me quick results. I'll scroll through drum loops and toppers, drop a few into my arrangement, combine them, cut them up, move them around—and in minutes, I've got the backbone of a track. Once the track starts to take shape, I'm likely replacing most—if not all—of those loops.

Loops are incredibly useful tools. Just don't lean on them too heavily. The best approach is to manipulate them, replace them, or build your own from scratch. That way, your work remains original—and yours.

So, use loops. But use them wisely.

MIDI

Most programmed tracks use MIDI, which stands for Musical Instrument Digital Interface. Unlike audio recordings, MIDI itself produces no sound—it simply transmits data related to musical notes, timing, velocity, and other performance parameters. It communicates through messages like "note on/note off" and "pitch bend," which tell a synthesizer or sampler how to respond.

All DAWs include MIDI functionality, and most producers use a MIDI controller—such as a keyboard or drum pad—to program or perform MIDI parts. Many, if not most, drum beats in modern productions are MIDI-programmed. That's unlikely to change anytime soon, though advancements in MIDI technology will continue to shape how we use it.

MIDI technology has remained largely unchanged since the early '80s, but MIDI 2.0 is an evolving update that expands its capabilities. It offers higher resolution, bidirectional communication between devices, and more detailed articulation control. While it hasn't yet been widely adopted, it's something to keep an eye on—it's likely to make virtual instruments feel even more expressive and natural in the coming years.

One of the biggest advantages of MIDI is its editability. If you record a MIDI piano performance and hit a wrong note, you don't need to re-record the entire take—you can simply move the bad note to the correct pitch. You can also quantize the performance to tighten the timing. While quantization exists for audio as well, MIDI allows for more granular control, including the ability to edit individual notes within a chord—something you can't do well with recorded audio.

That flexibility makes it possible to program entire productions without ever recording an instrument through a microphone. This can be incredibly useful, especially for genres like electronic music, pop, and hip-hop. But MIDI often falls short when it comes to recreating the organic feel of a live band.

That's because live musicians naturally push and pull against the beat, creating a dynamic groove that's nearly impossible to replicate with MIDI. Technically, you could program those subtle variations—but doing it well requires so much time and skill that it's either prohibitive or a complete non-starter. Live performances also benefit from natural acoustics, while MIDI parts, even high-end ones, are often built from isolated samples, which can lack the acoustic depth and interaction of real instruments in a space.

To work around these limitations, many producers introduce humanization techniques—slight variations in velocity, randomized timing, and dynamic automation. Some DAWs and sample libraries even offer built-in humanization tools to help MIDI parts feel less mechanical.

Sample Libraries

High-end sample libraries help bridge the gap between MIDI and organic performance by offering multiple articulations and expressive controls. This makes it possible to create far more realistic performances of instruments like horns, strings, guitars, or drum kits.

For example, Logic's stock string and horn libraries now include articulations like staccato, legato, pizzicato, and swells—all of which mimic the way real musicians play. Many third-party libraries go even further, using tools like key switching, velocity layers, and round-robin sampling to bring more life and realism to MIDI performances.

Round-robin sampling is particularly effective at preventing that robotic MIDI sound. It cycles through multiple recorded variations of the same note or articulation, so you're not triggering the exact same sample each time. That subtle difference mimics how a real musician would play and helps avoid the repetitive, machine-gun effect often heard in programmed drums, strings, and brass.

I recently recorded a horn section for a track and needed to add a bari sax part to the final chorus. Thanks to the articulations, dynamics, and expression tools in the sample library, I was able to program the part exactly as a bari sax player might perform it. Some notes were staccato, others overblown, some legato. By switching between articulations, I created a performance that felt natural and believable. Within the full section, nobody would guess it was MIDI.

That level of realism is impressive—but only in some cases. MIDI still struggles to convincingly replicate a live drummer. Even high-end drum libraries packed with detail often feel flat or sterile. Some libraries offer incredible velocity layering and articulation control, but they rarely make you feel like you're hearing a great drummer in a room.

The same goes for MIDI-programmed guitars. You might get fret noise, slides, bends, and other artifacts of real playing, but something about them always feels a little off. Oddly enough, composers have managed to build believable orchestral performances with MIDI and sample libraries, but when it comes to modern rock and pop instrumentation, the illusion tends to fall apart.

That said, sample libraries can be extremely useful in hybrid workflows. Many producers record real drums, bass, and guitars but use MIDI for things like strings, horns, or auxiliary percussion. This approach blends the flexibility of MIDI with the authenticity of live performance.

Another strategy is to use MIDI as a placeholder. It allows you to work quickly, sketch out parts, and refine arrangements before committing to live recordings.

MIDI paired with quality sample libraries can be an incredibly powerful tool. Used strategically, it adds tremendous flexibility and can dramatically elevate your production. Just be mindful of where it excels and where it still falls short.

Amp Sims

While amp sims aren't strictly programming tools, they do allow us to capture a performance without the use of a microphone, and if you have enough of them, it opens up your sound design options tremendously.

Amp sims have completely changed the game when it comes to producing electric guitars and bass. Sims aren't new. The Rockman—which came out in the early '80s—was all the rage when I first started recording. Frankly, the tones from the original Rockman are almost comical now—but then, so are a lot of things from the '80s. Since then, there have been countless amp simulators—most of them atrocious, especially for producing organic rock music. That's no longer the case.

There are still plenty of guitar purists who wouldn't dream of using a sim over a real amp, and I'm not here to convince anyone otherwise. At the end of the day, you need to be happy with your production. If you prefer miked analog amps, then that's what you should use. But for most producers, amp sims are indispensable and aren't relegated to processing guitars. I certainly wouldn't want to work without them.

I've used numerous amp sim packages, but none come close in quality and sheer size to IK Multimedia's Amplitube V. It offers an enormous variety of guitar and bass amps, and they sound remarkably like their real-world counterparts. When mixing bass, I often receive both a DI and an amp track. More often than not, I end up replacing the amp track with one of Amplitube's bass sims—and I almost always get better results. The same goes for guitar DIs.

Amplitube V frequently goes on sale for around $100, which is an insane price considering what you get. Aside from its vast amp selection, it lets you shape your tone with the kind of precision you'd expect from a pro studio setup. You can swap speaker cabinets and amplifier heads, insert virtual pedals and effects processors anywhere in the chain, introduce room ambience, adjust mic placements three-dimensionally as well as their blends, create stereo effects, and add in some of the direct signal—all from a mixer built into the plugin itself. The result is near-limitless tonal flexibility without ever having to mic a cabinet. That just makes my life so much easier.

Back when I was producing rock bands entirely in the studio, we'd spend hours dialing in tones—swapping amps, adjusting mics, and tweaking pedals. The amps were often blaringly loud, which made mic placement fraught. The process was both physically exhausting and time-consuming. And while it could be creatively rewarding, I have no desire to go back to that workflow.

Of course, having access to dozens of amp models can be overwhelming. Even in a studio with just a few amps, finding the right tone can take time—especially when multiple guitars are involved. The goal isn't to exhaust every option; it's to find the tone that best serves the production. More often than not, that just means cycling through amps until something jumps out, then shaping it from there.

One of the biggest advantages of amp sims is the ability to refine the tone later. When recording real amps, you have to commit to a sound at the time of tracking. That said, tone affects how a guitarist plays—particularly in terms of sustain and feel—so you can't go overboard. But even within those limits, sims offer considerable flexibility.

For newer producers, that flexibility is invaluable. Even after decades of producing, I often tweak tones as a session evolves—and amp sims make that possible.

Miking a guitar amp well is difficult. It takes years of experience, and even in well-isolated rooms, bleed between the amp and control room can make real-time tone judgment difficult. That's not an issue with a sim. I plug into a DI, run it through Amplitube, flip through a few options, and lock in a tone that fits the vision—then tailor it from there.

If a guitarist shows up with a fully curated tone, I'll absolutely record it. But that's rare. More often than not, I'm chasing a variety of tones based on the needs of the production—which is a far more efficient process with amp sims.

Live guitarists often rely on pedalboards for quick tone changes. In the studio, though, I recommend bypassing the pedalboard entirely and keeping the DI clean. Amplitube includes a wide range of virtual pedals, and you're better off maintaining flexibility. If you print external pedals to your DI signal, you lock yourself in—and unless you document your settings religiously, recreating the sound later can be a problem. That said, if an external pedal does something amazing, then by all means print it. There's nothing wrong with locking down a tone.

Many keyboards—Rhodes, Wurlitzers, organs, and even some synthesizers—can benefit from the tone of an amplifier. Even vocals, horns, and violins can take on just the right sonic character when run through a guitar amp or a pedal. I don't think there's a single instrument I haven't run through an amp at some point or another. Even if you're not working with guitars right now, a virtual amp package gives you the opportunity to experiment creatively with tone and texture. The more tonal tools you have at your disposal, the more flexible your productions will be—regardless of genre.

Amplitube's base package already includes a wide range of officially licensed amps from brands like Mesa/Boogie, Fender, Orange, and Marshall, with even more available through expansion packs. IK also offers separately available artist collections modeled after the exact rigs of players like Slash, Satriani, Brian May, and Hendrix. And then there's Tonex—a powerful AI-based tool for creating custom guitar tones, even if you have zero analog experience.

The best part? You can demo anything from their Custom Shop before making a purchase. IK's Product Manager app makes it easy to authorize and manage all your gear and expansions. It handles downloads, updates, and license tracking in one place. This means you can try out a product and, if you decide to buy it later, just unlock it directly in the app.

Amplitube is an amp sim I use daily. It helps me craft rich, layered tones and gives me a level of sonic depth I couldn't get otherwise. For any Home Producer, it's a must-have—I really can't recommend IK Multimedia's amp sims highly enough.

I reached out to IK Multimedia to sponsor this book specifically because I think they deliver a great product at a stupendous price point. I'm deeply appreciative of their support. They offer a wide range of excellent tools for producers, including high-quality sample libraries with detailed articulations and a full suite of engineering plugins under the T-Racks banner—all of them at accessible price points, and all well worth checking out.

CAPTURING AND REFINING STRATEGIES

Overdubs

Overdubbing is how you layer recorded parts into your production—whether vocals, guitars, keyboards, or anything else that requires capturing a performance. There are strategies involved in the process, most of which come down to the level of refinement you seek. As much as we'd love to nail a perfect performance from start to finish, that's rarely how it works. More often than not, performances are constructed from multiple takes and are sometimes enhanced with electronic processing to maximize their impact within the production. Where it comes to the initial capture, there are two primary strategies: comping and punching.

Comping and Punching

A comp is a compilation—or composite—of the best parts from multiple takes, stitched together to create one seamless performance. Most DAWs offer built-in comping systems, often placing takes in an expandable folder where you can quickly switch between sections, phrases, words, or even syllables. We call that convenient.

Suppose you recorded three vocal takes, none of which are perfect on their own. You could use Take 1 (T1) for the first line, Take 2 (T2) for the next, switch back to T1 for a few words, grab a single word from Take 3 (T3), and return to T1 for the remainder of the phrase. This continues down the track until you've built a complete performance. Whether that compiled performance is good enough—that's for you to decide. But this is a very effective procedure for constructing a more refined performance.

A great singer might need only a few takes, while a less experienced singer may need considerably more. That said, Whitney Houston reportedly recorded over 100 takes of "I Will Always Love You", and she was an undeniably great singer. That just goes to show how silly things can get when money is no object. She sang that song live too—and often in amazing fashion—so the idea that she needed 100 takes for the record is somewhat absurd to me, and always will be, but I digress.

If you don't like your first three takes, then you can always have your performer sing the track another three times. You could have them sing it ten times if you like, but then you have to go through all of those takes, and that can become rather time-consuming and draining to boot.

I recommend you always record, even during warm-up takes and even as you adjust your input levels. You can always throw those takes out later. But if your performer does something genius by accident—this happens—then you'll want to capture it.

Performers don't always remember what they did, and hard drive space is cheap. Anytime someone is performing—even just to practice—you want to be in record.

During overdubbing, monitoring is typically done through headphones, although some singers perform much better with monitors. This works best when you apply aggressive analog compression, which can push the bleed mostly—or even completely—out of the signal. Place the singer between the monitors, fairly close, and try to find a balance that allows for a strong performance without introducing too much bleed. This strategy can be quite helpful for singers who struggle with tuning.

You'll generally want to hear the mix as it stands but may need to mute certain elements to avoid headphone bleed. Shakers and tambourines, for example, tend to leak into vocal mics and are often best removed from the monitor mix (also called the cue mix).

Given the perfect recall of DAWs, it's common to mix as you go. Over time, your session can become bloated with processor-heavy plugins, creating issues when recording new parts. Even if you're monitoring vocals through your interface's low-latency software, heavy processing in the session can cause latency. Some 2-bus plugins can introduce horrendous latency—even in bypass—which may force you to remove them in order to record overdubs. Now you're unraveling your running mix just to lay down a part, which is far from ideal. The better solution? Create a separate overdub session.

Before any new overdub session with a performer, I prefer to work in a lighter session. I'll tighten my monitor mix, mute any problematic tracks, and bounce the mix as it stands. Then I import that stereo mix into a fresh session for overdubs. Not only does that keep the overdub session light, but it also keeps me from futzing with the mix while recording—and helps me stay focused on the task at hand.

This is especially useful when recording guitars through amp sims. Sims are resource hogs, and the only way to monitor them is through the DAW, which introduces latency and forces you to lower the buffer—further taxing your system.

If you're uncomfortable recording to a stereo bounce because you want more control over the mix, or you're not confident in your balances, you can export stems (stereo submixes) instead. This gives you a bit more flexibility with the cue mix while still keeping the overdub session lean. If the performer has trouble with timing, bring up the drums stem. If they're struggling with pitch, bring up the harmonic information.

Once the overdubs are complete, I import them back into my running mix session and integrate them into the production. By the end of a project, I might have multiple overdub sessions: "Guitar Overdubs," "Horn Overdubs," "Vocal Overdubs," and "Mix."

This strategy has the added benefit of serving as a backup archive. You can flatten your vocal takes into a single file in the mix session without locking yourself in—because the raw takes live safely in the overdub session. If you need to fix something later, you can always go back and pull an alternate take.

If there's any doubt about whether you've captured the performer's best take, it's often worth trying to beat the comp—especially with vocals. Having a completed comp removes the pressure, which can lead to a looser, more compelling performance. You can then decide whether to replace the comp entirely or just fold in the improved sections.

If the performer outdoes the comp—or even part of it—great. If not, it confirms you've already captured their best. But if they're not clearly outperforming the comp after a take or two, it's best to move on.

Now, there's no point recording an entire part just to fix a single moment. In that case, a punch-in will do—dropping into record at the exact spot needed. Most DAWs handle this by adding to your take folder, so you can later bring them into your comp.

When you're recording by yourself, a tight punch-in can be difficult. Most DAWs will allow you to set an automatic entry and exit point, which will make the task considerably easier, but that also requires annoying programming time. You can put your DAW into a loop, which allows you to record the same section multiple times without resetting. While that can be a great way to shed a part, at some point, you need to stop and give your brain a moment to process. There's a big difference between playing notes and performing music, and repeatedly singing or playing the same part over and over is generally not performing but rather practicing.

When I'm running the session for my artist, I prefer to punch in at the precise entry point. This is a habit developed from years of recording to analog tape. Given the non-destructive nature of the DAW, you can punch in early without losing any of your take, but that can also throw your performer off. I find that allowing your performers to hear their previous take up until the exact moment of the punch leads to better results and increased efficiency.

When recording vocals, I try to capture full takes of the song whenever possible—but sometimes, that's not practical. Overlapping sections may require a new track, and physically demanding parts are often best saved for later. I avoid recording screaming vocals until the end of the day—or even the end of the project—unless I specifically want the extra rasp. That said, pushing a vocalist to the point of vocal strain for purposes of tone is risky, as it can do more harm than good.

If a vocal part is particularly challenging, I might choose to record in sections rather than to ask my vocalist to perform the entire song down. Some transitions can be difficult to make, and certain parts might sit right on the edge of a performer's range. In both cases, that can make working in sections ideal.

Instrumentalists often benefit from a sectional approach, especially when the player is still working out the part. For example, if the chorus guitar part is the same every time, it might be more efficient to record those choruses one after the other. You can record just one chorus and fly the parts to the other choruses if you like but tracking them all gives you natural variation—and gives the player a chance to build excitement as the song progresses. It also gives you more to harvest from, and it might even lead to a happy accident. Don't deprive yourself of that opportunity purely for the sake of time.

Sometimes vocal takes don't go especially well. Once I sense the singer won't recover, I stop recording and let them regroup. This gives me a moment to offer suggestions and gives them space to reset. I can work a guitar player hard for hours—but vocalists have only so many takes in them. If you let them struggle too long without intervening, you make everyone's job more difficult.

Editing

There will be times when you've recorded a take that requires some editing in order to place it in better time. How aggressively you choose to edit depends entirely on how refined you want your production.

Editing is a tough way to derive feel—but a great way to lock things perfectly to time, which by its very nature tends to strip the feel away. If there really is no feel to speak of, or if you're going for a tightly programmed sound, then by all means, edit aggressively to the tempo grid. If you want the record to feel raw, then you should leave all the mistakes—other than perhaps the most distracting ones. It's the treatments that fall between raw and polished that require attention and taste.

There are two ways to edit: you can time-stretch, which allows you to slide notes using time compression, or you can cut and slide.

Cut and Slide

Before time compression was readily available in DAWs, editors had to manually cut and slide parts into time. This involved slicing notes at the transients, shifting them into place, and then adjusting region boundaries to create seamless transitions. Compared to time-stretching, this method is highly inefficient, but sometimes necessary. If a performance falls too far outside reasonable time-stretching tolerances, cut and slide editing may be the only option.

A hybrid approach can work—sliding the most problematic notes while using time-stretching for smaller corrections. This may require bouncing the part after your initial edits, since region cuts can interfere with stretching functionality. When working with multi-mic recordings, phase alignment is critical. Shifting individual regions without maintaining their phase relationships can introduce unwanted sonic artifacts, especially on drums.

In Logic, you can phase-lock regions by enabling the Group function and turning on phase-locked editing. I'm not sure how every DAW handles this, but the concept remains the same: any time you edit multi-mic sources, you need to ensure they move as a unit. Otherwise, you could get some rather surprising results.

Frankly, if a performance is so far out that time-stretching isn't a viable solution, you're far better off re-recording until it is. If you're the one struggling to perform? Why, that's just practice.

Time Stretching

Many DAWs offer the ability to correct timing discrepancies through time-stretching. As with any tool, there are tolerances—push beyond them, and you'll introduce obvious artifacts. Different DAWs use different time-stretching algorithms, which vary in how transparently they handle the processing. Some DAWs allow you to choose the algorithm and selecting the right one can make a noticeable difference in sound quality.

Many also offer automatic quantization via time-stretching, making it easy to snap a super rhythmic part into time. Once again, if you recorded that part with multiple mics, you must phase-lock the channels before making adjustments. Otherwise, things can get sonically weird—shifty transients, hollowed-out frequencies, or phasey artifacts.

While quantization is handy, we don't always want everything perfectly locked to the grid—at least, I don't. Unless I seek a fully programmed sound, I'm far more likely to selectively time-stretch problem areas while leaving everything else as played. If my goal is to preserve the human feel of a performance, I'll only fix the most distracting timing discrepancies.

As a mixer, I've used time-stretching to great effect on performers who tend to hold notes too long—especially at the end of their phrases. As a producer, I prefer to address phrasing issues during tracking, but some performers just can't help themselves. A little time compression can help rein in bad phrasing habits without losing the feel of an otherwise great performance.

Here's my recommendation: Use comping and punching to refine the feel, then use time-stretching to fix minor timing issues. If you want a strict programmed feel, quantize to the grid using either method—or both.

Tuning

There are two ways to tune parts: audibly and invisibly. The nature of your production, the abilities of your performer, and your overarching vision will dictate your approach.

The most popular and expansive third-party tuning package is Celemony Melodyne, which allows for various manipulations—including pitch centering, amplitude adjustments, formant shifting for vowel control, timing correction, pitch modulation control for vibrato adjustment, note separation to deal with non-linear tuning fluctuations, and even polyphonic pitch editing for adjusting individual notes within chords.

Logic's Flex Pitch works similarly to Melodyne, minus polyphonic tuning, and other DAWs have their own versions of tuning functionality—though not all are created equal.

If you don't care about obvious artifacts—the kind you'd hear on a T-Pain record—you can either use an auto-tune plugin set to stun or aggressively center all the pitches and flatten pitch modulation with tuning software. That said, hard pitch correction can sometimes force notes onto the wrong pitch entirely, requiring manual adjustments.

Auto-tune is likely the most efficient way to achieve a vocal sound laden with pitch jumps and artifacts. While you can apply pitch correction to a finished vocal, it can also be effective to let the performer monitor the aggressive tuning in real time as they sing. This gives the singer some control over how the tuning responds, allowing them to manipulate the effect in a more apparent way. That said, this strategy could easily distract a singer from delivering their best. Depending on the plugin, it can also introduce intolerable latency, which can interfere with their ability to sing in time.

If your production calls for a more transparent approach, you'll need to tune with precision and restraint. Invisible tuning requires practice, and there are limits to how much correction can be applied before artifacts become audible—even with for-mant shifting to counteract chipmunk-like vowel distortions.

As with editing, how aggressively you tune is a matter of taste and refinement. Sometimes the best way to keep things natural is to fix only the most distracting notes—but that often results in more extensive tuning than you anticipated. Tuning can be a slippery slope. The moment you tune one note, you've exposed discrepancies on the preceding and subsequent ones. It's like a cancer in the way it spreads. To tune one note will often force you to fix three. And then even more need tuning. Before you know it, you've managed to tune nearly every vocal note on the track.

Tuning both the lead vocals and the doubles can introduce phase anomalies, especially when pitch modulation is aggres-sively flattened. You can usually center the pitches of both the lead and the double without issue, but if you overcorrect vibrato, you can kill the natural chorusing effect—negating the purpose of the double, which is to smooth out tuning anomalies. This issue is even more pronounced with harmonies. Over-tuning stacked vocals can strip away the richness that comes from nat-ural pitch variation. In many cases, it's better to tune harmonies relative to each other rather than strictly to the pitch grid.

Chromatic tuning isn't always musically appropriate. Cer-tain notes should be slightly sharp or flat depending on the scale and chord progression. Some tuning software allows for alter-native tuning systems or scale-based adjustments, aligning notes based on harmonic relationships rather than rigid equal temperament. If a performance is solid, small tuning discrep-ancies often go unnoticed—and sometimes, leaving them in place is the best choice.

Some singers naturally sing a few cents flat as part of their sound and style. Bringing them fully up to pitch can destroy the sonic fingerprint that makes them unique. We aren't naturally meant to sing in perfect tune, and some singers come off far more honest when presented in their natural pitch location.

While tuning is most commonly used on vocals, it's also a useful tool for instruments. You can tune bass lines, string performances, brass, and guitar lines if needed. A slightly off-pitch bass note can make the entire production sound out of tune and can subtly muddy a mix. Tuning a bass part can improve both of those issues.

If you're aiming for a natural presentation, use comping and punching techniques first to build the performance, then apply tuning only as necessary. If you want a programmed sound, then fully commit—quantize, center the pitch, and adjust vibrato and pitch modulations to match your aesthetic. Just be aware that the tighter you make it, the more you risk losing the musicality of the performance. If the musicality isn't there to begin with, aggressive tuning surely won't make it any worse. Otherwise, you may want to be judicious in your tuning efforts.

Now that we've covered the tools, techniques, and mindset for producing your own music, let's turn our attention to producing others.

CHAPTER FOUR

The Many Roles of the Producer For-Hire

As a Self-Producer or even a Songwriter Producer, your work is often largely speculative. As such, you have no limitations on your time. But when you're paid a fee to produce others with existing songs, all of that changes. Now you carry the responsibility to deliver the record on time and within budget, and all the pressures that go along with that. You're in charge of the vision, the budget, time constraints, and the personnel. You also answer to a client, an artist, or even a band, which complicates matters considerably. As a Producer For-Hire, the scope of the job expands dramatically.

A great producer delivers a superior product efficiently and keeps the technology out of the way. For those of you who have come to this book as a Self-Producer, consider these next few chapters your primer, either to help you find the right producer in the future, or to help you make the transition to producer yourself. If you haven't worked with a producer before, or don't fully understand what the for-hire role entails, this chapter should prove enlightening and will even help you to better produce yourself.

The Producer For-Hire is enlisted for their ability and willingness to make the best record possible and is not relegated or restricted to recording at Home. Artists and bands who seek to make an organic record require a proper studio, and the budget to pay for it too. The Producer For-Hire will do whatever is necessary to produce the best record possible within the available and agreed-upon budget.

Producing is not purely a creative job. It's half organizational in nature. Good organization promotes exceptional creativity. There is nothing creative about making your singer wait during their moment of inspiration all because you weren't prepared. It is through organization that you make the technology invisible, and this allows both you and your artists to concentrate on delivering a great performance.

Let's face it: all but a handful of funded records are made outside the constraints of a budget. As the producer, you not only need to operate within that budget—it's the very mechanism that allows you to accomplish your goals in a timely manner. Staying on budget requires a modicum of efficiency and a willingness to stick to the basic structure of a plan.

Vision and leadership require creativity, but you can't lead if you're so unpredictable that no one can keep up. Making a record requires structure—just like music itself. One of your duties is to keep everyone comfortable and working together. And if you leave all logical convention behind, you'll stress out your artists and performers in the process.

Suppose you announced your intent to cut three songs a day in a commercial studio, and then you inexplicably abandon that plan to begin overdubs on the first song. Not only is your artist likely to revolt, they'll wonder what the hell is wrong with you. You're paying for a tracking room. You have a limited number of days in that tracking room. Why are you recording overdubs?

That said, there are times when momentarily abandoning a plan makes sense. If the horn section you intend to hire is leaving town, recording them a day early is a reasonable accommodation. If your artist just started playing the most amazing song you've ever heard, then there's a good argument to investigate it, no matter how far along you are in the process. As the producer, you must constantly weigh creative payoff against organizational discipline. But if your budget is tight, and you have no room for error, then that is the time to remain disciplined and focused.

Producing requires the ability to work politically to keep everyone on task without making the process so rigid, or so nebulous, that it stifles creativity. Believe me, that's a balancing act of epic proportions.

Overall, you have two main jobs as the producer: organization and leadership. These two jobs, however, break down to a number of specific roles. You operate as: Budget Manager, Time Manager, Personnel Manager, Product Manager, Arranger, Leader, and finally as the Creative Visionary. How you approach each of these roles will affect the quality of your output. Since the record that you make hinges entirely on the budget, we should probably start there.

Budget Manager in Chief

If you heed only one thing from this book, heed this: you cannot produce a project if you don't have complete control over the budget. Without that control, you can't possibly guarantee delivery at, or under, budget. To do so makes you the producer in name only. You have no power. You have no leverage. You have no control.

You also can't budget your time, which means you have no way to gauge where you're at in the process. If you don't control the money, you have no ability to plan your time. You are at the mercy of the person pulling the purse strings, and always in danger of failing to finish the project. Worse yet, you could be blamed for a failure that's someone else's doing. You never want to put yourself in that position.

Side-Players

Side-Players are musicians for hire. They were called side-men in more exclusionary times. They are not a part of a core group, and do not have a direct stake in the project. It's not uncommon to bring in Side-Players for horns, strings, percussion, and specialized instruments.

Side-Players can be rehearsed or arrive at the session unfamiliar with the music. This depends on how comfortable you and your players are with working on the fly. If the Side-Players are also the tracking band, then I prefer to rehearse them like a band entity, although they typically need to be paid for the rehearsal time too. Fair.

When working in the studio on lockout, scheduling Side-Players for overdubs requires coordination and preparation. You certainly don't want your players sitting for an hour because you got yourself into something unexpectedly time-consuming. You also don't want to twiddle your thumbs for an hour as you wait for your players to arrive. Poor planning can result in the interruption of a productive session or promote an unproductive one.

Budgeting Your Time at Home

When you operate out of a production room in your house, your overhead is fixed. You're paying for the space whether you're working or not. And ideally, you're charging for your services, not for your room—because services are worth far more than your time, space, or gear.

That said, charging by the project doesn't mean you can ignore how long things take. Time still matters. Whereas studio time costs force you to make the record in an allotted period, working from home removes that pressure. As such, how much time you spend on a project is far less important than your ability to free it up.

The longer a record takes to finish, the less bandwidth you have for others. If you don't complete projects in a timely manner, you could end up passing on work you might otherwise take. Which means you need to finish projects efficiently in order to stay available.

A record takes the time it takes—it's not done until it's right. And I'm not suggesting you put time ahead of quality. But that doesn't mean you don't have a strong incentive to stop fucking around and finish the record already—something I have to remind myself of all the time.

Budgeting for Studio Lockout

Some projects demand a full-scale recording facility. A commercial studio environment forces you to work on one project at a time, which requires a whole slew of strategies in order to operate efficiently.

When you rent a studio for several days (or more), you want to lock the studio out. A typical lockout restricts you to twelve hours of working time a day (sometimes ten), but the "lockout" means it's your room for a full 24 hours. You won't have others coming into the room behind you—nor would I recommend you ever accept such a scenario. Since you're paying for the room daily, you have to budget your time (how many days you need), along with the funds to pay for that time (how much those days will cost).

Before you ever walk into a studio, you need a budget that accounts for every possible expense for the totality of the project. This includes external hard drives, equipment and instrument rentals, outside engineers, rehearsal and preproduction space, tracking studio time, overdub studio time, Side-Players (outside musicians), food, hotels, airfare, per diems, mixing, mastering, and of course, your producer's fees. And while mastering and reproduction costs don't go into a major label recording budget, they certainly must be accounted for on an independently funded project.

Not all of these costs will apply. If you're mixing the record, there's no need to budget for an outside mixer. If you're overdubbing at home, you won't have room costs. That said, if the budget is somehow exceptionally large because you're producing a well-known branded artist, then surely you can charge for your mixing services and your room too, and you probably should. But most records are not that.

When estimating how much time you'll need in the studio, there are a lot of variables. First, if you're tracking a group of players, you need a facility with the space, equipment, and pricing that fits your budget. Then there's the endless array of questions to consider:

How tight is the group? Are they good players? Can they nail takes with minimal editing required? Do you envision working to a grid? Are you recording a singer who only needs a few takes—or one who needs to be hand-held line by line? If it's the latter, does it really make sense to record vocals in an expensive tracking room? How many songs are there? How involved are the arrangements? What are the runtimes of those songs?

A five-minute song takes significantly more time than one that's three and a half. Seven-minute songs are time sucks. Twelve-minute songs make you question your life choices.

Song length doesn't scale linearly with production time— it's exponential. You have to get through the first eight minutes just to reach the last four—repeatedly. That time adds up. Every 12-minute song I've ever mixed has taken days to finish.

You will need a rehearsal with the group in order to determine the answers to many of these questions. Rehearsals let you test how well the players take direction. If you're hiring Side-Players, the equation is simpler: pros generally work fast, have good tone, and don't require constant supervision. And if someone isn't up to snuff, they're replaceable. Bands, on the other hand, are fixed entities. One weak link can throw off the whole tracking timeline, and replacing that player isn't really a viable option.

Heavy-handed Gridiron editing also needs to be factored into your estimates. Editing a usable performance is far less efficient than capturing a great one. Taking tracks home to edit—or hiring someone else—is more economical than editing in the studio as your players wait. Sometimes you have no choice, but it's best avoided.

Editing is a far easier process on a click than off. The tempo restraints allow you to record using a take folder or playlists, so that you can easily switch between takes anywhere in the song. Where that fails, you can always harvest from other sections of the song.

When you're off click, you can't effectively use a playlist, and your takes are best recorded one after another in your session. Harvesting from other sections doesn't always work due to tempo fluctuations. Flex quantization becomes unviable, which means editing must be done without the benefit of a grid. This can be exceptionally time consuming. That said, it can be worthwhile to abandon the restraints if you really want to use tempo as a natural dynamic and if your drummer plays better without a click.

Recording off-click can produce an organic and raw product. Unfortunately, if the captures require extensive editing, you've lost the main advantage to working in this manner.

You can record to a click without having to completely abandon tempo dynamics. A tempo map created in advance allows you to manufacture changes in tempo without losing the benefit of the click. For example, you can map the click to 100 BPM in the verse with a jump to 102 BPM in the chorus. Of course, tempo-mapping requires some pre-planning and preparation.

Budgeting Your Tracking Time

How much you can spend daily on an outside studio has everything to do with the time you need to track. This is where estimations can get a bit tricky. I hesitate to offer you any hard values, because there really are none. Your time allotments depend on the abilities of your players, how much instrumentation you intend to keep from your tracking sessions, the density of the arrangements, the runtime of the songs, how raw or polished you intend the product, and the speed at which you work. Experience will make these calculations more accurate over time.

Some rock bands in the '90s only required a day per track to record the entire production. That's an exceptionally fast pace in the grand scheme of things. It also happens to be a good pace if you seek a raw product. Conversely, many early-'00s bands required days to record just one track in order to accommodate for heavy manipulation and polish in the DAW.

A highly polished product through technical manipulation takes time. A raw product is best achieved by restricting your allotted time. Your vision in this regard should be considered when budgeting your time.

When you plan to bring a band entity into the studio, rehearsals can help with your time estimations. It's a common strategy to record the entire band only to keep the drums. This can greatly reduce the time required for making takes, because the feel of the drums is the only consideration. That said, you still need the rest of the band there for vibe, cues, and context.

If you're hiring a band of Side-Players, your goal should be to keep everything. That's what you're paying for—the ability to lay down a keeper take as a unit.

For my part, if I'm aiming for a relatively polished product, I plan to capture ten basic tracks in a four-day session. That's true whether it's a band entity for purposes of a drum capture, or a group of Side-Players where I intend to keep everything. Of course, if the band has limited studio experience, more time may be required.

The first day in the studio is mostly setup, and I'm happy if I only capture one track on setup day. After that, I'm looking for an average of three beds per day (basic rhythm tracks: drums, bass, guitar, keys). That pace gives me three to four hours of time on each track. Some tracks require more time, others less— and it's not unusual to capture as many as five songs on the third day once we really get rolling. This puts us in very safe territory for completing ten songs in four days.

These time estimates do not account for all variables. I'm offering you the time estimates that align with how I work and the types of acts that I'm attracted to as a producer. I also won't go into the studio until I'm satisfied with the rehearsals. You need to factor in your realities and make your estimates accordingly.

If I plan to rework parts around the drums in overdubs, then I focus mostly on drum tones during tracking. I still want decent tones on everything else—good enough to inspire and serve the song—but I won't chase perfection on parts I know will need my attention later.

Record More Than You Need

Sometimes things don't go your way on every song in the studio, and if you're hired to produce an album or EP, you may want to protect yourself against this possibility. When you're cutting basic tracks in the studio, consider recording more tracks than you need.

It takes time and effort to set up to record a group of players in a studio, anywhere from just a few hours to six hours—even a day—depending on the complexity of the setup. As such, it can be far more efficient to record some extra basic tracks and put them away in case they're needed later. This strategy protects against another full setup day should a track become an issue down the line. You can record a well-rehearsed extra track in under an hour once you're fully set up. But to go into the studio again could require a full day.

This strategy is merely a matter of quality control. If you record six basic tracks for an EP of material, there's really nothing to prevent you from delivering six tracks, even if you're not entirely happy with one of them. But if one track is proving to be a problem and you have some alternatives available, then you can pivot to another track, and keep the overall quality of the album at a high level without altering the scope.

Should you find yourself in a bind, there are other options. COVID hit my tracking session with local Asheville band *Krave Amiko*, and I found myself a song short of my obligation as we began overdubs. Rather than to go through another full studio setup, we pivoted to another song—one that was well-suited for a more programmed approach. This also allowed me to put a trendier production on the album, which happened to serve the project well.

Recording an extra track or two can be a good strategy for your artists too. These days, artists must create constant content to keep their fans engaged. Many independent artists record EPs and singles rather than full albums, which allows them to maintain a constant flow of material. It's far more efficient to track five or six songs than it is three. Even if you only intend to finish the three for purposes of an EP, you can set your act up for their next EP. Of course, you'll want to include in the contract that any tracks you record are yours to finish. In order to ensure compliance, you should hold on to the sessions.

That said, major labels will insist that you give them everything you record, and won't generally negotiate that away, so you really need to consider just how many free basic tracks you want to provide a major label. There is no guarantee that you will be the one to finish those tracks once you lose control over them.

Sustenance

I almost always include food in the budget when operating in a studio lockout. It's worth it to set aside enough money to feed everyone two proper meals a day together. This ensures a higher quality diet and consistent blood sugar levels and prevents disparate and out-of-sync eating. It's better for everyone to come to the session fed, and to schedule a thirty-minute sit-down meal (or two) as a team, than to have people eating at various times throughout the session. Besides, there is nothing like the camaraderie of breaking bread together to help maintain good morale within the group. Eating together gives you time to socialize and connect with your entire team. It also allows them to perform at their peak.

On those occasions when things aren't going as smoothly as you'd like, think of dinner as one giant reset button.

Rentals

Depending on where you're located, you can often rent equipment and instruments that will help speed up the process. If you're working with a band, and they have suspect instruments, then you should consider renting some more appropriate equipment.

Whenever you look at possible tracking rooms for a project, you must also meet your musical gear requirements. If the project features a pianist, there's really no point in investigating studios that don't have a piano. You can always rent a piano in some locations if needed, but the delivery costs alone can be breathtaking. Once you have a list of rooms that meet your needs, you must weigh the costs against all other factors. Saving $100 a day in studio time makes little sense if the piano rental is $300 per day.

Recording facilities tend to carry a plethora of instruments these days, making rentals a less usual path. The equipment list can be an important consideration when choosing a studio. Quality instruments can easily save you half a day of unnecessary hassle while simultaneously improving your results. While there's no doubt that the player and the room are the biggest factor where quality of tone is concerned, the instrument itself is part of the source. Guitars with intonation problems will certainly cost you time. Of course, if the record calls for a ratty guitar tone with tuning issues, then you would be foolish to spend money renting a high-quality guitar. Find a ratty guitar. There's lots of them.

Networking for Gear and Talent

If rentals aren't readily available because of your location, and the local studio is short on instruments, then you need to do what I do in that situation—beg, borrow, and steal.

This is where networking comes in handy. If you build relationships with the musical people in your area, there isn't much gear you won't be able to find. Granted, you might not locate a specific and valuable piece—like a 1959 Les Paul. Even if you could, I'm not sure it's a good idea to borrow an insanely valuable guitar and put it in the hands of a sauced up punk rocker. I believe there are comparable and less costly instruments you could borrow for that situation. There are musicians everywhere in the world, which means there are fine instruments within your vicinity; you need only find them. The best way to do that is to network with anyone and everyone who likes to make music.

Local music stores are a good place to start. Not only will they have equipment that you may be able to borrow or rent, but the staff and owner will also likely know all the local musicians, engineers, and producers. They'll probably even know who owns a particular instrument in the area. Most local stores will also have a bulletin board for people to post flyers and business cards. Contact them all. Invite them to your production room if you have one. Or meet them for coffee. But get to know everyone in your local scene. You'll need them one day, and they will likely need you in return.

Local clubs are a good place to frequent, too. Especially if they book acts from out of the area. Live shows are a great way to make connections and can widen your networking scope significantly. This also happens to be a fabulous way to find talent, although some advance research on the Internet would probably be advisable. Of course, if you're so isolated that none of these suggestions are useful, I do wonder how you're supposed to operate as a Producer For-Hire in such a remote location. I suppose there's always the Internet.

It's staggering how many professional relationships I've made on the Internet. All that's required is a willingness to participate in audio boards, engage in discussions, and build relationships with people who also make music. If I find myself in need of some professional help while I'm in a less populated location (and it happens), I can put up a post on an audio forum and have the information I seek within an hour. There are millions of people involved in music all over the world. The Internet community should reduce your personal connections to one or two degrees of separation from just about anyone in this business.

I needed a tuba player once for a project I was producing in Asheville (before I moved here). A single post on the Internet garnered me three names in under an hour. Bam! I had a professional and wholly competent tuba player on my session before the end of the day. Granted, I'm well known in audio Internet circles, but then that's the point. Make yourself known, participate in the community, and you'll make all sorts of new and mutually useful connections.

If I need something big, I'll make a direct trade. Like a mix for some musician services. For smaller requests, the trade is implied. I mean, if you're going to borrow a fine instrument from a veritable stranger—or even a buddy, for that matter—then you should be prepared to do the same in return. Sometimes you don't get the opportunity to pay the favor back directly. We call that paying it forward. I borrow from some. Some borrow from me. All is well in the Universe.

Padding Your Budget

No matter how good you are at reading the tea leaves, you can still misjudge matters. You make your time estimations based on incomplete and imperfect information. The more information you can gather before you set foot in the studio, the more accurate your estimates will be. Regardless, you must leave yourself some wiggle room, and this is achieved by padding the budgeted time.

If you believe it will take a band three days to make 10 takes, you should budget for four days, if feasible. This may force you into a slightly less expensive tracking room. As long as you're meeting your acoustical needs where the recording is concerned, this compromise can save you from a difficult budgeting situation.

Some studios will allow you to book a fourth day as a pad, and then only charge you for what you use. This is especially true for producer-owned studios, since they have the flexibility to use the studio for their own work when it's not rented out. Other studios will have no interest in that kind of arrangement, because if you don't use the fourth day, they have no way to sell it.

Whatever you do, don't completely sacrifice your acoustical needs due to time and budget constraints. You're not doing yourself any favors by recording in an inadequately sized room.

Budgetary decisions must be weighed against the overall needs of the recording, and time is only one consideration. You need a room that matches the sound you seek. If the room costs are such that you can't reasonably record all the songs in the time allotted, then you may have to consider reducing the scope of the project. Since you're likely paid by the track, that could mean less money in your pocket. This reality can add a lot of pressure to your decisions.

You could also just trust your estimations, forget about a pad, and operate without a net. This might result in studio overages, which can cost more than a padded extra day. Perhaps that's a risk worth taking, but if extra hours are an impossibility, then you could very well force yourself into producing tracks that fall outside of your vision. I mean, if restraining your time is how you most effectively produce a raw product, then that principle holds true whether you do it on purpose or not. If your vision is for a polished product, operating without a time pad could push the productions to a place you weren't intending.

Many of you reading this book probably have a space of your own, and you might even have the space and equipment to successfully record drums. But are they the right drums? While your own room can certainly help with budget constraints, it shouldn't prevent you from renting outside studio time for the good of the project. If your recording space is inadequate for your vision, you should rent an outside room. When your budgetary compromises prevent you from making the record you envision, you're not doing your job as a producer. Not well, anyway.

To cut corners on a low-budget project can be a necessity, but you must execute those cuts in the places that don't affect the quality of your product. These budgetary compromises should be planned out rather than left to chance. Once you've determined you can't make the record you envision within the available budget, it's incumbent upon you to present this information to your client. Reducing the scope of the project is often your best solution.

Look, no matter how much you want to make a record, if you can't make the record you envision, then you're failing. What are you going to do? Put a disclaimer next to your name in the liner notes? "This album would have been exactly the way we intended it, had I just $3,000 more with which to make it."

I'm thinking not. For the listener, the record you put forward is the record you intended. There are no excuses available. So, if the budget is insufficient, then you need to propose the necessary budget, or alter the scope of the project to match the proposed budget. If that's not a possibility, you should pass on the project.

Let me repeat that. If you can't make the record you envision, you will waste your time by taking on the project. In all likelihood, nobody will be happy with the results. We will discuss vision and all that it entails a little further along in this chapter, but your vision isn't your own private little secret. You actually need to sell your artist on that vision. You have a vision, you've expressed this vision to your clients, and now you'll make decisions that prevent you from accomplishing it?

Now, if you think that you can take the gig and then just go over budget, that's a rather risky option, one that could result in money coming from your own pocket. If you're unwilling to negotiate your fees before you've begun the project, then why would you be willing to spend those fees on overages to complete the project later? And what happens if you're not willing to do that? That's not a situation you want to ever put yourself in.

There are many projects in which going over isn't an option—and the overages will undoubtedly come out of your fees. If you're in control of the budget and still go over, that's on you. And if it's somehow not your fault (and that can happen), then you can always attempt to renegotiate the terms. Just keep in mind, you can't increase a budget with money that doesn't exist in the first place.

There are also projects in which the client can clearly sustain overages should they occur. You'll usually know you need to go over budget well in advance, and you'll have some time to renegotiate terms. But I would highly advise against ever purposely taking on a project that's obviously inadequately funded. It puts too much pressure on you, the artist, and the project itself. The better strategy is to insist on reducing the scope of the project. This way, if things go well, and you record one or two extra basic tracks, the client has the option to expand the budget to include more songs. As the producer, you're the expert in how long things should take, and the further off the mark you are, the less competent you appear.

I'll show you how to build a project budget in the business chapter. For now, let's move forward.

Time Manager in Chief

You already know that time is a currency—and as the producer, you're the one who spends it. One of your most effective tools for keeping a project on schedule and under budget is how you leverage your day-to-day time management. On occasion you'll spend an inordinate amount of time on one track or even one part. Working out parts is to be expected. You can't reasonably shut down what could be a brilliant, game-changing idea just to keep to a rigid schedule. You must leave yourself time to be creative, otherwise what are you making? A widget?

Falling behind on a project is a given and can be a useful session tool as it tends to ratchet up pressure. It can also bring down morale, particularly if you get too far off track. Conversely, getting ahead relieves pressure, and allows everyone to relax. But then people can also become too relaxed.

Between the push of falling behind and the pull of getting ahead, you can improve the efficiency of your session. If you base your time-management decisions on this principle, you will know where you're at on your session in regard to your time. So will your team. If you allow yourself to fall way behind, you could be so focused on catching up that your decision-making suffers. Parts that deserve thoughtful attention might get sloughed off due to time pressure. Where it comes to producing, you should avoid sloughing off anything.

While you don't have total control over how things go on a session, you do have considerable influence. You should certainly have some idea of which tracks will be a breeze and which a struggle. Of course, you'll be totally wrong at times, but that will usually go both ways and will ultimately result in a wash. Simply put, if you're ahead, work on something that you believe will require time. If you're behind, knock out something easy.

There's a certain ebb and flow to the creative process and recording sessions in general. Twelve-hour days on a creative project will all but guarantee hours in which seemingly nothing is accomplished. This is a given, and such waste can't be eradicated from a recording session. In a full day's session, the most efficient work typically occurs after dinner. A slow start to the day is common, although many producers are their own worst enemy where this is concerned.

One of the more destructive habits you can get into is to work *more* than twelve hours, regardless of your client's wishes. Any hour of time you might gain at the end of the night will almost always be frittered away the next day. Worse yet, the more days you work on a given project, the more inefficient and exhausted everyone on the session becomes, especially if you work long days. Even when you're on hour fourteen and kicking ass, you'll pay for it the next day—both in morale and in studio overages. That said, there are occasions when it might be necessary.

Deciding when to cut off the session for the day is a judgment call—one that you will get wrong many times in your career. At least, you'll think you got it wrong when you find yourself in hour six with nothing accomplished, all because you didn't have the discipline to shut your session down at a reasonable time the night before.

Often, the solution is to start later, but that only works so many times before you've completely flipped everyone's schedule. Will you really be able to cut the session off at hour 10 when you lacked the discipline to leave at hour twelve the day before? Of course, that's probably what you *should* do, but that inefficient first six hours looms large toward the end of the day.

Personally, I don't like to work more than eight hours a day, ten at most. Honestly, I totally scoffed at the idea of an eight-hour session for most of my career. The idea was pure madness. The LA studios that I frequented often cost anywhere from $1500 to $2000 per day. I had to use all of the available time, whether it was efficient to do so or not. Nowadays, I rarely go over nine hours of tracking time in the studio, and I find eight-hour days considerably more efficient than twelve.

Just because your lockout gives you twelve hours doesn't mean you have to use it all. Where you lose on studio time, you gain in efficiency and the well-being and good feelings of your artists. All of that said, I certainly understand why you might want to use the full twelve hours available. That's what I did for most of my career.

Breaks are also useful for keeping a session on track. Given the nature of the creative process, calling breaks at regular intervals is a nearly impossible task. It's hard enough to work around dinner. Besides, the last thing you want to do when you're accomplishing good things is to call a break. Your group might have had another hour of efficiency in them!

We can't time our need for a break with anywhere near the same kind of accuracy as we can predict hunger. Given the challenges involved, full-team breaks are usually best for "re-set" purposes.

If your team is going strong, and you find yourself in need of a break, delegate the producer's role for a few minutes and take one. It's important that you get out of the room on occasion. For the most part, the band and the artist will have all sorts of down time. You need some yourself.

Be Flexible (Just Not Too Flexible)

As much as you must adhere to a budget, it's useless to be militant in your approach to time management. No one makes a list of songs and records them in that order. At least no one should. In fact, your management choices should generally be based on the team's overall state of mind. If your whole team is beat up from hours of working on aggressive tracks, finish the day on something mellow. If the band is up and inspired, pull out an energetic track—one they can nail in short order, especially if you're up against the end of the day. This can have the effect of sending everyone home on a high, which will often translate into an efficient start the next day. If everybody's totally stoned, pull out the stoner piece. If the singer is absolutely inspired to sing on a track, let them, even if you're still tracking the band. Give them two takes and call it a day.

If you haven't figured it out by now, let me just say it plainly: time management in record-making is about keeping the team in the right headspace. The goal is to make constant adjustments in order to keep the team and the project on track. "Win One for the Gipper" speeches as Motivator in Chief can help, but ultimately, the project itself must be the most motivating factor.

Countless hours of inefficiency have a debilitating effect and lower spirits. If you don't make the necessary calibrations, you risk feelings of concern and possibly despair from your artists. To date, you're recording the most important work of their career. This is how they see it, and so should you. As a result, slow progress can freak your team out. I can assure you; a freaked-out artist (or band entity) is a fabulous way to bring your session to a grinding halt.

People tend to get along when things are going great—and can become quite contentious when they're not. So, if you want to keep your session running smoothly, you must adjust course—if only to eradicate the relatively poor mood of your team.

Personnel Manager in Chief

As the producer, you're in charge of the entire team. This includes the musicians, engineers, and studio personnel involved on your session. That's right: you're the boss. But don't get a big head. The kind of boss you are will have great ramifications on how well your team works with you.

Assistants and/or Interns

When you're in an outside studio environment, you need help. Your assistant comes with the studio, should know where everything is, and is there to help facilitate a successful recording session.

If you treat your assistant like a second-class citizen, you could inspire them to work against you in the most insidious ways. Be exceptionally nice to your assistant—but don't be a pushover. They work for you. But they are also an important part of your team, and it's best to allow them to feel that way.

I rely heavily on a good assistant, but then I generally record my own sessions, which means I'm doing two jobs at once. I can't reasonably judge the performance of a take if I'm also checking levels. My assistant is therefore critical in watching my back on the engineering side of things.

When you find yourself in a situation where you're both the producer and the recordist because of budget constraints—especially if you're not actually a qualified recordist—it can be a good idea to delegate the engineering duties to your assistant. When you book a room for a tracking session, request an assistant who is a somewhat *bona fide* engineer, interested in credit. The studio manager will typically be more than happy to accommodate you, and the staff assistants will be ecstatic to act as recordist, particularly if they know they'll be credited for their work. Credits are valuable early in an assistant's career, since this is what allows them to make the transition to freelance recordist.

The most important attribute I look for in an assistant is vibe. There is nothing worse than attempting to record a project with an irritant in the room. Personally, I'd rather work with someone green with a great attitude who appears to be into the project, than a super-qualified assistant who annoys the shit out of me. The latter is cancerous to a session and will have an obvious negative impact on the work.

The longer someone has been an assistant, the more likely they are to bring a bad vibe to your session. Notice I said, "more likely." It's not always the case that a lifelong assistant will bring a bad vibe, and frankly, it's less true in smaller markets given the lack of opportunity. But if you find yourself with a surly longtime assistant, it's probably due to career frustration. You really only have two options. Bring them under your wing and involve them as a recordist. Or request someone else. Be forewarned: if you don't get some basic respect from your studio assistant or engineer, you must replace them.

If you're working in your own room and you don't have an assistant, then you can always take steps to get someone to help you. The local recording colleges are a good place to start. There are far too many recording graduates for the jobs available, and the competition is so steep that you can find help. The trade-off is that your assistant learns as they earn, but then don't we all?

Notice I said, "learns as they *earn*." I don't subscribe to interns or internships that aren't paid. People should never work for free. Not for exposure, not for experience, and not for purposes of learning. If someone is making your life easier, then as far as I'm concerned, that has value, and they should be paid.

Engineers / Recordists

I'm not fond of the term "engineer." Mostly because I find it insulting to both the person who's spent four years in college and the guy in charge of recording the coolest project ever. To find work as an "engineer," one needs a degree, and for good reason! Actual engineers can cause death with their decisions. You know, like the people who design bridges or build jet engines. All an audio engineer can kill is a record—that is, barring some bizarre studio accident or an A&R rep intent on murdering you (that's a story for another book). Personally, I prefer the term "recordist," although admittedly, I do use the term engineer too.

The job of recordist is largely a left-brain one. In simplistic terms, the left hemisphere of the brain is the analytical side, responsible for minutiae and detail. Conversely, the right hemisphere of your brain is responsible for evaluating the big picture. It's also where most of your creative thinking occurs. As a result, producing is largely a right-brain-dominant activity, or at least you want it to be.

Whereas the recordist is recording and capturing *sound*, the producer is recording and capturing *performances*. Sound and performance are inextricably attached, but evaluating sound requires attention to technology, and evaluating performance requires attention to musicality and feelings.

It's impossible to concentrate on the details and the big picture at the same time. If you're focused on the details, you're metaphorically zoomed in. If you're focused on the big picture, you're metaphorically zoomed out.

I usually operate as producer and recordist concurrently, and for many years, I felt as though one of those jobs was suffering at all times. If I was in my producer's brain, the recording was suffering. If I was in my recordist's brain the producing was suffering. And it's not easy to switch back and forth.

I've found the best way to combat the problem is to simply camp out in my producer's brain. I no longer separate sound and performance, they are one and the same to me. As such, the fix is almost always performance related which makes life a lot easier because I'm no longer distracted by technical fixes.

That's not to say there isn't a time to focus on the technicalities of capturing sound. Surely there is. And the instrument and the room you're in are a part of the capture. But once I've adequately pulled tones, subsequent problems that arise with sound are dealt with for what they are—performance issues. Rather than to constantly slip into my recordist brain to fix a problem through technical means, I stay in my producer's brain and approach all problems from the performance and musical side of the equation.

I've operated for many years as a dedicated recordist, so that part of it is almost second nature to me. I have immense trust in myself where it comes to my capture. As such, I don't make many recording mistakes, and my assistant is there to prevent any slip ups. Even so, I can assure you that when you start with good tones, they don't just magically fall apart on their own. Unless a mic has moved or the source has been compromised, sound issues are almost always the result of a performance issue.

Many things can cause performance issues—a poor monitor mix, the tempo, the excitement of making a take, exhaustion, hunger, being altered, and so on. You can resolve a performance issue in any number of ways, which might even include an engineering solution, but the key is to identify the root of the problem first.

If you have limited experience as a recordist, then anything more than a one mic capture can be daunting. Fraught too. So, if you have room in the budget for a competent recordist, that is always best. Ten years ago, it was unheard of for a record to be produced without a recordist. Now it seems to be the opposite of that.

A quality recordist, separate from your assistant, will make your life easier, particularly if you don't have a tremendous amount of experience in the studio. Your recordist can be your most valuable commodity on a session since they can cover much of the left-brained thinking as you stay camped out comfortably in your right hemisphere. Unfortunately, not all recordists grasp the producer–engineer relationship. Therefore, you need to choose carefully and spell out your expectations clearly before you set foot in the studio.

How you approach these sorts of conversations is obviously up to you and depends on your personality. But setting up certain boundaries will save you awkward and problematic situations on your session. These are the expectations that you might consider relaying before your first session with a recordist.

If I'm trying to sway my act, then either back me up or abstain from offering an opinion.

Some producers like constant opinions. Others prefer that the recordist do as they're told and shut up. While I don't mind consultation if I'm struggling, I certainly don't prefer to debate ideas with my recordist, especially if I have a clear vision for what I wish to achieve. It can be a problem when you have a recordist who is on a different page from you.

Whatever you do, never allow your recordist to become the go-to de facto tie-breaking vote against your favor with the team. That will make your job impossible. If you give your recordist an equal say to the band, or if your recordist begins to align with a band or artist against you, this will prove catastrophic to your session and your sanity. Don't let that happen. Making a record isn't a democratic process when you're the one with the vision. Not only should this be expressed to your recordist before you start your session, if your recordist begins to weigh in against you, then you need to have a conversation with them immediately (away from the team) in order to reset the protocol.

Watch my back.

At any given time on a session, you could have 20 things on your mind. Screw ups happen, especially early in your career, but you should do all that you can to minimize them. It's up to you and your team to work together to accomplish that. If you somehow forget to record an overdub on an internal chorus, it's the job of your recordist to catch that before you move on. Under normal circumstances, this shouldn't happen at all, but if you're working against the clock, or if it's late at night, shit happens. Not only will such a mistake make you look incompetent and unprofessional, it will also cost you valuable time.

I'm reluctant to name the countless stupid errors I've made in my career, not that I could. We all make mistakes. Everyone. Most of my missteps have translated into lessons, and it's the lessons that I remember at this point, more so than the specific errors. Many times, a lesson isn't fully learned until you repeat the mistake, maybe multiple times, which is maddening. *This time will be different*, you might think to yourself, and on occasion that's true. When it's not, you'll have solidified the lesson.

The process of producing an artist's record is a team effort, and the team must work together to prevent mistakes. Yes, you want your recordist to watch your back, but you also need to watch theirs. Given that record-making is a creative process, it can be slightly lax at times, and that's when slip-ups happen. The trick is to keep up the illusion of a relaxed atmosphere as you pay constant attention to everything that's going on around you. But you can't be the only one. Everyone needs to participate in this, particularly your recordist.

I don't want you to think for even a moment that hiring an outside recordist for your session is a risky proposition. It's not, especially if you get some recommendations. But I promise you, there are people in this world who will somehow, for some reason, go out of their way to make your life more difficult.

I've developed Protect Systems upon Protect Systems throughout my nearly four decades of making records. All of those systems are designed to prevent repeat episodes of ineptitude and chicanery that should have never happened in the first place. I never want such jaw-droppingly absurd episodes to ever happen again, and hence the Protect Systems.

You might read some of this and wonder how often I've gone through hell with a recordist or assistant, and all I can say is, shit happens and some of it you may need to experience for yourself in order to even fathom it. I just want you to be aware of all the worst case scenarios so that you can nip it in the bud the moment it happens to you.

Any time anyone attempts to usurp your power as a producer for any reason in any situation, whether they're testing you because you're green, or because they have no respect for you, or because they're jealous of you, or even if they're just a clueless little git, you have every right to immediately remove that person from your periphery. I'm here to tell you that you should. Sometimes, it's to your advantage to be intolerant to the nonsense, because it lets everyone on your session know that you'll be the sweetest person on earth until someone who works for you decides to eff around and find out. And now back to our regularly scheduled program.

Document, document, document.

There will be times when you'll want to revisit a part or match a particular sound. When I recorded Ben Harper's *Burn to Shine* album, he had 100 guitars and 20 amps available for the recordings. That album took six months to make—go figure. Consider that even as few as five guitars and five amps allows for 25 possible combinations. Add to that equation mics, mic preamps, compressors, pickup choices, amplifiers, pedals, tone settings, etc., and it becomes nearly impossible to return to a particular tone without documentation. If you think that you'll need to return to something, then you'll want your assistant to document the entire chain, starting with the source. This way you can get back to it later. At the very least, include the guitar/amp combo in the filename.

You only need to experience the "matching tones" game once before you decide that this is something to avoid. It's easy enough to figure out which snare you're using out of five, it's far more difficult to determine the guitar/amp combo. Sure, you can just re-record a part, assuming it was a breeze to lay down in the first place, but the new tone (and certainly the new performance) could very well be second-guessed for the remainder of your session and beyond. There's nothing worse than that nagging feeling that your track isn't as good as it would have been. To make matters worse, it's a negative thought that festers and spreads to others. No matter how preposterous or irrational that might be, this is a mindfuck of epic proportions.

Of course, only the analog gear really ever needs to be documented. Amp sims settings certainly don't need to be written down. The computer retains those, greatly enhancing your speed. This is one reason I prefer recording with Amp Sims over analog amps these days.

Not all projects are candidates for extensive documentation. In fact, there could be times when documenting is prohibitive due to time and budget restraints. One of the most important purposes of a budget is to force restraint, and sometimes that means working in a way that prevents any second-guessing. You pull the tone, record the part, then move on. That's a perfectly legitimate way to work.

It's not a bad idea to keep a pad and pen near you (or your favorite device) so as to notate your thoughts or preferences throughout the session. You can take pictures too.

Never send a player or singer into the room to perform before we're ready to start recording. If you need some time to get tones, let me know, so that I can prevent people from becoming frustrated.

I'd rather have a killer take with less-than-optimum recording quality than to allow a performer to rot in front of the mic because we were unprepared. If you or your recordist sends the artist to the mic only for them to wait as you all get your act together in the control room, you risk frustrating them. I promise you, of all the emotions that can be used for an effective performance, frustration is rarely one of them. On those occasions when frustration is called for, you now know exactly how to achieve it.

To send a performer into the room before you're ready to record them is often an error in judgment that could reduce the likelihood that you'll capture a magical take from your artist. At least at that moment. It's best to make all the necessary preparations before a performer enters the room: make sure the headphones are working; blaring headphones scattered throughout the room are unplugged; mics are ready and scratched out (on large sessions with many mics in close proximity the assistant literally scratches the mics so you can be certain which mic you're hearing); water (or tea) is available in the recording room; pencils are on music stands, etc. When your recordist needs some time to get tones, be sure to let your talent know this in advance.

I often request the performer's patience as I pull tones and usually treat the setup as a separate process. There's the time that we get tones. And then there's the time that we make takes. There's usually a break between the two. The recordist needs to pull tones as quickly as possible but take as much time as is reasonably necessary.

Frankly, I prefer to have the mic and the singer in the same room with me. This means I usually must listen through head-phones, which isn't optimal, but I far prefer the ability to directly communicate with the artist in an interactive manner over dealing with talkback. Besides, control rooms are generally great sounding vocal recording rooms too.

You work for me.

You should be wary of ambitious recordists. If your potential recordist tells you that they too are a "producer," you might want to extend the interview and make sure they really under-stand your expectations and boundaries. If they seem to have an undesirable attitude, look elsewhere. That said, a recordist who understands producing and is willing to stay out of your way is a huge asset to your session. But when a potential recordist vol-unteers that they are a producer and doesn't follow that up with how their experience as a producer will benefit you, be wary.

Frankly, if you lack studio experience, it might be worth-while to hire a veteran recordist if you can. Or find a studio where a veteran recordist resides. People who have made a ca-reer of recording tend to know how to operate with a producer. You don't have to shy away from hiring someone who knows more about record-making than you do. This can be beneficial to your session, and a veteran can keep your session on track in an invisible manner.

Just as you want your recordist to respect your role as producer, that's a two-way street. Let your recordist do their job. While all aspects of the recording are within your purview, the recordist is there to cover much of the left-brain minutiae. As such, the recording process choices are best left to them.

If you start to dictate the tools your recordist uses, you will completely throw them off. They work how they work. Not how you work. Should you find yourself unhappy with a particular tone, it's certainly fair to point that out, and even offer solutions. But if you hired a good recordist, you need only explain the problem and let them come up with the strategy to fix it.

I came into a session as the recordist about a week into the process. Drums had already been recorded, and they were set up for guitars. The producer—someone I'd worked with many times—insisted I keep the last recordist's setup. But they did nothing like I did. I was completely lost and had such a hard time adjusting to someone else's approach that the producer—recognizing his error—rescinded his order and insisted I set things up to my preferences. Once I did, the session went far more smoothly.

The more experienced you are as a producer in the studio, the less experience you need from your recordist. If you're lacking experience in the studio, you really want someone with a track record to help keep the process running smoothly. If you've made many records and understand the technical side, the vibe your recordist brings is of far more consequence to the session than their skills.

Musicians

Whether you're working with a band entity, or a group of Side-Players, you're in charge of the musicians. So long as you have some basic understanding of music, you shouldn't have any problems leading them. Where things start to get a bit fuzzy is when one or the other of you is unfamiliar with basic musical lingo. I've worked with producers who have little-to-no musical knowledge other than what they like and dislike. This always makes for an interesting, if not amusing, session. Equally amusing are those sessions with a musically illiterate band member. A thesaurus might be your best weapon. That's because other than specific musical references, bizarre adjectives become the only viable way to convey a musical concept. Get used to it.

Musical literacy has little to do with one's quality of musicianship. There are plenty of great players (and producers) with absolutely no grounding in any kind of music theory whatsoever. They operate by ear and feeling alone and are free from musical rules beyond their own innate recognition of them. At times, that can be a disaster. Other times it can prove both refreshing and beneficial to the session.

Even when dealing with knowledgeable musicians, feeling adjectives are the best way to get across a concept. If a guitar player is too precise on a raw rock track, I might suggest that they take off their "red velvet jacket" and start to play with some "reckless abandon." If the bass player is a bit "herky-jerky" on the groove, I might recommend a "smoother" line. If the singer is uncompelling, I might tell them, "Sing it like you mean it." I might also remind them that we need a *performance*.

Concrete examples are an exceptionally good way to communicate. I produced an album many years ago where I spent an hour recording a guitar solo, to no avail. At least it felt like an hour. Whatever it was, it was far too much time to invest without intervening. The problem is, I didn't have a solution myself. Sometimes producing isn't about knowing exactly what you want at a given moment. Sometimes it's about waiting to hear what you want. Of course, you can only wait so long before you bring undue stress into your session.

Before pulling the plug on a struggling musician, you should consider the consequences. Whether you pull it early or late, either choice can frustrate a player. In the case of my guitar soloist who was now wondering why he was playing this solo so many times, I probably should have stepped in earlier. My hope was that he would hit on something by accident—some theme that we could build upon. I would much rather wait for an accident and build upon it than to spoon-feed a part to a competent player. Unfortunately, after many takes of solo wankdom, we really didn't even have a worthwhile musical phrase.

In this case, we were recording a track that had been completely reworked in preproduction. The track was originally a rather mundane country/folk song. For purposes of a richer production, and to accentuate the band's rather eclectic ways, I introduced some disco and ska elements to the production. Regardless of what you might think of that concept in the abstract, the guitar player had no clue what to play on this rather new interpretation of the song. Truth is, I was equally befuddled. Perhaps that was the reason why I didn't interject earlier.

With a guitarist just moments away from suggesting we cut the solo (okay, okay, maybe I did let him go too long!), I had several options. I could move on and revisit the solo later. I could write a solo myself, which could take even longer since I'm not a guitar player. Or I could give him a concept that might inspire him. I chose the third option.

"You know the solo on Michael Jackson's 'Beat It'? The one that was played by Eddie Van Halen, and that is so outside the scope of the production itself it's almost comical, yet somehow works? Give me something like that."

He chuckled at the suggestion, not because he thought it was ridiculous, but rather because he somehow understood it. How do I know that? He played the perfect solo in one take, and frankly it was nothing like the Eddie Van Halen solo. My example pulled him outside of the box that was constraining him (and me). Before that, he was still stuck on his approach to the original demo. A single, simple suggestion, based on something concrete and well known, can immediately break down communication barriers.

Now, I purposely didn't play "Beat It" for him. I didn't want him to play a solo like Van Halen's, not that he could. What I wanted was for him to draw from the feeling he *remembered* from that solo. Feelings are powerful, as is our memory of them, and even the most illiterate musician will understand this. In this case I wasn't dealing with an illiterate musician. Far from it. But too often we try to communicate in specific theoretical terms, and sometimes all that crap needs to be tossed aside as we engage in feel-speak.

Had the guitarist continued to struggle, I might have considered other examples, or I might have played him the Michael Jackson track. There are no guarantees that a proposed solution will magically work. This just happens to be a nice little success story that I can share with you.

I guess the lesson here is to avoid frustrating a player with a complete lack-of-direction. You'll destroy the morale of your musicians and artist. They look to you for guidance when they struggle, just as you should look to them for guidance when you're at a loss. At some point, however, you need to be willing to come up with a concept—preferably one that inspires the right performance.

Union Musicians

There will be times when it will be necessary to pay your Side-Players through the American Federation of Musicians. It is a requirement of major label sessions. There are different scales for musicians, depending on the type and purpose of the session, but they are far too numerous to list here. Besides, the Union will be more than happy to supply you with that information on behalf of their members.

Union sessions are structured in three-hour intervals. If you go over 3 hours—even by a minute—you owe another full block.

Some musicians command multiples of scale, depending on their demand. Typically, the best musicians in Los Angeles get triple scale for sessions, and that can amount to nearly $1,500 per three-hour session. Other markets with mostly single scale players will be considerably kinder to your budget.

You also have to pay one of your session musicians "Leader" scale. If you hire an ensemble of string players, for instance, you must designate one of them as "Leader," and they will be paid double scale at a minimum. Oftentimes, the leader will put together the group of players for you, so this is a worthwhile extra expense. You can also hire your leader for scoring assistance, and if you need a plethora of string players, regardless of scale, you'd better have a score. Sectional string players in general aren't great at winging it. Your results will likely suffer without a score. You've been warned.

You can mock up your string parts using MIDI and make charts with scoring software. You can also hire someone to write the arrangement for you. You might be inclined to score your own parts for a quartet, and you should, but there are many musical rules involved in four-part harmonies (called voice leading), and you may not want to leave that to chance. Try it for yourself as a mockup, but if you struggle, seek help before you pay out an exorbitant portion of your budget to a union section.

Horn players, particularly those who typically perform rock, pop, or funk, are often able to play by ear, and if that's the case you can get away with bagging the score, but your session will take much longer than it would with charts. You'll have to listen carefully for rubs, but a good horn section will naturally stick to the voice-leading rules. The parts will likely be simple and not all that inventive in nature.

Frankly, if you want kick-ass horn parts, you'd do well to arrange them in advance. The good news is, modern sample libraries can generate remarkably realistic horn sections, giving you a solid idea of what works before you ever set foot in the studio.

Paying for musicians through the Union is usually more expensive than negotiating outside of that structure. Even union musicians will work for less than scale on certain projects, and there's a low budget record scale that exists. Regardless, if you produce a record for a movie or a major label, you will be required to adhere strictly to the union pay structures. Frankly, that's good for our business. People need to be paid.

If you're making a local record outside of the major music markets of Los Angeles, New York, or Nashville, then you likely won't deal with a union. That means you can negotiate any rate you want based on your budget. But if your project is ever picked up by a major label, the Side-Players that you hired will likely get paid again through the Union.

Editors

Editing organically recorded tracks can make or break the feel of an album, especially drums. It can also be an exceptionally time-consuming job. An aggressive edit job on organic drums, performed by hand (as opposed to through flex quantization) can take hours for a single track. Frankly, it doesn't make much sense to bring your tracking session to a grinding halt to edit drums. For starters, a tracking room serves as a grossly overpriced editing suite, and you risk deflated musicians if you use it as such. You can either edit after tracking is complete, in which case you want to be very sure that you've captured everything that you need for a take, or you can hire someone to edit as you continue to track.

If you choose to edit the drums after your tracking session is complete, you would be wise to make a rough cut by section, so that you can be certain you've captured what you need. Of course, not all recordings require editing. Great players don't generally need editing, beyond perhaps cutting together large sections between takes. And if you seek an especially raw product, editing your tracks would tend to work counter to the goal.

When I operated as a recordist on mega budget albums in the early aughts, it was common for us to have an editor on the session. They typically operated out of a production suite somewhere in the complex. This allowed the producer to continue the recording process in the tracking room, as basic tracks were edited down the hall.

Every kid who goes to recording school knows how to edit. Not only is it the easiest job to learn, it's also the safest job to perform due to its nondestructive nature. Given this, finding a good editor should be neither difficult nor expensive. The tricky part is finding someone who is both musical and able to follow direction.

Editing strictly to grid removes much of the decision-making, so even a relatively green editor can handle it. If the goal is to leave the "good" time discrepancies intact, you need to find someone who is not only skilled at editing by ear, but also able to make those kinds of judgment calls on your behalf. You may want to make sure that you've established a protocol with your editor before releasing them to make subjective decisions for you. Once they understand your preferences, they should be able to work on their own without constant monitoring.

A highly experienced professional editor should be able to quickly adjust to your preferences on a per track basis. There should be no need for hours of handholding. Frankly, fifteen minutes of your time should be adequate. Besides, whether your editor errs on the side of aggressive or conservative, it's quite easy for them to make the necessary adjustments upon receiving your feedback. If your project requires significant editing, or if you have a budget that can afford it, you are well advised to hire a designated editor. If not, your assistant should be able to help. Or you can do it yourself.

I'm not trying to downplay the importance of a good editor here, but it's not a destructive process. Certainly, it doesn't do you much good if your half-priced editor takes 4 hours to do a two-hour job. Nor does it make much sense to hire an editor who can't get the job done right the first time. If your project will likely require heavy editing, it's best to find someone who can do the job both quickly and properly. This is true regardless of the budget.

Third-Party Mixers

If your experience mixing is limited, you may wish to seek out a third-party mixer—preferably someone with a verifiable discography. Mixing is a highly specialized position, and it's a skill set that takes thousands of hours and many completed projects across a wide range of genres to master. Mixing well also requires a highly accurate monitoring environment. None of that prevents you as a producer from mixing your own productions, especially if you're a Songwriter Producer, given the speculative nature of your work.

If you've never sent a production to a mixer, this can be a somewhat daunting prospect, so we should first address expectations. Let me start by explaining my process as a third-party mixer to alleviate any stress in this regard.

I will generally spend between six to eight hours mixing your production. By the time I make my initial bounce of your mix, I'll know every nuance of the track. I'll know what parts come in where and why. I'll underdub (remove or mute) parts that aren't serving the production. I'll maximize the payoff through my balance decisions. I'll automate the parts so that the balances can help to push the listener forward through the song. I'll be able to explain every arrangement decision and every pan decision. I'll recognize where you may have gotten confused along the way and will have addressed those sorts of issues.

All of this will be based, not just on what I think is best, but on what you reveal to me through your tracks. Your decisions in recording the track will dictate my decisions in the mix. My goal throughout the process will be to maximize impact in order to cause a reaction from myself, so as to trigger that same reaction from you and ultimately the listener.

After the initial bounce, we will go through a notes process in which you tell me the issues you're having with the mix. I'll listen to you, share my thoughts and offer you my perspective, and then I will implement your first set of notes. We will go back and forth once or twice like this, which can include a negotiation and sometimes pushback from me, because I'm not there just to do what you tell me. I'm there to provide my expertise, my consultation, and ultimately a great mix.

Ideally, by the time we're through the second or third round of notes, I won't even be able to get through the song because I'll keep losing my focus as it causes me to react. Same with you.

Now, I can't speak for others. There are lots of ways to work. Some engineers will work hourly and allow you to direct the process throughout. While that may work for certain projects, that's not how mixers typically operate—and certainly not how any mixer I know works. Mixers are hired to deliver a mix that leverages their sensibilities and taste. In other words, mixers are paid for their work, not their time.

If you're the kind of producer who can't imagine hiring an expert with a strong point of view (which is entirely your prerogative), and you're simply looking for someone to execute your instructions, then you're probably not looking for a mixer. In that case, it would make far more sense to hire an engineer who works hourly and will follow your direction precisely. That's not how mixers typically operate.

It's also important to understand that the quality of my mix is wholly dependent on what you supply me. If your production really doesn't match your vision, then I won't match your vision either. The clarity of your vision will be apparent from the tracks that you provide me.

If you have total control over the production, then you should keep working it until it matches your vision before you send it to me as a mixer. If you're stuck with certain compromises due to circumstances beyond your control, or perhaps even a mistake on your part, then you should do all you can to fix the issues before you send it to me. Otherwise, you're just hoping and praying that I can do what you couldn't. Maybe I can, maybe I can't.

If you can't make it good, then don't go in with the expectation that I can make it great. I can surely help it. In some instances, I will indeed be able to make it great. But only if the necessary elements already inherently exist. If it's just broken? There's nothing I can do to fix it. Which is why I listen to the rough before I accept the job. My success is based on your success, and before I put my reputation and sanity on the line, I need to understand the job that I'm accepting.

Let's say, as an example, you recorded drums in an under-sized room, and you're unhappy with their tone. If you're stuck with those drums due to budget constraints, then you would do well to fix them to your liking before you start building upon them. The other option is to change your entire approach of the record to match the drums. But to build the rest of your production on a foundation that you find lacking is madness. Forget the notion that the problem can be fixed in the mix. That strategy merely leaves everything up to chance.

Now, if you make a production that does all that it should, and you send it to me as a mixer, then I'll be in a very good position to maximize its impact and to cause the listener a reaction. A great mix isn't about the sound. It's about the reaction it causes. We use sound to cause that reaction—but that largely comes down to the arrangement decisions.

If you send me a dance track, then I'll mix it in such a manner that it causes you to dance. I'll get that KIK drum thumping, and I'll get the internal rhythms such that I can't stop myself from moving. We use sound to make that happen, but the goal is still the reaction.

You want to receive a mix that causes you all the right reactions and feelings. If the mixer accomplishes that, you'll love the mix. If they don't, then you won't. It's that simple.

That's not to say you won't ask for changes that will improve the mix, especially if the arrangement is dense with parts. I expect more notes from larger productions with many parts. But once we're through the notes process, you should notice the reaction the mix causes you, not the minutiae of many tiny balance decisions.

There are some things that you can do as a producer to make the process easier for everyone involved. You can supply a rough mix that closely represents your vision. That can be very helpful to me as a mixer, especially if you're sending me the multitrack session files remotely.

Frankly, when sessions were attended, I preferred to avoid the rough until I had the track pumping. I didn't want my decisions to be influenced by it. I wanted to allow the track to unfold so that I could naturally discover how it best fit together. But the producer was also usually there to answer questions. These days I need to reference a rough just to be sure that I have all the right parts. So, be certain all the parts are in there.

As a mixer, I'm operating as an extension of you, the producer. A mix is really just the final presentation of the production, and as such, I need some modicum of control over that arrangement—at least until we get to the notes process. Believe it or not, people often add far too many parts and then struggle to let go of them. I have no loyalty to any individual element; my loyalty is to the production and the song doing all the right things. But that's exactly why hiring an outside mixer can be so valuable. It's far easier for me to underdub parts as a mixer than it is as a producer.

The easiest way for me to improve the arrangement, which then makes for a better mix, is to trim some of the fat. If a part doesn't have a clear purpose, if it's merely taking up space, then I'm likely to underdub it. That's what you want.

Now, if your vision is so clear that you know exactly what you want from the production and you have the capabilities and the monitoring to make that happen, then you should absolutely mix the track yourself. Mixing is just a process, and if you build the production and make your arrangement and processing decisions as you go, by the time you've finished adding parts, the mix should be close to done. Of course, if your monitoring is severely flawed, and most home monitoring environments are, then you really should consider hiring a mixer.

I would generally advise against sending me a list of conceptual instructions before a mix. Trust enough in yourself that you have made your intentions quite apparent in your tracks. Trust enough in me as your mixer to decipher your intentions. That said, if your expectations are completely out of whack with the reality, then this can be a difficult process for us both.

Attended sessions are somewhat unusual these days. I really don't even offer them other than for purposes of the Notes process. If you do happen to be present for the actual mixing process, then you need to give your mixer some space before you start second-guessing their decisions. They need the latitude to experiment with everything in ways you may have never even considered. This allows your mixer to find opportunities for lift and contrast, which can be powerfully beneficial to the track.

The far more common scenario these days is for your mixer to work remotely, in which case you will send your audio files to them through a file sharing service. There are certain protocols and conventions that you should follow in preparing your files for delivery, and they may vary slightly by mixer. I will offer you mine.

You've likely been listening to your mix with plugins on the channels, and you may even have plugins on the Stereo Output channel or the Master Fader. I don't want any of that processing or automation. I just want the raw audio files bounced out such that they all start at zero. This way, I can put them in a session in perfect alignment, and they all play as they should. Your mono files should be mono, your stereo files stereo, and there should be no processing and no effects on the tracks.

If you use the same DAW as I do, in my case Logic, then I'll probably ask you for the session itself. I will likely replace all of your processing with my own. It's really not any faster for me to start with your session than to start from scratch with my own. In some ways, working in your session is actually more of a pain. As such, many mixers may prefer you send them the bounced unprocessed audio files.

If you know for a fact that you want a part to sound a certain way, like if you want the Bridge to have a filtered vocal, then send the part processed as you hear it. The advantage to sending me a part exactly as you hear it is it will appear in the mix that way. The disadvantage is you remove alternative options from me. Of course, if a committed processing decision causes me problems, then I can always have a conversation with you about it. This is a communication medium, after all.

Science Experiments, which are sounds or parts that you've spent significant time designing, should be bounced out as you hear them in your session, including the processing, the panning, and the automation. There's no reason for you to think that I can do a better job recreating a Science Experiment during the mix phase. As a mixer it's best if I can work fast, and recreating your good work will slow me down significantly. I can't think of a single instance of a Science Experiment that I felt I could improve. As a mixer, I'm not here to remake (or even judge) your art. I'm here to help you evoke a reaction.

There are occasions when I might go way off the reservation in terms of what you might expect. But then, people often hire me specifically for my take. If you send me a rough, and I plan to diverge greatly from that vision, I'll usually have a conversation with you first, if only to warn you. But at the end of the day, if you don't like my treatment of a mix, I'll adjust the record to how you hear it as a producer, that is, until we get into silly season—where notes become excessive or arbitrary—at which point, you'll get pushback from me.

In most cases, mix Notes are somewhat minimal, although it really depends on the complexity of the arrangement. Occasionally, you could feel I completely missed the mark. In those cases, don't make a long list of specific notes. The problem is conceptual in nature, and that's what I need to address first and foremost. This requires a conversation, which will allow me the opportunity to rework the mix to better fit your vision. Once I do that, then a list of notes is very much appreciated.

My mixes are delivered mastered. That means they're already the appropriate loudness. By the time we're done the Notes process, the record is done, and I will deliver you a Final Mix, an Instrumental, and an *a cappella* of each song, all at the session sample rate and bit-depth, and all bounced through the mastering chain. I'll also deliver a 16-bit version of the Final mix for CD. Stems—which are 8 stereo submixes of your tracks used for sync licensing opportunities—can be made for an hourly charge. Once all the versions are complete, and the project has been released, I'll zip up your session(s) and send you links to them for you to download. This way, you maintain your backups.

Now, that's how I approach mixing. Most of these protocols are common, possibly even standard, but other professionals might diverge slightly and could have their own systems and policies. Certainly, not all mixers deliver mastered mixes. Other mixers might master the mix after the Notes process is complete. But this should give you a good idea of what you can expect from a *bona fide* third-party mixer.

Choosing a Mixer

Choosing a mixer can be difficult. How do you pick? You could look at the liner notes of your favorite records. You could ask around. You could search the Internet. But ultimately, once you have a list of mixers, you have to choose one.

Some of you might decide the best way to find your mixer is through a shootout—a mini-competition in which you are the judge. I've participated in shootouts over the years as a mixer. I no longer engage in them, despite a pretty solid record of winning. I've been mixing too long, and my discography is far too extensive to compete in that manner.

If you don't want to work for free, and you'd rather not have to prove yourself repeatedly, then you should have the same respect for the time of other professionals. You charge for your work. Pay others for theirs. That just seems reasonable to me.

Developing a rapport with a mixer is a process. My first mix with you won't account for your preferences. But the more mixes I do for you, the more each one will naturally reflect your personal tendencies—especially when it comes to balance relationships. Some people prefer their harmonies 3 dB down from the lead. Others want them nearly even. While those decisions may differ between songs, most producers gravitate toward a certain consistency.

I've been told a mix of mine was "way off the mark," only to perfect it with one tiny change in balance. As it turned out, the difference between a ruined mix and the perfect one was a 2 dB reduction of the harmonies. That's how significant balance preferences can be.

I suppose the best way to choose a mixer is to have a conversation. That gives them a chance to explain how they work and offer insight into how they'd approach your track. Of course, that means they'll need to hear your roughs first.

If a mixer doesn't ask for your roughs and simply quotes you a price, that's a red flag. Be wary. They aren't protecting themselves—and they're certainly not protecting you. They're just trying to fill their time.

It's also impossible to accurately price out a project without hearing the roughs. Songs with long runtimes and high track counts take more of my time, and that affects the rate. There was a time when the price of a mix was high enough that those parameters didn't matter. But today, time is absolutely a consideration.

Many inexpensive mixers—the kind you'll find on freelance platforms like Fiverr—see mixing as a process, not an art. Processing sound is part of mixing, sure, but the goal of a great mixer is to cause a reaction, not just clean up your track. That takes time, commitment, and a willingness to address the arrangement.

You want someone who charges by the mix. If the price seems too low, there's a reason: they don't intend to spend the time your mix requires. You also want someone with a discography that includes known records. That's your best strategy—because a real discography and longevity in the business likely means they know what they're doing. That said, a high rate is no guarantee of quality either.

Mastering Engineers

Theoretically (and traditionally), the Mastering Engineer's sole job is to prepare the client's finished record for its intended delivery medium—whether that's vinyl, CD, or streaming. All delivery mediums have parameters that must be adhered to for proper reproduction. A 12-inch vinyl record has a maximum run time of around 30 minutes and an optimal run time closer to 15; a playback speed of 33 or 45 RPM; and a limitation on the amount of low- and high-frequency information that can be reproduced based on the length of each side.

A CD has a maximum run time of about 72 minutes, with a bit-depth of 16 bits, a sampling rate of 44.1 kHz, and a maximum level of 0 dBFS. The Mastering Engineer (ME) accepts your record in whatever form you deliver it—tape, reference CD, WAV file—and then creates a master that conforms to the specifications and limitations of the destination format.

The ME also attempts to maximize the impact of your mix through the use of a processing chain. That chain can include EQs, compressors, clippers, faux tape-saturation devices, and brickwall limiters. All of that may sound fine, but at some point, maximizing *impact* was confused with maximizing *level*. There was a time when the credo of a well-regarded Mastering Engineer was "do no harm." That noble sentiment has since been replaced with a "take no prisoners" mantra of war. More specifically, the loudness war. Although at this point, it's more of a standoff.

Loudness is the apparent level at which a record plays through a consumer playback system relative to other records. Loudness began as a way to get a perceived advantage. The thinking was, if your CD played back louder than other CDs in your player's carousel, then people would more readily take notice. Today, most records are streamed, and the streaming platforms apply normalization so that everything plays back at a similar level.

Streaming normalization is merely the application of gain— more often than not, negative gain. Basically, the loudest records are gained down in level by the streaming service so that the consumer doesn't have to constantly adjust their volume. Negative gain doesn't affect the sound of your record in any way.

The problem is, many producers choose to turn off the normalization from their streaming services and then feel less-than about their record compared to much louder records. This pressures the shamed producer to maximize the loudness of their records, prompting others to follow suit, to the point that loudness becomes the goal. Meanwhile, music fans are oblivious to the variance in level between tracks because the large majority of them listen with the default normalization *on*.

The argument by producers for turning off normalization is to hear the record as it was artistically intended. But the negative gain applied by streaming sites doesn't change the intention or the sound in any way. It has only one purpose. To improve the listening experience for the consumer, because nobody wants to constantly adjust their volume (other than people who make music, apparently). The large majority of consumers have no idea how loud one record is compared to another.

Loudness certainly matters, just not for competitive edge. The purpose of loudness is to reduce the dynamic range of your track so as to help your record translate better in noisy environments. If your chorus explodes in level, that's a dynamic that can prove exciting in the quiet of a studio. We love that. The problem is, when you bring the mix to a noisy environment (like the car), you could find yourself losing the verse in the din. If you turn up the verse so that it's audible, the chorus could very well tear your head off. Loudness evens this dynamic out so that your record will translate better in noisy environments. In other words, loudness has mostly to do with how your record is perceived over the course of the entire record.

The current preferred method to measure loudness is called LUFS (Loudness Units Full Scale). Most of the streaming sites recommend you submit your record at -14 LUFS (-16 LUFS on Apple Music). A -14 LUFS record is not especially loud, and most producers reject that recommendation. Certainly, the major labels reject it. In fact, many mixers do too.

If you hire an ME, then you either hire them for their ability to achieve exceptionally loud masters regardless of the sonic consequences, or you hire them for their taste. There is no taste required to make a record as loud as possible, and if that's what you desire, then you should hire an ME who is adept at such things. If you want the appropriate loudness for the record at hand, then you should seek someone whose philosophy on loudness matches your own.

There was a time when mastering was somewhat specialized in nature. Not only did MEs have their own set of specific tools, often located in an analog rack, they also required super accurate monitoring environments. For most of my career, I sent my mixes to an outside mastering engineer.

A great ME made my mixes better. I was delivering 2 mixes a day, often in a new room every week, and the ME could touch up my mixes with some corrective EQ for continuity, and a brickwall limiter for purposes of some loudness. This allowed me to focus my attention on causing a reaction, leaving the ME to fine tune how it will play back in the outside world.

There are many Mastering Engineers who will deliver excessively loud masters by default. As one somewhat well-known ME told me—when I asked why he would make my mixes on a Blues album so unusually loud, he replied—"because if I don't it will come back!" This is a buddy of mine, so I respect his position, but it was at this point that I decided to start mastering my own mixes. Many mixers now master their own mixes since we have the processors necessary to deliver a fully realized master.

As I already pointed out, when I deliver a mix, it has essentially already gone through the mastering process. It's ready to go. Since brickwall limiters don't layer well, a Mastering Engineer would be hard-pressed to apply another limiter. Frankly, any competent Mastering Engineer would quickly recognize they really have to run my mix flat (without any processing whatsoever). There's nothing they could do without clearly damaging it.

The problem with aggressive limiting on a bounced 2-track mix is it alters the balances. Rather than to have an ME slam my mix with a brickwall limiter, which would skew my preferred balances, it makes more sense for me to slam it myself and then integrate my balances to the limiter. The process is the same. I mix the record as I've always done. But once the mix is close, I add my mastering chain, including the brickwall limiter for loudness. It then takes about ten minutes (if that) to rebalance the parts.

What I find strange–and I've never really been able to figure out why—my mix can sound perfectly balanced and go out of whack once I apply the limiting. But once I adjust the mix to the limiter, I can bypass it without any negative repercussions. Surely the balances have changed on the unlimited version of the mix, but I don't seem to mind them.

I can all but predict my vocals will be at least 1 dB too loud once I apply a brickwall limiter. You would think I'd automatically adjust for that as I mix. I certainly compensated for what tape did. I suppose I just require hearing the vocals at a certain level as I mix, even if I know I'll have to lower them once I apply a brickwall limiter.

For many years, both online and in my books, I recommended that mixers mix through a 2-bus compressor. Not only did the 2-bus compressor make mixing easier, but it also protected the balances from an ME who might be inclined to apply a compressor. Of course, that didn't stop some MEs from trying it, and it really pissed me off when they did. My mixes rarely needed additional compression (still don't), and any ME who added a compressor to my mix obviously wasn't listening. They had a process and stuck with it regardless of what was sent to them. This is why I always steered the producer and label towards my preferred MEs.

I suppose that's just a long way of saying, if your third-party mixer recommends a specific Mastering Engineer, then you should hire that person to do it. And if they master their own mixes, then you won't need to hire a separate Mastering Engineer.

Product Manager in Chief

As the producer, it's up to you to guide your artist toward their most effective songs. If your artist doesn't have any songs (which makes them a performer) then your job is to find a suitable collection for them—whether that means poring through publishing company catalogs or writing them yourself with the artist. These days, an artist in need of songs will almost always seek a Songwriter Producer.

When working with an artist with their own songs, your first job is to sort through all of their existing material. You want to listen to every song they have, including previous releases and every demo they've ever made (within reason). If they have some songs without an existing demo, you can have them perform them for you in a rehearsal or gig.

Shows are particularly useful for evaluating an act, mostly because you can watch the reaction of the audience. Of course, if your hard rock band is performing at a country bar, audience reaction is unlikely to tell you much. Even the poor reaction of a more appropriate audience shouldn't automatically disqualify a song, particularly if you have a vision for how to best present it. A positive reaction, on the other hand, should rarely be discounted.

When evaluating an artist for the first time, it's not unusual for me to pore through as many as 30 songs. I want to hear every demo they've ever made of unreleased songs, and I want to hear their releases too. That's far too many songs to do anything with, so I need to whittle the list down to the most viable songs in order of priority. The new songs are the most viable contenders, but sometimes it's worthwhile to revisit a song from earlier in their journey.

I'm always very careful not to single out a particular song as the "most important," and if I do, *I don't tell the artist!* This puts too much pressure on the song and works to the detriment of the project as a whole. Besides, at this stage of the game, I'm not in a position to determine which is the best track, regardless of my optimism. There are too many variables to make such a blatant predetermination.

Your song prioritization allows you to compare how you see the artist with how they see themselves. If your priority list doesn't remotely intersect with that of the artist, then you either need to sell them on your vision or pass on the gig. Whatever you do, don't realign your vision to match theirs. Your gut instincts are almost always right, and if you ignore those instincts, you'll regret it.

Choosing songs is often a bit of a negotiation process. Unfortunately, if your favorite songs continually fall off the list at the insistence of the artist, you're probably not the right producer. Think about it. If your vision diverges significantly from theirs, you'll find yourself at odds with them throughout the entire recording process. You can't implement your vision if you find yourself recording the least compelling songs. Avoid this scenario like the plague.

There will be times when you'll need to get involved in changing the song itself. If you're not known as a Songwriter Producer—and if that's not the kind of help they seek—then this can be uncomfortable territory for the artist. A great song requires a strong melody and strong lyrics. If one or the other is weak, you should address that problem. You don't have to get involved with the actual songwriting process, but you surely should fix any blatant systemic problems, particularly on songs that have considerable potential. You are not relegated solely to the arrangement.

When you do get involved in the songwriting, you're entitled to a credit and publishing, but this must be worked out in advance and should be in your contract. Artists will often balk at this suggestion, particularly if you don't have a definitive track record as a writer or producer. Furthermore, the lines aren't always clear.

I wrote the cello part that was integral to the payoff to Pete Murray's song "Better Days." It acted as both a melody and a countermelody. Should I have gotten writer's credit and songwriter's royalties? Frankly, I wasn't in a position to ask for it at the time, and it's debatable as to its function in the arrangement. So, I decided that this was a producing contribution, not a songwriting contribution. But if you feel that you're making integral changes to the song, the kind that will be sung, then you have every reason to discuss your role as a songwriter.

Tempo and key are also important considerations. Singers will often overshoot their range. The true range of a singer is what they can sing on a daily basis, not what they can sing on their best day. If the singer is struggling on a track in preproduction, you'll want to alter the key before recording it.

You want to lock in tempo and key in preproduction and before any studio sessions—especially key, since harmonic bleed from acoustic instruments can make changes impossible after the fact. If there's even the tiniest amount of harmonic bleed contained on the drums, you really can't change the key without re-cutting them. The rub will be untenable. We'll discuss preproduction at length later but use this time to evaluate your singer's ability to hit their notes. If they're struggling, consider a key change.

Changing the key of a fully programmed production is far easier to do, but if you've recorded any parts, they may need to be cut again. Pitch shifting recorded parts can sound quite un-natural at times.

Market Considerations

Whenever you set out to make an album, or a single track, you should consider the target market. For instance, if your act will appeal mostly to jazz lovers, and you put an outrageously distorted, balls-out electric rock guitar in your production, you will likely alienate your intended market. So, you need to con-sider who the music is meant to attract. Young tweens? Angry 20-somethings? 30-somethings?

Will it appeal to girls more than guys, or vice versa? What region of the country will this product appeal to most? Is the goal radio airplay and streaming? Sync to video rights? To tour the festival circuit? Is this an established artist or a new one? Established artists have a legacy and an identifiable sound that should be taken into consideration. A relatively unknown band or artist still needs to establish a sound, one unique to them.

Of course, you can always just copy what everyone else is doing. Certainly, fashion and trendiness have a place in music production. It just tends to date your material. If you follow a fashion trend on your artist's record, and they have a massive hit, you could find yourself with a one-hit wonder. The song "It's Raining Men" is basically a disco song that hit as disco was exiting stage left, and the Weather Girls never recovered from the genre's demise.

Trendy Techniques

If you're producing a modern pop act, then more often than not you'll want to implement trendy production techniques. The problem is, if you try to cram every trendy technique there is into your production, it will come off as uninteresting and safe.

If you want to make your production familiar and generic in the hopes of capitalizing on a musical trend, you risk presenting your artist in such an uncompelling manner that their likelihood of failure increases exponentially. If you create a production that makes an artist sound unique without coming totally from left field, you have a far better chance of becoming a trendsetter rather than a trend-follower. Trendsetters make the big money in this world, and then all the little trend-followers capitalize on that trend until a new one comes along.

That doesn't mean we want to avoid trendy production techniques. It only means we need to be aware of how we use them. If you use a production technique that will soon fall out of fashion, you could very well kill your track before it's even had a chance. So, choose your trendy production techniques carefully.

Current production trends in pop music include: tuned 808 KIK drums that function as a bass; the presence of audible autotune artifacts; highly syncopated and intermittent 32nd and 16th note hi hat patterns, super sparse arrangements; filtered drops; bass drops; bull-horned vocals; and mixes that pulse rhythmically with the beat via sidechain compression.

All of those production and arranging techniques are hot (as I type this) but will, at some point, go out of fashion without warning. There is no way of predicting when that point is. The good news is, anything that goes out of fashion will likely return to fashion again, but it could be years or even decades before that happens. Frankly, bass drops may already be out, seeing as you hear those on reality-based television productions.

Once a trend goes out of fashion, then any *new* production that uses the technique is automatically dated. If you seek sync opportunities, super dated productions can be useful for placement. If the song in question was already a hit, then it's already firmly attached to the time in which it was released. If the goal is to break the act, then it's critical that your production techniques aren't completely out of fashion.

Retro Techniques

When a technique has been dated for long enough, then it becomes a retro production technique, and if that retro technique is used by enough others, then it can once again become current.

Retro production techniques are useful for placing a production into another time. For instance, were you to combine several busy percussive loops into a production, it would immediately reek of the '90s. If you put a big, gated reverb on the drums, it would instantly remind you of the '80s. But if you implement a trend that only recently went out of fashion, then your production will merely be dated.

We have such a long and rich history of recorded music that a modern track does not necessarily require modern techniques. The reverberant guitar was big in the '60s and came back in vogue in the '80s (everything was reverberant in the '80s), but just because you used a reverberant guitar doesn't mean you've made a '60s production, unless you create a production that's supposed to sound like it came from that era. In which case, copying those production techniques is almost essential to the sound. This is especially true if you're producing a song for a period movie.

Overtly placed gated reverbs on drums was big in the '80s and was so overused that it's tough to put that into a production without completely dating your music to that era. If you want to make a song feel like it's from the '80s, that's fine, but if you've chosen to add a prominent gated reverb, you probably want to make sure that everything else sounds as modern as possible. Perhaps this would be the time to insert that lovely Auto-Tune artifact that's only gotten trendier in recent years.

Genres have their own trends. You wouldn't likely hear tuned 808s or syncopated 32nd note hi hats in a hard rock production, although, it would probably be pretty interesting if you did. You will, however, hear machine gun KIK drums in perfect time on that hard rock production, which have more top end snap than low end bloom. As far as I'm concerned, that particular production technique just about defines the genre at this point. I don't disparage the sound, except to say, there isn't currently all that much variance in how these productions are approached. When you choose to use every trendy technique available to you, your production will end up as nothing but a caricature of itself. If you want a breakout hit, then you would do well to try to influence trends by doing something unique.

Raw vs. Polished Productions

Just how raw or polished you wish to present your production is one of the more significant decisions you'll make. The level of refinement you present directly impacts how the listener feels, and it can be powerful to reflect the emotion of the song through the production itself. This is a decision best made early, because it dictates your overall approach to the record.

Raw productions are typically simple and tend to promote bold moves over nuance. As such, you can take full advantage of dynamics. There's certainly no need for a click track. Obvious performance mistakes become desirable, allowing players to perform with reckless abandon. Sound quality is of little consequence—which can be quite liberating, because it puts you in a place of evaluating how the track makes you feel over all else. And once you discover that place, you never want to leave it.

Raw productions also call for overt noise. Aggressive compression can cause a part to breathe and distort, which brings with it all sorts of glorious raw artifacts. In the case of vocals this can manifest as lip-smacking, excessively loud breaths, a strident tone, and saturation distortion. Where it comes to a raw vocal presentation, that's the good stuff right there.

Then there's the quality of the players. If you put a group of top-tier musicians in a room, they might struggle to deliver a believably raw performance. Professional players spend their lives shedding bad technique from their repertoire. To play poorly can become so foreign that their attempts come off as downright comical. So, your available personnel may dictate your approach.

The best way that I know to make a band production come off raw is to limit my time polishing the track and the performances. There's no editing. There's no tuning. There may be little-to-no automation. I pull tones as quickly as possible, with a band that isn't exceptionally polished, and we leave it mostly as is.

As with anything there are degrees. The rawest possible production will sound as if you stuck a single mic in a compromised room with a band of total novices. The quality of the players isn't really the issue. It's the locked-in ambient capture that's best avoided, if only because anyone can accomplish it. As such, it's a technique that carries no real intrinsic value.

Now, if you genuinely believe a single-mic capture is the best way to present your art, by all means—let your genius shine through. I just don't prefer to give anyone the opportunity to think, "I could have done that!"

A raw presentation is just as contrived as a polished one, because at all times, you maintain control over the level of refinement you present. Still, if you can contrive something by doing nothing to it, that would seem efficient to me. I'm always appreciative of times when laziness becomes an asset.

Fully polished productions typically require considerably more time than raw ones. Every part is either tuned and timed to the grid or brought into compliance through aggressive comping and editing. Both are forms of polish, and you have full control over how far you want to take it.

I suppose the biggest pitfall with a polished production is that new producers have a tendency to take it too far. If you polish a production too aggressively—if you make everything so perfect that nothing stands out in any way—your "perfect" production will come off just as uninspiring as a one-mic capture of a band. Uninspiring is uninspiring. It doesn't matter how long it took you to accomplish it. Applying just the right amount of polish is one of those things that takes discipline and practice.

Eclectic Projects

In the '70s and '80s, and even in the '90s to some extent, it was typical for a band or artist to have a particular sound, and to stick with that sound. Beginning in the '90s, and continuing until the present, it has become more and more common for artists to create rather eclectic albums that jump styles and genres seemingly from song to song. I call this an eclectic album.

Eclectic albums are a ton of fun. They also tend to require more work, more overdubs, cost more, and make an overall vision and identifiable sound more difficult. Therefore, the sonic landscape must be dealt with on a song-by-song basis. Given that people tend to stream songs rather than full albums, continuity isn't anywhere near the concern it once was. Besides, the singer will provide some semblance of continuity. Of course, if you're recording a band entity that has alternating lead singers, then all bets are off.

I like to actually visualize music. If I'm working with a hard rock band, then I want the record to sound tough. If they're pop, I want the record to have a sheen about it. If the group falls within the indie genre, I might want a rattier, less polished sound. But sound is a major part of producing, and if you hone the sound at the source, you won't need a ton of engineering chops to pull it off.

Leader in Chief

If you haven't figured it out by now, as the producer, you're the leader. As such, you must lead. Somehow, there are all sorts of people who think that one can lead by following. One can't.

As the leader, it's your job to keep your finger on the pulse of your session and to adjust when needed. All sessions have an ebb and flow to them. There are highs and lows. If there weren't, your session would be dull and severely lacking in passion. When morale is high, productivity tends to be high. When morale is low, productivity can be nonexistent. Conversely, when productivity is high, morale stays high. When productivity stops, morale can tank. This is especially true when working with a band entity.

As you produce, you should watch for indications that morale is headed in the wrong direction, preferably before it bottoms out completely. Still, there will be times when your session will become a tough slog. Don't bother beating yourself up over this. It happens to everyone on every session.

All things being relative, there will be tracks that give you little-to-no resistance, and tracks that make you wonder why you got into this business in the first place. While you can often predict which tracks will prove difficult, that's not always the case. On those occasions when you find yourself mired in a difficult problem track it can be tempting to move on to something easier, but that carries with it risks. Giving up on a problem track can tank the morale on your session. Besides, if you spend your session avoiding the difficult work, all you'll manage to do is pile it all up to the end, and then you've completely lost control over your time and risk going over.

Hopefully, you're not working with a crew of dainty little flowers, unable to deal with the natural headwinds of your typical recording session. The more seasoned the act, the more of a workhorse mentality they'll typically have. Veteran acts understand and expect the grind.

Personalities will also dictate how hard you can push. If you're working with a performer who seems to take every criticism personally, or who gets frustrated at the first hint of a problem, then you may have to soften your approach. If you're working with a supremely optimistic workhorse, you can push them hard without concern.

I suppose the point is that you should allow your session to alternate between the tough grinding work and seemingly effortless free flow. This way, the aggregate of your session is kept on a somewhat even keel. Just as important, don't ignore how a session is affecting *your* judgment. If you're in a crap mood, or down in the dumps, you're not helping your session morale. Compartmentalization is almost a requirement to good producing. Stay in the moment of your session and leave the external problems for later.

Conflict Resolution

Conflict happens. Sometimes you're in the middle of the conflict. Sometimes you're the arbitrator of the conflict. And if you believe you have a personality that can avoid all conflict, think again. There are people in this world who won't allow it.

I'm not saying you should constantly engage in fights. But if you give in to your artist's every whim, then how exactly are you serving their needs? You're the one who is responsible for finishing under budget, and that requires keeping the session focused and moving forward.

What are you going to do when the artist wants to put a violin response part right on top of the vocal? Will you allow it? It's a response part—it should go between the vocal lines. That's Arranging 101.

Situations will arise on sessions when you must make a political calculation, and sometimes in politics things can get a bit ugly. Even if you whisper your objections, you're still in the midst of a conflict. The definition of "conflict" does not include yelling. It's a disagreement that must be negotiated and resolved.

Since you're responsible for delivering a final product on time and on budget, you don't have the luxury of allowing your artists to endlessly experiment, especially where it comes to tried-and-true principles of good arrangement. Even if you work for them as a dedicated Producer For-Hire, they've brought you in for your expertise. If you don't stand up for your expertise, then you don't help the project. Worse yet, you could go over budget.

At the same time, it's important to recognize when to give a little rope. I mean, if your Child of Brain has a wacky idea, you should probably try it out. You want to investigate your bold ideas. Why shouldn't you investigate theirs? That's all perfectly reasonable. But if your artist wants to explore countless ideas to the point that it's distracting from your vision, that needs to be addressed.

I rarely want to get into a conflict over something abstract, at least not if I can possibly avoid it. It usually only takes but a few minutes to try a reasonable idea and make a determination as to its merit. To debate it in the abstract can take more time than to try it and offers no resolution in the process.

Band entities are often conflict machines. Of course, if they've been together a while, they should have the ability to settle their conflicts on their own. That said, don't let your crew argue for an hour before weighing in. That's just a waste of everyone's time. Offer your opinion (or solution), try it out, and move on. That's part of leadership.

With bands, there is almost always one person who wields the power. Typically, the power player is the primary songwriter, although there are exceptions to that. It's pretty easy to pick out the power player, because they're the one to whom the band acquiesces. They're also the person you've probably been talking to from the start.

You should assess the personal dynamics within a band entity in the first few minutes of a rehearsal. Once you've pegged the person in charge, that's the person with whom you want to develop your primary relationship. The power player's opinion will naturally have more weight with the band and will know precisely how to lead them. Therefore, nearly anything that you work out with them, they can then work out with the band.

It's not that you have to do everything through the principal songwriter of the band. You work, and develop your relationships, with them all. But when there's a dispute between you and another band member, the songwriter will have the weight necessary to help resolve the issue. Hopefully, so do you, but you're not a dictator in the process. For the purposes of making the record, you're the leader, but there is already an established leader of the band, and that person can make the session considerably easier or more difficult. So lead, but don't discount how you leverage the politics.

I recently worked with one band in which the primary songwriter refused to use his natural leverage with the group to back me up on my decisions. It was a nightmare. No matter how many times I explained it, he wanted to foster a "band feeling," even though the band was perfectly willing to acquiesce to his wishes as the songwriter. He was the Child of Brain. Without him there was no band entity. By shirking his position and his leverage, it made my job infinitely more difficult.

Unfortunately, I have no lesson for you on this. It's an unusual circumstance, and I relay it so that you can understand the importance of leverage and politics where it comes to producing a band. I wish that I could tell you how to deal with *any* of the countless strange situations that occur over the course of a producing career. Sometimes politics don't work the way you expect them to, and you'll have to adjust to that reality.

Honest Communication

In my experience, the best way to deal with artists is to be completely honest and blunt at all times. It's surely shocking at first, but artists soon realize they can trust what I say, and I find this crucial to making a great record.

If I tell an artist my negative feelings about their work, they'll believe me. If I *only* offer them positive words of encouragement, they will question my sincerity.

Some people like to communicate in circles so as to avoid a direct criticism. We all have different personalities, and I'm not proposing that you change yours if this is how you operate. But I can tell you, it's extremely inefficient to avoid direct, honest, blunt communication.

I never lie to my artists. If I don't like something, I tell them. If I think something is terrible, I don't sugarcoat it beyond, "I've heard better." If I think something is mediocre, I say it straight up. Everyone performs badly, probably more often than they perform well—especially when working on relatively new material—so it makes no sense for me to pretend otherwise. I promise you, it can be galling to hear praise at a time when constructive criticism is needed most.

Trust is the cornerstone of your relationship with the artist. If you don't have their trust, you can't operate effectively as their producer. You will be second-guessed at every turn. Trust is so critical to the working relationship between performers and producer—it's so necessary to the process—you shouldn't even consider engaging in contract discussions until that trust has been firmly established.

Let me just highlight this concept in clear, blunt terms: Do not squander or risk established trust under any circumstances.

Don't blow smoke up their ass. They'll know it. They'll resent it. And they'll never trust your encouragement again. Even if you are somehow incredibly talented in your bullshitting abilities, at some point you'll be caught, and everything nice you've ever said to that point will be tainted and questioned as to its sincerity.

Don't patronize your musicians by praising an idea you have every intention of muting later. When you're honest, it gives your artist a chance to reconsider their approach, which could ultimately lead to something brilliant. If you cheat your act out of a compromise, you risk a confrontation later. You might even box yourself into needing a part that you hate come mix time. After all, every subsequent overdub will be recorded with that part in the equation.

The most compelling argument for total honesty is that it tends to open the channels of communication in both directions. You lead by example here. If your singer is uninspired by the track and doesn't feel they can be fully forthright about it, then all your hard work could be for naught. You can't reasonably demand honesty from your artist if you're not setting the tone.

Now, just because you're honest, even brutally so, doesn't mean you shouldn't select your words carefully. Of course, how carefully depends on the personalities involved. If proclaiming "that sucked" will cause your singer to crumble, I would suggest softening your delivery. You're not engaging in effective and efficient communication if your criticisms bring the session to a screeching halt.

In general, you should tailor your style of communication, and even your working methods, to the artists themselves. A singer in need of constant encouragement and direction is not a good candidate for setting the DAW to loop record. Conversely, a singer who likes to work their parts out would probably love it if you looped a section. That's not to say you should never push your musicians outside of their comfort zone if you believe it will solve a problem. But you need to understand what that comfort zone is in the first place and then use that information to everyone's advantage.

In general, you want to gauge what works best for your act, and work within those confines, even if it takes you out of your own comfort zone. When criticism becomes a problem, you should likely seek out positive examples of what you're trying to express. Rather than to focus on how badly the artist performed the second verse, you could present the first verse as the model. "Sorry, but you did such a killer job on the first verse, that this is now the bar," is considerably more palatable for the Dainty Artist than "You call that performing?!"

Fortunately, the Dainty Artist isn't all that common. Besides, if you're straightforward right from the beginning and your artist accepts this about you, even the Dainty Artist can handle direct communication. Just make sure you're consistent in how you communicate. You don't want to be pure sweetness during preproduction and abrasively blunt during the session. Let them see who they'll be working with, and if you lose the gig, that's probably a good thing.

The Struggle

There will be times on just about every session when your artist will struggle and need some coddling. All artistic people need that on occasion. Even you. This is all part of the leadership job. Sometimes a good 10-minute love fest is exactly what a stalled session needs. And why not? You chose the project because you loved it, so it's good to express your adulation.

Let your artist know you still adore the project and why. Remind them of everything that's gone right with the project. Take a moment and review your successes. Play the tracks that are kicking ass, regardless of what stage they're at in the recording process. Talk about what's good about them, how they make you feel, what kind of physical reactions they cause. This sort of positive feedback is a great way to reset and can often serve to inspire your talent enough to get you through the tough times.

Track review is also a good idea when you're the one struggling. At the very least, it gives you a basis of comparison and a break from the grind.

Visionary In Chief

Vision, quite simply, is your ability to picture the final product before recording a single note. Vision alone is your most powerful asset as a producer, and more specifically, as the leader of a project. Without vision, you leave everything up to chance. If you don't know how to present an act, if you don't have a clear concept of the project at hand, then you have no business producing it.

Whereas you can produce a record with large gaps in your knowledge base, you cannot produce a record without a vision. Certainly not with any kind of consistency, and probably not well either. As we've already established, an Engineer Producer could have minimal knowledge of music, and a Musician Producer can be weak in the engineering, and both of them can produce an effective record. Those gaps can be compensated for by employing others. Who are you going to hire to fill in for your lack of vision? A producer? *That's you!*

I can promise you this: if you don't like the act, the song, or even the genre, then you will have no vision in regard to the project. You can't possibly. You can't lead if you don't know where you're going, and you can't rightly know where you're going with a production if you don't adore the material. And I mean *adore.*

Clearly, your vision for a project is not so clear that you can predict, with absolute accuracy, the final result. There are far too many variables for that. The free will of your talent alone would make that impossible. So, vision isn't some form of clairvoyance. Vision has to do with the basic conceptualization of the album, in both sound and approach.

Your vision should take the genre into account. A hard rock band requires a different approach than a pop artist. While the genre will dictate many of the conventions you adhere to, music is far too complex to stay rigidly within the stereotype of a genre. Oh, believe me, there are plenty of producers out there capable of producing only one genre, and who seemingly make the same record over and over again. How boring is that? Your goal is to create something stunning and new, but also recognizable. To accomplish that goal, you need to operate within and outside of convention simultaneously.

Admittedly, there are some genres in which to break from convention in terms of production aesthetic is to be viewed as an almost amateurish and out of touch presentation. Genres can get into ruts so deep that they almost become comical in their adherence to current trends, such that any deviation puts it into a new classification of genre. If that describes your favorite genre, the scope of your vision will be limited to those accepted conventions.

The recording process itself can and will carry great influence over the final product. Thirty days of recording time will yield a considerably different record than one completed in just 10 days. Unfortunately, if you have an act that requires 30 days of polish, and a budget that barely covers 10 days, it becomes impossible to accomplish your vision. In other words, vision dictates budget, and budget dictates vision, and if you can't reconcile the two, you can't make the record. Not properly, anyway.

Now, you don't typically conjure your vision out of whole cloth. All the information is there for you in the form of an act's past records, demos, and live performances. You just have to figure out what it's all telling you. This is true even if an act's vision is on point. Merely recognizing this is a contribution on your part.

When you listen to every available track from a potential artist, you should start to form a clear picture of how you wish to approach the album creatively. It's not enough to listen to one track and decide you have a vision for the entire project. That may be a fine vision for one song, but that song could also prove an anomaly within a collection of several songs. If you immerse yourself in the complete recorded history of the band or artist, you gain the benefit of understanding how they developed and transformed over time. This is true even if your act has only recorded demos.

Demos and previous recordings are an absolute treasure trove of valuable information. The strengths and weaknesses of the act become apparent. The style that fits them best will be revealed. Subgenres will be discovered. And all of these realizations go into the manifestation of your vision.

For instance, you may discover that the singer sounds best in a particular range. This could make certain songs pop more than others. Helping an act home in on a set of songs that seems to fit them best is a major part of carving out a vision. The artist might show a tendency to cut their tracks too slow. This could drastically change the audience they attract. If an act's style and genre don't jibe with their approach, they could very well make themselves unattractive to all.

Your artist's arrangement choices are also quite revealing. As you investigate an act, you should find little threads that make them more interesting than the generic standard of their genre. What makes an artist unique is what sets them apart from others. If you can find all those glorious distinguishing characteristics, you can take advantage of them in your presentation. It's not enough to accept what makes an artist unique from everyone else. You want to *exploit* those qualities.

Some of those tiny threads are considerably more obvious than others. If you dig a little deeper, and with a little imagination, you will often find influences that fall completely outside of an act's overall genre. A country act could have blues influences. A hard-rock act R&B influences. These could be obvious influences or subtle ones, but they're important to both recognize and include as part of your vision. Cross-genre influences pull a song and production out of the mundane and gives them their own character.

There will be times when a cross-genre influence is a sum negative for a given production. You may wish to quash an influence if you think it's getting in the way of a feeling you wish to evoke.

Certain parts can change the overall genre landscape of a song. A piano on a roots song can pull it into the country realm and risk alienating the intended audience. It could also be fresh and work brilliantly. Only you can make these determinations on your production.

Genre influence can be contained within the fabric of the music too. Certain melodic modes, chord changes, and even lyrics can define the overall genre impression. These sorts of systemic genre influences can't be eradicated through production. They can, however, be significantly reduced.

The song "Gabby," which I produced for the Josh Phillips Folk Festival (*Get Outside*) was systemically a folk/country track, and outside of my vision for the song. Frankly, I found the demo boring and one-dimensional, particularly within the context of the collection of songs as a whole. It was like they said, "We need a folk/country song," and then made it. Fortunately, there was a subtle ska thread contained within the demo, and ska would certainly change the vibe considerably. So, we pulled on that thread and made the ska feeling a feature rather than an influence. This made the song infinitely more compelling. It also made it more appropriate for the eclectic nature of the band as a whole.

I worked with Australian hard rock band, Mammal in 2009. I'd produced and mixed many rock records to that point, but nobody would have ever classified me as a hard rock producer. But then, I didn't view them as a hard rock band. I mean, yes, technically they were hard rock, and any punter would classify them as that. They were also unique, and as such, that made them interesting to me. I had a vision for an album that was far outside the constraints of their genre.

In the course of our initial interview, one band member asked me what kind of album I would make with them. It was a somewhat odd question, one that would be difficult for me to answer were I to lack a vision. But it certainly wasn't an unfair question. So, I answered.

"I want to make an R&B album with you guys, but when people will listen to it, they'll think it's hard rock."

Apparently, that's what won me the gig.

There were a ton of R&B influences in the vocals. The singer was singing in a hard rock style but seemed to take an R&B approach to his melodic phrasing. Frankly, those particular influences are what made the band special to me. I'm not sure whether any of those influences will come out on the album to anyone other than myself (and perhaps them) at this point. My goal wasn't actually to make the band sound more R&B, or R&B at all. The balance was already there as far as I was concerned. I just had no desire to eradicate those influences. It's what I found compelling about the band. The bottom line is the concept made sense to me, and it clearly made sense to the band. The best part of all? I didn't come up with the concept. They did. All I did was recognize that element in their music and chose to utilize the influence so as to avoid making a purely conventional hard rock album.

It's not good enough to act as an organizational force for a project. You must be a creative force too, as that is what makes you valuable as their leader. The band (or even the artist) is so mired in being themselves that they have no perspective. They can't pore through their music and determine what they are. That's what you bring to the party. And if they're a long established act, then you need to pick up on where they're at musically in their journey. As an outsider, you not only have the ability to evaluate an act and help them discover their true strengths and unique qualities, but you also demonstrate it to them in the form of their recordings.

The Sonic Landscape

The overall sonic landscape is critical to the production and should be a significant part of your vision. It's a mistake to believe that this part of the vision should be left in the hands of a recordist or mixer. The sound of the record has influence on the listener; as such, it is wholly within your purview.

Nowhere is this more evident than with organically recorded drums, which can set the tone for the entire production. Tight, dead, Al Green–style drums recorded in a veritable anechoic chamber are not likely the best sonic choice for a huge ambient rock track. That's not to say that you wouldn't or couldn't choose an Al Green drum tone for a rock track, so long as you choose it purposely. There have been many rock tracks with dry, tight drums, like AC/DCs "Back in Black." But if you've been using words like "huge" and "ambient" to describe your desired drum sound, a large room seems a more appropriate place to record them.

Of course, if the '80s taught us anything, it's that you can always add your drum space in the form of reverbs and delays, which isn't an unreasonable strategy for some records. But that doesn't work all that well if your drums sound like pure trash.

Those reverb laden drum tracks from the '80s were typically well recorded in acoustically designed rooms. You really can't hide a trashy sound with reverb. You can't hide anything with reverb. In fact, reverb can often make overt flaws more apparent. If the telltale markings of an undersized room are contained within the recorded tracks themselves, your large hall is typically an inadequate solution.

The reality is drums generally sound trashy in small rooms with parallel walls and eight-foot ceilings. They can get quite strident and ratty since the reflections return too quickly to the microphones. I'm not suggesting that you must always record your drums in a fantastic acoustic space with the best equipment. I only seek to explain why you might not be happy with your drum tones after you record them in your bedroom with four dynamic mics.

For the right production, like a punk rock record in which the goal is to agitate, that's a perfectly reasonable way to record your drums. For just about any other kind of record, you could find yourself unhappy with the tones, and unable to adequately create the feeling you envision. No amount of sonic manipulation can fix that.

Yes, you could replace the KIK and the snare with samples, or use sonic repair tools that ostensibly remove space, but then you still have your overhead and possibly room mic, which will contain the bulk of the trashy room information. Tools like Ozone's RX don't work well on overheads.

You can certainly overdub the cymbals to go with your sampled KIK and snare, but now you've managed to completely remove a performance from the equation, which could also run counter to your vision. Your good feelings, to boot. You could even bring your cymbals way down in the balance.

All of those are reasonable strategies for dealing with a problematic drum capture, but none of those solutions will ever alleviate the crux of the problem, which has nothing to do with sound and everything to do with the feelings those sounds evoke, particularly in relation to how they make you feel. When the sound coming from your monitors runs counter to your vision, you won't be happy with it, and the tendency is always to fix the problem with tools, rather than to fix the problem at the source.

I can promise you that there have been many hit records that didn't match the vision of the producer or artist. None of this has anything to do with the success of your record, but rather your own good feelings towards it.

The reality is, the tools that we use to manipulate sound are far more effective for mangling a pristine tone than repairing a problematic one, especially where it comes to removing space. In the event that you can't seem to match your vision with your tone, it's probably because you refuse to fix the actual problem. The source, which always includes the room.

The most important consideration where it comes to the sound is how your tones work together. You want your tones to blend to create one unified sound. If you're recording a stylized track, then you need tones that fit the style appropriately and they need to be somewhat consistent.

Now, in general, I think people place way too much importance on sound. But that really only relates to sound itself. The reality is, your tones can generate a feeling, and how you make people feel is everything where it comes to producing music. So long as you evaluate the sound purely on how it makes you feel and move, then the sound is of great consequence. If you evaluate your sound outside of that context, it has no relevance.

When I recorded Ben Harper's "Steal My Kisses," J. P. Plunier didn't like my initial tones. We were well into the recording of the album, and this was our first hitch, but my initial drum tones clearly didn't match his vision on this particular song. After two failed attempts to come up with a tone that inspired him,

I asked in exasperation, "Can you give me an adjective that I can use to understand what you're going for?"

"New Orleans," he replied.

"New Orleans" is hardly an adjective, but it was most certainly a place, and places can have a sound. So, in that respect, the term "New Orleans" describes a sound. I'd spent time in New Orleans, so it was a term I could understand.

I changed out Dean Butterworth's KIK drum for something a bit rounder. We swapped out the snare drum for one that was tighter and higher pitched. I exchanged Juan Nelson's five-string bass for a Hofner (I won't lie, he wasn't happy to abandon a fifth string, but he was so absurdly good it really didn't matter). Admittedly, a Hofner bass isn't necessarily a bass that screams New Orleans, but it's distinctive midrange and lack of a fifth string forced Juan into a rather brilliant new part. In fact, the tones changed how everyone on the session played.

I didn't use EQ and compression to change the tones. I adjusted the instruments. And the only instruments I needed to touch were the bass and drums. In most cases, the bass and drums dictate the sound of the record. I know that sounds crazy, but it's true. Just changing out a snare drum can completely change how the production makes the musicians feel. Once players hear the drums and bass, they typically adjust their sound and possibly even their parts to match. Not only did Juan play a new part, but Ben swapped out his guitar and amp the moment he heard the new drum tones.

The use of electronic processing to create a tone is the least effective means to do it. As such, I treat it as a last resort. If you can get the instruments sounding right in the room, then they will sound right on the recording. J. P. wanted New Orleans, so I addressed the instruments themselves, and the players adjusted their parts. With everyone on the same page conceptually, we had New Orleans.

Then J.P. decided he wanted a beatbox on top of that New Orleans sound, which one could argue is completely out of left field and defies my suggestion that all the tones should work together. I would retort that they do work together. The disparate styles don't prevent that. More importantly, the beatboxing brought the production somewhere far more interesting than to stay strictly within the confines of a New Orleans sound. Besides, it's a city with a large black demographic, and as such, the tapestry blend of styles worked perfectly. To this day, "Steal My Kisses" is Ben's most well-known song, and we surely can't discount success.

Frankly, that record wouldn't have been nearly as compelling produced as a straight folk/country track. Would it still have been a hit? Hard to say. Would it have been as playfully fun? Certainly not. And a playfully fun feeling fit the lyrics, so in that respect, the production and the song work in synergy to create that feeling.

Sound is feeling.

The Big Superfluous Change

I'd like to take a moment to save you from one of the bigger mistakes you can make as a producer. The most effective way to make an uninspiring record is to completely overhaul your talent to the point that they're performing completely outside of their strengths. If your whole purpose for taking a gig is so you can turn an act into something completely new, don't.

It makes no sense to take a strong, riffing singer and constrict them to singing a rigid melody in a light and airy tone. A style outside of what a performer naturally does well will lead to poor results. Yes, you want to follow the song, but you also need to do so in the way that best fits your talent. To make matters worse, a drastic change in style requires an immense preparation and practice, and if that process occurs in the studio, a compelling performance will be difficult to achieve.

You can't reasonably turn a hardcore band with weak melodies into a polished pseudo-punk pop act. That's not what they do. That's not what they hear. And that won't be what they perform most effectively. If they don't resent you for trying to make them something they're not during the process, they will certainly hate you for ruining their record once it's finished. And rightly so.

Young producers often feel compelled to make an indelible mark on a record. Sometimes our purpose is to merely confirm goodness. That's important feedback. The longer you produce, the more content you are with staying out of the way. Believe it or not, that's not laziness. That's a Protect System, for the benefit of everyone.

Staying out of the way requires more discipline than just about any other skill in producing. Even if you find yourself on a project in which an aggressive touch is necessary, there should be times when you don't have to do anything beyond offering a few well-placed suggestions. The old adage "If it ain't broke, don't fix it" is one to live by when producing, although I would add: "If it's fundamentally broken, don't take the gig in the first place."

All artists need guidance, no matter how great they are. I promise, you will never make a record in which your only role is to sit and quietly admire the genius before you. There will, however, be *moments* like this, and when those come, enjoy them. And I mean *really* enjoy them. Lie down and take a nap if that's the only way you can shut up. But don't muck things up by sticking your nose into a process that's working beautifully without your guidance.

The one time it's acceptable to bring an artist to an entirely new place is when it's time for a reinvention. Alanis Morissette was a Canadian teenage pop singer before she co-wrote her album *Jagged Little Pill* with Songwriter Producer Glenn Ballard. That was a total reinvention of her as an artist. As it turns out, a far more appropriate and successful model for her, since she'd outgrown the whole bubblegum-pop angle. What better way to shed her teenage pop image than by singing about a blowjob as an adult?

Even with the changeover, Glenn didn't ask her to work outside of her strengths. If anything, he helped her make both music and productions that fit her abilities in the best way possible. That would seem to explain the album's massive appeal.

I can assure you, the plan to make an edgy album was established well before they ever recorded a note. That, my friends, is vision.

Sweating What's Important

Far be it for me to dictate to you what's important to a hypothetical production, but let's face it, as much as you need to sweat the details, you don't want to do so in a debilitating manner. You have to pick and choose your battles, not only with the artist, but also with yourself.

I frequently have internal debates as I work through decisions. I don't involve the artist in every consideration. If I constantly spit out my thoughts and concerns, it won't be long before my team is convinced I'm an absolute lunatic. I have way more bad ideas than good ones.

The point here isn't to hide your bad ideas. You'll reveal plenty of those. But many of your thoughts can be rejected without involving anyone else.

There's another reason to keep your thoughts close to the vest. You want to give the artist an opportunity to confirm them independently. For instance, if you're certain that a keyboard part isn't helping the song, there's no reason to waste time beating around the bush. Kill the part and go in a new direction.

If you're merely unsure about the keyboard part, and your artist expresses similar thoughts without prompting, that serves as a clear confirmation. This strategy can save you from some unnecessary consternation.

At those times when I struggle with a decision, then I present my concerns directly to the talent in the hopes that we can solve the problem together.

Frankly, if I were to mention every thought or idea that came into my head while producing a record, I'd never shut up. It's impossible to listen if you're talking, and despite the incredibly obvious nature of that statement, there are plenty of people on this earth who have yet to learn that lesson.

Arranger in Chief

As the producer, the arrangement is in your domain. Arranging isn't just about instrumentation and parts. We discussed much of this in the Arranging chapter, but it bears repeating. An effective song and arrangement focuses the listener's attention and propels them forward through the song. Since songs unfold over time, they must keep the listener's interest, and this is achieved through both writing and arranging techniques.

Believe it or not, you don't need to go to music school to learn arranging to produce most records. If you need parts and charts for a string or horn section, you can hire an arranger to perform that service for you. Most other arranging techniques can be learned by rote purely by listening and mimicking.

Modern songs and productions are generally extremely simple, particularly when compared to genres like jazz and classical. As such, anyone can become an effective songwriter and arranger.

CHAPTER FIVE

The Business

Let me just start with a warning: Do not ever finalize or sign a contract without consulting an attorney with experience in Entertainment Law. Proceed without one at your own risk.

I am not a lawyer, and any advice that I offer has to do specifically with my knowledge as it relates strictly to my own contractual negotiations over the years. My negotiations and demands may not always align with yours, as those have everything to do with your position, the nature and scope of the project, and the expectation of success. Nothing that I offer you in this chapter should be taken as legal advice. Nor should any of it be considered some sort of template for your own contracts.

The best resource for how money flows in this business is Donald Passman's *All You Need to Know about the Music Business.* I highly recommend this book where it comes to understanding the business aspects of producing. That said, we should go over the general concepts and practical strategies for how and when you get paid.

Please Note: for the sake of clarity and consistency with industry contracts, the terms "Producer," "Artist," "Band," and
"Label" are capitalized throughout this chapter.

Producer's Contract

A Producer's contract with an Artist outlines the responsibilities, rights, and obligations of both parties during the
production of a music project. Recoupment alone can be a significant negotiating point, which can affect how and when
you're paid royalties.

Most Producer's contracts—whether major label or indie—
will include a range of standard provisions. For some projects,
especially in early stages or indie scenarios, these points might
first be outlined in a simple term sheet before a full contract is
drafted. Here are the major areas typically addressed:

Scope of Work

Project Details: Specifies the number of songs to be delivered
for the project to be produced.

Producer's Role: Outlines duties such as arranging, recording, mixing, and overall creative input.

Timeline: Defines the deadlines for deliverables and production milestones.

Compensation

Advance Fee: Upfront payment for the Producer's work,
which is typically recoupable from royalties.

Points/Royalties: The Producer's share of the record's income, usually expressed as a percentage (e.g., 2–5% of the
Artist's earnings from sales, streams, or royalties). 3% is the
most common Producer's share.

Payment Schedule: Details when payments are made, such as upon signing, start of production, and delivery of masters.

Producer rates are almost always negotiable, and so is the scope of the project. In the higher echelons of major label producing, the real money is made on the back end in points, not the front.

The front end is your guaranteed payday, regardless of how successful the album is. Your back end is where you make your money should the project prove successful. The stronger your track record, the more leverage you have. A proven track record of hits means you can demand higher Advances, better recoupment terms, and even publishing percentages.

That said, if an act is already successful and known, I'm less willing to negotiate my Advance and fees. For starters, we have sales and streaming data available with an existing Artist. So, we can make reasonable projections based on that data.

It's only reasonable that you demand an Advance that's in line with those projections; otherwise the Artist is merely deferring your payment, which can extend more than a year from when you finish the album. But on an unknown act? If you honestly believe you can make an album that will be an enormous streaming and radio success, then a smaller Advance than you'd prefer might be worth the risk.

All that said, the only reliable indicator you have of a client's commitment to the project is their willingness to put up the money to make the product. If you feel that you're in such a strong position for a project that they will meet your Advance requirements, then by all means demand it. Just be prepared to lose the gig if they don't meet your number, and understand that a great many major label records have been shelved because they cost too much to make.

The typical payment schedule with major labels is 50% up front upon signing the contracts, and 50% upon completion. For

Independent projects, it can be a good idea to schedule the final 50% to be paid before mixing. This way you greatly mitigate your risk of getting stiffed.

Yes, that can happen. This is the Music Business, and not everyone will prove scrupulous or trustworthy. You need strategies to protect yourself, especially on independent projects. This payment schedule is one of my Protect Systems, and it has served me well.

Ownership and Copyright

Master Ownership: Specifies who owns the final master recordings, whether that's the Artist, Producer, or Label.

Publishing Rights: Addresses any shared songwriting contributions, entitling the Producer to a share of the publishing revenue if applicable.

Work-for-Hire Clause: May state that the Producer's contributions are "work-for-hire," granting ownership solely to the Artist or Label.

Credits

Producer Credit: Ensures the Producer's name is properly credited in all media, including album artwork, streaming platforms, and promotional materials.

Recoupment

Recoupable Expenses: Defines which costs (e.g., recording studio fees) will be deducted from the Artist's or Producer's royalties.

There are many ways to define the recoupment of costs, and this can be a serious sticking point in the negotiations and will greatly affect how and when you're paid royalties.

Your Advance is essentially a pre-payment on future royalties. You won't see another dime until that amount is recouped.

If you take a small Advance and recoup early, you'll make the same amount of money as taking a large Advance and recouping later.

As the engineer on a project, you're "work-for-hire" and you don't typically collect royalties, which means your payments aren't considered Advances. Therefore, if you're recording and mixing the project too, it's worthwhile to request less in Producer's Advances and more in engineering fees since you don't have to recoup those.

Let's say you seek a $30,000 total Producer's fee, which you'd need to fully recoup. If you charge $5,000 for engineering services, and $10,000 for mixing services, your Advance now drops to $15,000.

Those engineering fees aren't Advances; they're part of the recording costs, which must be recouped by the Artist. So now, instead of recouping the full $30,000, you only need to recoup $15,000 before you start to collect royalties. This is a negotiating point, because you shift some of your recoupment on to the act, so don't be surprised if the other side balks.

For much of my career, Producer's royalties were based on Mechanical Royalties, which are generated from the reproduction and distribution of music, such as streaming, digital downloads, and physical sales. Mechanical royalties are collected by organizations like the Harry Fox Agency, Music Reports, or Mechanical Licensing Collective (MLC) in the U.S.

Performance royalties are earned when music is publicly performed. This includes radio airplay, live performances, streaming platforms, and music played in public venues like bars or clubs. These royalties are collected by Performance Rights Organizations (PROs) such as ASCAP, BMI, and SESAC, which monitor public usage and distribute royalties accordingly.

Streaming Clause

A streaming clause in a Producer's contract outlines how you will be compensated for revenue generated from streaming platforms. This clause has become increasingly important as streaming has overtaken physical and digital sales as the primary source of music revenue. Here's a breakdown of what a typical streaming clause might include.

Percentage of Streaming Revenue

The Producer is typically entitled to a percentage of the Artist's net revenue from streaming income. The industry standard ranges between 2% and 5% of the Artist's share of streaming revenue, depending on the Producer's experience, reputation, and contribution to the project.

For Producers who also contribute significantly to songwriting, they may additionally earn a portion of the mechanical royalties generated from streams. As always, have a qualified music attorney review any contract language related to streaming revenue or mechanical royalties.

Gross vs. Net Revenue

This clause specifies whether the Producer's share is based on gross revenue (total revenue from streaming before deductions) or net revenue (revenue after costs like label recoupment, distributor fees, etc.). Most agreements calculate the Producer's share based on net revenue.

Pro-Rata Allocation

If the Producer worked on multiple tracks on an album, their percentage is typically applied pro-rata (based on the number of tracks they produced relative to the total tracks on the album).

Payment Terms

This clause should specify when and how the Producer will receive their share of streaming income (e.g., quarterly or semi-annually). The Artist (or their label) is responsible for providing accounting statements and ensuring payments are made.

Accounting and Audits

I know it may sound crazy, but you can't always rely on the accounting of others. Given this, the Producer is entitled to request an audit of the Artist's (or label's) books to verify the accuracy of the streaming income and payments. The burden of costs is usually on the Producer, although there can be stipulations.

Many agreements include a clause stating that if the audit reveals underpayments beyond a specified margin, the audited party (the Artist or label) must reimburse the Producer for the audit costs in addition to correcting the payment discrepancies.

Approvals and Deliverables

Approval Process: Sets expectations for the Artist's involvement in approving mixes or final masters.

Deliverables: Specifies what the Producer must deliver, such as final mixes, stems, and masters.

This section specifies the tangible materials the Producer must deliver to the Artist or label upon completing the project. This information is contained in even the simplest of contracts. It ensures clarity about what is included in the Producer's fee and what the Artist can expect to receive.

Deliverables often include final mixes, stems, instrumentals, a cappellas, mastered mixes, and possibly alternate versions. It's surely in your interest to provide your clients with everything they need to make the project a success. That said, this doesn't necessarily include the session files themselves.

Maintaining possession of the session files is one of the few ways you can retain control over your production. Major labels will almost always require delivery of the full session before issuing final payment, and that expectation is non-negotiable in most major projects. However, on independent projects, you may want to negotiate when and under what conditions you release the session files. If you deliver the sessions too early, you risk losing control over the final sound of the project—or worse, having your work altered without your input or approval.

If you hand over the sessions, you could later hear an entirely new mix of your production—one you never approved. I can all but guarantee you won't be happy with this new production. As if that's not bad enough, your name could still be attached to this new abomination—or removed entirely. It's difficult to say which would be worse. Prevention is your best strategy here.

Termination

Termination Rights: Details conditions under which either party can terminate the agreement, such as failure to deliver or meet obligations.

Kill Fee: Outlines compensation owed if the project is canceled. I've never actually had a kill fee in any of my contracts. Personally, I consider the full schedule of agreed-upon payments to be the only fair kill fee.

Warranties and Representations

Producer's Assurance: Guarantees that the Producer's work is original and does not infringe on third-party rights.

Artist's Assurance: Ensures the Artist has the authority to engage the Producer and use their contributions. Also guarantees their work is original and does not infringe on third-party rights.

Indemnification

Purpose: Protects both parties from financial and legal harm resulting from claims made by third parties due to actions related to the project.

Producer's Indemnity: The Producer agrees to indemnify the Artist (and/or label) for any claims arising from issues such as copyright infringement, unlicensed samples, or unauthorized use of third-party materials in the production.

Artist's Indemnity: The Artist agrees to indemnify the Producer against claims related to the project, such as disputes over ownership of material, unlicensed use of samples provided by the Artist, or other liabilities stemming from the Artist's actions.

Key Considerations: Specifies who is responsible for covering legal fees and damages. Often includes a clause requiring prompt notification of any claims and cooperation in resolving disputes.

Publishing Points

The big money in record-making is publishing. Songwriters often earn the lion's share. It's not uncommon for the writing member of a successful Band to be a multimillionaire while the others make a comparably modest living.

Given the predominance of streaming, along with its generally low payments (labels take 85% of streaming revenue and independent Artists share in just 10% of the total streaming pie), it can be worthwhile to seek points from publishing. In fact, I recommend it if you can pull it off. Here are the situations that warrant asking for a piece of the publishing.

Substantial Creative Contributions

If the Producer contributes significantly to the songwriting process—writing lyrics, creating melodies, or crafting instrumental parts—they should negotiate for a share of the publishing rights.

Example: If the Producer creates the hook or instrumental foundation that defines the song, they can argue they are co-writers and deserve a share of publishing. (Publishing is typically split 50/50 between the writer and the publisher, so a Producer credited as a co-writer would earn from the writer's share.)

High-Profile Producers

Established Producers with a proven track record and strong reputations often negotiate a percentage of publishing as part of their deal. This is more common in genres like hip-hop, pop, and EDM, where the Producer's creative input is integral to the songwriting.

Independent Artist-Producer Deals

When working with independent Artists, Producers sometimes accept a smaller upfront Producers fee in exchange for a share of publishing rights as a way to invest in the project's potential success. So, if you find the Advance insufficient, this is a great way to mitigate your risk.

It's not unreasonable for a Producer to ask for a percentage of the publishing, especially for an independent project. That said, it can sometimes be difficult to convince the songwriter to give up this percentage.

In many standard industry deals, Hip-Hop Producers who create the beat are credited as co-writers and typically receive 50% of the songwriter's share. Given this, it's totally reasonable for a Producer who is in charge of the vision, the sound design,

the arrangement, the presentation, the inspiration, and the organization—who puts the Artist in a position for success—to be
rewarded for such. A percentage of the publishing offers you a
much higher probability of a back end payout down the line.

5-10% of publishing is standard if the Producer's role is limited to recording and mixing the song with little to no creative
input in songwriting or arrangement. 10-25% of publishing is
reasonable if the Producer contributes meaningfully to the
song's structure, arrangement, and overall creative direction.

If you're not in a strong position to request a percentage of
publishing, or if that proves to be an absolute non-starter, then
points on sales and a percentage of Streaming revenues is really
your only protection should the project succeed. That said, the
record has to be an enormous success for these kinds of points
to pay off, given the structure of Streaming revenues these days.

Independent Projects

Since many Independent projects are far less likely to generate significant Royalties, it dramatically alters the calculus on
how to approach your contract as a Producer. In lower-budget
indie situations, it may not be feasible to hire an attorney—but
even a short consult could prove valuable if there's any long-
term potential.

The reality is you must weigh the costs of a Producer's contract with the likelihood of an actual payout. Some projects really
have almost no chance of paying out a back end, which admittedly makes them glorified vanity projects. For these kinds of
projects, you can always create a simple contract using online
resources or AI tools. Just be aware that a generic or poorly
structured contract could be challenged down the line—especially if it doesn't follow standard industry practices. AI-
generated agreements can also lack important specificity, which
could negatively impact your ability to get paid should the project gain traction. As such, they should be reviewed by a qualified

attorney when money or rights of consequence are involved. While some protection is better than none, this strategy carries risk.

At the very least, you should make a contract that spells out your role as the Producer, how many records you intend to deliver, your fees, the totality of the budget, and the schedule of payment. This is especially true if we're talking about the kind of money that can be litigated in Small Claims court. Every state (and country) has its own cap for Small Claims, so it's worth a quick search to know whether your contract falls within that range.

The Production Company Contract

There will be times when you will find an Artist with no deal, no money, and no prospects. On the surface, that doesn't sound particularly appealing, but if you find the Artist compelling and you have a clear vision, then it could make sense to fund their record. Much of that funding can be accomplished through sweat equity.

Typically, the goal is to make the album and seek a record deal. This is an exceptionally difficult road to take, one that will require many hours of perseverance upon completing the record. If you really believe in a project, it can be a worthwhile venture on your part.

Production company contracts often heavily favor the company over the Artist, and many acts avoid them unless they're desperate. But with risk should come reward, and if you plan to fund a project (covering recording, mixing, mastering, and other costs), it is reasonable for your company to expect a significant share of the revenues and rights generated by the project. This kind of agreement is called a Production Company Contract.

A 50-50 split is a common structure in these agreements, where the production company and the Band or Artist share net revenues equally after costs are recouped. The production company often recoups its investment (recording costs, marketing, etc.) from gross revenue before the profit split begins. These agreements usually cover multiple albums (commonly 2-5), which gives the production company some security in case the first album underperforms.

It is common for production companies to take a percentage of the publishing rights as part of the deal, especially if the Producer contributes to songwriting or arrangement. This can range from 25-50% of publishing, which includes income from performance royalties, mechanical royalties, and sync licensing.

An eventual record deal is typically made with your production company. You operate as the liaison between the record company and the act. If the label prefers to sign the Artist directly, you'll probably be pressured to let them go (although you can always decline). In that case, your contract should include contingencies in the form of point overrides—a built-in royalty you retain if the label bypasses you and works directly with the Artist on future projects. It's a way to ensure you're still compensated for your early investment and development, even if you're no longer part of the production process.

The stakes are high in production contracts, and small errors or omissions can lead to significant financial or legal disputes. An experienced entertainment attorney is essential to draft and negotiate these agreements to ensure that your rights and revenue are adequately protected. It's also in your best interest to insist the act has their own attorney to go over it with them.

A Band or Artist that is successful enough to be its own business does not need to sign a production company contract. It's generally viewed as an option of last resort, given how much the Artist must give up. But hey, 100 percent of nothing is still nothing, and that is always the argument from the Production Company's perspective.

Personally, I'm not too keen on funding records with my own money and would rather help a Band find funding that pays me for my services than take that kind of risk. If you want to shop the Band—that is, pitch them to labels or managers—you can have an attorney draft a separate agreement for your shopping services, which pays out in the form of points or publishing. However, unless you're well connected, you'll likely need to give up a portion of your points or publishing to incentivize an attorney or manager to shop the act on your behalf.

The good news is, many records can be made fully in your own room, so you can often fund the making of a record with nothing more than your time. That doesn't mean you don't have costs associated with the project, including the attorney's fees and travel costs associated with shopping the act. That alone can get quite expensive.

Preparing the Budget

The cost to make an album can't be left to chance, and you will need to put together an itemized budget of costs. For all intents and purposes, it's a plan, which estimates costs based on your experience making records.

Let's say we're recording a somewhat successful Band and the proposed budget to make the album is $60k. While $60k may seem like an enormous budget to many of you reading this book, it's not an inordinate sum of money for a project that requires studio time and personnel.

The more that you charge as a Producer, the bigger your budget needs to be. Given a $60k budget, it's not unreasonable for me to start out at $3k for my Producers fees. Rather than to limit myself, I'll put in all the costs at a high level, understanding that I will likely blow past our budget in the process. This way, we can discuss strategies for paring the budget down.

BUDGET

Studios

Rehearsal Room	$50 per day	3 days	$150
Tracking Room	$800 per day	5 days	$4,000
Overdub Room	$400 per day	20 days	$8,000
			$12,150

Per Diems

Producer	$30 per day	25 days	$750
Didgeridoo	$30 per day	2 days	$60
			$810

Side-Players

Union Fiddle	$445 per session	1 session	$445
Union Piano	$445 per session	1 session	$445
Church Choir	$200 donation	Flat fee	$200
Union Perc	$445 per session	1 session	$445
Didgeridoo	$1000 project rate		$1000
			$2,535

Rentals

Hammond B3	$200 per day	1 day	$200
Les Paul Jr.	$75 per day	3 days	$225
REDDI Tube DI	$50 per day	4 days	$200
Snare Drum	$50 per day	4 days	$200
			$825

Miscellaneous

Drumheads	Ambassador White	$200
Drumsticks		$40
Guitar Strings		$100
Bass Strings	Flat Wound	$40
Bass Strings	Round Wound	$40
Drum Tech		$200
Guitar Tech		$200
		$820

Tape and Drives

1 TB Hard Drive	$100 per	2 drives	$200
			$200

Sustenance for the Team

Food and beverage	$100 per day	25 days	$2,500
			$2,500

Producer and Engineer Fees

Producer's Fee	$3,000 per track	12 tracks	$36,000
Outside Engineer	$500 per day	25 days	$12,500
Outside Mixer	$1,500 per track	12 tracks	$18,000
			$66,500
		TOTAL:	$93,290

I've included everything I would desire on this budget in terms of personnel and rooms, but we are currently $33,290 over budget. We have some serious cutting to do.

Budget slashing is the ultimate exercise in compromise. At this point in the process, I've put in everything I might want or need, and now I have to consider where and how I can reduce the budget without compromising quality.

What makes it so difficult is that some expenses can't be removed. Getting rid of your sustenance line item might seem like a no-brainer as it would instantly save you $2,500 on your budget. Unfortunately, your Band and personnel still need to eat, so all you do is to shift that item from the budget to the pockets of everyone on the session. If you don't put the food in the budget, you'll often end up buying food for everyone, and then you'll start eating badly, because the record is costing you a fortune. Take it from me: sustenance should be removed as a last resort.

Frankly, I don't think my fees are too high for this budget. So, we'll leave those for now. Since I'm recording everything on this project in outside studios, I can probably use the engineer

who comes with the room. So, let's cut out the outside engineering costs.

Producer and Engineer Fees

Producer's Fee	$3,000 per track	12 tracks	$36,000
~~Outside Engineer~~	~~$500 per day~~	~~25 days~~	~~$12,500~~
Outside Mixer	$1,500 per track	12 tracks	$18,000
			$54,000

That saved us $12,500. We were over by $33,290, less
$12,500 now puts us $20,790 over budget.

There's not much we can do about travel costs. My ticket is
only $400, so it's not like I'm flying first class here. I could
surely find less expensive accommodations, but I do want to be
comfortable if I'm going to be away from home for an extended
period of time. But the didgeridoo player? They live in Australia,
and it's a $2,500 ticket to get them to our session, another $300
to put them up in a hotel, $1,000 in session fees and $60 in per
diems. That's $3,860 for a didgeridoo player on what should be
a $60K budget. 6 percent of the budget for an ancillary sideman
is pretty outrageous, and I have to wonder how this Band doesn't
have their own didgeridoo player if it's such an important instrument to their project. Besides, didgeridoo is a drone
instrument. It's worth nearly $4000 to avoid using a sample for
a drone? Unless I'm buying the Band's insistence that a didgeridoo sideman is an absolute necessity (and I'm not), all of those
line items need to be cut. Of course, a real didgeridoo player is
superior to a sample, so instead of cutting it, I'll record the
player remotely.

Travel Costs

Producer Airfare			$400
Producer Hotel	$150 per night	25 nights	$3,750
~~Didgeridoo Airfare~~			~~$2,500~~
~~Didgeridoo Hotel~~	~~$150 per night~~	~~2 nights~~	~~$300~~
			$4,150

Per Diems

Producer	$30 per day	25 days	$750
~~Didgeridoo~~	~~$30 per day~~	~~2 days~~	~~$60~~
			$750

That saves us $2,860 in travel costs and per diems. So, we're currently $20,790 over, less $2920 brings us to $17,930. Since the Band has their heart set on a real Didgeridoo on this imaginary project we'll record our performer remotely, which requires a local studio. So, we'll keep the $1000 project rate fee under "Side-Players," which will be plenty of money to cover both the player and a local studio, and whatever technology we use to broadcast and monitor the session live.

There aren't many more places to cut. I've budgeted for some modestly priced rooms that fulfill my acoustic and equipment needs. So, I'm locked in there. The Union sets the prices for the Side-Players, so there's no negotiating those prices. I need a B3 for this session, and the guitar player has a shoddy guitar and the drummer a suspect snare drum. So, I don't want to cut out my rentals. I want the players to have new heads and new strings since that will make recording easier and more efficient. And while I could leave it up to the individual Band members to cover those costs out of their own pocket, many times they won't because they're broke, and I'll end up having to pay for them myself.

I could probably get a mixer for $500 less per track, which would save $6,000 from the budget.

Producer and Engineer Fees

Producer Advance	$3,000 per track	12 tracks	$36,000
~~Outside Engineer~~	~~$500 per day~~	~~25 days~~	~~$12,500~~
Outside Mixer	$1,000 per track	12 tracks	$12,000
			$48,000

We are currently $17,930 over, less $6,000 brings us to $11,870 over.

And now it seems I'm out of fat to cut. Either I need to mix the track myself and save the remaining $12k on that line item, or I need to trim my producer's fees by $1k per track and save it there. Let's say I've decided to mix the album myself.

Producer and Engineer Fees

Producer Advance	$3,000 per track	12 tracks	$36,000
~~Outside Engineer~~	~~$500 per day~~	~~25 days~~	~~$12,500~~
~~Outside Mixer~~	~~$1,500 per track~~	~~12 tracks~~	~~$18,000~~
			$36,000

Now there are only the Producer's Advance and no engineering fees. I'd like to shift some of my Advance money to mixing fees, so I can reduce the total amount that I need to recoup.

Producer and Engineer Fees

Producer Advance	$2,000 per track	12 tracks	$24,000
~~Outside Engineer~~	~~$500 per day~~	~~25 days~~	~~$12,500~~
Outside Mixer	$1,000 per track	12 tracks	$12,000
			$36,000

Now I'm charging $24,000 as an Advance on my royalties, and $12,000 to mix the album, which is recouped by the Band. The total for producing and engineering hasn't changed. It's still $36,000. What's changed is how I recoup.

Let's review our budget as it stands:

Studios	$12,150
Side-Players	$2,535
Rentals	$825
Drives	$200
Misc.	$820
Travel	$4,150
Per Diems	$750
Food/Bev	$2,500
Prod./Eng.	$36,000
Total:	**$59,930**

Clearly, this would be a much tougher budget to cut down if I require a recordist and a mixer. If I didn't have to travel, I could record the overdubs in my room and save there. But it costs way more to bring a Band to me than it does to pay for an overdub studio, so that's not really a viable option here.

I also have a lot of experience recording and mixing, which gave me some flexibility on those costs. The reality is, I would never put a third-party mixer on my budget because I will always mix the album myself. If I weren't skilled at mixing, and if my room was inadequate for the task, then that's not a line item that can be cut. And while you can request that your studio assistant operate as the recordist on your session, you could regret that decision if you end up with a uselessly green assistant. So, you have to really consider whether those are good places for you to cut, and if not, then you need to find other places.

Should you find yourself over budget and you're having trouble reconciling it, then you have a variety of options at your disposal.

Reduce the amount of time scheduled to make the album, and/or completely change the recording plan.

This is not an ideal solution, and you risk going over budget should you try it.

A budget isn't an exercise in wishful thinking. It's a projection that should be as accurate as possible. You have budgeted your studio time based on the information you've gathered. Unless that information has changed, recording the project faster is unlikely to happen. The only way you could really reduce your studio time is by changing the overall vision from a relatively polished album to a rather raw one. Your vision should be based on the music and the Band, not on the money required.

Pass.

Come on. You're going to pass at this point? You love the music, and you knew the budget going in. Unless the available budget was slashed for some reason, you should be pretty much committed at this point.

Work for a reduced Advance on the strength that you'll make it up later on the back end.

By doing this you remove the protection the Advance offers you for your time. However, if you find yourself having to cut your Producer's Advance, you might consider charging it as something other than an Advance. If you're going to give up that much, then the Artist or Band should be willing to recoup your fees.

Attempt to reduce the scope of project.

If a Band or Artist asks you to produce ten songs for them, but you can't make the budget match the vision, then you may seek to reduce the scope of the project to fewer songs. There's no rule that says you have to record ten songs. That's a fine length, since the Artist is paid for all ten songs, but it can certainly be 8 songs, which would immediately save thousands in

Producer's Advances, studio time, mixers fees, and engineering fees too.

Attempt to expand the budget.

Depending on the real numbers (rather than these hypothetical ones), if I find that I'm really taking a drastic hit on my Advance due to expenses out of my control (like if the Band insisted on working in a $1,500-per-day room for the duration of the project), then I will most definitely attempt to expand the budget. This puts the onus on the Band to reconsider their demands. Your success at expanding the budget depends partly on your ability to sell the concept.

If you were a slightly less scrupulous person, you could purposely underestimate the time required to make the album in order to hit your mark on paper, knowing you'll go over in reality. Going over budget happens on occasion. Setting aside the moral issues, technically if you go over budget, the money comes out of your Advance monies. Going over budget may mean you don't get your full final payment. The money may not even exist once the Band bank account is nearly empty. Remember, you were in control of the budget, which puts the onus on you to manage the budget accurately.

Of course, collecting a $36K Advance on a $60K budget might be a bit steep. There's no basic range regarding what percentage of any given budget should go to the Producer—not that I can figure. But in this example, that's 40 percent of the budget going into my pocket.

I can't tell you how much you should charge, or how much of the budget you're worth. Only you and the market can make those determinations. But if you make a budget that is so heavily weighted toward you, in combination with an impossibly short recording schedule, that may not be the best look.

As much as this is a business, it's one in which the final results are actually more important than how much you made in the process. If you make great albums, the payoff will come. If you make mediocre albums, you will remain a second-rate Producer. So, in terms of the big picture, you might be better off making less in the hopes of putting yourself in a position of demand.

The records you make manifest as your brand. If you want your brand to say "quality," then don't do anything to undermine that perception.

Now, let's take a look at a somewhat smaller budget. The Artist is paying for the record themselves, and the proposed budget is $20,000. I'll be mostly programming the project, and my room is sufficient for anything that I may want to record. As such, there will be no need for any outside studios, and I will handle the engineering duties myself.

Drives

1 TB Hard Drive	$100 per drive	2 drives	$200
			$200

Producer and Engineer Fees

Producer's Fee	$2,000 per track	10 tracks	$20,000
			$20,000
		TOTAL:	$20,200

Well, that was easy. Of course, if I need instruments or if I want to add sustenance, then the only place to take from is my Advance. The beauty of working in my room is that my time is my own. So I don't need to budget time, I merely need to trust in my discipline to finish the project in a reasonable time frame.

I do want to reduce those Advances and charge for my Mixing though.

Producer and Engineer Fees

Producer Advances	$1,000 per track	10 tracks	$10,000
Outside Mixer	$1,000 per track	10 tracks	$10,000
		TOTAL:	**$20,000**

Now that we've covered key contractual considerations and budget planning, it's time to dive into the many strategies behind producing a full-blown studio project.

CHAPTER SIX

Studio Projects

Not all projects are candidates for producing at home. If you're working with a band entity, an artist with a backup band, or even an artist in need of Side-Players, you'll likely need to rent an outside studio to accomplish it. Not only does this complicate matters, it also makes for a considerably more expensive project to produce.

Producing an artist with Side-Players is far less complex than recording a band entity. You're working directly with the artist, and they're the only one with a say. You also have control over the quality of the Side-Players you hire.

But with a band entity? Not only does everyone have a say—which involves politics—the lineup of players is locked in. The band also has to be able to perform the songs live, and you'll need to operate within those limitations to some degree.

This chapter lays out the process of producing existing songs with a band in the studio—particularly band entities, given the politics involved—but all of this information translates to any record where existing songs and a group of players are part of the equation.

Choosing a Winner

Operating as a Producer For-Hire requires a high degree of selectivity. I never take a producing job unless I'm convinced it's a winner. And there are three cardinal rules for choosing a winning project. They are, in order: the songs, the songs, and the songs.

Sure, you might love the songs and still despise the band. Maybe you find the singer's voice annoying. Maybe the band are generally atrocious performers. Both are valid reasons to pass on a project. But there's really only one critical consideration when it comes to accepting a project, and that's the quality of the songs.

I can promise you this: if the songs are great, I can make a production shine—even with the most novice of performers. But if I don't like the songs? The most amazing band of inspired players can't overcome that fatal flaw.

Surely you can understand why I'd much rather produce a suspect band with great songs than an amazing band with mediocre ones. The former offers me the greatest chance of success. Some of my favorite albums were made by bands that were practically infantile in their playing abilities. The 1983 Violent Femmes eponymous release comes to mind. U2's 1980 debut Boy is another. Neither of these bands were technically great at the time those albums were made—yet I find them magical. Why? Because I love the songs, of course.

It can be tempting to take on projects purely for the money— because, well, you need to eat. Since most of us don't start our careers as Producers For-Hire, you likely have some other primary way of earning a living. I'd say, lean into those skills when you can't find a project worthy of producing.

If you fill your schedule with projects you don't believe in, you're well on your way to killing your prospects as a producer.

Producing opportunities present themselves in a number of ways. If you're particularly aggressive (and not very busy), you can actively seek out acts you'd like to produce, both online and in person. Sometimes, talent finds you—through a former client or the buzz generated by your good work.

Regardless of who finds whom, descriptive hype only goes so far. In fact, whether showered upon you by others or self-generated, hype is useless information. Don't fall for the hype.

You'll hear all sorts of claims about record company interest, multi-platinum producer interest, celebrity interest—et cetera, et cetera, blah, blah, blah. Not only will most of it be overblown, but it also often precludes you from involvement—unless you're in a position to pick up that kind of gig.

Hey, even if the hype is true—and it rarely is—you still need to make your decision based on how you feel about the songs. Believe me, when you or anyone else presents a project that's undeniable, no words are needed to convince you. You'll know the moment you hear it.

So set aside those Grammy visions for a moment and focus your emotional response where it counts: the songs and the music.

The projects you select to produce are your first point of failure. Be picky.

Evaluating Demos

Nearly every act has recordings and videos of themselves available online. Frankly, if the first three tracks make you hit the skip button, there's no point in listening to more. In fact, you can reject most acts within a matter of seconds.

They might not even be bad. They could just be outside your lane, or maybe you find them boring. Either way, there's little reason to sift through more material.

Once a project gets you excited, it's time to have a conversation with the leader.

The Interview

Your first conversation will typically occur with the Child of Brain—the driving creative force behind the band. This initial interview is the first step in the process, and it's very similar in nature to dating. Just as you're judging the Child of Brain, they're judging you—and by the end of that conversation, you'll both have determined whether you're interested in taking the next logical step.

Your greatest tool in the courting process is enthusiasm. Generally speaking, there's no point in playing coy so as to gain some perceived advantage through feigned disinterest, like an A&R rep might. It's best to tell them exactly what you love about them—and in full detail—based on what you've heard so far. Let them know specifically what it is that interests you.

That said, you do yourself no favors by offering false or over-bearing praise. You want to reveal your enthusiasm, but you also have to establish trust. If you go on and on about how they're the next big thing—or drop any other trite hype-producer line—you risk losing the gig.

It's also fair game to express your concerns. If you think there are weaknesses that need to be addressed, there's no reason to withhold that information—especially if you have a clear vision for the project. How aggressive or pointed you are with your criticism really depends on the dynamics of the interview and how much material you've heard.

Some people have an unrealistic view of themselves. If you get the sense that the band won't allow you to lead them appropriately, it's a worthwhile strategy to knock them down a peg or two rather than to stroke their ego. You must establish yourself as the expert in charge, even if that requires a somewhat aggressive stance.

This lets everyone know you're not there just to hit record and be awed by their genius. Yes, you work for them—but your results are what make you valuable. You need some power over the direction of the record. Your name goes on it too.

It's possible that ego-checking will cost you the gig, but if the band or their leader comes off completely delusional, and you can't immediately establish your position as an expert, it's not a gig you want. You can't effectively produce an act that doesn't believe they need you.

The interview process typically shouldn't be contentious. Quite the opposite, really. Your goal is to get as accurate a picture as possible of the band—the lineup, their history, their goals, and most importantly, their personalities.

You'll be spending many hours with this group of people. You need to know what you're getting yourself into.

Your questions will vary depending on their past work and current demos, but I can certainly give you an idea of the kinds of things you might ask:

Who writes the songs? Is it a collaborative effort? Is the band ostensibly comprised of sidemen? Or is it a band entity?

These are usually my first questions, mostly because the answers tell me whether I'm talking to the right person. It also helps me understand whether I'm negotiating with one person or several.

The Child of Brain in a band entity is almost always the person with the most power—followed by either the front person

or possibly the most talented player in the band. If it's a collaborative effort where everyone in the band writes together, you'll
need to figure out who the actual leader is. You want to deal
directly with the power player as early as possible. If you align
yourself with the least important member of the band, you risk
alienating the others. Your main connection must be with the
Child of Brain—or in their absence, the leader of the band.

On those occasions when you're talking to an artist with a
backup band, your job is to determine whether the band is a
tight-knit group who plays together frequently, or a loosely as-
sembled lineup with little to no real stake in the project. The
stake the players have in the product is important information.
An artist with a backup band could be perilously close to becoming a band entity. Your interest in them as a producer can throw
all of the expected politics into chaos. When a project starts to
look promising, the backup band sometimes wants a stake. That
situation is ripe for a blowout—which could result in a full band
entity, or an artist suddenly in desperate need of new players.
Neither outcome bodes well for the success of the project—let
alone the completion of it.

Make sure you know the band's full history, including any
personnel changes. You need to know exactly how long this particular lineup has been in place. You could be listening to fully
produced demos performed by an entirely different set of players—which can lead to some surprising results come first
rehearsal.

*Where are you from? What kind of following do you have? How far
from home do you perform, and how often? How long have you been
performing with this particular group?*

By the time you get to the interview stage, you'll likely know
much of this already. The size and scope of their following will
be apparent from their streaming numbers and tour schedule.

It's inadvisable to take on a project with a band that's only recently formed, has no following, and limited experience playing together. This holds true regardless of your level of experience as a producer. Chances are, you'll end up producing what are essentially their demos—just to help them book club dates.

Remember, if your goal is success, you want to involve yourself in projects that show real potential. As it is, you can expect an unfortunately high number of projects to crash and burn—completely independent of your involvement. This is especially true if you get involved too early in the process.

Now, if you find a band with so much talent and musical promise that you have to get involved during the embryonic stages, just know this: you'll be as much their manager as their producer. That means you'll be investing a lot of time and effort into a single group, which will limit your ability to take on other projects. If you believe it's worth spending a year or two developing and nurturing one act, then be my guest. Just understand, you can do everything right, and the whole thing can still implode on you.

Band members can have babies (with each other, even). Singers can lose their effing minds. Irreconcilable differences can happen. And not everyone is replaceable. In fact, the less time a band has been together, the less likely it is that a replacement player will work out. There's simply not enough infrastructure to withstand that kind of blow. And one could argue the band never really existed in the first place if it couldn't stay together long enough to build even a modest following.

Developing acts appeals to many fledgling producers. After all, if you don't have a discography yet, and you wait until a group is in a position to hire a professional, you might miss the gig entirely. That's a valid argument for getting in on the ground floor. Just keep in mind: far more things can go wrong with a band entity than with an artist. And when there's no track record of the band's work ethic or seriousness of purpose, you're taking on a massive risk by getting involved too early in the process.

What are your goals?

You can ask this question early on or save it for later, as the conversation itself will often give you a clear sense of the band's direction. Still, it's worth getting the Child of Brain to state their goals explicitly. The answer may not be as clear-cut as you'd expect—because you're dealing with artistic types, not businesspeople. That said, these days, many artists are surprisingly adept at the business side too.

"I just want to make a living playing music."

That's a common answer, and while we can probably all understand the sentiment, it's a rather broad goal. Buskers make a living playing music, after all.

"I just want to make music that I can be proud of."

This is another broad and useless goal. What exactly does that mean? Statements like this give me pause—mainly because they signal a lack of expectation for any kind of monetary success. As much as we all produce records because we love music, this *is* a business. And we can't eat if we don't make money from the records we produce. If a Child of Brain is under the delusion that a successful record wouldn't also make them proud, that's a potential problem.

"I want to be rich beyond my wildest dreams with my killer songs."

Here we have the other end of the spectrum. This is someone willing to sell their musical soul to make money. While we all want a salable product, there is a middle ground.

None of the above statements really count as goals. Businesses need goals. And when there's a band bank account set aside for making a product, then that band is a business.

So, what are the business goals—both short-term and long-term? What are the goals for the album? Is it to land a distribution deal? To hit the road and play 250 shows a year? To get onto the festival circuit?

Is the goal to make an album they can license for film and commercials (otherwise known as sync)? To create a product they can sell at shows? To parlay a record into a television career for the Child of Brain? To deliver a finished record their major label can promote?

Who's the market? Who likes the act now, and who will like them in the future?

All of this information will help you make the album that best suits the band and their stated goals.

How were the demos recorded? Was there heavy editing involved?

Once you've determined the band's likely trajectory, you'll want to gather some intel on how their demos were recorded—especially if the group is located far from you. If you can't see the band live, then you'll need some idea of how enhanced those recordings are. That information is critical for proper budgeting.

A band that requires heavy editing will also require more time overall—and how *Gridiron* you intend to be about the production depends entirely on the vision you plan to sell them. That's right. You need to sell them on *your* vision.

How many previous albums have you released? How many songs do you have written as a band? How many are in demo form? How many of those do you perform regularly?

These days, you can get a pretty good sense of how prolific a band has been with just a little online research. Nearly everything they've ever recorded will be available for streaming. The more songs that exist, the better—even if half of them are no longer performed. A deep catalog shows a clear track record and gives you some indication of whether the band is truly ready for a producer. Of course, so does the budget.

What kind of a budget do you have?

If you're feeling good about the act and you believe you can help, you need to understand the scope and viability of the project. Without a budget, you can't even begin to assess whether it's something you can realistically take on. If you discover early on that a band is completely delusional about what they can accomplish with their proposed budget, then there's no point in spending hours poring over all their tracks. Unless you plan to develop them on a speculative basis, you simply can't take the gig if the budget won't support the record you envision.

After a while, you develop a pretty good sense of whether there's a reasonable amount of money available. Oftentimes, the plan is to fundraise, and the band will probably have a decent idea of their ceiling. So, this question must be broached directly—but whatever you do, don't lead with it.

Opening with money makes you seem more interested in the cash than the music. And the truth is, the money isn't even relevant until you have a basic sense of the project's scope. A $25,000 budget can be minuscule for one project and enormous for another. You can't judge whether it's adequate until you understand fully what the project will entail.

I'll warn you now: bringing up the budget can be a bit shocking—and slightly uncomfortable—for an act. Some potential clients may not want to reveal their budget, but there's absolutely no justification for withholding that information. While it's true that the bigger the budget, the more you'll be paid, everything is relative. If there's a $100,000 budget, your client isn't going to stand for you taking $90K while everyone slums it in a crappy studio on the remaining $10K.

Conversely, *you* won't stand for spending months in the finest, most expensive studio around only to work for pennies. The budget is the budget—and your job is to make the best record you can within it. That includes your fees and/or Advances.

The difference between an album that costs $100,000 to make and one that costs $10,000 is time and personnel. The hundred-thousand-dollar record can afford a top engineer, a caterer, a cartage crew, a guitar tech—and yes, an in-demand producer. But none of those things are a requirement for making a record or album.

Furthermore, whether you're paid a $10,000 or $100,000 Advance, your royalties pay out exactly the same. The Advance is recouped out of your royalties—and once that recoupment is complete, you're paid additional royalties beyond that. In other words, the Advance protects you against *failure*, not success.

If you find yourself considering a project that, in your estimation, is underfunded, you can always attempt to expand the budget. Unfortunately, it's tough to do that before you've built any trust. And a band can't possibly perceive your value until they've worked with you. Sometimes it makes sense to invest some time into a project in the hopes of increasing the budget—but you shouldn't bother unless you're genuinely willing to make the album for the proposed budget.

Whether you take on an underfunded project depends on how much you love it, how you believe it will benefit your career, how much time you can realistically devote to a gig with limited upfront funding, and how good you are at the beg, borrow, and steal game.

Typically, a label or band won't hand over the entire budget—so don't take that literally. Control over the budget simply means you're in a position to designate and authorize all expenditures. There's no reason for a potential client to withhold this information from you, and there's no way you can commit to—or even *plan* for—a project without having that control. So, ask the question. And if there's any hesitation, explain the realities. No matter what the budget is, your decision—and ultimately your fee—will be based on that number.

When dealing with a major label, you will occasionally be asked to submit a budget based on the needs of the project. In some cases, this is slightly trickier than working within an established budget; in other ways it's easier. In this situation, you charge a per track price, and you propose the budget required to accomplish your vision. If you're in demand, that price will be high (in relative terms), and so will the cost of the album.

Typically, labels don't ask you for a budget unless the band or artist fully intends to hire you. They probably already have a sense of what you charge and what to expect from a budget. That said, you could submit a budget of $100,000 only to be told you need to halve it. No worries—now you know the actual maximum budget. Aren't you glad you didn't start at $40K? Personally, I wouldn't worry too much about overbidding on a major label project. These are institutions full of superstitious people. The more you cost, the more likely they are to have confidence in you.

Whew! All that for one simple little question. Money always complicates things, doesn't it? But it also *simplifies* things, because once you know your budget, you can strategize how to make the numbers work. There are plenty of ways to cut costs without sacrificing the ultimate quality of your product. We went over many of them in the last chapter.

The interview process is your best defense against wasting copious amounts of time. You'll only treat this part of the process as unimportant once in your career. After the initial interview, you'll start investing significant time and energy into the project—and you still might pass or lose out on it. As you gain experience, you'll come across scenarios that are instant deal breakers. These usually come from hard lessons.

When a project implodes because the singer is dating the bass player, you may start asking whether anyone in the band is hooking up. This is natural (both the hooking up and your questioning it). Your deal breakers are yours alone. Use the interview to flush out any and all potential red flags. Knowledge is power, and even if you choose to overlook a particular problem, at least you'll know to monitor it. So, make sure to use the interview to find out everything you possibly can about your future project.

Give Me Everything You've Got

Once you've determined that everyone's goals are in alignment and there's a sufficient budget available, you need to get your hands on every piece of music the group has ever recorded and performed. This includes past albums, rejected recordings, and current demos.

Honestly, I can't tell you how many times I've emphasized my desire to hear *everything*—to clearly define what "everything" means—only to receive some paltry collection of tracks that barely qualifies as a small portion of their repertoire. I want to hear everything they've done.

So do you.

This is far less of an issue these days, because you can usually find a band's entire repertoire online. That said, there may be demos that aren't publicly available, or unfinished ideas with massive potential.

Once you're reasonably convinced that you have the full picture, you can pore through all of their music—past, present, and unfinished. This material paints a portrait of the band: their capabilities, their tastes, their strengths, their weaknesses, their focus, and their evolution. This is how you'll formulate your vision.

When evaluating previously recorded material, pay attention to patterns and trends more than the specifics of any one song. There's no point in tearing apart a record that's long been completed. It's a snapshot in time—but one that can offer critical insight into how to approach their next body of work.

For example, if the bass parts (and playing) are weak on earlier recordings and strong on later ones, it's worth figuring out why. Did the bass player improve? Were they replaced? Or did another producer work out the parts with them?

Whatever the reason, that's valuable information in terms of time calculations. If you know you'll need to spoon-feed the bass player their parts by rote, you need to budget for that accordingly.

Previously recorded material is a treasure trove of the band's own past lessons—many of them yet unlearned. Let me give you a few examples:

If the singer tends to work outside of their effective range, you can make adjustments in preproduction by changing the keys of songs. If the band's earlier recordings are consistently too slow, you can push tempos to better match their energy. If arrangements are too busy and distract from the vocals, you can clean that up. Whatever the issues, make note of them.

Evaluate the band's strengths, too. If the singer sounds best in their upper register, that could explain why certain performances pop more than others. The band might be more exciting without a click. They might even play better without the restraints. Anything you notice across their body of work is valuable information. Use it to help shape your vision—which you will then pitch to the band in your first rehearsal.

Depending on the band's location, a shortage of available material might require you to travel. Unless you plan to sign the act to a production deal, they should be covering your travel costs—at which point you only risk your time. I mean, if there's a budget to make a record, part of that budget should go toward finding the right producer. If the band isn't willing to pay for that, they're not serious about hiring you. Pass. Of course, if the band's local, this is hardly an issue. Just set up your first band meeting at a rehearsal.

The First Rehearsal

First things first: bring beer.

At least a six-pack, if not a twelver. And pull it out the moment you walk in the room. This nominal act of gift giving is such an effective softener it can actually mean the difference between winning and losing the project. As much as your purpose here is all business, you want to create a relaxed atmosphere, one in which defenses are lowered. A couple of beers per person will serve you well in this regard. Even if you don't drink, you should bring beer, preferably at a level of quality the band appreciates most.

Once beverages have been adequately dispensed, I always take a moment to work the room. I tell the band everything that I love about them. I talk about what I feel each member brings to the band. I extol their strengths, and at the very least I touch upon my overall vision for them in abstract terms. I'll often discuss how and why I can best help them to achieve their goals. All the while, I monitor their reactions, because I can't work the room if I don't read the room. My first meeting with a band is my best opportunity to sell myself, and first impressions matter. Why do you think I bring beer?

The best place for me to get to know the band is to join them in a rehearsal. It gives everyone a chance to showcase their abilities, including me. And it provides me with the opportunity to address their weaknesses in concrete terms. This way, they can witness the improvement. In fact, I actively engage in preproduction on at least one song on the very first rehearsal meeting, even if I'm just there for a meet and greet.

There's not much point in getting all protectionist about your ideas. If the band loves what you bring to the party, they'll hire you. It's unlikely they invited you in so they can take all your great ideas and work with someone else. That wouldn't make a whole lot of sense. So, if you're coming in as a dark horse, or if you feel you're against some stiff competition, or if the band seems dubious of your qualifications, then you might as well go for it in as bold and convincing a manner as possible. This is really the best way to win the gig anyway, so there's no point in being cautious with your ideas. You always want to approach the band with absolute confidence. Don't even think about losing the gig. It's irrelevant. If you're the right producer for the job, everyone in the room will know it.

The best way to win over a band is to provide them immediate, undeniable improvements to their music in a short period of time. If the band hates your ideas, you'll lose the gig, but who cares? Do you want to produce a band that balks in every way to your vision? If they don't buy into what you bring to the party, you're done. You can't produce them, nor would you want to. Don't waste your time or theirs.

Whether you're the dark horse or the frontrunner for the gig, the first rehearsal gives you the opportunity to wow the artists and gather information. Really, you either impress them or you don't, based on your bedside manner and the quality of your ideas. The information gathering happens concurrently with the wowing. You want to determine anything that will be useful where it comes to the process or the politics of making the record.

A rehearsal with the band allows you to hear them without edits, sweetening, overdubs, or illusions. It's just you in a room with the core band. Everything is stripped down to its most basic form and hearing them live compared to past recordings can be telling. Not only can you more accurately evaluate individual playing abilities, but you can also analyze the simplified arrangement without the distraction of a full production (demo or otherwise). This comparison can reveal both strengths and weaknesses you didn't realize from the recordings alone. It can also provide you with that final bit of inspiration that solidifies your vision. Most importantly, you can make your first adjustments and evaluations without the pressure of studio time.

In order to suss out the politics you need to pay attention to everything. Is the Child of Brain their clear leader? How quickly does the band kowtow to them? Is there an irritant in the band? Is there any kind of power struggle going on? Does the power shift based on who wrote a particular song? Does anyone seem like an outsider to the band? If so, why? Is there an apparent partnership in the band? Who runs the band business? If it's a backup band, do they clearly respect the artist's wishes? Are they close to becoming a band entity?

Any and all information regarding how members of the band interact or how the duties are distributed is valuable. This is somewhat more complicated than the musical evaluations, because much of your political evaluation will be inferred from the interactions within the band. As such, you want to pay attention to their dynamics. Every stolen glance, every verbal jab, every action and reaction should tell you something about the band and its members. This information should be gathered and considered as you move forward with your suggestions.

You don't need to—nor should you—perform, preproduction on the entire album in a first rehearsal. All you want to do is get across your overall vision, and that can be done in just a few songs at most. The rest of the time is best spent discussing the project, including your impressions and goals. This is your opportunity to put into words how you hear the project and how you wish to approach it. You want to discuss the songs, including the collection that you feel best represents the band, along with your vision for them.

Essentially, this is a sales call, and you are there to sell the band on who they are, who you are, and why you should work together. It's a sales call for the band too. After all, they want to attract a producer.

The best way to exchange information is through effective communication, and by the end of the rehearsal, both the band and you should have some idea of how you wish to proceed. If it's not a good fit for everyone, then you've only lost a few hours of your time.

Once everyone is ready to move forward and the band has fully bought into your vision, it's time to discuss the contract.

The Contract

At this point, you have a good idea of what the project entails. You've sold the band on your vision, and you have the group excited at the prospect of working with you. Now it's time to work out the broad terms of your agreement with your future client, including your fees, your Advances, your back end points, and your recoupment. This way, when you present your contract, they all know what to expect. Of course, we discussed the usual contract terms in The Business chapter.

Some of you are probably wondering why I'd wait this long in the process to even think about a contract. Surely, if you feel strongly about it, you can work out a contract before you go into preproduction. You can even work out a contract before your first rehearsal. Hell, you could command a contract before you even listen to demos, if you think you're in high enough demand and you don't care what you produce. Unfortunately, that's not reasonable, nor is it how things work in this business for anyone other than perhaps the most super of super producers (and not even for them).

Let's think about this logically for a moment. You want to pay to have contracts drawn up for a project you're not fully convinced you should take? Contracts are an agreement, and an agreement can't be made until all parties understand the expectations and until there is some modicum of trust. How could you possibly enter into an agreement if you don't even know what you're getting yourself into? What if you have the band sign the contract only to realize they're unproduceable? What if you find them insufferable as people?

There's no point in drawing up a contract until all the parties are ready. If you're a veteran producer, you most certainly want to keep your options open. If you're a young producer, you want to increase your perceived value before you negotiate terms. Besides, as I've already explained, the budget is the budget, and your fees are based on that budget. Sure, if you're a super producer in high demand, you can name your price and turn down anyone unwilling to pay it. But what happens when you fall in love with an act you believe will make some noise? And what if they've only got a budget that can pay you half your Advance? Will you turn it down?

Preproduction

Preproduction is the process in which you prepare for a recording. You might hear it referred to as "prepro" for short. This is the time when you work out the song tempos, keys, basic parts, form, and anything else that can help your efficiency in the studio.

Preproduction is without a doubt the most critical phase of making a record. All the major decisions are best made at this stage. It's the framework for your record—the foundation. Everything that follows this process builds upon it. Not only is this the time when you get to explore your ideas, it's also when you fully solidify your vision.

Before you set foot in the studio, you want to relieve as much pressure as possible from the process. Make sure the band fully understands your vision, wholly buys into your vision, and is completely prepared to implement said vision. This way, there's a stated plan, and everyone agrees to that plan.

Now it's time to set some ground rules.

No matter how wacky an idea may seem, it can't be shot down until it's been tried.

It's futile to argue over an idea in the abstract when you have the tools necessary to demonstrate it. If an idea can be easily implemented and heard, then it should be tried, not debated. The moment it's heard, everyone might reject it, and you've saved yourself an unnecessary debate.

Presenting ideas to a band for the first time can be an awkward experience. Certainly, if your very first suggestion causes some members to recoil in disgust, you could have a problem. It's often best to save your more controversial suggestions for later in the process. Attempting to convince a hardcore punk band to open their album with a string quartet is a risky strategy, no matter how brilliant the idea.

I'm certainly not suggesting that you shy away from your convictions, just that you time them well. Consider your current level of trust. A radical change will likely freak the band out significantly. Unless your goal is to rattle the cage, as it were—and there are times when that's a good strategy—I would recommend you start with your less controversial changes.

If you think that a band or an artist needs to go a completely new direction somehow, then you very well may want to introduce your more provocative suggestions early in the process. Shocking them is a good way to establish both your position and your vision. It also sets the tone that everything is subject to scrutiny.

That said, over time you will develop strategies as to when to bring in some controversy. More often than not, it's best to begin with a track that you feel you can improve with some relatively minor musical or conceptual changes. If you think that changing the KIK drum pattern can greatly enhance the feel of the track, that would be a good place to start. If you feel the band missed a rather obvious musical opportunity (like a drop before the chorus so as to maximize the payoff), that would also be a contender. These kinds of minor changes can demonstrate an immediate and noticeable improvement.

When presenting a radical idea, I like to couch it in such a way that prepares the act. "So, I had this idea, and frankly, it's a rather crazy idea, and it could be the worst idea I've ever had in my life, or it could be brilliant. I'd like to try the idea to see if it works, and if it doesn't, we'll move forward."

While that whole monologue may be a bit much, playing coy does several things. It prepares the band to accept my idea no matter how outside the box, which opens them up to just about any idea. It also gives them permission to agree that it's probably the worst idea I've ever had. My willingness to accept such criticism goes a long way to reduce their angst. Lastly, I've let them know that I view the concept as a long shot and have no intention of spending time defending it if it falls flat.

Even after I've fully established trust with a band, perhaps even deep into the recording process, I'll still couch edgy ideas as potentially awful or brilliant. I never want a band to think they can't shoot down an idea, just so long as they're willing to try it in the first place. Of course, it doesn't do much good to try out an idea with the band if they're not offering their full-throated effort. When this happens, I like to remind them of our agreement to try things before we shoot them down and point out that I give them the same latitude, within reason.

By the third time I present something in this manner, everyone in the room understands that I just want to get an idea out of my system, and the group will begin to couch their more wacky ideas in a similar manner.

The fear every band or artist will have is that you will alter their core. While it's true you'll make alterations, your goal shouldn't be to change them. It's to present them in the most effective manner possible, and sometimes there is creativity involved in that. Suggested alterations are based on your vision and the songs. Ultimately though, you're there to help them make a record they adore.

Not everyone will agree with every decision. A band producing themselves won't agree on everything, so why should you be held to such an unrealistic standard? It certainly doesn't do you any good to make an album that the band hates. That's why I prescribe such a careful courting period before you jump into the studio, and believe me, you're still courting come preproduction. I mean, we haven't even discussed an agreement yet, right? Besides, there are almost always multiple solutions to any musical problem, so any particular idea that makes the band uncomfortable can be followed up with alternative ideas that address the same issue.

Frankly, if you pay attention and you're sensitive to the overall dynamic of the band, it's unlikely that you'll pull the band so far outside of their comfort zone that you'll inspire a mutiny. There certainly could be specific instances or songs when this is a good strategy. But in general, any group that's ready for a producer has an identity, one that is best maintained to some degree. Be sure to ease any fears that might exist in this regard.

Once we make and agree to a plan, we're going to stick with the plan until the track is done.

It's critical that you trust yourself and your vision. I'm not saying there won't be occasions when you'll discover a brilliant, missed opportunity that completely changes how you might approach a particular record. But that should be a somewhat rare occurrence, and the band needs to be willing to take that journey with you. They also must trust your vision, and once the band signs off on it, they need to understand there's no turning back. In reality, nothing is set in stone until the record has been released. But the argument for abandoning the initial plan must be so compelling that there can be little debate as to the merits of the new plan. Otherwise, you won't finish the record before the budget runs out.

There's a very good reason for sticking to your vision. You may not always be perfectly clear-headed during the recording process. If you don't treat your original vision as a plan, you run the risk of changing your mind at a time when your judgment is impaired by exhaustion. There are many ways to make any given record. Once you pick one, you need to stick with the plan until you're absolutely convinced your production fell short, and even then, it's probably too late.

You'll undoubtedly be tempted to change course throughout the record-making process. Doubts will come into play, both from you and the band. While there's certainly nothing wrong with doubts, if you allow every minor struggle to force you into an overcorrection, you'll never finish the record. And even if you do, your production will come off equally as unfocused as you. Go figure.

Adhering to a plan also serves as protection. If your band is unfocused, it's easier to hold the line. That's the beauty of demonstrating and explaining your vision. You can prevent a complete change in course.

Only one person runs the session at a time (and that's usually me).

This may seem rather obvious, but inexplicably, some people have a difficult time understanding the concept. This isn't about who is capable of running a session. This is about how many people are running a session at any given time, and that can never be more than one. If you are stepping out of the room for a moment, then you can pass the metaphorical producing baton to someone else in the room—whomever you trust the most to take care of the job. If you have a close relationship with your recordist, then have them take the reins. If your Child of Brain is working out an idea with another band member, hand the responsibility to them. But someone must have clear control of the session at all times. I go so far as to announce who is in charge at any given moment.

"Alex is producing the triangle part," I might say.

That may seem silly, but if you don't announce it, you could come back to a clusterfuck of a session, with some poor soul in the room absolutely frustrated because they're fielding four different sets of opposing instructions. I even go so far as to designate a producer for meals.

"Terry is producing dinner tonight!"

Even sillier, I know. But putting one person in charge of something as important as dinner means it's likely to get done. Dinner duty is also a good strategy for redirecting someone who's getting in your way, although I do prefer to delegate the job to the person with the best taste in food.

It can be a good strategy to ask the Child of Brain to take the producing controls every now and then. This can give you a much deserved break from the room and allow you to step back and evaluate a more complete idea. Such a strategy is especially effective during mundane tasks like working out a part. It's also a great technique to use for ideas from your band that you don't quite understand.

Just be sure you don't hand off the producer controls as an act of petulance. That will only cause bad feelings and lower morale. Running the session for a period allows the band member the opportunity to fully develop and present their concept.

It's always a good idea to record the preproduction session. I don't get any fancier than placing a device in the middle of the

room. The recording is strictly for reference and especially helpful if some time passes between preproduction and the actual
session. Band members often forget the changes, and those recordings allow you to reinstate them. Personally, I like to
schedule preproduction as close as possible to the recording
dates.

Song Selection

As we discussed, you will enter preproduction with a list of
available songs in order of priority. Remember to keep your specific prioritizations to yourself. Everyone knows that people have
favorites, and some songs are better than others. You're not trying to hide your overall preferences. You just don't want to put
undue pressure on specific songs by foolishly labeling them "hit
singles."

A hit song is not defined by the high hopes of a few, but
rather the undeniable reaction of the many. You also don't want
the band thinking that the lower-priority songs aren't worth
your full-throated effort. Believe me, everyone will have their
own priority list, and you need to figure out how your list relates
to the band's list without revealing your detailed priorities.

As the producer, you need to understand the shortcomings
of each song. Not every track is a hit—some are meant to be
album cuts. That said, if you're working on a song where the
lyric or melody could clearly be improved, it's well within your
job description to fix it—either by pressing the songwriter or
getting involved yourself.

You can use your preproduction session to evaluate the songs
that don't have demos. Unless you're a Songwriter Producer, I
recommend you avoid getting involved in songs that could qual-
ify as a "ditty." Of course, if you find a song in the embryonic
stages that is undeniably compelling, then you can always prepare it for recording. Tracking a fresh song increases the

excitement level of a session considerably, because there are no preconceptions. There's nothing quite like recording a song for the first time, and if the song is great, then why not?

Between recording new songs and making improvements to old ones, it's highly likely that your priority list will change throughout the course of preproduction. This is especially true if the band has a cache of relatively strong songs that haven't reached the demo stage. Your priority list will likely change during the recording process too, although it's unlikely that a song will go from a high priority to a low one. As far as I'm concerned, there's not much difference between the top 5 songs. They're all in the top five, and number one is somewhat irrelevant when they're all supposed to make the album or EP.

Since you're prioritizing, you should also have a goal in mind for the final track count. Personally, I like 10-song albums. It's far better to release 10 killer songs and leave the fans wanting more than to include five weak and uninspiring songs. Given the current streaming habits of consumers, there's really no point in keeping any of the fat. Major labels only pay you on 10 songs anyway, so you might consider that too.

There's even a strong case to be made for avoiding albums altogether and releasing singles or EPs instead. As such, you should base the track count on the budget—not the other way around. If the band wants to record eight songs but only has enough money to properly record five, it's your job to convince them to reduce the scope of the project. That decision will serve them better in both the short and the long term.

Tempo

Rhythm and tempo are just as responsible for how a track makes a listener feel as the melody and lyrics. They all work together. If the lyrics are upbeat and happy, the rhythm will generally follow suit. A brisk, skippy beat supports an upbeat message. A slow, brooding eighth-note pedal pattern suits a darker one. The overall rhythmic feeling and tempo you settle on should take the content of the song into account. Most song-writers will do this innately. You should be conscious of it as the producer.

While rhythmic pattern and song content will often dictate the general tempo, performance considerations are paramount when it comes to nailing down the optimal BPM of a song. That's true whether or not you're on a click. One beat per minute can be the difference between an undeniable groove and an unsettled performance. It doesn't do you much good to record a song at 120 BPM if the band plays it best at 121 BPM.

Further complicating matters are the needs of the vocalist. If your singer can't perform the song comfortably at that tempo, then that would be of primary concern. Typically, this isn't a problem unless you've radically altered the tempo, but you should always be conscious of the singer's needs. Believe it or not, the singer may not protest until it's too late to engage in anything other than damage control.

To put this as plainly as I can, never lock down a tempo without first checking how it affects the vocalist. You must find an adequate compromise that allows the track to cause the phys-ical reaction you seek while serving the performance needs of both your singer and the instrumentalists. Typically, that isn't a difficult compromise to reach, but on occasion it can be an is-sue. When in doubt, the vocalist wins. If that means you have to change the groove to accommodate the singer's needs, so be it.

You'll probably want to have a click track available even if you don't intend to use the restraints. At the very least you want to have a metronome app, or even a stopwatch so that you can quickly determine the tempo any time the band finds a groove. The tempo you designate in preproduction is just a starting point. It's far easier to judge tempo with focused tones coming out of studio monitors than in the smeary chaos of a rehearsal PA.

Tempo can, at times, be a bit of a headfuck. How you're feeling, or what you heard last can affect how a certain tempo hits you. I have been convinced that I recorded a track at the wrong tempo, only to realize the next day that the tempo was perfectly fine. Just as you need your team to trust you, you also need to trust yourself.

Even if you recorded a song at a less than ideal tempo, arrangement techniques can offer a solution. You can speed up or slow down the overall feeling of a track just by how you present the internal rhythms, which means the arrangement could be the likely culprit. So, don't beat yourself up unnecessarily. First, trust yourself, then figure out how to solve the problem—but only after you're certain it's actually a problem.

Key

It should be rare that you change the key of a song, and the primary reason to do it is for the sake of the singer. If the singer struggles to hit the top notes of a song, you're far better off bringing down the key to fall within their true range. They do have to perform it live, after all. Just be careful not to pull the song down beyond their lower register in the process.

I might also change the key if it compromises the overall sound design. There is an enormous tonal difference between playing in the key of G as compared to E, because the guitars and bass are all playing way up on the neck. I much prefer to be in lower keys so as to gain the advantage in the overall low end presentation of it.

Depending on where you are in the process, changing the key can be a drastic decision that triggers a cascade of other issues. A guitar player may have to alter their part. It can even introduce technical problems. The earlier you can lock in the key, the better.

Song Form

The more effective the song is at forward push, the less you need to concern yourself with structural tweaks. If the energy is carrying you along, then the form is probably doing its job. But if the verse feels too long—or worse, it starts dragging—you may want to cut it in half. That's a structural fix for a songwriting issue.

There are plenty of ways to fix lacking forward push, and cutting sections is just one of them. It also happens to be the simplest—and often the easiest to implement, especially when you're up against deadlines or tracking schedules. Still, you should always ask *why* a section feels long before you start chopping. Is it the lyric? The melody? The lack of movement? Form is just the frame. If the song isn't pushing forward, then there's a deeper issue you need to identify and address.

You can also solve songwriting issues through arrangement. For example, you might hold off on introducing the drums until halfway through a long verse. You could add a rhythmic or countermelodic part to keep the second half more engaging. You might even accelerate the rhythmic structure. Anything that buys you more time is a good thing.

Inexperienced songwriters tend to write in block format— melodies and lyrics set across evenly measured bars. If you pair that technique with mundane lyrics, you've got a song with no real forward push. If you can't get Music Fan through the first verse, it doesn't matter how great the payoff is—they've already skipped to the next song. Besides, a disappointing verse that goes into an exceptionally strong chorus doesn't provide a payoff, but rather a *relief*.

You may or may not want to get involved with the songwriting. That depends on your skills in that area and on how open the songwriter is to input. At the very least, you can point out the part that isn't working and challenge them to come up with something stronger. The best time to bring this up is in preproduction. All of that said, if the song is broken, it would seem to make more sense to choose another song.

I'll warn you now: getting involved in songwriting can be touchy, and the subject should be broached with some politic. If your Child of Brain really trusts you, they'll be far more open to songwriting suggestions. If you're a Songwriter Producer, they likely got involved with you because of your writing skills. If you're coming from any other position, you need to approach songwriting issues with a modicum of sensitivity and finesse.

The Recording Plan

How deep you get into working out specific parts in a preproduction session is up to you and depends on the lineup and skill of the players. The more parts you can nail down ahead of time, the more parts you can keep during the tracking session. If you can record the band all at once, that's certainly a valid way to work, but you must have the space, the isolation (if desired), and the quality of musicianship to pull it off.

If your lineup is drums, bass, electric guitar, acoustic guitar, keys, percussion, background vocals, lead vocal, and horns, you'll need an exceptionally large space and plenty of baffles for isolation. The less isolation, the more skilled your band and recordist must be.

Recording a sizable band all at once takes considerable practice, and you would do well to hire a veteran recordist to help you with that. Frankly, most young recordists aren't skilled at recording in this manner, mostly because it's now an unusual way to work.

How far you microscope beyond the drums in preproduction has to do with what you hope to achieve during the basic tracks. If you seek to keep both the bass and drums, then you'll need to suss out the bass parts during preproduction. This is not a reasonable course of action if your bass player doesn't have fully worked out parts. There's not much point in dragging the entire band through a bass part overhaul during preproduction when you can accomplish that in the studio or even at your crib.

Granted, it costs more to work parts out in the studio, but it's a bit tough on everyone when the band must act like some sort of live looping mechanism. You're far better off shaping the part at the recording stage. Of course, if any player accidentally comes up with something brilliant in preproduction, you should stop and figure out the part right then and there; otherwise, it will surely be lost. And if you're not recording the prepro session, the part will likely be lost anyway.

If you intend to use your own recording space for the tracking session, an argument can be made to perform preproduction in your studio. If it doesn't add to the budget, then why not? If you're charging the band top dollar for your room, there's no justification for doing prepro there unless you're also recording.

As far as I'm concerned, if you're producing an act, you shouldn't be charging for your room anyway; in fact, you should even make it part of the deal. You're the producer. As such, you're in charge of making the best product possible. If your room assists you in that goal, then it should be part of the benefit of working with you. It's always better to charge for your expertise over your space.

Now, as we've discussed, there are cases where it's totally legit to charge for your room as part of the package price, but certainly not if your room is insufficient for the task at hand. In other words, if you have a small overdub room, one that is completely inappropriate for the band's basic tracks, then you shouldn't be recording them there. You will appear to be bilking your client. Notice I used the word "appear." Well, appearances matter, particularly when your band is pissed off at you because you're using digital reverb to mimic a large room after selling them on an organic sound.

So, figure out what your recording requires in terms of space and studio time, come up with accurate estimates, and make sure your plan aligns with your vision *before* you go into the studio.

Renting Studios

When it comes to selecting a room, one of the more important considerations is acoustic space—primarily the size and nature of the main tracking space. After that, I evaluate equipment—musical instruments in particular. There are certain consoles that I prefer as a recordist, but many studios don't even use a console anymore, in which case the mics are routed through outboard preamps instead.

If you're hiring a recordist, then you might want to involve them in the room selection process. Since so many decisions are engineering ones, you might even be better off allowing your engineer to choose a few rooms and provide you with some options. If your recordist has relationships with these studios, consider having them negotiate the rate for you.

When renting a room, you want to be sure that you fully understand the terms. Will there be charges for going over the allotted hours for the day, and if so, how much? Is everything on the website and/or the equipment list available, in working order, and included as part of the price? Do the musical instruments come with the room as part of the deal? What amenities come with the room? Some studios put out food every day. Others provide a runner for the entire day, or only part of the day. The formula is rather simple: the more you pay for the room, the more amenities you get as part of the deal.

Your overdub room doesn't require nearly as much space as your tracking room. For the most part you'll be recording one part at a time during overdubs, although acoustics still matter. You want to avoid recording in an overdub room that's so small and poorly treated that it makes everything you record sound boxy. Horn sections and percussion are best recorded in a slightly larger acoustic space than your average overdub room.

Aside from the recording room itself, the next most important consideration is the control room. If you end up in a control room where the monitoring is skewed, nothing you do will translate in the real world, and you could find yourself miserable. This is a good argument for getting your recordist involved in selecting the studio.

How soon after your tracking session you schedule your overdub sessions is up to you, but there are risks to waiting too long. If you let your artists go home and listen endlessly to the tracks—or worse, take the sessions home to experiment—you could be in for some surprises when you return. On many projects, I don't even offer roughs, because I don't want my artists obsessing over an unfinished version of their record. I never hand over the sessions—they always stay with me.

A lot of young producers and engineers are willing to take a year to make an album—some even prefer it. That's all well and good when you don't have a mortgage, a family, or responsibilities. It's all but impossible if you actually wish to maintain a career.

If you want to take a few days between tracking and overdubs so you can get some editing done, that makes sense. But unless you have a logistical reason for delaying the overdubs, you should probably schedule them soon, if not immediately, after tracking. Even if you're taking time to organize and edit, schedule the overdubs so your players can plan—and so you can maintain momentum.

Preparing and Organizing Your Session

As you can see, there is an immense amount of organization required to prep for a session, and that work doesn't stop once recording begins. In fact, it gets considerably more challenging, given that you might be working 12 hours a day on the recording. That leaves only a few hours each day to take care of business, lest we forget unwinding and sleep. The better organized you are, the less you'll have to deal with your own screw-ups in the studio. There are a few things you can do to help with the organizational aspects of producing.

I like to keep a running document with my thoughts throughout the process. This includes a prioritized list of songs, what I think about the songs, a documented list of changes I made to the arrangements in preproduction, the tentative tempos, the keys, and an overall description of my vision (which can be as simple as one word). I often keep the Notes app open on my phone (which syncs with my computer and other devices) and use it to track thoughts and information about the project and the individual songs. I highly recommend this, because it's easy to forget something.

Before you go into a tracking session, you'll want a basic schedule, especially for Side-Players. Obviously, if all of your players are for hire, you need to nail down their schedules before you book a studio. This can be more challenging than you might imagine, particularly if you have to deal with touring schedules and competing sessions.

There's not a whole lot of point in hard-scheduling your Side-Players for the overdub process, certainly not before you've begun tracking. You could end up dropping songs, which in turn could conceivably change your Side-Player requirements. You'll also have plenty of work to do during your overdub sessions, so you can schedule your Side-Players a bit more loosely. That said, I prefer to book them for the first part of the day.

When you're dealing with the band, and they're just as tired as you are, it's easy to fritter away the first few hours. But when a Side-Player comes, all of a sudden everyone is eager to be productive.

The best argument for scheduling a Side-Player for hour one is timing. In general, you don't want to abandon a creative task, as that is an exceptionally inefficient way to work. Imagine starting a vocal session an hour before your Side-Player is due to arrive. What are you going to do if it becomes more involved than you anticipated? Stop? Or are you going to have your Side-Player sit there for two hours as they wait for you to finish? Not only would that be unfair, but in the case of a union musician, it would be rather expensive since you pay them for the time you scheduled.

As much as it's usually best to schedule a Side-Player for the beginning of your day, there are some performers who do better in the evening. Many singers prefer that time period, so unless your sessions start at 7 p.m., scheduling of the night-owl performer for the beginning of your session will be undesirable, since any efficiency you hoped to gain could be lost.

Then, of course, you will come across a Side-Player who has no earthly shot at ever making a session before 11 p.m. and will need an hour to roll and smoke an immense blunt full of the most potent marijuana one can find. I call this the Blunt Side-Player, and they are often highly efficient once you've got them in front of the microphone. The problem is getting them there in the first place. The best procedure is to schedule your Blunt Side-Player for the end of your session. Please be advised, this is a very loose and tentative engagement. In all likelihood, you will have to make several attempts to get the Blunt Side-Player there, and they will ultimately require a ride. Save yourself some time and make the necessary transportation arrangements in advance.

None of that is to denigrate the Blunt Side-Player. It's just a common side effect of the drug.

The Studio

When recording in a large commercial facility with a locker of mics and racks of outboard gear, there are a number of strategies that I can offer you to make your time there more efficient and more effective.

Whether producer or recordist, I *always* listen to the source instrument in the room before I listen to it in the control room. This way I have some idea of how the sound is translating through the monitors. While this may seem like it's in the purview of the recordist, it's still useful for you to know what the instrument sounds like in the room.

During studio overdub sessions, I find it useful to have a plethora of mics set up and distributed around the room. If you have a variety of mics—large-diaphragm condensers, small-diaphragm condensers, dynamics, and ribbons—all set up and ready to go, then you can quickly grab one for any overdub. This has the added advantage of providing you a near-instantaneous room mic should you want one.

Mics set up in the room are a massive time-saver. It allows you to quickly listen to multiple mics on a source without having to wait for them to be set up. Of course, if the player is seated and ready to go, forget it. Grab the nearest mic, get in the control room, and press record. Once your talent is in position, there's no more fucking around. Start recording.

The beauty of placing multiple mics throughout the room is that it's easy to bus and combine them, particularly when a console is involved in the process. Speed in this regard is more important than choosing between mic A and mic B. If you're ready the moment the performer is, then you have a better chance at a great take. Whatever you do, don't spend half an hour seeking the perfect mic for a woodblock, unless it's some-how the feature instrument (not even then, really).

On the other hand, it's probably worth a little extra time ex-ploring different microphones with a vocalist. This has as much to do with sonics as with the singer themselves. If they don't like how their vocal sounds in the headphones, then they will lack the necessary inspiration. That said, you don't want to waste 20 minutes testing out different mics on your vocalist ei-ther. You risk frustrating them. So, consider trying out different mics as you're tracking, especially if a high percentage of those vocals will end up as scratch takes. This allows you and your singer to hear how they sound on various mics in advance of an actual vocal overdub session.

Some productions call for a particular kind of mic. The broad sound of a large-diaphragm condenser isn't always the best op-tion. A dynamic mic could sound best on a particular track. Even if you find a mic that you like on a particular singer, you might consider switching it out for something else depending on how it sits in the track.

Clearly, when you test your microphones throughout the tracking phase, there will be occasions when your singer delivers an undeniable vocal on a less than optimum mic. Your recordist might feel like you threw them under the bus if you insist on using that vocal, but your instinct to put performance over sound is a good one.

Believe me, I've had some wretched-sounding vocals deliv-ered to me as a mixer. Don't let your recordist convince you to re-record a great performance unless it's somehow unusable, and the only way that can happen is if there is some artifact that can actually hurt people.

The Whiteboard

When making an album, or even an EP, you're juggling mul-tiple songs, all of which have potentially different arrangements and requirements. As effective as computers are for organization, sometimes you just want to have your basic checklist right there in front of you, easily seen by anyone and everyone involved in the project. For this, you need The Whiteboard.

I didn't come up with this concept. I can assure you, it's as old a technique as the whiteboard itself. Of course, you'll want to use dry erase markers for maximum flexibility.

The bigger the board, the better (within reason). You want to be able to see the board from anywhere in the room. On the left side of the board, you'll list all of the songs on the album. Across the top of the board, you'll list all of your instruments. Then you can make a grid and keep track of where you are in the recording process through various notations and markings.

Whiteboard Example

SONG	Drums	Bass	E/Gtr	A/gtr	Keys	Vox	BGs	Hrns	Perc
1	X	X	X	X	N/A	X	X	Tpt?	?
2	X	X			X				
3	E					**		N/A	
4	N/A	N/A						N/A	X

There are all sorts of codes that you can come up with for marking the whiteboard. In the example above, we're recording four songs. Any box with an "X" means we have a keeper take of that particular part. The "E" means the part is recorded, but in need of some editing. The "N/A" means "not applicable" given that the part or instrumentation doesn't exist in the production. The "?" indicates some question as to whether that particular instrumentation will be on the track, or it could mean you're not sure about the performance. I might recommend you have a discussion with the player before you rudely insert a question mark there. The asterisks are the equivalent of a gold star, which I give to players when they perform something exceptionally. Admittedly, the desire for gold stars—and the good feelings that come with them—often leads to even more gold stars. By the end of the session the entire board is usually full of them. This is all good for morale.

The whiteboard serves a number of purposes. For starters, it prevents you from forgetting a part. When you have many songs, and you're working for weeks on end, it's pretty easy to forget something. Let's say you had a brilliant idea at the end of a long day to record a trumpet part on a song. With a whiteboard, you can add "TPT" in your horns column as a reminder. This way, when horn session day rolls around, you won't forget to take a stab at that part.

Now you could easily enter this information into your computer as well. Far be it for me to tell you how to remind yourself of late-night ideas. But there are other, more important, reasons for using the whiteboard. It lets everyone else know where you're at on the session too.

As much as you're the producer and you have the trust of the band, you will on occasion have ideas that are treated with disdain. Clearly that breaks one of our rules of engagement, but there will be times when this is an expected reaction. Marking a concept you wish to try on the whiteboard serves to give notice of that to everyone on the session. There will be a trumpet part recorded. It's on the board and remains on the board until the horn session is complete. The question mark tells the band there is some doubt in your mind as to whether that trumpet part is a good idea. This relieves any angst that the pending horn part might be causing the group.

Lastly, the whiteboard is a powerful visual organizational tool that involves everyone on your project. When you're ahead, it helps to boost morale. And although the board can also illuminate how far behind you are, this is not something to fear. It's far better for the session overall if your entire team can view the board and plan around it. You will find that when you get behind, your team will often step up to the occasion and serve up a kick-ass day. Furthermore, you can use the board to acknowledge an exceptional individual or even a group performance. Kudos can go a long way toward inspiring your team, and you can use the board to give praise on regular occasion.

The beauty of the whiteboard is it travels well. So, if you only track drums and then head to your home studio for overdubs, you can continue to use it. As such, it's a good idea to bring your own whiteboard for this purpose. You can buy 4x8 sheets of whiteboard material at your favorite big box hardware store and have them cut it in half. This is far more economical than purchasing a whiteboard at an office supply store.

Setup

Your main organizational task before your first tracking day is the setup. Much of this falls within the purview of your trusted recordist. Whether you're using a staff engineer or your own freelance recordist, you should probably get together with them to discuss your goals and vision. If you invited your recordist to the preproduction session, this discussion has already taken place. If not, this conversation can't be put off any longer.

The setup for a session can take anywhere from a few hours to a full day. How long it takes depends on many factors, including the size of the band, their skills as musicians, and the quality of the instruments and the room. There's really no reason to rush the setup process, particularly if you'll be camped out in the room for an extended period of time. It's well worth it to burn some hours to get the right tones and create a recording environment that's comfortable, as this will save you countless hours down the line.

I like to create comfortable little "apartments" for the musicians—a designated space that each musician can call their own. Every instrument that has been brought to the session is out and ready to record at a moment's notice. Guitars are put on stands, acclimating to the room. Extra snare drums are laid out behind the drummer on blankets with the snares off. Pedalboards are hooked up, plugged in, and neat. Every musician gets a headphone box, a music stand with pencil and paper (or device), an appropriate chair, and creature comforts. Cases and junk are removed from the recording space entirely. The goal is to create an environment where the transition from idea to implementation is as short and simple as humanly possible. If you think this sounds silly, try it once.

Your needs will often diverge from those of your recordist, at least on the surface. As the producer, your main concern is comfortable musicians who are able to perform to the best of their abilities. Sight lines are also of concern, since eye contact is critical between musicians.

Your recordist will want to place instruments in a manner and location that is beneficial to the sound over other considerations. In reality, all of it matters, and a compromise may need to be negotiated. You don't want to put your recordist in a position of failure because you value sight lines over acoustic considerations, and your recordist should understand that a good performance makes for good sound. You work together to find a solution that works for everyone on the team.

Most studios have a to-scale map of their room, which you can use to mark where you'd like your players. If you can physically go to the room, that's always best, but you most definitely want to put together a mic and instrument placement plan *before* tracking day. Otherwise, you're in for a very long first day in which nothing other than setup gets accomplished.

Some producers *like* to take the first day purely for setup, regardless of how long the process takes. While setting up gear is physically exhausting and pulling tones is mentally so, unless you're working with a crew of dainty flowers, I don't think a designated setup day buys you much. Besides, the band is excited. I say try to make some takes.

Your recordist should put together a setup sheet listing the source, the mics, the mic pres, and the processing gear. This list may change as you and your recordist pull tones. Frankly, you really shouldn't worry too much about the mic selection. Even if you're skilled in such matters, it's best to allow your recordist to work within their own comfort zone. For starters, that's what you hired them for, and if you undercut their preferences at every turn, they won't be happy, or effective. You'll also slow them down. What you need to be concerned about is the recordist's approach to the recording. Not their tools.

Many years ago, I came into a session as a recordist that was already in its second week. This was a project with a big budget, and the producer insisted that I stick with the first recordist's miking and processing decision. I was completely lost, and unable to operate effectively. It was so problematic, that the producer (who I had worked with many times before) soon revoked his mandate. I was no longer hamstrung and could perform to my usual standards.

People have systems that they develop, and while it can be good to operate outside of one's comfort zone on occasion, it tends to slow down the creative process. This is less of a problem with a green recordist, because those systems and methods haven't been fully developed, and they may not have discovered certain techniques. Even so, to micromanage your recordist is inadvisable. If what you hear doesn't match what you want, then give your recordist the opportunity to address the problem as you describe it, rather than for you to dictate the solution.

Recording Approach

There are two basic approaches to recording a band, whether as a band entity or a group of Side-Players. There's aggressive recording, in which the recordist captures the tracks with bold processing—like compression or distortion—to lock in the sound. And there's passive recording, in which the goal is to capture everything as cleanly as possible, and to apply most sound design decisions later. With aggressive recording, you mangle on the way in. With passive recording, you mangle on the way out.

Aggressive Recording

I've spent a portion of my career as a dedicated recordist on high budget albums, and I can promise you this: I am quite capable of placing a part in a sonic box from which it has no chance of being extricated, that is, short of re-recording it. I know, I did it on regular occasions. Not to the producer, mind you. I always announced my intentions to the producer along with the strategic reasoning. It was the eventual mixer whom I wanted to put in a box. The purpose was to protect the producer.

You have to understand, when we were operating within a $500,000 budget range, the politics changed considerably with major labels. I say this to you in the past tense mostly because a $500,000 record budget doesn't really exist anymore. At the height of the madness in the early aughts, it was not atypical for the label to take away all power from the producer come mix time. High-priced mixers were cherished for their ability to make records sound similarly consistent. The best way to protect a producer from the homogenization of our hard work was to employ highly aggressive recording techniques.

By the time we were printing takes to tape, the tones were so dialed in, you could simply pull up the faders and hear a static mix that already sounded like a record.

This kind of ultra-commitment can be a good modus operandi for both producer and recordist alike. You should know what you want, so why not try to make it sound exactly that way right from the start? Granted, this won't leave you much room to change your mind, but that has the benefit of keeping you to the plan. It doesn't make much sense to second-guess early decisions—made fresh and with laser-like purpose—at a time when you're exhausted, oversaturated, and hypersensitive. How often do you think that's going to work out? The answer is rarely.

There's another equally compelling reason for aggressive recording techniques: you have access to analog gear at the recording stage that may not be available when you're mixing. Digital compressors, limiters, and EQs don't have quite the character or color of their analog counterparts. You can generally be far more aggressive with quality analog gear than you can with emulations, which often present artifacts too early in the process along with somewhat unimpressive distortion algorithms. If you're likely to process the mix entirely in your DAW, you can gain enormous benefit from analog processing while tracking.

Now, aggressive recording doesn't necessarily mean you're pushing compressors to the point of breathing and distortion (although sometimes that's exactly what you want). It means you're recording in a manner in which the tones are fully realized as you record. The goal is to avoid the need for aggressive processing of the tracks come mix time. The beauty of this method is that everyone knows where they are at all times in the recording process. There are no surprises. The words "We'll fix it in the mix" are never uttered. Your act feels comfortable because they can hear the record as it develops.

If you're the kind of person prone to changing your mind, you might seriously consider operating in an aggressive manner, as it is highly effective at locking in your decisions.

Passive Recording

A passive recording approach is one in which you leave yourself as much wiggle room as possible. This is how you record if you find yourself unable to commit to a sonic vision, as it offers you the greatest flexibility. The goal is to capture everything as cleanly as possible, leaving you the space to shape your tones in your DAW. I couldn't even fathom working this way just a decade ago. Now? I find it a totally valid approach.

Passive recording does not mean you avoid compressors and EQ. That will only make your life more difficult. You certainly want to take advantage of analog tonal shaping and dynamic control. You just don't want to lock yourself in a sonic box.

When I wrote the first iteration of this book back in 2012, high-quality distortion algorithms were limited. As such, it was still critical to derive your distortion with analog gear on the way in. Now? Distortion plugins are so convincing and abundant that you can adequately shape and control any flavor of distortion you seek in the DAW. This offers you enormous flexibility in how you capture your tones.

Regardless of whether I'm taking an aggressive or passive approach, when I want an uber distorted presentation of the drums, I want the players to monitor that tone as we make takes. The sound affects how people play, and I want to take advantage of that. So, either I need to distort the drums with analog gear going in, or I need to distort the drums on playback using plugins. Either way, the players aren't just imagining how the drums are supposed to sound. Of course, latency can become a problem when you strap your favorite boutique plugin saturator onto your tracks, which may force your hand.

Your recording won't necessarily play back perfectly the way you imagine it as you're tracking, nor will that prevent you from making the record how you intend. It takes many years of practice to reach that level of precision. What's important is that the overall tones trigger your players to produce the desired emotional response with their performances. You generally don't want to leave that up to chance.

All of that said, regardless of which recording philosophy you subscribe to, should you find yourself on a session with a recordist who is unskilled at aggressive recording, it would be inadvisable to work in this manner. If you're not paying close attention to the tones, you could find yourself unpleasantly surprised later.

It's not the end of the world. These are the kinds of mistakes that offer us our lessons. Just make sure you don't learn the wrong lessons in the process. If the goal was to purposely lock yourself into a sound, you accomplished that. The mistake was locking yourself into an unintended sound. Now you just have to be creative with how you build the rest of your production. If you locked yourself into the wrong box, don't fight it, use that box to your advantage.

As you go over your setup with your recordist, you want to discuss your preferred strategies in this regard. If you see only four drum mics on the setup list, and an outboard compressor on every mic channel, you probably have a rather aggressive recordist. The less mics you place on a set of drums, the less room you have to maneuver later. If you seek a more passive approach, then you need to have a conversation with your recordist regarding the kind of flexibility you require. A good recordist will operate in a manner that best serves your needs, whatever those are for you.

Commitment to a Vision

Now that we've discussed aggressive and passive philosophies of recording, we need to talk about your commitment to a vision.

All DAWs, while useful recording platforms, allow the producer to work in a rather noncommittal fashion. Between playlists that allow one to keep every take of every part throughout the process, and virtual amps, which allow one to change the overall guitar tones at any time, the temptation to leave your options entirely open is a powerful one.

Given that kind of flexibility, why would you ever choose to operate in an aggressive manner? Why should you commit to a guitar tone if you can change it any time you like? Why should you commit to removing a part that absolutely doesn't work, when it very well could work tomorrow, or come mix time, even?

If you find these questions reasonable and deserving of an answer, I have a question for you:

Do you really have a vision for your recording if you're unable to commit to parts and tones?

The problem is, if you record in a passive manner at all times so as to provide yourself with maximum flexibility, you put your discipline to the test. You can't stick to a plan if you never commit to it in the first place, in which case, you've already abandoned it.

Just because you can completely change the sound design of your production, doesn't mean you should. Think about it. You've spent time developing trust with your band, artist, or cowriter, you've insisted that what they hear is what they'll get, and then you want to reserve the option to completely and gratuitously change it at the end of the process? If you insisted to your team that you make a plan and stick with the plan, then there could be significant confusion and consternation from your act when you avoid the plan.

For most of my career, I operated in an aggressive manner, in which I mangled my tones going in, such that they really couldn't be changed significantly later. That's still the case when I rent out a room for tracking, because I want to take advantage of the available analog gear. But most of my work is now done from home, and so I often record passively and mangle on playback. That's a big change in how I work. But the discipline has remained the same, because I still develop my tones as we go. And once I decide on a tone, unless there's some problem, I largely stick with that decision.

If you keep every part that you record, regardless of how it works with your track, you're not committing to a vision. I have worked with producers who are loath to remove parts from a session under any circumstance, even after it's been determined that there is no use for it. Every bad violin take, every poor guitar solo, every stupid attempt at a bad idea, is fair game until the day the record is finished.

This combination of data collection and total lack of commitment is not a philosophy of recording, but rather a disease. One in which the final results are nearly as random as the collection process. Not only will your act have no idea what their record is until it's too late, they'll likely hate the final product.

I've certainly made radical changes to tracks as a mixer, but only when the producer's vision is muddled and unclear. When you find yourself with a track that falls short of your vision, the power of the DAW can come in handy. You can certainly salvage a production gone awry, especially if it's a great song. The production might even turn out brilliant by way of some happy accident. But that particular good fortune is the exception, not the rule.

As much as you can change your mind, alter direction, or go back to a part that should have long been deleted, it's an inadvisable way to work. Your artist will not have confidence in you if they feel lost in the process. They're not hiring you to stumble your way through the record and hope it all comes out all right. They could have done that. They're hiring you to provide vision and leadership, and if you rarely commit, you deliver neither. This will result in an act that doesn't trust you, and rightly so.

You have a responsibility to your client to make a record with purpose and forethought. This doesn't mean you can't change your mind. It doesn't mean you can't completely alter your original vision if the creative process has all but forced you there.

Making a record is not a fully planned out process. It's one in which you must constantly evaluate what you have in order to create what you seek. But if you treat it as a wholly malleable process, one in which everything is fair game until it's complete, you leave the quality of your results largely to luck.

Kismet, happy accidents, and unplanned events are critical to making music and art in general, but not when you allow chaotic serendipity to completely rule the process and the results.

Stick to the Plan

As you record, be sure to keep your budget in mind. You most certainly don't want to blow your budget on a song that amounts to nothing more than filler before you've nailed down the top 5 contenders. That may seem like basic math, but bands can be exceptionally unfocused and free-spirited in this regard. As they should be. That's why they need you—someone who can keep the project on course and prevent wild shifts in the plan. Bands in the studio can be like mobs, and mobs can be unpredictable in their course. This is why you're the leader: to keep that from happening. So, don't become part of the mob. Stick to the plan.

I've worked with producers who are highly unfocused, to the point of being a one-man mob. When this happens, it forces someone else on the team to step up and be the voice of reason. Sometimes that voice will come from the band, sometimes from the recordist.

I suppose if the producer is making creative improvements to the project and the team is somehow able to prevent mayhem, then all is good. The clusterfuck happens when the unfocused producer ends up with the free-spirited band. Not only will the album most assuredly go over budget, it will be a complete disaster if it ever gets finished at all.

Someone needs to keep to the plan, and an inherent inability to focus does not mean that you're somehow lacking in creativity. It *only* means you lack basic organizational skills and focus. This is not a virtue, especially in a producer. There is nothing creative about lacking discipline. Creativity is most effective within the confines of a definitive and proven structure. That's a basic law of art, if not life in general.

Tracking

It's the big day!

The musicians are ready. You're ready. Your band is ready. You have a vision and a plan. Your team knows and understands your vision and plan. You have the band prepped. You have your initial tempos mapped out. Your song forms sorted. Now all you need to do is implement the plan. Easy!

Ahem.

Plans are notoriously fickle where it comes to creativity. Oh, I realize I've told you repeatedly that you must stick to the plan where vision is concerned, and I shan't back away from that position now. But let's not confuse the end with the means by which we get there. While you can use the process of recording to assist in your goals, there are far too many variables outside of your control to rigidly depend on a plan. You can't hear the record you're about to make in your head precisely as you intend it to turn out. You can only envision the feeling you wish to evoke. There are many ways to evoke a feeling, and you would do well to be flexible in your approach.

We are wholly dependent on the talent when it comes to making a record. It's all well and good to budget six hours to get tones, but that's nothing more than an estimate. I require all of ten minutes to pull tones with a high-quality, experienced studio drummer. Even a decent band drummer could require hours. The difference is consistency in tone. Great players have a knack for pulling consistent and compelling tones from their instrument. Where a player may lack in their consistency, that's when we pick up the slack on the technology side.

As much as microphones will color the tone of an instrument, whether the resonances "sing" in a compelling manner, or merely "sound" in a rather uncompelling one, *all* microphones pick this up with marked accuracy. Sure, two different mics in two distinct positions can yield wildly divergent tones. But both mics will capture the *performance* with absolute accuracy. When the performance lacks, so does the tone, at which point mic choice and position will have a more significant effect.

The very first thing a great drummer will do when they sit down at a kit is adjust the drums themselves. In order to pull the best tone from an instrument, one must fine-tune it. This is especially true of drums. A snare drum with a nasty overtone ring that causes a beating resonance with the first tom is a problem that can't be fixed with mic placement or processing. A KIK drum that rattles is picked up by every mic in the room. You have only one effective way to fix these kinds of issues, and that's to adjust the source.

That's right, I'm hammering this concept once again. In fact, quite a bit of what we discuss in this section could be considered review. Repetition helps to solidify information in your brain. Besides, you've chosen a field in which repetition is a major aspect of the job. You'll listen to the same song hundreds of times before you finish. Consider my use of repetition practice.

Unless you plan to completely mangle the tones that you capture, you need to get the instruments to sound right at the source. If you want a clicky KIK drum, and there's no hole in the front head, you'll never get the tone you seek—not organically, anyway. Sure, you could sample replace it later, but that doesn't deal with the sound of the KIK in your aggregate mics, like the overheads or rooms. A sound of a clicky KIK drum is organically achieved with a hard beater and a hole cut into the resonant head in conjunction with the aggressive foot of the player.

When pulling electric guitar tones from an analog amp, the first step is to audition guitars and adjust the tone at the amp. There is nothing your recordist can do to make a Les Paul Jr. into a Marshall amp sound like a Tele into a Supro. That must be achieved at the source. Once you have the appropriate tone in the room, then your mic placement and processing will serve you well. Compressors and limiters are exceptionally useful tools for managing inconsistent tone and dynamics. So, you need to fix the problems first.

Mic Placement Strategies

Once you have the right instrument, the player is responsible for the quality of the tone. A great player makes an instrument sing, and with a marked consistency of tone. This tone translates easily into the control room by simply sticking a mic in proximity of the instrument. A weak player does not have nearly the same command of their instrument, and mic placement can help tremendously toward maximizing their tone.

The less accomplished the player, the more significant the mic placement becomes, to the point that a one-centimeter adjustment can make a world of difference. This is especially true with drums, which are recorded with many mics in close proximity to one another. The best way to find the optimal placement on a source is to move the mic.

In order to understand the benefits of mic placement, send your assistant out into the room to slowly move the mic around the vicinity of the source. As they move the mic, you'll hear the tone go in and out of sonic focus. Often, there will be a sweet spot in which the mic sounds best. The better the player, the larger the sweet spot.

If you'd like to remove confirmation bias from the process—and you do—don't watch your assistant as they move the mic about the source—or even the room for that matter. Wait until they've hit upon the optimal location, the one that causes you to yell *"Eureka!"*, and have them lock it down. Then, take a look. Where that mic lands can be nothing short of shocking. I've had mics end up in the strangest places using this technique.

Setting the Tone

Historically, the producer is the person who can walk the line between the technology and the music. You're most effective as a producer when you can make the technology nearly invisible to your band or artists. The best way to achieve this is to make the band sound the way you want in the room, so your recordist can capture and shape the tone appropriately. As much as you want a fast recordist who is able to think ahead and keep you from leaving the producer's head space, setup is not the time to abandon them. If they need an entire day to get tones, it's probably a problem with the source.

As the producer, I may be the boss, but that doesn't mean I don't pitch in to accelerate the setup procedure. I'll move instruments, move headphone boxes—whatever I have to in order to push the session forward. But I never pull my tones based on the clock. Recording is a building process, and if I don't have a rock-solid foundation from the start, the production will ultimately crumble.

All of that said, we do have a schedule, and I want to get at least one song down on the first day. If all I accomplish is the ability to hit record the moment I walk in on day two, that's fine—but it's better for morale if we can finish one of the beds.

Even if your only goal is to walk out of your tracking session with drums, you don't want to completely slough off the tones of your scratch tracks. You want the recordist and the band to have a decent depiction of what the record will sound like. It also becomes more difficult to judge the track if your tones aren't coherent. It's exceptionally difficult to pull drum tones if everything else comes off anemic. Of course, the most important reason to pull good tones on everything is because you want to "wow" the band. If you can do that, then you will have gone a long way towards solidifying trust.

The more trust your band has in you, the easier it is to produce them. When you blow your band away on the very first day of the session, you set yourself up for the remainder of the project. You send the message to your entire team that you seek to accomplish something special. Not only will they appreciate you for this, they will never worry about it again so long as you don't do anything to erode that trust. There is nothing quite as effective as removing all doubt from your band, and no matter how much they trust you before your tracking session, this is the time that they verify that trust.

Happy and excited players are good players. The more excited you can get your team, the easier your job will be. This is true at all times in a session. Pulling poor tones—followed by reassurances and caveats—can be unrecoverable. Job number one on the first day is to solidify the band's trust in you. If you can do that, then when things go awry, you have the necessary latitude to get things on track. If you fail to impress, all of your decisions will be second-guessed, and you will completely lose control of your session.

When the band listens to their first legitimate take of the first song, you want them grinning ear to ear. You want them inspired. You can only accomplish this if you blow them away, and you'll only blow them away if you take the time necessary to do so in the first place.

Making Takes

When making takes with a band (for hire or otherwise), the basic parts are worked out in preproduction and rehearsals. What you want from your band more than anything else is an inspiring performance, one that can be built upon in the overdub phase (if there is one). There will be times when a band's very first take is magic, and there will be times when they will require many takes. Just how many takes a band requires depends on many factors, and can vary by the song, but fewer takes are better for both morale and time.

In general, it's best to limit your takes to no more than three at a time. This is usually true in any phase of recording, but particularly so in tracking. Even if those takes are abominable and unusable, it's good to let your band get off their instruments and out of the recording room to reset. Playback provides your players with a connection between the physical act of playing and the reproduction of their work, and you should not underestimate the power of this comparison. Sure, their bad playing could very well disgust them, but it's far better for your band to come to that harsh conclusion on their own, when possible. Of course, there's no point in stopping to listen if your band can't even get through a full take.

There are times to abandon the three takes suggestion. The problem is that you will put yourself and your band into complete and total oversaturation if you attempt to evaluate too many takes. Oversaturation is a common malady in recording, one that will make you unable to discern even not-so-subtle differences in timing, tuning, expression, musicality, and balances. That's not a good state of mind to be in when it comes to picking takes.

Occasionally, your band will need to rehearse a particular track in the studio. This isn't ideal, but it shouldn't bust your budget. When this happens, you need to stop the recording process in order to transition back to the rehearsal process. The difference between this rehearsal and one executed outside the studio is that you have the ability to capture a take at any moment. You're all set up! Therefore, your recordist should stay in record at all times—just in case. In all likelihood, you and the band will work on sections and transitions before you actually make takes again, but you never know. Recording a rehearsal in the studio could capture magic when you least expect it—if not in the form of a take, then in the form of a brilliant mistake.

I'm sure some of you are amenable to this idea of rehearsal in the studio, given the advantage of an immediate capture. This is certainly *one* way of recording, and it works great with a group of high-caliber professional Side-Players. It's a rather risky strategy to take with a band entity.

Studio musicians will come in without any preconceptions and are skilled at changes on the fly. Bands, on the other hand, have to relearn their parts once you make changes, and may require more practice than anticipated. Those dedicated rehearsals are also for *you*. That's the time you experiment without concern for the clock or budget, and it allows you to make accurate projections and plans. To abandon dedicated rehearsals is to leave much to chance.

Everyone performs poorly sometimes. When a band is struggling with a take, they are likely thinking about their parts as they play them. It's okay to let your band struggle for a spell, but then insist on a break. The brain has this remarkable way of sorting things out in the background while it's at rest. I'm not sure how that works, but I can promise you, a break can have the remarkable effect of solidifying parts and often leads to a killer take upon return.

Once your band nails that amazing take, it's not unreasonable to let them make another take right then and there. No matter how unlikely it is that they'll beat it, at least you give yourself a take to harvest from for edits (if necessary). It also puts to rest any doubt that they've peaked. Don't underestimate the value of setting aside doubt.

I almost always make my way into the room to greet my band so as to personally discuss a take. There are a number of reasons for this. For starters, it boosts morale when I get off my butt and communicate face to face with the band. Secondly, talkback through headphones sucks. It's a necessary evil at times, but for complex instructions and interactions, I prefer to deliver my notes personally. Lastly, and most important, you get a chance to look around the room.

You would think that with several people in a room, someone might notice a microphone drastically out of place, but you can't rely on that. Equally problematic is a room littered with unused and blaringly loud headphones. This is a fantastic way to get that click track (among other things) burned into several takes, rendering them unusable.

While it's certainly within the purview of your recordist to check the room, the buck ultimately stops with you. Even if you think it's your band's stupid fault, you're the one that must deal with the ramifications of the error. If your band didn't notice something out of place, it's probably because you didn't ask them to watch out for it in the first place.

It's really a drag to capture a perfect performance only to discover it's been compromised by an inadvertently bumped mic. This is especially true if it's one of the drum overheads. It can put you in an exceptionally awkward position. Do you keep the performance and deal with the recording mistake as best you can? Or do you attempt to beat the performance? It's catastrophically deflating to everyone on the session to try and beat a killer performance. The best way to avoid that is to stay on top of your session.

I've produced, recorded, or mixed more than one song with just a single overhead. Shit happens. If a recording mistake occurs on a compelling take, then I'll likely choose to keep the take and deal with the recording issue later. I may try to capture the group again, but I certainly won't ask them to chase perfection. I can always revisit the track again once we have some wins. And if I'm forced to deal with a capture issue on an undeniable take, so be it.

Such is the nature of *undeniable*.

Judging Takes

Playing back a take is an entirely different experience from listening to it as it goes down. The mild anxiety that comes with an unfolding performance is enough to color your evaluation. Your first impressions can be completely shattered upon play-back. For this reason, you want to evaluate each set of takes in the presence of the band.

You'll find that it's rare to get a split opinion about a keeper take. One player may be unhappy with a single moment in their performance (that's what overdubbing and editing are for), but if everyone is aligned on the overall vision, there shouldn't be much debate over which take is the keeper.

And remember: when the performance is great, the sound will follow.

Recording Drums

Drums are acoustically loud instruments that cover the entire frequency range. Placing many microphones in close proximity to one another makes drum recordings challenging at best.

Typically, you want to record all of the drums for all of the songs during your tracking sessions, even if that's the only instrument you keep in the process. The other option is to record one song at a time, but this is a far more expensive way to record, since you must camp out in a proper tracking room. It's also a logistical nightmare, given that so much gear is locked down on the drums and unavailable for recording other parts.

Even if my only goal is to capture drums on my tracking session, I often bring the bassist into the control room to play down the track again immediately after we choose a take. It's way easier for the bass player to perform in time while playing to monitors than through headphones. A good bass player with a solid part can help confirm you have what you need from your drum capture.

As we discussed earlier, it's best to record the drums within the kind of space that matches your vision for the track. The closer your room mics are to the source, the less ambient they will be. If you find yourself in a room that lacks the size or acoustic makeup to produce enough ambient tone, then you will be forced to either re-amp the drums later in a larger room (which is essentially a chamber) or simulate the space through the use of digital reverbs. There are certain styles of music and production where a digital reverb is desirable, but if you seek wholly organic tones, digital reverbs always fall short.

When your drums are in an overly reverberant room, you can easily attenuate the perceived space within your capture by employing large baffles. This is especially so where the close mics are concerned. In fact, you can completely choke the drums if you're too aggressive with your baffling.

As much as I'm a proponent of commitment when it comes to tones, it's not a bad idea to leave yourself some wiggle room. By putting your room mics outside of the baffle zone, you can add as much room as you like. This is especially useful when you have a limited harmonic context in which to evaluate the drums in the first place. In other words, it's very difficult to judge the overall drum presentation against the bass alone.

It's not a bad idea to subtly switch up your drum tones from song to song. I try to have several choices of snare drum on hand when producing an album. The tone of the snare can completely change the impact of a track, particularly if you seek to accentuate other genre influences.

For instance, if the goal is to bring out a bit of ska from a hard-rock track, then a wide-open, high-pitched, ringy snare works brilliantly. If you want an old-school '70s-style R&B tone, a deep snare with a wallet on the head will do the trick. The disparate tones of the open ringy snare compared to that of a deep dead snare will significantly alter how the tracks feel. It will also influence how the drummer plays.

KIK drums also significantly affect the overall drum presentation, and I like to have a few of those around too. And some tracks might even call for a change in cymbals. Just a few strategic adjustments can completely shift the drum presentation—adding tonal variety across the record and allowing you to shape the drums to fit each song and production.

The actual recording of drums falls within the purview of the recordist. A competent recordist knows the room, the mic collection, and the outboard gear, and should be able to capture the tones you need.

Editing Drums

As with any of our manipulation tools, you must consider the feel that you seek. Your aggression in this regard matters. An organic rock track edited to grid will yield a completely different feeling from that same rock track left raw. One is the sound of compliance. The other, the sound of rebellion.

There is surely a time for the sound of compliance, and when that's what you seek then editing to grid is a very good way to achieve it. A track edited to grid has a certain monotonous and trancelike feel to it, and that can be powerful. But then so can a tempo dynamic. Base that decision on how you want the record to feel.

If all you want to do is edit large sections between takes, that's a rather easy process that can be accomplished with cut-and-slide techniques (see the *Home Producer* chapter). It's when you seek to adjust every KIK and snare that things get a bit labor-intensive, and that kind of job requires some practice to do invisibly. The KIKs and the snares are easy to move using flex-time compression techniques. It's the internal rhythms of the hats and cymbals that can get a bit squirrely.

I don't typically prefer aggressive edit jobs on drums, but on those occasions when I do, I hire someone with the necessary skill set to do the job. I would recommend you do the same. It would take me many more hours to do a big edit job than someone who does it on a regular basis, and even the biggest edit jobs won't be prohibitively expensive.

All of that said, many of you will edit your own drum recordings, which I also get. I do all sorts of things that I could hire someone else to do. Sometimes it's just easier to do something yourself, and often it needs to be done in the here and the now.

The best advice I can give you for an invisible, organic drum edit is to retain as much of the feel as you can. If you find something distracting, fix it. Otherwise leave it alone.

Bass

The bass is often both the musical and sonic foundation of a track. Musically, it defines the root of the chord, performs an important rhythmic duty, and anchors the bottom of the record. If you get the bass right, your chances of a compelling record increase dramatically, and that's not an overstatement.

The weaker the bass part, the weaker the production. The weaker the player, the less your track will groove. You should make special note of the bass player when budgeting your time.

I spend an inordinate amount of time making sure the bass part is great. There's a good reason for this: it allows me to place it prominently and audibly in the mix. Low end is critical to the stability of a mix, and if the bass part is sloppy and unfocused, this will affect the impact of the track. Think of the bass as the foundation of your house. Without a solid, concrete foundation, the integrity of your house is weak. That's how important the low end instruments are in music.

To me, there's nothing more disappointing than a bass part that merely takes up low-end space. Even the simplest of bass parts should mean something to your production. Clearly you don't want the part so prominent that it distracts from the mix, but it should most certainly be audible and apparent. I'll even spoon feed the player a part if that's what's required.

Bass is often well-served with distortion, especially on rather dense productions. You can distort the living shit out of a bass, and that distortion can be nearly inaudible within the context of the track. Distortion affects the upper harmonics most and can make the notes audible without losing a robust low end. This is an especially useful treatment for a somewhat dense arrangement.

Electric Guitars

When recording an act that involves electric guitars, it's helpful to have a reasonable supply of amps and guitars available. You can certainly record an entire album with a single guitar-amp combo, and if you're after a raw, super honest presentation, that's a perfectly valid approach. But if you want to tailor your sound design to the songs, then you'll need a wide variety of tonal options at your disposal.

Learning the basic characteristics of guitar-amp combinations is a bit like learning about wine and food pairings. You need to taste a whole lot of wine over the course of many meals before you even have a baseline—and even then, you're just scratching the surface.

A Strat through a Marshall sounds nothing like a Gibson Les Paul Jr. through a Rectifier, which sounds nothing like a Gibson 375 through a Supro. The Strat is a solid-body guitar with single-coil pickups—which are bright and scooped in tone and prone to buzzing. A Les Paul Jr. is a solid-body guitar with humbucker pickups—which are fatter, warmer, and offer more output and therefore more sustain. And the 375 is a large hollow-body guitar, so it offers a resonance the other two don't—which its pickups tend to exaggerate.

Each guitar reacts uniquely to the amp you pair it with. So, if you have three guitars and three amplifiers, you already have nine combinations—and that's before adjusting gain or switching pickups.

The neck pickup rounds out the tone, and the bridge brings bite and presence. The middle position is a mix of the two. Each setting changes the character of the tone. Gain controls on the amp determine the level of distortion, as do the tonal controls. Every amp reacts in its own way as you gain it up, which opens up an even wider array of tonal options. Add more amps, more guitars—even a handful of pedals—and the tonal possibilities become endless.

I've recorded countless electric guitars for every imaginable genre of rock music. I knew nothing about guitars and amplifiers when I first started recording. I had to learn it all along the way, mostly through trial and error.

As a result, I've developed a broad knowledge base of how various guitars and amps sound. But even with all that experience, I can't just call out the perfect combo without some experimentation. Not that it would matter if I could—I'm always limited by what's available.

Some larger studios carry a collection of guitars and amplifiers, which makes tonal variety easier to achieve. But that also means spending hours swapping guitars, moving amps, adjusting mic positions, comparing cabinets, dialing in pedalboards, and possibly even tailoring parts to work with the tone. This can be a fun and rewarding process—I highly recommend it—but it's also quite time consuming.

It's not uncommon for a band entity guitarist to have a rather limited supply of amps and guitars. It's also not unusual for a young guitar player to have but one usable combination—and it might not even produce the tone you seek for the production at hand. When your supply of guitars and amplifiers is limited, you should just do what I do: use amp sims instead.

We covered amp sims in detail back in the *Home Producer* chapter. Large sims packages (like IK Multimedia's *Amplitube*) offer me quick access to a huge variety of tones. I can fire through dozens of amps in seconds—and still leave myself the flexibility to tweak the tone later.

I even use sims when I'm cutting bands in commercial studios. Amps often get shoved into undersized iso booths, which compromises the tone—and they frequently bleed into the drum room, which only makes things worse. But the most compelling reason to track with a sim is that the DI lets me keep a great performance—even if I decide to overhaul the tone later.

That said, if a guitarist already has a curated tone—one they've dialed in over years—you won't convince them to use a sim. Nor should you try. If it's the right tone for the song, mic up the amp (just be sure to record the DI signal too).

RECORDING AN AMPLIFIER

Many recordists like to capture guitar amps with two mics, which makes the process far more complicated than necessary. Often, this is done to compensate for a deficiency in tone, although I find it a rather ineffective way to do it. If the tone is right at the amp, you should be able to adequately capture it with just one mic. As always, the source is king.

If you like what two mics offer you, then carry on. But as a mixer, when I receive two mics on a single amp, they're usually a phasey mess, which forces me to discard one of the mics. Occasionally I'll get a pair of mics that work well together, but that's rare. It takes skill and a lot of practice to do it well. For an engineer, that may be a worthwhile pursuit. For a producer, there are bigger fish to fry.

If you're working as both the producer and the recordist, it's always best to simplify the engineering as much as possible. Capturing a tone with one mic is far easier to get right, and it takes considerably less time to place. This way, you can keep your focus on the parts and the performance—both of which will affect the tone far more than any other factor.

Of course, if the studio comes with a recordist, and they have a two-mic system that produces quality results, then let them do their thing. You can always ditch one of the mics later. But if tinkering with two mics seems to be costing you precious time, I would suggest you put an end to the madness and insist on a one mic capture. Yes, you should allow your recordist to operate within their comforts, but not when it encroaches on your efficiency as a producer.

My go-to for accurate electric guitar capture is the Royer 121—a $1500 ribbon mic that's worth every penny. Clearly, that's not an inexpensive solution. The good news is, I'm not the only one who swears by it, and given its popularity, most commercial studios will have at least one available.

Like most ribbon mics, it has a figure-8 pattern, and the rear side of the capsule is slightly brighter. That can lead to some unwanted room tone. A baffle placed behind the mic can help with that. Generally speaking, we want guitar tones to feel immediate. And if you do want more space around them, you can always set up a room mic for added flexibility.

Many recordists prefer the Shure SM57, a $100 dynamic mic with a prominent midrange bump. Like most dynamics, it has great off-axis rejection, which makes it particularly useful when the amp has to go in a small iso booth. It's a reliable choice for nearly any guitar tone, and works especially well for gritty, high-gain parts.

The drawback with dynamic mics is that they're highly sensitive to placement. Even a small shift can cause a significant change in tone, which can make them tricky to position—especially when dealing with excessively loud amplifiers. That said, they're rugged, affordable, and you'll find them in every studio.

Condensers can be a great option too, especially for clean or chimey tones. And while you can certainly use them for higher-gain guitars, they tend to accentuate the rather grating top-end sizzle from the distortion. Mic position can help tremendously with that issue. Aiming the mic toward the edge of the speaker cone, angling it off-axis, or pulling it back from the cab can help reduce excess brightness.

Where you place the amplifier itself also affects the tone. Putting the cab on a rug will reduce floor reflections and produce a darker sound. Elevating the amp on a chair can clean up the low end. All of this is worth experimenting with when you seek to shape the tone, but as always, the most effective strategy is to dial in the tone at the source.

Most tonal issues come down to the player. The overall character of the tone may come from the guitar and amp, but the quality of the tone is all in the hands. The more skilled the player, the more consistent the tone. There is no bypassing this reality.

If the tone is anemic at the amp—that is to say, thin, weak, or lacking sustain—it doesn't matter where you place the microphone. That won't fix the problem. Certainly, compression can help, whether with a pedal ahead of the amplifier to promote sustain, or with an analog compressor in the chain to control the dynamics. But they aren't a magic bullet for poor tone.

As much as we all would like to believe we can fix a performance issue with our tools and techniques, it's really just damage control. Sometimes, a new part is needed, one that is easier to play. Other times more practice is required. But tonal issues are always best addressed at the source, especially from the perspective of the producer.

THE SECRET TO BIG GUITARS

Everyone wants big guitars—especially in rock productions. Where it comes to achieving size in a mix, less is almost always more.

Newer producers often try to make guitars sound bigger by layering them, but that usually has the opposite effect. Stacking high-gain guitars tends to schmear the transients, reduce clarity, and create a chorus-like wash that acts more like a sonic airbrush than anything powerful. If you want your guitars to sound big, you'll want to avoid all of those maladies. The best way to do that? Limit the number of guitar parts—often to just two. One on the left, one on the right.

If the guitars are relatively clean, and the parts are distinct, then layering can be a useful way to add depth. Clean guitars take to chorusing well, and you avoid the phasey artifacts that come from stacking heavy distortion. But then clean guitars aren't what we'd typically describe as "big guitars."

You *can* layer a clean electric with a high-gain guitar, especially if they sit in different registers. That can certainly add some depth. So, there's nothing wrong with layering guitars *per se*. But if your goal is for your guitars to sound "big," then layering is a technique that's best avoided.

This is a matter of space. The more parts you cram into your arrangement, the more sonic space you fill—and the smaller everything begins to feel. The more you obscure parts, the less impactful they become. That's not to say a wall-of-sound approach is wrong. Everything is fair game when it comes to creative production. But it comes at a cost. And if *size* is your priority, you get there by *leaving* yourself space—not obliterating it.

Your distortion plays a big role in this too. Excessive distortion compresses the guitar's dynamic range and eats up clarity and low end. There's nothing quite like a guitar laden with beautifully unstable, oversaturated distortion. But for *big guitars*, you want enough gain to produce sustain—just not so much that the tone collapses under its own weight. We typically refer to these as "crunch guitars."

Two crunch guitars panned hard left and right give you both power and width—whether the second track is a tight double, a loose double, or an entirely different part. For added texture, you can vary the tone on the double or back off the gain. You can even run an acoustic guitar through an amp opposite your high-gain electric. Believe it or not, it can be hard to tell they're not both electrics.

Acoustic Guitars

Acoustic guitars pose a number of challenges. For starters, depending on how it's recorded, an acoustic guitar is a rather broad instrument that takes up an immense amount of frequency space in the sound field. This isn't a problem on a production consisting of acoustic guitar and a vocal, given the sparseness of the arrangement. It's drums that are easily dwarfed by a broad acoustic guitar.

Most recordists are reticent to record acoustic guitars, or any instrument, in a manner that doesn't hold up in isolation. This is understandable from the perspective of the recordist. But if your vision is that of a small and dusty acoustic guitar (just as an example), then you should record it that way. Like everything else, the tonal quality of the acoustic guitar starts with the source and the player. So, if your guitar player is strumming a big Taylor, and you're looking for a much smaller, trashier sound, then you should get the right instrument for the job. There is no amount of mangling that can change a beautiful guitar into a trashy one.

There are times when it's best to record a performer who plays acoustic guitar as they sing. This requires a bit of finesse, as two microphones in such close proximity on a shifting source are fraught with phase-coherency issues. Even the slightest movement from your performer will cause the vocal to momentarily shift within the stereo field. This will also cause select frequencies to cancel out in a seemingly random fashion. This is called comb filtering, and in combination with the phase shifts, it will cause a vocal to sound downright swirly.

The fact is that some people sing better when they play and sometimes play better when they sing. If we are to put performance above all else, and we are, then in those instances it's best to record the guitar and vocal simultaneously, regardless of the sonic issues. Fortunately, there are ways to reduce the swirliness.

In general, I avoid pickups on an acoustic guitar because most of them sound like an unnaturally plucky distorted mess. My preferred solution is to use Seymour Duncan's Mag Mic (as of this writing, Seymour Duncan still manufactures it), a modular guitar pickup that is half mic, half actual pickup. The device easily clamps right into the sound hole and features a wire terminating in a ¼-inch output for the pickup, and an XLR output for the mic. There is a thumbwheel on the device that lets you adjust the ratio of mic to the pickup. This combination allows you to reduce the awful sound of most modular pickups along with the phase-coherency issues caused by an external microphone. There are other similar products on the market these days. I encourage you to explore them.

If you don't have an acceptable pickup, you might try a dynamic microphone on the vocalist since it will better reject the guitar. The problem is dynamic mics are terrible on moving targets. You will have significant tonal changes if the singer is somewhat animated and doesn't stay squarely on mic. There's nothing wrong with an active singer, but once you know this to be the case, you'll probably want to rethink this option.

The last solution is to use one mic for both the acoustic and the vocal. This technique is highly dependent on mic placement, and you'd better lay some tape—around the player's stool, the mic stand, and under their feet—in case you decide to punch in on a take. Even taking these precautions, you could find it difficult to match the tone between takes. This technique also relegates your vocal and acoustic guitar combination to mono, which is why I rarely employ it.

Many recordists and producers think it's a good idea to record acoustic guitars in stereo, which I always advise against. Stereo acoustic guitars will wrap around the listener's head unnaturally due to phase-coherency issues.

We discussed this earlier, but it bears repeating. A stereo representation of a pinpoint source requires a time differential between two mics. To achieve that differential, there must be distance. There is no possible way to get enough distance between two close mics on a single acoustic guitar. All you will accomplish is what I call *faux* stereo, which can be problematic.

Now, if you're in a relatively neutral room, and you use hyper cardioid mics from some distance, that might work. So, it's not that it's impossible to do. I've heard recordings that offered a solid stereo field on a solo classical acoustic guitar. But to accomplish this well requires an engineer, the right space, the right equipment, and a devotion to sound as much as to performance.

The number of people who will defend this method of recording an acoustic guitar on the Internet is simultaneously horrifying and hilarious. When your acoustic guitar clearly wraps around your head, you lose control over your balances in all sorts of playback scenarios. This is the primary reason to avoid phase coherency issues. There will be cancellation of frequencies and a reduction in the guitar's balance when reproduced on small systems. The close proximity of the L and R speakers will cause more cancellation than you might notice on your monitors or your headphones. As it is we lose a tremendous amount of control when our music leaves our rooms. We don't want to also cede our desired balances.

The use of faux stereo guitar has everything to do with one's own hang-up with asymmetrical mixes. There's nothing wrong with having a single acoustic guitar on the left, and only the left.

There is overwhelming precedent for this, both on records and in real life in general. If you're unwilling to accept some asymmetry in your music, then you will at all times use symmetry, which lacks contrast.

The best way to make a guitar appear stereo is to derive the image from the surrounding space, which can be captured with mics in the room, or with a digital reverb.

You may now commence with ignoring everything I've just said. Do be sure to write when you hear your song playing from the pharmacy ceiling, only to realize your beautiful stereo acoustic guitar mysteriously comes in and out of audibility. I love those emails.

Piano and Keyboards

Stereo pianos pose many problems for a producer. You may not have noticed, but they're rather large instruments, and every single one of them has unique sonic characteristics. Given budgetary and logistical constraints, finding the right piano for your production can be challenging.

If the piano is meant to be a lead instrument in your production, then the piano itself and how you record it will have a profound effect on the production. A nine-foot Steinway recorded in a giant hall and miked from distance sounds nothing like a seven-foot Yamaha with the mics directly above the hammers. Combine that with the vast differences between pianos of the same make and size and finding the right piano can be a daunting task.

If you have all the time and money in the world, this is not a problem. Take the time and spend the money necessary to get the right piano on your session. If you have a budget like the rest of us, you have to do the best you can with what you have available.

If you're recording a superstar piano performer, then you'll surely get their preferred piano shipped in for that session—

probably two. That only makes sense for a superstar. If you're producing the local jazz pianist, then you not only need to find one piano they're comfortable with, but you also want to record them in the appropriate space for the record. Therefore, it might be worthwhile to invest a significant portion of the budget to get the right piano in the appropriate space. While I'm all for finding a precise tone for any given instrument on any given production, budget constraints will usually preclude perfection when it comes to instruments like pianos. Ultimately, if the piano takes a back seat to a vocal, "close" will likely be the reasonable goal.

How difficult it is to find the right piano in the right space depends on where you're located. If only two studios in your area have pianos, then you'll either have to use one of them or get a bit creative.

You can find pianos all over the place, and a little bit of cash (and the offer of a free tuning) can often give you access to instruments that aren't necessarily available to the public. You can find pianos in churches, schools, and even local bars and clubs. You might find that coveted detuned honky-tonk piano somewhere close by, and if you do, make note of it. If it's important that the piano player and band play at the same time, and a remote recording isn't an option, then you can always attempt to rent the piano and move it to the studio for your session.

You can also travel with the band to a studio in another city for an appropriate piano. You can record the band together with a scratch piano and then overdub the piano part on location. You can record the piano on location and then record the band to that part. Now, on the face of it, you may not prefer any of these solutions. I know I wouldn't. I especially don't prefer to record the main driving instrument of a production as an overdub. It's no longer driving once I do. But sometimes plans must adhere to reality, regardless of preference. At the very least you must choose between negatives.

Which is better? The perfect piano that appears slightly dis-connected from the band? Or the less-than-ideal piano performed in perfect harmony with the band. I would probably prefer the latter, but not always. And surely, editing can be used to help with the overdubbed piano. Ultimately, when faced with two situations that aren't ideal you need to decide which is best. That's why you get the big bucks.

Keep in mind that a piano should usually be tuned before a session. As large as a piano is, it's a delicate instrument that will go out of tune when moved. So be sure to move it at least several hours (if not a full day) before your session and allow it time to acclimate to the recording space before you have it tuned.

As with any instrument, mic placement will influence the sound. Two mics placed well off the piano will produce a far mellower tone than two mics over the hammers. How far you can pull the mics off has much to do with the amount of space surrounding the piano. If you're in a small room, then the sound doesn't really have time to blossom, and this will lead to all sorts of dead and overblown frequencies. So, if you're looking to mic the piano from a distance, make sure you have a room that can accommodate.

In my estimation, recording a piano/vocal is even more chal-lenging than recording an acoustic guitar/vocal. If you want any kind of isolation between mics, then you have to close the piano lid and cover it with blankets to create a cocoon, which produces a highly unnatural sound. If it works, great! If not, you might have to get creative.

If the studio has a large enough glass between the iso booth and the room, you can encase a grand piano in such a way that the keys are in the iso, and the body of the piano is in the room. Depending on how crazy you want to get with this (and how long your talent can survive in the iso booth), you can get great iso-lation this way.

The default for many recordists is to record a piano stereo, with two mics in close enough proximity to the hammers, such that the piano takes up the entire stereo field. For many situations that's a reasonable way to record a piano. For many others, it's a ridiculous way to record the piano.

On rock productions, particularly ones where the piano is the secondary instrument to the guitars, a stereo piano tends to take up too much space within the mix. This is true with just about any full range keyboard, particularly when the player is using the entire breadth of the instrument.

Keyboards are space-eaters, and you should carefully consider how much space you want a keyboard instrument to take up in your production. Oftentimes a mono piano panned to the side (possibly soft panned) is a better choice. As such, it would make sense to record the piano in mono, which will avoid some of the phase coherency issues that can occur once you combine the two mics.

Hammond B3s and Rhodes offer movement. The B3 is typically played through a Leslie cabinet, which literally spins the sound. The Rhodes suitcases have a stereo tremolo function, which acts as a panning effect when set to its widest setting. As a result, these two instruments record well in stereo.

The movement from a Leslie speaker can be captured nicely by placing a mic on each side of the top rotor, which captures the motion of the rotor in stereo. But just because you can record these instruments in stereo doesn't mean you should feel compelled to do so at all times. Ultimately, you should allow the track and the arrangement to dictate the best placement and use of the instrument, stereo effect notwithstanding.

Synthesizers, like all keyboards, can also take up the full breadth of frequency space in a production. They tend to create a subtle faux stereo spread and usually sit in the middle of the stereo field. That makes them a bit of a space hog—especially when you're already working with a dense arrangement. If filling in the middle with a synth pad helps to glue the track together, then that's fine; otherwise, you might want to place the synth as a mono instrument panned off-center.

Horns and Strings

When you're recording a horn section of four (or fewer), you don't necessarily need charts. Horn stabs and unison parts are especially easy to work out on the spot with a good section. If, however, your arrangement calls for four-part harmony within the section (whether that's for horns, strings, or voices), you'd do well to make charts. Writing four-part harmonies using proper melodic motion is called voice leading, and you can get yourself into a little trouble if you attempt this on the fly.

Voice leading has very specific and stringent rules, all of which can be broken under the right circumstances. You just have to know when. Learning the rules is the easy part. Actually writing four parts that abide by the rules is difficult at best and learning when to break them takes considerable practice and overall experience.

In voice leading, the goal is to create four discrete melodies that work together to create one harmonic part. No part may cross lines with the other parts. You must avoid parallel fifths, sixths, unisons, or octaves in motion. And it's best to avoid large melodic jumps (although the bass voice can jump more than the others).

Crossing lines is the most common mistake. Once you establish your melody as the top line of your voice leading it must remain the top line. If you suddenly allow your harmony to go above the melody, your harmony becomes the melody in the ear of the listener. So, if you have a male singer on the melody, and a female singer on the harmony, and then you cross lines, the female is now singing the melody. This is confusing to the listener and will cause you fits when mixing. In a four-voice composition, the melody isn't dictated by who is singing it, but rather by its established position within the other voices.

The stronger each individual line, the better the voice leading. That said, writing four fully self-sustaining melodic lines that never cross is almost impossible. It's far more important that the lines don't cross, than to have the perfect melodic makeup for each line. This is a basic description at best, and if it's something that interests you then I would suggest you seek out a college course on voice leading.

While learning the rules of voice leading is a worthwhile endeavor, it's certainly not a prerequisite to producing (if you haven't figured it out by now, little is). Your horn section leader should know these rules, and you can always hire an arranger. If you have a very specific part in your head, you can mock up the parts with a synth patch, but you will soon realize why voice leading is an actual college-level class. At the very least, if you give an arranger your top line or melody, they can fill in the rest.

Sectional instruments like horns and strings are best recorded together—as a section. A good section will operate as one instrument, and recording each part individually won't offer you the natural interactions that occur between players and sound. Horn players play best when they're able to hear each other for tuning and timing purposes and will often use only one ear of their headphones for this purpose. If you can record a section together, you should.

Orchestra

Recording an orchestra requires hiring a director, an arranger, a properly sized and outfitted studio, and a recordist who knows how to record an orchestra. There is no room for error on this kind of session. You will have anywhere from 30 to 120 players, each paid somewhere between $445 and $1500 for 3 hours of their time. A 60-piece orchestra (which is typical for scores) will cost tens of thousands of dollars for one 3-hour session. If you're on a project that has the budget for an orchestra, then you have the budget to hire the appropriate personnel. Unless you're a legitimate orchestral arranger and director, your job at this point is as Overseer-in-Chief.

The problem with recording strings is that once it's done, you're stuck with the result—whether it works or not. I wouldn't consider recording an orchestral section, even a somewhat small one, without a MIDI mock-up of the parts. I'd also want to live with those parts before scheduling the orchestral session. Throwing out a $25,000 string section is a political nightmare, one that will not win you any friends at a record label. So, you'd better be sure you know what you want before your orchestra sets foot into the studio.

Percussion

The genre you're working in usually dictates the prominence of percussion. R&B and pop music, which are often programmed, typically rely on percussion parts to carry the internal rhythms of a track. In rock music, the drums carry most of the internal rhythms, and percussion is often used for lift and excitement. Tambourines are the odds-on favorite in a rock chorus, since the surge in high-frequency rhythm is exciting to the listener. The more integral the percussion is to the internal rhythm of the track, the earlier in the process you should consider recording it.

If the percussion isn't a critical part of the internal rhythms, I prefer to save it for last. I judge whether a percussion part is good by one simple criterion: is the track better with it?

As much as it might seem like a good idea to capture a plethora of percussion parts and sort them out later, it's a highly inefficient way to work. It is far better to select your percussion parts by how they improve the track.

When adding percussion, keep in mind the frequency needs of your track. If you have a track laden with high-end information from cymbals and shredding guitars, a tambourine could very well be overkill. Egg shakers should be used with caution in rock music, because they tend to make the guitars sound dull in comparison. Be highly attuned to how percussion affects the track. If a part provides a lift because it fills in a much-needed frequency and internal rhythm, then that's a great choice. If not, try something else.

If all you want to do is lay down some tambourine parts, and the band has someone with the skills necessary to do this (there's usually one), then there's no point in hiring a percussion player. If you intend to have a plethora of percussion parts, then a professional player is recommended. Not only will a high-caliber percussion player have great rhythm, they will often play parts that work well within your production. The time you save can make it well worth hiring a professional percussionist.

Vocals

There's a reason why the vocal sits prominently in the middle of our most popular and enduring songs—it's the money. It carries the melody and the lyric—the entirety of the song. When rapped, it's the part that pushes us forward through the song.

This is not to dismiss the importance of a track or an arrangement. The functions of harmony, countermelody, response, rhythm, and bass are what make a production compelling. But make no mistake, they are there to serve the vocal.

The best strategy for capturing a killer vocal performance is to deliver a track that excites your artist. You're far more likely to get a moving performance when your performer is inspired. Think about it. How on earth will you ever get a compelling vocal if the track itself doesn't emotionally move your vocalist to perform?

The answer is you won't.

As far as I'm concerned, the goal is to compel your singer to ask *you* to lay down their vocal. Once they do, you can be sure you have a track that's doing everything it should.

This is the reaction that I strive for when I build a production. If I can cause the singer to react, they can cause the listener to react. So can you.

Recording Vocal Overdubs

There are two basic strategies to overdubbing a vocal—comping and punching. A comp is a vocal that is compiled from several full performances.

Sometimes it's advantageous to record a song by punching in on lines or sections after the initial capture or comp. This technique is especially useful if there is a challenging section. There's no reason to make a singer perform an entire song just to capture one difficult line.

Anytime you can record a full performance you should. This is what the singer's main gig is—to perform. And once you're done the record, they are likely to perform the song repeatedly live. At some point they will have to sing the entire song. The recording phase would seem an ideal time for them to start that process.

You capture a great vocal performance any way that you can, but if the singer comes unprepared, you're kind of wasting your time. Yes, you can punch in one line at a time if you have to. You could punch in one word at a time, but that's a tough way to collect a performance. There's a big difference between singing lines and performing. If you immediately launch into punch-in mode, you don't provide your singer an opportunity to find their best approach. Performers need to get into a flow.

Believe me, if your singer's woefully unprepared, you're better off letting them discover that for themselves. That's usually as simple as allowing them to sing the track down three times and stitching together a comp to fully illuminate the problem.

The issue is often so glaring that your singer will interrupt the comping process. Personal shame can be such a wonderful motivator. If that doesn't work, then bluntness is probably your next best option.

"You're not ready to sing this."

The idea isn't to beat your artist up, but rather to give them the opportunity to deliver their best. If your vocalist can't be bothered to demand a high standard of themselves, then how can they possibly demand that from you? Your best is wholly dependent on theirs. Once your singer is faced with the mediocrity of their own take, they will often recognize the reality of the situation—you can only coach them; you can't deliver the goods. That's their job.

Of course, as the psychologist-in-chief, we must take into account our singer's morale. As much as I want my singer to learn a lesson about coming to the session unprepared, I don't want to crush their confidence. Rather than to send them home on a low note, I'll move to another song—one that I'm certain they can perform well. This allows them the opportunity for some success and allows us to set the bar for any remaining songs. I'll warn you now, this strategy can totally backfire if your vocalist struggles with an easy song.

In general, you want to avoid comping more than a few takes at a time. You increase your comping time considerably with every take you introduce. If it's the first vocal session of the day, you might record a few takes for warmup. Even if they did their proper vocal exercises, it can sometimes take a few takes to get them into the zone.

Of course, warmup takes are generally atrocious, so you may end up with six takes on your first run at the track. Save yourself some headaches and start by comping the later takes. Reserve the warmup takes for filling in what you're missing. If those takes prove insufficient, you may need to record another set.

When all goes well, you can cut large sections of vocals together from about two takes of material. That's the ideal scenario, because it means everything's clicking. If only things were always that easy.

Many times, you won't really know what you've got until you attempt the first comp. There is nothing wrong with making a comp purely so the singer has something to beat. Once you have a take, it can really take the pressure off.

It's not a bad idea to let a comp sit a day or two before making a final judgment on it. Comping a vocal can require an enormous amount of concentration and energy. When a comp is fresh, you're often far too hypersensitive and oversaturated to evaluate its overall effectiveness. You may want to set it aside until you've moved on to other tracks.

If I get one great comp from my singer, then I want to follow that up with another. There's nothing like a string of successes to bring a performer into the zone, and I want to capture them while they're hot.

As much as comping is preferable to punching, there are times when you will have no choice but to record by section. For instance, if you have six takes, and the first verse falls short on every take, it's totally reasonable to focus on that section of the song until it clicks.

You might also come across a note that causes your performer issues. A difficult note can cause your singer to falter, both on the approach and on the subsequent lines, which can be a tricky bit of business. It may require you to focus on that section until you get what you need.

Then there are physical considerations. If a certain section is going to blow your singer out for the day, then you should surely avoid that section until you have the rest of the take. And if the plan is to record several vocals in a day, then it would be best to reserve that section for the end of the day.

Vocals in the Studio

It's perfectly fine to record a vocal in the studio if we're capturing a performance. Once the process gets more involved than that, it makes more sense to record in a less expensive setting.

When recording in a studio I personally prefer to bring the singer into the control room with me. Not only does it make communication more efficient, but it also allows me to kick everyone else out of the room. If the singer responds to an "audience," as it were, then others on the team are welcome to stay. But the moment they become a distraction, everyone has to go.

Of course, if your singer prefers to perform in the live room, then that's where you should put them. Just be sure you're rolling the moment they're ready to sing. This is not the time to allow your recordist to go into anal mode. Set the preamp and the compressor, make sure you have good level, and roll.

An important part of a producer's job is to keep the process invisible. Performance is about being in the right headspace. When the technology gets in the way, you've failed a fundamental part of your job. Hey, whatever—dust yourself off, and do better next time. Even the most veteran producer will be caught unprepared occasionally.

For the most part, I find it's best if I don't interrupt a performance for notes and suggestions. I'd rather let the singer sing the whole track down and then offer my notes between takes. That said, if I'm not getting anything usable from a take, I don't allow them to struggle. That will only generate frustration. Sometimes people just need a reset.

Encouragement is surely a useful tool to keep your performer's spirits up, but false praise can do more harm than good. It's okay if you have nothing to say beyond, "cool, let's make another one." Believe me, it's better to say nothing than to spit out a bunch of crap that could easily be misinterpreted, all because you're not comfortable with a little dead air. Both you and your artist are there to work. They seek your expert guidance to help them deliver their best. If you have nothing to add at that moment, it likely means you're not sure of what you think. Wait until you are.

When comping a vocal, tuning is typically my last concern, but it is certainly a consideration in the selection process, especially if I want the tuning invisible. The goal is to assemble a *performance*—one that I can emotionally connect with and keeps my attention. The tuning of your singer can have some role in that connection, although I can promise you, a great performance can withstand some klunkers.

Typically, I send the performer out of the room while I comp the vocal, but it really depends on the singer. Some artists prefer I make the take alone, which is probably the most efficient way to work. Others prefer to be there for the decision-making process. I'm fine with either unless the singer starts working against me, at which point I'll tactfully request some time to make the comp. I may couch it as needing them to stay fresh.

Selecting the best takes for a comp is not something everyone can do well, especially when it's their own performance. Singers can focus on all the wrong things when it comes to their vocal takes. If the singer has good instincts, or is just observing, they're welcome to stay in the room with me. Otherwise, it's best if they get some distance so they can evaluate the compiled *performance* with a fresh ear.

If a vocalist is delivering something great, I don't want to get in the way of that. I'll merely praise them and suggest we record more takes. If they're struggling, I need to figure out why. Is it a monitoring issue? Are they still not fully warmed up? Is their mind elsewhere? Sometimes, they just need to hear playback for themselves, which will help them to make the necessary adjustments. It also allows me the time to formulate my thoughts and offer some direction.

The Cue Mix

The vast majority of tuning and timing issues are a result of an improperly balanced cue mix. What your singer hears in their headphones will directly affect how they perform.

When you find a competent singer unable to deliver the basics, then your first course should be to investigate exactly what they're monitoring. This way, you can make the necessary adjustments to the cue mix.

If your vocalist can't seem to sing in tune, it's usually because they aren't hearing enough harmonic information in their mix. If they struggle with their timing, they likely need to hear more rhythm. They could also have too much of themselves in their headphones. Most singers go flat when they're too loud in the cue, and sing sharp when they're not loud enough, but you can only rely on that to a point, because it's not *always* the case.

Latency can also cause timing issues. If you don't need plugins, then you can monitor the input of your vocal through your interface software panel, which will eradicate latency.

Monitoring with reverb can also cause tuning problems. Digital reverb generates complex early reflections which can mask a singer's pitch. It also hides flaws at a time when you want them readily apparent. As such, it's best to monitor the vocal dry as you're recording.

Occasionally, I'll come across a singer who prefers to sing with reverb. If I can't dissuade them from this, then I'll set up a stereo delay with short delay times and enough feedback to generate a reverberant sound. This treatment will satisfy your singer's requirement for reverb with less likelihood of tuning issues that come with reverb.

Whenever I notice a performer is struggling, I always check their monitor mix on a set of headphones. Many studios have multi-channel headphone systems, which gives the performer some control over their cue mix. While this is generally a useful feature, some performers have trouble setting their balances. I've discovered some rather shocking and useless cue mixes.

Since I record my overdubs on clean sessions, I usually only offer the singer a stereo mix which is balanced to allow them to hear everything well. But then I've been doing this a while. If you'd like to keep your session light, but still maintain some control over the cue mix, you can always import stereo sub-mixes.

Singing to Monitors

When headphones or in-ears aren't cutting it, try setting some monitors on stands and place the singer in the middle of the stereo field. You can do this in the room, or you can just bring them into the control room.

Some recordists will flip the polarity on one of the monitors when recording vocals this way. The thinking is that the center information will cancel, and you can put the mic in the null spot. In my experience, this doesn't buy you much more than the annoyance of listening to an out-of-phase stereo image. I've recorded many vocals with monitors. I've found the bleed to be the same regardless of monitor polarity.

You may want to consider a dynamic mic when recording a singer with monitors, though you can certainly use a condenser. If you place the microphone so that it's flush with the front plane of the monitors, you will minimize the bleed. Be sure that the monitors are loud enough for your vocalist to perform—but not so loud that you're picking up excessive bleed.

A healthy bit of compression can work to all but eradicate the bleed during the performance. It's the tacit parts in which the leakage will be most apparent, and you may have to strip the audio between vocal lines to deal with it. Setting your compressor to a slower release time will help, as it will give you a little time before that bleed creeps in. Just be sure you don't send parts to the monitor mix that you're still debating. Monitoring with parts that might be abandoned can prove problematic come mix time due to the bleed. This is especially true with percussion parts.

While you certainly need to be wary of the bleed, I record with monitors all the time with great success. It just requires a little diligence on your part. If your singer performs better standing in front of monitors, then that's all that matters. Besides, headphone leakage can be just as problematic (if not more so) than monitor leakage.

Miking a Vocalist

When recording in the studio, you should audition microphones to find the one that best represents your singer within the context of the track. Notice I said within "context." You could find a mic that does everything you want for a singer in the abstract, only to find it lacking on a particular track. Context is not something to be ignored.

The procedure for auditioning mics is simple. Pick five contenders, set them up, and record a section of the song on each mic. Choose the one that sounds best.

Your singer could very well prefer a mic that you don't favor. No mic or preamp will ever matter more than your singer's confidence. If the price of the artist's confidence is a mic that is less than ideal, it's usually a worthwhile cost, and you're likely best to acquiesce.

Fortunately, not all artists and singers are this sensitive, and if you can shake your performer off a poor mic choice without any ill effects, then by all means, do it. But if your singer likes what they're hearing, they're more likely to perform their best. Besides, you buy yourself an enormous cache of good will when you put your artist's needs above your own.

By far, the most commonly used microphone for vocals is the LDC. They're big, sensitive mics that capture the full range of the frequency spectrum. They also look impressive in front of a singer, which can have the added benefit of boosting the singer's confidence. But an LDC is not automatically the best choice, and not all LDCs sound great on all singers.

Dynamics will shine on singers with an obvious dearth in their mid-range—often described as hollow, broad, or even smokey in nature. Dynamics are also a major pain in the ass, especially on vocalists who tend to get excited as they perform. Even slight shifts in position on a dynamic microphone will manifest as an obvious change in tone. That said, if a dynamic offers the best presentation of your vocalist, then that's the type of mic you should use, even if it makes you work a little harder down the line.

Once you accept that there isn't a single mic that you can use for every vocalist, and once you concede that your most expensive mic available could very well be the worst choice, you will be well on your way to the right headspace for judging vocal mics. Forget about how much the mic costs. Pick the mic that sounds best for the production.

In order to neutralize a room of size, you can use three large gobos to create an open booth. One gobo goes directly behind the singer, the other two gobos flap off at 45 degree angles (or so), and the singer stands within their boundaries. This will control much of the room ambience from returning into the mic. It's a standard setup when recording a vocalist in a large tracking room.

Pop screens are often a necessity when recording vocals so as to control the plosives. The "P", "B" and "T" consonants will produce a rush of air. This will result in a short burst of low end every time one of those consonants sounds, which is nothing short of distracting. Excessive plosives could force you to pull out a high-pass filter later, which often sacrifices low-end weight. Where a filter fails, you may have to draw out the plosives by hand, which is a time-consuming process best avoided.

The presence of overt plosives and esses is almost always a mic placement issue. Everyone wants to put a condenser mic right in front of the singer's mouth for the proximity effect, but raising or lowering it somewhat can often garner a better result. When you lower the mic, it will derive more low end from the chest cavity. This can be overbearing on a male vocalist in their lower register, but quite useful on female vocalists who tend to get strident in their upper register.

The problem is it can be a bit disconcerting for a singer to perform on a mic that appears out of proximity to their mouth. The mic position could cause them to crane their neck or awkwardly alter their stance. To avoid this, you can use the pop screen as a decoy target for the singer. That usually works like a charm. Just make sure you tell them where to aim.

The "S" consonant produces sibilance, and this can be just as problematic as plosives. Unfortunately, a pop filter doesn't help much with sibilance. If the esses you hear from the mic are especially egregious, you should either consider another mic or adjust its placement.

Don't be afraid to experiment a little with mic placement. Compression, even applied in stages, will bring those esses forward, so it's best to minimize them as much as you can at the time of recording.

While a de-esser can help, it's inadvisable to use them as part of your recording chain. They are far too unpredictable and can cause your singer to have an intermittent lisp, and there's no easy way to fix that. Compression later will only make the lisp even more apparent. As such, de-essers are best reserved as a mixing tool.

If you have a solid collection of mic pres available for your session, then you're merely looking for the pre that best pairs with the mic. I can assure you it's not worth comparing five pres in combination with five mics for a total of 25 vocal tests. No one wants to go through that, and it's totally unnecessary. Any quality pre should be adequate for recording a vocal.

Once you've chosen your mic and positioned your singer, the next factor to consider is how you'll control the vocal's dynamic range.

Compressing Vocals

Copious compression is the norm for modern vocals. Music must compete with all sorts of external noise in the real world, and an overly dynamic vocal doesn't maintain consistent audibility. The right analog compressor can help a vocal tremendously, but some compressors introduce obvious artifacts almost immediately. While there is nothing wrong with audible compression, if you record that way, then you are committing to that sound.

Don't be afraid to move the meter on your compressor. There are some analog compressors—like 1176s and LA2As that you can hit quite hard before you hear any obvious artifacts. There are others that will introduce woolliness and distortion the moment you insert them. That's not something to be afraid of, but rather something to use to your advantage when it suits you, and to avoid when it doesn't.

While it's true you may want to avoid over-compressing, you don't want to be timid either. It actually helps most singers when they hear themselves somewhat aggressively compressed, and it's probably going to end up like that anyway. Overcompression isn't something to fear. It's something to listen for—then dial back if it doesn't suit the sound.

Double Vocals

Double vocals can be recorded as an effect, or as a way to support a weaker vocal. A loose double will flam, which produces a carefree feeling. A tight double will chorus and offer a feeling of ensemble power.

Perry Farrell (Jane's Addiction, Porno for Pyros) frequently sings as many as seven lead vocals on his productions. Each take has slightly different phrasing and timing, which creates a party-like atmosphere—in this case, all the guests happen to be Perry Farrell. He likely chose this technique to hide the relatively thin nature of his vocals. It also happens to be a pretty cool effect.

The main reason to double is to blur imperfections and even out the tone. It's also effective for making a somewhat weak singer sound more powerful. When you double a great singer, you're washing over their nuances. If it's their subtleties that make them compelling, then you're better off avoiding doubles.

When recording loose doubles, you can run the track from the top. When recording tight doubles, the singer has to learn the phrasings from the comp and mimic them. Given this, it's best to work tight doubles by section: long enough so that the singer can get some flow, and short enough that they can remember their phrasings. Make sure they hear the original vocal at least as loud as the new pass. This procedure could require a few passes. Once your singer starts nailing lines, keep those and punch around them.

Background Vocals and Harmonies

Background vocals can range anywhere from a single vocal harmony to stacked harmonies in which each note is doubled or tripled—possibly even quintupled if that's the desired sound.

Given that the vocal is the focal point of most songs, the way you treat it will have a huge effect on how the track is perceived. Any track in which all of the backing vocals are stacked as overdubs by the lead singer has a far less organic sound than harmonies performed by someone else.

This isn't a value judgment on my part. Organic doesn't equal better, it merely means it sounds more natural and less produced. This all ties into your early decision of a raw or polished presentation.

Harmonies in general are far less intimate when doubled and tripled due to the natural chorusing effect. If the goal is to create the illusion of a highly polished pop record, then stacked vocals are a good technique to use. If the goal is to create a raw, heartfelt track, then any more than one background vocal would work counter to that goal. The more precise you are in your vocal stacking, the more polished the record will sound.

Esses that flam make for sloppy stacked vocals. You can combat this malady by asking your performer to duck their esses on the tail of their harmony parts. They can try to duck the front esses too, but those are much harder to do. Internal esses are usually tight and not a problem.

When you want your backgrounds super tight, it's best to work in small chunks. Your vocalist needs to learn what they did on their first pass in order to match it with their second.

If they're having issues singing their double in tune, have them slide one of their headphones to the back of their head. Then have them cup their hand against their jaw so that their fingers touch the entrance to their ear canal. This allows them to hear their voice more directly, which can make it far easier to sing in tune.

It doesn't make sense to inject a whole lot of personality into a stacked background part. Vibrato can get a little weird across multiple passes. If you keep the background stacks relatively motionless, it makes stacking easier and leaves more room for your lead vocalist to riff. In general, vibrato as a technique has gone out of favor, largely due to the advancement of tuning software.

Be mindful in regard to how aggressively you tune your background vocals because they can get a little phasey and weird when you do. If strange phasing artifacts on your backgrounds don't bother you, then carry on. But if you want those vocals to sound relatively natural, then you'll have to get the preponderance of them in tune as you record. This just requires attention to detail. Keep recording them until they're in tune.

Some singers don't blend well together. Often the suggested solution is to have the lead singer perform the harmonies. But that may not produce the sound you seek, in which case you're far better off either hiring a Side-Player or having another band member sing the parts. Or you could sing them yourself if that's in your wheelhouse.

A harmony part can completely change the feeling of a track. If the proposed part doesn't do good things, then you should get in there and change the parts until they do. This is within your domain as the producer.

When the harmony is in a higher register than the melody, you have to be careful about how you balance the parts because the higher vocal will be perceived as the melody. Therefore, an upper harmony should be noticeably quieter than the lead in the mix.

Keep Them Comfortable

When it comes to vocals, all rules go out the window, particularly singing rules. Open vowels are useful for keeping a singer on pitch, but classical-style pronunciation is rarely desirable in modern music. It's one thing if you're recording a pure singer, where incredible technique is combined with soulful singing. But singers like that have technique ingrained.

Most vocalists are not technicians but rather performers with their own quirks and style. The only time to bring technique into the equation is if it will improve their ability to perform. More often than not, it will only serve to put them in a space of thinking rather than performing. You generally want to avoid that.

Only address posture if your singer is having an issue with their tuning or breath control. Beyond that, it's not worth thinking about. It doesn't matter if the vocalist wants to stand on their head—if they're convinced they'll deliver a great vocal, let them. In fact, sometimes it's best for your singer to perform in a manner well outside their norms.

I had an artist who was so used to singing in bed that they performed better on their back. If something makes your singer more comfortable, forget about convention—encourage them. Keep this in mind when you're recording vocals, especially when your singer struggles.

Didgeridoo, Dulcimer, and Bagpipes

Throughout your producing career, you'll come across all sorts of wacky instruments you've never heard of, never seen in person, and certainly never recorded—like didgeridoo, dulcimer, and bagpipes. I've recorded all three, and not a single one came with a "how to record" instruction manual. Go figure.

I can save you a whole lot of stress where it comes to recording an instrument you've never seen before. The advice I am about to give you is not only ridiculously simple—it's the secret to recording in general. If the thing sounds good in the room, no matter how exotic, mic placement is the key to capturing it in all its glory.

If you can find a location where all the important aspects and notes are picked up evenly, you can successfully record the instrument. It's as simple as that. Listen to the instrument in the room. Locate the spot that seems to best capture it. Place a mic there. If it sounds off, move it until you find the sweet spot. If it sounds right, start recording.

If you and your recordist are unable to find a position that captures the instrument evenly, that's when you begin to introduce more mics. The reason we use so many mics on a drum kit is to control the balances. When there's some aspect of the tone that needs to be boosted, bring in another mic to help even things out.

See? I told you it was simple.

Okay, yes, yes—if you stick an SM57 mic 10 feet off a dulcimer, you'll likely be disappointed. But even the greenest assistant would suggest trying a large- or small-diaphragm condenser instead. It doesn't take long before you start recognizing the basic characteristics of different mics.

Overdubbing Side-Players

When working with a band entity, it's not unusual to bring in Side-Players as part of the overdub phase, especially if you include instrumentation that doesn't exist within the band itself. In general, you should have a fairly good idea of what you're looking to achieve with a part. You may have specific parts in mind, but it's often smart to keep those in your back pocket until you hear your musician's take on it. This has more relevance in the overdub phase, given that you're often hearing a Side-Player for the first time.

Every musician has a unique personality and brings some of themselves into the session. Good musicians tend to listen and react to what the other musicians are playing. In an overdub situation, your player has a concrete bed from which to work. As a result, the musical interaction is one-way—they're responding to a fixed track rather than interacting live against other players. As you layer new parts on your record, the new players will interact with what's already there.

In most cases, you would do well to allow your Side-Players at least one pass before you offer direction, and at least several passes before you decide to dictate parts. Presumably, you've brought them in because they're an expert on their instrument, so it makes sense to give them some time to familiarize themselves with the track. This provides you with an opportunity to understand the flavor they bring. It also allows you to compare what's in your head (which may be no more than a feeling) to your Side-Player's initial musical response to the track.

A quality Side-Player will often come up with something brilliant, and guess what? You just managed to improve the record by staying out of the way. They'll also play a part that goes well with their instrument (which is a critical component to a quality part that makes sense). Of course, sometimes you get nothing even remotely useful, at which point you can offer some guidance.

This would be the time to pull that great part or idea from your back pocket and sing it to them. If they're a good musician, they'll shape the part in a manner that works best for them and their instrument. You could encourage that, even. If they can make the part their own or build on your idea, fantastic. If not, ask for alternatives—or consider whether the problem is the instrument, the player, or both.

You could very well decide your Side-Player is far better suited for another track, even if that goes against the original plan. As you work with more Side-Players, you'll start to develop favorites. Whenever someone new joins a session, figure out what they bring, and use them for their strengths—now and in the future.

Occasionally, you might find someone on your session who is quite obviously in over their head. A session player who is either underqualified or brings the wrong sensibilities to the track, is not worth the time sap. I understand that we all have different personalities, and you don't want to be rude, but one of the more important functions of a producer is to be the hammer.

I promise, if you allow a musician to flounder as you burn time, you're not doing your job, which is rude to your artist. And while several hours of hard work might yield you something useful—perhaps even brilliant—the far more likely result is wasted time. Unless you have a limitless budget, it is not a sum positive to end up with a single magical (and seemingly incidental) note that happens once in the song—especially if you spent hours to get there. This has happened to me on more than one occasion, and my takeaway was the same each time.

I could have played that!

The longer you produce, the less patience you'll have with musicians who don't fit the project. It's nothing personal. You're not the right producer for every project either. Seasoned producers will cut their losses early and come up with a new solution. How you go about it really has to do with your personality, but if you allow unfruitful experimentations to go on unabated, you could run out of time.

The injection of a problematic player in way over their head tends to happen most often when the artist brings in a buddy, oftentimes playing an unusual instrument. Don't get me wrong: these situations have their benefits. At the very least, they're often downright comical, and can reset the headspace and morale of your entire team. That has some value. But comical tends to quickly transgress to annoying, followed by painful—and eventually painfully annoying. What's worse is when your Child of Brain is the one who brings the Side-Player into your session, they will tend to feel a responsibility to get something useful from them, so as to spare their feelings (artists are sensitive folk). If firing the Side-Player is politically problematic, this is often a good time to pass the producer's baton to your Child of Brain as you take a break. Then they can learn this valuable lesson too.

Even if you're initially dubious of your Side-Player's abilities, provide them with enough time to acclimate. Oftentimes, unknown players are last second additions, and they may be hearing the track for the first time. Some people need more time than others to get their bearings. They might even be nervous.

This is particularly true for musicians with minimal studio experience. If the musician is seemingly competent, give them the time they need to work out a part. If your Side-Player is clearly *in*competent, I would suggest you make two takes, thank them for their contributions, and move on. You'll have them if needed, but you won't waste valuable time hoping for a miracle. Many times in producing, you must weigh the politics against your budget when making this kind of call.

There are advantages to sending the track in advance to a Side-Player. Presumably, they'll come to your session prepared, either with a part or ideas. They'll also know their way around the production. This is an essential strategy if you're tracking a group of Side-Players. It's also a good idea if you just want the Side-Player to perform an existing part as presented on a demo. Sending the demo ahead of time would be nothing short of efficient.

Personally, I like to be there for a player's first musical response to what they're hearing. Good musicians have keen instincts, and if I send a track ahead, I miss out on their gut responses. The sooner I can get the Side-Player on the mic and recording something—anything—the better. After a few passes (maybe less), I'll invite them to listen to what they've done. This gives me the opportunity to point out what I like, and the musician can hear for themselves what they're bringing to the track.

CHAPTER SEVEN

Mixing & Mastering

The Mix

A mix is the final 2-track—left and right—presentation of a production, which contains the performance of an arrangement of a song.

Let's expand on that a bit.

Once the recording process is complete, the production is ready for mix. Our job is to take the many individual recorded parts—anywhere from two to a hundred to outrageous—and combine and arrange them into a stereo track that can be played by the consumer.

Given such a broad definition, it's fair to say that anyone can make a mix. But few can make a *great* mix, which is probably the more relevant definition.

A great mix is one that brings a production of a great song to its fullest potential by effectively manipulating the listener's emotions and focus, thereby forcing an appropriate and desired physical reaction while simultaneously causing the listener to sing.

I realize that's a mouthful, but essentially: if a track makes you sing and causes some other physical reaction—whether it makes you dance, stomp, or raise your fist (even goosebumps count)—then it's a great mix. If you can't stop singing to your own production, if it does everything you intended when you set out to make the record, you can't ask for much more. Your production has most certainly been brought to its fullest potential.

The whole goal is to get a reaction from the listener—preferably tens of millions of them around the world. This is how an unknown song becomes a hit: many people react to it. If a track doesn't make *you* react, how's it going to make anyone else react? You're producing it! I mean, you already adore the song, right? So, if something you adore doesn't move you to sing or move, how's it going to do that for anyone else?

Most people think a mix is about sound. But sound is merely the medium we use to manipulate emotion. So long as you're not inducing pain, there's no such thing as good sound or bad sound. There's only the reaction you generate with it—and there are tried and true production and mixing techniques to make people feel and respond in specific ways.

We place a four-to-the-floor KIK drum prominently in the balance of a production to make the listener move. We place an amazing vocal of a great lyric forward in the mix to make the listener sing. We accelerate the rhythm in a prechorus to generate excitement and forward push, hurling the listener toward the payoff. We contrast a sparse verse with a denser, wider, and louder chorus to heighten the natural payoff. We drop the arrangement momentarily to just the vocal—or perhaps the bass—to help the chorus explode out of the verse.

All of those are primarily production and arrangement decisions. None of them are actually engineering tasks. Yes,
balancing the vocal is technically an engineering task, I suppose.
But where that vocal sits best in the mix—that's a production
decision. And as the producer, you have the final say on that.

Most new producers place too much focus on the engineering, as if that's what makes a mix great. The questions online
are never "How do I cause a reaction with my mix?" They're
always "How do I make my mix sound good?" or "How do I
make it sound professional?"—as if the recording, the performances, and the arrangement have nothing to do with it.

More often than not, a good sound is somehow conflated
with loudness. Music Fan doesn't understand loudness and
won't even know how loud your record is. They don't care about
the sound either. They like the song.

Surely, there's engineering involved in mixing. This book
would be half as long if there wasn't. But it's important to understand that the best mixers in the world—every one of them—
think first and foremost about how the mix makes them react.

When I focus on sound while mixing, the result is boring—
and I have to pull myself out of that mentality before I can fix
it. When I focus on how the track makes me feel, I deliver an
exciting mix. In all my decades of mixing, there has never been
a case where either of those statements proved untrue.

It's not about the sound. It's about the reaction.

The mix is the culmination of all your efforts, and I've armed
you with everything you need to set yourself up for success. I've
shared with you my Five Planes of Space, including the importance of contrast for dynamic effect. We discussed the Six
Musical Functions in an Arrangement. I explained frequency,
masking, and the importance of presenting a prominent midrange. We talked about the concept of "what happens now,
affects what comes next," and how to use that principle to create
excitement and forward push. And we covered how critical

performance is to good sound. All of those concepts affect the sound of your mix far more than any of the engineering.

There's no bypassing the engineering, of course. If a part is coming in and out of focus, apply compression so it stays audible. If bass movement isn't cutting through a dense mix, saturation can add resonance and clarity without bloating the soundscape. If a vocal isn't present enough, a midrange boost can help it cut through. These are engineering solutions used to promote audibility and clarity. Without audibility, the parts can't function as intended. It's not about whether a part "sounds good." It's about whether it serves its function in the arrangement—especially in terms of how the track causes you to react. If that's working, then it sounds good.

This is why I employ underdubbing as a third-party mixer. I only have so much space to work with. When I get a track in which five instruments are all fighting for the same upper-midrange register, my best tool becomes the mute button. If independently performed parts are completely masking each other from audibility, then they clearly don't all serve an important function within the arrangement. When parts get in the way, something has to go.

Don't confuse masking with layering sounds to create a single part. That's sound design—a legitimate and often powerful strategy. The purpose of layering is to manifest a more complex and interesting tone. But even that can get a bit problematic, especially where it comes to organic instruments that have some dynamic. There are times when one of the layers fails audibility, at which point it's a candidate for an underdub.

I've been asked, on occasion, to place a part in the mix such that it's effectively inaudible. This request always gets pushback from me. I can't even wrap my head around the concept. If a part isn't audible, it's merely taking up space for no benefit. Space is at a premium in a production. I won't readily cede space in a mix for a part that has no relevance to how the track makes me feel.

You can use your engineering tools to promote audibility, but that only goes so far if your arrangement decisions work against it. Good arrangements allow parts to occupy their own frequency space so they can fulfill their role. That said, don't take this principle too far—there will always be some overlap.

Your bass and KIK drum are the perfect example of parts that overlap frequencies. To be perfectly honest, that relationship can still challenge me at times. It can cause people such fits, that they end up doing way too much. Sidechains on compressors are activated. Multiband compressors are pulled out. VU meters are examined. Saturators are engaged.

Saturators on KIK drums and bass are often a good thing. The question is: how audible do you want the distortion? Those 808-style KIKs that double as bass almost always have loads of beautiful buzzy saturation, which accentuates the fourth harmonic above the fundamental, making them audible across all playback systems.

I'll only reach for multiband compression if I'm working with a loop and I need to muscle its internal balances into submission—and even then, it's my last resort. There are simpler ways to achieve similar results, and if you're not a full-time mixer, simpler is usually better.

When you operate as a dedicated mixer, and you mix every day for many years, you come up with all sorts of processes, procedures, and Protect Systems that are your own. Some of those processes may appear somewhat complicated, but they are developed to solve problems and then implemented in a somewhat automatic manner to promote speed. Where it comes to third-party mixing, speed is a crucial component to quality results. For anyone unsure of how to use a compressor, a multiband compressor will only slow down the process to a crawl.

At its core, the decision to apply tone-shaping processing—whether compression or EQ—is best made to solve a clear, identifiable problem. Don't add a compressor just because you think you should. You add it to control dynamic range, add punch, or shape tone. If none of those apply, you don't need compression.

Until you know the problem, the solution is nothing short of elusive. So, to attempt complicated solutions before you've even learned how to implement relatively simple ones is to bypass learning. That will only result in confusion and frustration.

You'd do well to make all processing decisions based on the problem at hand and to keep your approach simple. What's the problem? What's the simplest solution? If your vocal is still popping in and out of audibility after one compressor, add another. Add a third, if needed, to control the dynamic. If it's too dark, add EQ. If your processing helps the vocal maintain presence throughout the track, that's all you need.

The mixing process as a producer is a very different beast from that of a third-party mixer. As the producer, you know every part in the arrangement because you put them there. There's far less discovery involved. You've probably been mixing your record all along—and if you haven't, you should be.

Mix as You Go

Mixing is always discussed as a separate, critical process—and if you send your productions to a third-party mixer, it surely is. But your arrangement, recording, and performances will have everything to do with the success of the mix. And if the song falls short, the mix falls short every time. People don't listen to a mix, nor do they perceive a mix. They listen to a production of a song, and it either moves them or it doesn't.

Since mixing is merely the culmination of the production process, it makes sense to mix as you go. This is how you tell where you're at in the production. It's how you discover compelling combinations of parts. It's how you find what's missing, and how you determine what needs improvement.

As we've discussed, I keep an active mix session at all times, which is separate from my overdub session. Once an overdub session is complete, the new parts are imported into my mix session. By the time I've recorded the last overdub, my mix is already in good shape. At that point, it usually just needs some refinement. And while there's still a dedicated mix phase, I don't have to start from scratch. I tighten up what I have, I seek opportunities to enhance lift, and I give the mix some love—particularly where my effects are concerned.

It took me a stupidly long time to really understand how to mix my own productions, because they required entirely different muscles. As a third-party mixer, I'm aggressive in the process. As a producer, I'm aggressive too—which doesn't leave room to be aggressive on the mix. So, when it comes to mixing my own productions, I had to learn to accept what I had already made and merely give it some love.

I suppose "love," in this case, starts with effects.

Effects

I've saved effects for the Mixing section since this is typically when I set them. While I may have some effects on my working mix, it's rare for me to give them much attention until I'm at least approaching the mixing phase. Reverbs tend to act as an airbrush—they can obfuscate, mask, and eat up space. For what should be obvious reasons, I prefer the sound focused and apparent while I work on the arrangement and evaluate performances.

That's not to say I won't throw a reverb or delay on a part early if it clearly calls for it. But there's little point in refining the overall reflectivity of the track until everything is recorded and the production is fully in order.

Reverb

There are three purposes for reverb: to create the illusion of space, to mask imperfections, and to soften tone.

There are seven basic types of digital reverb patches: Halls, Rooms, Chambers, Plates, Gated, Spring, and Non-Linear. These reverbs can be produced by convolution reverb units (which use impulse responses to recreate real-world spaces or devices) or algorithmic reverb units (which synthesize reverb characteristics mathematically). Springs, Gated, and Non-Linear reverbs are typically generated algorithmically.

Size

When choosing a reverb, your first consideration is the size of the space. Halls tend to be dark and large, with long decay times and a smooth, lush tail. Rooms are more contained, with generally shorter reverb times. A room can be large, of course, but there's a point where a room becomes so large it would have to be defined as a Hall.

Chambers simulate echo chambers, which are built with reflective walls, producing a smooth and rich reverberation. Plates emulate the sound of large vibrating analog metal plates found in units like the EMT 140. These create a bright, smooth, and dense reverb tone. Spring reverbs mimic the physical mechanical springs found in guitar amps, which produce a somewhat artificial, twangy, metallic sound. They can get quite trashy in tone—which can be an endearing quality. Gated reverbs supply a burst of space followed by the near-immediate dissipation of it.

Decay Time (Reverb Time)

The decay time controls how long the reverb tail lasts— measured by how long it takes for the reflections to dissipate.

Short decay times (below one second) create a tight, controlled space, while longer times (several seconds) result in larger, more atmospheric environments.

Pre-Delay

The pre-delay determines the time (in milliseconds) between the original sound and the onset of the reverb. A short pre-delay makes the reverb feel more immediate, while a longer one creates separation between the dry signal and the reverb tail. Long pre-delays can produce an unnatural effect—which might prove useful at times. Shorter ones can help the reverb maintain clarity in a dense mix.

Diffusion

Diffusion controls the density of early reflections. High diffusion produces a smooth, cohesive reverb tail, while low diffusion makes individual echoes more distinct—often useful for simulating hard, reflective surfaces.

Damping

Damping determines how quickly high frequencies decay compared to low frequencies. High damping mimics materials like carpeted rooms, where high frequencies fade more quickly. Low damping mimics reflective spaces like tiled bathrooms, where high frequencies linger and remain prominent.

EQ Controls

As with any signal, EQ allows you to shape the tonal balance of the reverb. Cutting low frequencies can help reduce muddiness, while rolling off highs can make the reverb warmer and less apparent.

Stereo Width

Controls the spread of the reverb in the stereo field. A wider setting fills more space, while a narrower one keeps the reverb more focused and centered. I rarely set a narrow spread—I typically want the width that reverb provides.

Tail Shape or Envelope

Determines how the reverb fades out, sometimes using non-linear options like gated or reverse reverb. Gated reverb cuts the tail abruptly, while reverse reverb swells in rather than decaying.

Early Reflections Level

Sets the volume of the initial reflections before the reverb tail begins. More prominent early reflections create a sense of intimacy and clarity, while lower levels result in a more diffuse, ambient sound.

Reverb Mix (Dry/Wet)

This control sets the balance between the dry (unaffected) signal and the wet (reverberated) signal. If you place your reverb unit on the track itself, then this control allows you to adjust your wet to dry ratio. If your reverb is on an effects return, then you want it set to 100% wet, since the dry signal is coming from the channel itself.

Reverb Designs

There are two primary types of digital reverb units: convolution and algorithmic. Convolution reverbs use sampled impulse responses to replicate the sound of real spaces or devices. Algorithmic reverbs, on the other hand, generate reverb characteristics mathematically, giving you greater flexibility to shape a unique sound. Each type has its strengths, and which one you choose often comes down to workflow and preference. Many use both.

CONVOLUTION REVERBS

Convolution reverbs are designed to emulate real acoustic environments or classic hardware units. They rely on impulse responses—recorded bursts of sound captured in a specific space or through a specific device—to recreate how that space reacts to audio. If you've ever wanted your vocal to sound like it was recorded in a cathedral, a stairwell, or through a vintage plate, convolution reverb makes that possible.

Think of an impulse response as an acoustic photograph—it captures how a space sounds when hit with a sharp burst, and that "photo" becomes the basis for your reverb. You're not designing a space from scratch—you're stepping into a space that's already been captured.

The tradeoff is flexibility. You're essentially choosing from snapshots of existing spaces rather than sculpting your own, which can make fine-tuning feel rigid or tedious—especially when you're under the clock. That said, the realism and character you can get from a great impulse response—especially for orchestral, ambient, or vocal productions—can be worth the tradeoff.

Frankly, I find it far too time-consuming to bother programming convolution reverbs as a producer—even as a mixer. With convolution units, it's more efficient to decide on the general tone you're after (room, hall, plate, etc.) and then fire through presets to find the best fit. Once you land on something close, you can use the controls to fine-tune it.

I realize that people will absolutely scream at you online if you ask for a preset. *You can't use a preset!*—they'll admonish. Sure you can. I mean, they're useless for EQs and compressors because there's too much source variance. But where it comes to convolution reverb, you're essentially auditioning room models. You're choosing a space.

The first step is to make your best guess as to the kind of reverb model you seek and quickly listen through the various options. Sometimes, when you're unsure of what you want, you just need to figure out what you don't want and go from there.

Once you've spent some time working with convolution presets, you'll develop an instinct for what works and what doesn't. And while they may not offer much in the way of customization, they absolutely deliver on realism—especially when you just need to drop something in and move on. But if you're looking to shape reverb in more detailed or musical ways, algorithmic reverbs are where things get interesting.

ALGORITHMIC REVERBS

If you like the idea of shaping your own space, an algorithmic reverb is likely the better fit. These reverbs don't rely on snapshots of real-world spaces—they build the space from scratch using mathematical models. That gives you more control over the texture, size, tone, and behavior of the reverb. You're not just selecting a space—you're shaping it in response to your production.

For years, I used convolution reverbs almost exclusively. They gave me what I needed: realism, depth, and authenticity. But over time, I found myself reaching for algorithmic units more often. Not only do they sound more natural to me now, but they also let me respond in real time to what the mix needs. I can make creative decisions quickly and precisely, without being boxed in by the limitations of a static room model.

My current go-to is the FabFilter Pro-R, which offers smooth tails, natural reflectivity, and highly usable tonal shaping tools. I can get solid results fast with just a few tweaks. But if I want to go deeper, I can still craft more complex and nuanced reverbs. The controls are intuitive and musical, which lets me focus on feel rather than menus.

Of course, we went through all the various controls and what they do, but I'd be remiss were I not to point out, I never actually think about reverbs that way. I don't have settings in my head that match a space. Most of the time, I don't even know exactly what kind of space I want—if any at all. I figure that out by auditioning and listening. Whether I'm firing through room models or programming the tone myself, choosing the right reverb is always a somewhat random process. But then, that's true of almost everything we do. We make our best guess, listen to the results, and reduce our options until we find something that feels right. This is a perfectly valid way to work. Embrace it.

The point is you don't need to know how the controls work. I even considered leaving those technical explanations out—that's how inconsequential I find that particular knowledge in practice. So don't be intimidated by adding space to your production. Adjust parameters until you hear something that sets your part off in the best way possible. Listen and react. When you react the right way, you've found the solution.

When to Use Reverbs

While reverbs offer us the illusion of space, they also tend to eat space within our production. Much of that has to do with how they mask, but that's also what we like about them. They hide things.

If you apply reverberation to everything in your production, you will significantly reduce your overall clarity and punch. Surely, I can understand the instinct to hide the obvious shortcomings of a singer who sounds like a dying seal by smothering them with reverb. Unfortunately, there comes a point where blatant attempts at obfuscation only serve to make the imperfections more obvious. If you add 3 seconds of decay time to an atrociously sung vocal, you're only prolonging the pain. In this case, by nearly 3 seconds.

I find the best way to deal with an almost comically questionable part that rightly can't be underdubbed is to put it stupidly forward in the production. I may even keep it relatively dry so as to fully expose it. This way, everybody who hears it believes it was done with intent. When your instinct is to hide flaws, consider exposing them instead. This way, you can maintain some clarity and punch from your production. Use as much reverb as you like for artistic reasons—but if you're using it to hide things, you may be doing more harm than good.

It's important to understand that a little reverb can go a long way. It's certainly not a requirement to smear verb on all your drums. In many cases, you can leave them bone dry. The absence of space is just as much an effect as the addition of it, and we can use that absence of space for purposes of contrast.

When you do apply reverb to the drums, the KIK, snare, and toms are usually sufficient. Reverb on hats and cymbals tend to wash out the mix, and if it's an analog kit, the close mics will contain some of that cymbal information anyway.

Bone dry drums in need of some slapback do well with a gated reverb. You can place a gated verb prominently in the balance for that big '80s drum tone if you like. But if you place the reverb more judiciously in the balance, it will often sound more natural than even a room patch. In general, the shorter the gated verb, the better. The trick is in how you balance the return. You can also use a slapback delay as a tail to achieve a similar effect.

String patches and pads are often treated with verb, but we really only notice the space either with note movement or a break in the action. Long sustaining parts are often best served with less reverb, not more, as that verb mostly eats up space. Where it comes to added space on sustaining parts, there's a point of diminishing returns. By the time the reverb is super obvious, you've masked your entire mix with it.

Crunch guitars—especially sustaining ones—are best left dry, as reverb tends to soften their tone by smoothing out the distortion. To soften tone is to mask imperfections. But it's the imperfections that we often like about the distortion. We want to obfuscate those imperfections, why? That is usually cross purposes. Dry crunch guitars are tough. Wet crunch guitars are soft.

There's just no way around it, there is a balance that must be achieved between space and clarity, and that ultimately comes down to taste. I can tell you that most new producers add too much reverb on too many parts without much consideration or acknowledgement of its negative impacts. If an overly reverberant treatment is a creative decision, that's fair. Otherwise, it's best to be somewhat judicious about what parts get reverb and just how much you apply.

Production trends have a big influence on how we use reverb. I spent most of the '90s avoiding it altogether. I've mixed entire records with no canned reverb whatsoever—including three Ben Harper albums. Once reverb came back into fashion, I started using a lot more of it in both my mixes and productions.

It can be advantageous to apply discrete reverbs to any given part that needs added space. Vocals, drums, keys, etc., get their own discrete reverb units in my mixes. This way, I can easily control the balances. If I put the drums and the vocals on the same reverb, then my return affects them both. This would require me to adjust my reverb levels between those parts at the individual sends, which is a bit tedious. Even if I wanted the same reverb tone for both parts, I'd still set up discrete units to do it, as it offers me quick independent control over return levels.

I can't tell you what too much reverb sounds like or where the line is. As always, that comes down to your taste juxtaposed to the general needs of the production. I can tell you this though: When you find yourself wondering why there's no clarity to your production, or if you find the whole thing just sounds soft, you want to apply your reverb more judiciously.

Organic Chamber

Sometimes we use digital reverb purely to create space that wasn't there during the recording. And while that's a perfectly valid approach, don't kid yourself—there's no canned reverb that accurately mimics the reaction of an organic room. Halls can be surprisingly convincing. Rooms? Not so much. Don't ask me why that is. It just is.

If your goal is a natural, organic-sounding room, the best strategy is to mic up the space during the original capture. If that's not an option, you can always create your own chamber by blasting a part through a PA and re-recording the generated room tone.

You can turn almost any reflective environment into a reverb chamber. Tile bathrooms, open living rooms with wood floors and vaulted ceilings, even stairwells, all offer space that can be worth exciting and capturing. If the space has reflections, it's fair game.

The size of the space and the materials within it will determine the overall action of the room. If your house is too dead, take a field trip. Churches, rec centers, empty houses—can all be good candidates. Just be sure to get permission first.

If a real-world space will help bring a track to life, then it's worth the trouble. You can even rent out a local studio for an hour or two—just to use the room.

When I was mixing in rooms with large tracking spaces, I would often have the assistant set up some speakers and mics in the main room. That way, I always had a natural chamber available. If you have space that could prove useful as a chamber, *mic it up.*

Intimacy

When it comes to reverb or lack thereof the main consideration should be intimacy. The more intimate your production, the closer everything appears to the listener.

The most intimate space occurs when you're wrapped up in the arms of someone you love. There is no reverb when your partner is singing in soft tones inches from your ear. Conversely, there is no intimacy at the back of a stadium filled with 60,000 adoring fans.

The addition of reverb serves to erode that intimacy. Introduce even a small room patch, and you create the illusion of distance between the listener and the artist. That space reduces intimacy compared to a dry vocal. As the size of the room increases, intimacy continues to decline. The song and production should dictate the level of proximity you choose to present. In general, the rawer the production, the more intimate it feels.

If you think along these lines, it will help you apply reverb with intent.

Delays

Whereas reverb gives us the illusion of space, delay can provide the illusion of both space and distance. Mono delays offer pinpoint placement of the repeats, while stereo delays are great for making a part feel larger than life. Unlike reverbs, presets don't tend to work as well with delays—especially mono delays—so it's important to understand the parameters and how to manipulate them to your advantage.

Time

The time setting determines the length of time between the initial signal and the delayed repeat. It can be based on note divisions (e.g., quarter note, eighth note, sixteenth note) or expressed as an absolute duration in milliseconds.

Back in the olden days, you had to break out some math to correlate your tempo to your note values. Or you pulled out your handy-dandy delay chart. These days, a delay unit will do the math for you. But I'll explain it just the same.

Let's calculate the delay times for a tempo of 90 BPM (the Devil's Tempo). There are 1,000 ms in a second and 60 seconds in a minute, which multiplies out to 60,000 ms per minute. To determine the length of a quarter note in milliseconds, divide 60,000 by 90 BPM to get 666 ms. So, at 90 BPM, a quarter note occurs every 666 ms. That means an eighth note is 333 ms, a sixteenth note is 166 ms, and a quarter-note triplet is... well, that takes a little more math.

A quarter-note triplet occurs over the span of two beats. A half note at 90 BPM is 1,332 ms. Divide that by three, and you get 444 ms. Fortunately, we rarely need to do these kinds of calculations anymore. Just set the delay to the note value you want, and you're done.

In most cases, you'll want your delay times to correspond to a note value—especially in productions programmed to the grid. But sometimes, you can create a subtle tension by slightly diverging from tempo, particularly on long repeating tap delays. Perfection can be highly overrated. Keep that in mind.

Feedback

Before digital delays, we had tape delays. On a tape deck, the playback head (repro head) is physically positioned after the record head. This setup introduced the original version of latency—you couldn't monitor playback without a 50–60 ms delay caused by the distance between the heads. Somewhere along the line, someone realized they could use that latency to their advantage.

Tape machines also had speed settings. Slow the machine down, and you increase the delay time between the two heads. A 60 ms delay at 30 inches per second (ips) becomes 120 ms at 15 ips, and 240 ms at 7.5 ips. Machines also featured vari-speed controls, which allowed more precise adjustment of the delay time.

If you send a vocal to a tape machine, it's recorded at the record head and reproduced a short time later at the play head. The length of that delay depends on the playback speed. But that only gives you a single repeat.

To get multiple repeats, you feed the return from the tape machine back into itself. The delayed signal is recorded again, and played back again, and again. The more return signal you send back in, the more repeats you get. If you send too much, the repeats become louder than the original signal, and every subsequent delay increases in volume. At that point, you lose control of your feedback loop. That's why it's called feedback— you're literally feeding the return back into the input of the delay device.

The beauty of tape delays is that each subsequent repeat loses fidelity, becoming darker, grainier, and noisier in character. A tape delay plugin gives you parameters to model those tape traits, including flutter and distortion. Many units even allow for pitch shifting. This mimics what happens when you manually adjust the playback speed as the sound repeats.

Delay Filters

Filters are critically important in delay processing. Part of the illusion of great distance is caused by a loss of top end. A trumpet played in proximity to your position will sound considerably more brilliant than a trumpet played a mile away. That's because top end is absorbed more readily than low end, and by the time the sound reaches you, much of the top end has been sucked up by the environment along the way.

A high frequency roll-off with a delay filter helps with the illusion of distance, and a low frequency roll-off can help the delay cut through. The further away you want that delay to sound, the more you should filter out the top end.

I suppose there could be times that you want your repeats to have the full frequency spectrum of the part, but it's rather unnatural and offers you no contrast between the part and the repeats. Even when used as an almost reverberant effect, I like to roll off top end, because a darker delay can help thicken the part and hide flaws more readily than a reverb.

It's almost routine for me to filter some amount of the top end from delays. It's not uncommon for me to filter the frequencies down to as far as 3 kHz, completely eradicating the top end of the delay. That said, the part and the sound you seek will dictate how aggressive you are with your filters.

Mono Delay Tails

If you apply a robust feedback setting of 50–60 percent with a relatively short delay time—somewhere between 50 and 200 ms—your mono delay will start to sound more like a mono reverb than a delay. This effect isn't ideal on super percussive parts, as it can sound like a machine gun. But when applied to more fluid parts—like vocals or electric guitars—you may find this spatial tone nothing short of useful.

As you increase the delay time, the repeats become more distinct, but with that much feedback, the effect still feels reverberant in nature. Go ahead and roll off some top end to enhance the illusion—doing so will help soften the attack of the taps. Once you balance the delay with the dry signal, it can sound a lot like a natural reverb.

The advantage of a mono tail is that it provides the illusion of space without eating up a ton of it in the mix. If you put stereo reverbs and stereo delays on everything, you greatly reduce the perception of width—making a mono delay tail a smart strategy when space and clarity are at a premium.

Short Delays

A 60 ms delay is super quick and is often referred to as a doubler. This effect causes chorusing and all sorts of wonderful masking. As a result, it's often used to obfuscate the unevenness of a vocal part. That said, it can also sound downright robotic— and if you're aiming for a more natural tone, you'd do better to record an actual double.

A slapback delay of around 120 ms with no feedback can also create the illusion of space. Keep in mind, though, that short delays work best on parts with some percussiveness—including certain vocal performances. Slow-developing keyboard pads, for instance, would derive little benefit from a delay this short.

A 250 ms delay with minimal feedback, or none, set back in the balance with a filtered top end is an excellent way to give a part the illusion of distance without losing any definition or clarity from a wash of reverb. A prominent 250 ms delay is useful too. But if the delay is balanced too loud, it no longer feels like distance.

Once you exceed 250 ms, you start moving into eighth-note and quarter-note time values, depending on tempo. At 120 BPM, a 250 ms delay equals an eighth note. At 90 BPM, an eighth note is 333 ms. As delay times get longer, they present more like rhythmic taps than spatial effects.

Taps

A delay that manifests as repeating taps can get a bit distracting when used as a tail—stereo taps even more so. In general, once you get above an eighth note in time, and especially when you reach a quarter note, you'll usually want to automate your taps so they only occur on specific words or hits.

There are a number of ways to automate a tap. I use *fx* sends to route to my tap delays, just like any other effects unit. This way, I can automate the send level whenever I want to introduce the taps.

You'll hear taps all the time on lead vocals. The last word of certain vocal phrases can often benefit from a repeat—typically a quarter note or an eighth note, but really, any value you like. Snare fills on reggae tracks also respond well to taps, often set to an eighth-note triplet with heavy filtering on both the top and bottom frequencies. Distortion too. It's the automation that makes these taps work.

If you're wondering why I automate an *fx* send rather than just mute the return of the delay, there's a very good reason for that: it's not clean. If I'm sending to the delay the whole time and simply open the return, I'll hear previous phrases. The point of the automation is to send only the word or phrase I want repeated—nothing else.

If your track isn't cut to a tempo, you'll have to adjust the delay manually—and you may never get it perfectly in time, nor should you try. Productions without tempo restraints don't typically call for rhythmic delay taps. If you want perfect placement on a shifting tempo, you'll have to cut and paste the word manually for each repeat.

Dry delay taps can really stick out, which can be useful. But if you want them to blend better, add a splash of verb. Just open an *fx* send on your delay return and route it to a reverb. It doesn't need to be discreet—I'll often apply the same vocal reverb to the delay taps for continuity.

You can get as creative as you like with how you mangle and manipulate the delay—distortion, tonal modulation, pitch shifting, flangers, automated panning, filters—all of these can be applied to your taps to create complex and engaging effects.

For whatever reason, I'm far more patient when it comes to programming delay taps than reverb. When I want something simple, I tend to use stock delays. When I want something more interesting or unique, I'll break out FabFilter's Timeless. It's not the fastest plugin to dial in, but it gives me deep control over how the delay evolves—and if I can imagine it, I can usually build it in Timeless. Taps are incredibly useful for pushing the listener forward, which is why I don't mind spending the extra time getting them just right.

Programmable Delays

Sometimes, you want the first delay tap to hit at a different time interval than the repeats. For example, you might want the last word of a vocal phrase to repeat first at a dotted quarter note, followed by quarter-note repeats. There are a few ways to achieve this.

One option is to use a fully programmable delay unit, which allows you to manually place the repeats, shape the filter dissipation, and automate the panning. This can be a bit labor-intensive if you're programming the unit from scratch—but it gives you a high level of control.

You can also accomplish the same thing by inserting two delay units in series. Set the first delay to a dotted quarter with no feedback, and the second to a quarter note with a higher feedback setting to generate the repeated taps.

Another approach is to duplicate the word you want repeated and move the duplicate to a new track. You can then place that duplicate on the timeline to act as your first dotted quarter tap and send it to a quarter-note delay for the subsequent repeats. This method can be tricky if your track isn't locked to a tempo grid.

Delays add color and personality to a production, which is why I give them so much attention. They create space, texture, and depth.

Stereo Delays

There's really only one stereo delay I consistently use, and it's the most plug-and-play processor I can think of: Soundtoys Echoboy. That delay sounds great on pop vocals right out of the gate, and it includes a long list of modeled delay units that make it easy to tailor the tone of your effect. If you don't have it, you should.

I have received sessions from clients in which every vocal had a stock stereo delay on it, with the left set to a quarter note and the right set to an eighth note and with no top end roll off. This is often the stock setting of your DAW's stereo delay, and it does nothing other than to distract when set forward in the balance, and to obfuscate when set back. I would generally advise against this sort of treatment, as it offers little subtlety or depth.

A quarter-note delay bouncing around at all times is something to avoid—even if it's just tucked to the sides. Sure, there might be trippy musical sections (or even entire productions) where this kind of treatment makes sense. But more often than not, you're better off automating a quarter-note delay than letting it ride the whole time.

Stereo delays can be incredibly useful for adding movement through the ping-pong parameter, which alternates the delay between the sides. You can achieve this effect with a stereo delay, a mono delay paired with a stereo tremolo, or with a programmable delay plugin that lets you get fancy.

Modulation (Motion)

Modulation includes choruses, flangers, Leslie speakers, ensembles, phasers, tremolos, automated filters, ring shifters, and the like. Each of those modulators does its own unique thing, but they all offer us motion.

We use motion to make a production more interesting, to obfuscate tuning issues, and to provide us with some width and clarity too.

Chorus is the effect that occurs naturally when two instruments play the same part. The slight variances in tuning cause the parts to react, which provides subtle motion to the part. A chorus plugin modulates the tone in a linear manner, which makes it less interesting than the natural chorus you get when you double track a part, but that doesn't make it unuseful. If you want to obfuscate tuning issues, a chorus is a great way to do it.

Modulation units like choruses, ensembles, flangers, and phasers also introduce distortion, and as you already know, that's handy for clarity. In other words, you can hide slight tuning issues and make the part more apparent at the same time using these types of modulation plugins.

Ensembles emphasize harmonics and introduce distortion. They often sound like a filtered version of a chorus, which can help vocal harmonies cut through a dense production. Ensembles, choruses, and phasers all work well on background vocals—even when they're in tune. In those cases, it's the added texture you're after. Still, it's wise to use these effects sparingly. Overuse of modulation can make a mix feel psychedelic, muddy, or just plain chaotic.

Tremolo plugins provide motion either in volume or pan position. A stereo tremolo bounces a part from left to right, while a mono tremolo oscillates the volume. Used subtly, it can sound like vibrato. Used aggressively, it can add rhythm, width, or even salvage a lifeless guitar part.

The latest fad in modulation is the pumping effect applied to the entire track. This can be created using sidechain compression, but it's often more effectively achieved with an LFO tool that allows you to control the envelope—Attack, Decay, Sustain, and Release (ADSR)—of the audio. Sometimes the pumping is on the low end. Sometimes it's on the synths. And sometimes, I can't even figure out what's pulsing in the track. All I know is, I like it.

Be careful with modulation. As with any effect, you can absolutely destroy the integrity of a production with too many instances of motion.

Taste

It's important to remember, the mix is simply the final presentation of your arrangement. The better the arrangement, the less need there is for trickery and ear candy. Well-placed delay taps, for example, can be nothing but love—but they can also be overdone.

It's not unusual for me to add taps or motion and then decide against them. If the tap isn't filling a space that needs it, or if it's not actively helping with the forward push, it gets removed. If a motion effect is gutting the tone, a different treatment may serve it better. In general, effects deserve the same scrutiny as the parts themselves. Does this make the mix or production better? What is this doing for me? Why am I implementing this effect?

If you put an effect on something and it's better, it's better. You don't have to justify every instinctive decision you make. I'm all about doing instead of thinking. But it's worth scrutinizing your choices to make sure you're not overdoing things. When in doubt, let the power of the arrangement and the song shine through—without getting in the way.

It takes time and practice to develop taste and restraint. Early on, you may find yourself slathering effects on everything just to see what sticks—which is fine. Experimentation is part of the process. But over time, you'll begin to recognize what actually helps the production and what's just cluttering things up for no apparent reason.

Reference Tracks

Many people will suggest you reference other tracks as you mix. This is always about sound. The thinking goes: if you can make your record sound as good as another, then you're good. Some even go so far as to use AI tools like iZotope Ozone to apply another track's EQ curve to their own—which is inadvisable. It's the arrangement and the parts that dictate the overall sonic curve, not how you EQ it.

Referencing tracks for the feeling they evoke is always a legitimate strategy. But referencing sound? That's nothing short of fraught—especially when you're monitoring in a space with serious translation issues. You can absolutely frustrate yourself to no end trying to match tracks in a compromised room. Your references become a moving target.

It's perfectly reasonable to listen to a few tracks at the start of your day, or after a break. That can be an effective way to get your head in the right space. The problem is the direct A/B comparison. For starters, you're probably comparing a fully mastered track to your own work in progress—which is never a fair comparison. You're also likely referencing a song you love, and no matter how hard you try, you can't separate that emotional attachment from your evaluation. The song you love wins every time, which can be demoralizing.

Mixing is a game of confidence, and anything that undermines that confidence will only make your job harder.

Contrary to much of the advice you'll read online, I suggest avoiding direct A/B sonic comparisons and instead focusing wholly on how your mix generates motion and emotional reaction. You really can't match the EQ curve of your track to someone else's—and even if you could, why would you want your production to sound so similar? Your decisions dictate the sound. Trust them.

Translation

How your mix translates outside of your studio is crucial. Ideally, you want a mix room that reveals everything accurately, so that you don't have to listen to it outside your room. Where that fails, you will probably want to hear your mix in outside playback systems.

One of the more popular places to evaluate your mix is the car, but there are a couple of things that can trip you up. First, if you don't apply brickwall limiting to your mix before you bounce, it could be difficult to get enough level in your car to play it at a sufficient volume. You'll also get lots of line noise because you'll have your volume all the way up. Even if you plan to hire an outside engineer to master your record, you should apply a brickwall limiter to your mix before you listen to it in an outside environment. You will likely find it immensely helpful.

Car listeners also frequently adjust their EQ settings—often with the bass boosted and the treble attenuated. When you've spent hours listening to your mix on the brilliance of your monitors, the car can sound downright dull in comparison. Keep that in mind.

Strategies for Wider Mixes

We've already discussed space in an arrangement, and the importance of using it all, but I often see people complain that their mixes aren't wide enough. Usually, that's because they aren't panning things hard, but there are other common mistakes that cause you to struggle with your width. Here is a list of strategies to help you achieve wide mixes that do all that they should.

1. **Pan independent mono parts hard to the sides.**
Don't avoid those hard pan positions. Panning hard

defines the total width of the production, and offers you space to more easily mix. It also prevents you from wondering why your mixes aren't wide.

2. **Keep the center clear for vocals, KIK, snare, and bass.** The low end of the bass doesn't appear in the center but rather at the bottom, due to a lack of directionality. Other elements—like a mono harmony vocal—can live in the middle, but not much else should occupy that space.

3. **Use internal pan positions for incidental parts.** The core driving elements of your instrumental arrangement should come from the sides.

4. **Limit stereo tracks to one or two at a time.** The more of these stereo elements you put into your mix— stereo overheads, stereo B3, stereo piano, stereo guitar— the less wide your mix will appear. Stereo tracks aren't as wide as independently panned mono parts. They fill in the whole sound field. Any more than two stereo parts at a time and you will reduce the overall apparent width of your production.

5. **Don't record small instruments in stereo unless they're stationary.** Instruments like acoustic guitar don't have enough physical width to justify stereo miking without introducing phase coherency issues.

6. **Avoid phase-induced widening tricks like the Haas effect or stereo imaging plugins.** These weaken your mix and can cause it to play back strangely on consumer systems—especially phones. The same goes for stereo-miked acoustic guitars. This isn't about stifling creativity—it's about maintaining control over your balances in the real world. Do what you like in terms of creativity, but when you hear your mix out in the wild,

and its seemingly missing parts, you'll understand why it's best to remove phase induced stereo imaging from your bag of tricks.

7. **Use asymmetry as contrast to symmetry.** It's perfectly fine to have one part on the left with nothing balancing it on the right. To mix with constant symmetry is to mix with timidity.

8. **If you want a big, wide record, keep your arrangement sparse.** The more parts you cram in, the smaller the record will feel—including on the width plane. There are some producers who virtually require a dense arrangement. They know no other way. That's fine, but the cost of that is less width, more masking, more compression, and a smaller record overall. I've yet to determine the advantage to dense productions.

9. **Use stereo motion effects to help push stereo parts further to the sides**. Leslie cabinets can make B3 organs feel massive. Ping-pong delays can widen a part. But too much motion can also blur your width—so be judicious.

2-Bus Compression

Whether your entire mix requires compression depends largely on how you processed the individual channels. If you were aggressive with compression on your tracks and busses, you may not need any on the mix itself—or you might just want a touch of compression to act as glue.

I prefer to apply 2-bus compression as I'm mixing, rather than waiting until the end. Even a small amount of compression can significantly alter your balances. And unlike limiters, compressors can offer value added to your mix and won't generally exhaust you over time.

If you're using a modeled compressor on your Stereo Output (or your ALL BUS, which is where I put mine), you'll need to carefully manage your levels to avoid any unwanted distortion it might introduce. This must be done by ear.

Your attack and release times dramatically influence how the compressor responds to your mix. A slower attack time (around 5–20 ms) allows the initial transients through, while a faster release time (200–300 ms) helps the compressor recover quickly. A ratio between 2:1 and 4:1 is generally appropriate for 2-bus work.

Your threshold and input controls determine how much compression occurs. The amount of Gain Reduction (GR) you can apply depends on the model, but once you push beyond 3–4 dB on your Stereo Output, you risk making your record sound small.

Different compressor types can also affect your 2-bus results. For instance, VCA compressors are known for their fast, transparent response and are excellent for controlling dynamics without coloring the mix too much. On the other hand, vari-mu compressors tend to add warmth and glue, subtly shaping the overall tone. FET compressors offer a more aggressive character, often adding a bit of edge or punch. Experimenting with these different circuit types can help you find the balance that best sets off your mix.

Organic mixes are generally better candidates for mix bus compression than programmed ones, due to their more controlled dynamics.

Automated Processes

Automated processes like sidechaining seem to be all the rage these days. Every week I read about someone who wants to know how to sidechain their bass to their kik drum, which can certainly create a nice breathing effect, but isn't really a solution for dealing with masking between the KIK and the bass part. An accurate space and practice will go a long way towards addressing that issue.

Now I see people asking about sidechaining their vocal to the instrumentation, so as to compress certain parts of the instrumentation in order to keep the vocal front and center. While that may sound handy, it lacks control.

Where it comes to a mix, you want to maintain control over all aspects. So, while an automated process might seem like it will speed things up for you, it could very well make mixing more difficult.

I don't use gates on drums, mostly because I don't like the sound of gated drums. But I also want to maintain precise control over muting, and that is best served by programming by hand.

Sometimes toms contain excessive cymbal information that I wish to control. The best way that I've found to do this is to make duplicate tracks of all the toms, strip one set of toms down to individual strikes and leave the duplicate fully open. This way, I can control how much cymbal bleed and shell tone appears in the blend, while retaining strong and forward tom hits.

This results in an automated process that has been programmed, which is far more accurate and dependable than a gate prone to mis-triggers. I can clean and adjust the toms in about 10 minutes, and the job is done. I could be screwing around with a gate for far longer than that.

Automated processors can create more work in the long run. They're great for quick-and-dirty results, but when it comes time for mix refinement, you want precision—and that's best done manually.

Automation

Automation allows us to refine balances, trigger momentary effects, and add motion to the mix. All DAWs include automation functionality, which can be applied to nearly every available channel and plugin parameter.

When it comes to track volume for balance adjustments, automation is a staple. But you're not restricted to using your DAW's programmable automation system—there are plenty of clever ways to automate.

For instance, if my verse vocal requires more compression than my chorus vocal, I'll split them onto separate tracks. This way, I can set the appropriate compression for each without digging into automation menus. The vocal flows naturally from verse to chorus without any automation programming.

Even if I can use the same compressor settings for both sections, I'll often split them anyway for purposes of balance. It's much faster than drawing automation lines to raise the chorus. If all the chorus vocals are routed to their own channel, I can simply bring up that fader to adjust their level collectively. Of course, sometimes the third chorus needs more level than the first two—that's when I use the trim function.

Trim allows you to adjust the overall level of an automated track while preserving the relative automation moves you've already written. If you adjust the fader manually, the automation will override your change. But with trim, you can make global level changes without affecting the nuance of your rides.

In my world, any part that requires unique processing in different sections gets split across multiple channels—as many as make sense. Guitars are often separated by section: Verse Guitars, Chorus Guitars, Bridge Guitars. This lets me set static balances that behave like automation—without drawing lines. While this results in more tracks in the arrange window, it also makes it easier to see everything that's happening.

If a part works with the same processing and mostly the same level throughout, I'm more likely to use automation than to split it up. Either method works. My strategies have everything to do with speed, and the best approach isn't always clear-cut. I use automation to make level rides or to automate panning and effects, but whenever I can avoid digging into the automation screen, I will.

However you choose to implement automation, it's an essential part of effective mixing. It offers precise control and allows you to inject excitement and dynamic into your mix. Sometimes, it even makes sense to automate the volume of your entire mix.

Say you want to enhance the contrast between a verse and a chorus—you can raise the automation line on your Stereo Output channel across the chorus section. Just keep your signal flow in mind. You'll usually want that automation to occur after your mix compressor (so the compression remains consistent) and before your brickwall limiter (since the limiter sets the final output level)—which is yet another argument for using the ALL BUS.

You can even automate EQ moves. For example, in a house production, if you want to gradually filter out the low end of your breakdown over the course of a measure, you can automate the filter parameter of an EQ—either on your ALL BUS or your Stereo Output channel.

Automation is how you refine your mix and give your levels some love. I use plenty of it because that's how I best maximize forward motion and payoff. The beauty of automation is that it lets you draw the listener's ear exactly where you want it, when you want it, helping you guide the emotional arc of the song in ways static levels simply can't. Done well, automation makes the mix feel almost as if it were performed.

The Payoff

In modern music, the payoff is often synonymous with the chorus. The chorus typically occurs multiple times in the song with the identical lyrical content. It's the section that is the most identifiable, the most likely sung, and we all look forward to it. A great song will push us toward the chorus by design, and we want to be sure our mix does everything to enhance both the journey and the payoff alike.

If the listener doesn't get a big payoff from the chorus, all is lost. As with just about everything we discuss here, the majority of the payoff should come from the song. We can enhance that payoff with the arrangement and the mix.

In AC/DC's "Highway to Hell," the verse is nothing more than drums, vocal, and a single guitar playing short choral bursts in unison with the bass. When the chorus comes in, a second guitar enters playing fully held power chords, along with an entire chorus of vocals. Not only does the song offer us a great melodic and lyrical payoff that's fun to sing, but the arrangement and the mix actually enhance the payoff using contrast.

The chorus doesn't necessarily have to get bigger. It's the contrast that offers us a payoff. Take Led Zeppelin's "Rock and Roll," for instance. In this song, the refrain actually breaks down in order to set it apart from the rest of the song. In the first chorus, the guitar stops playing at the refrain. If the guitar didn't drop out, the payoff line ". . . been a long, lonely, lonely, lonely, lonely, lonely time," wouldn't be nearly as effective. In the second and third chorus both the guitar and the drums drop out, further setting the line apart. This offers contrast, and contrast enhances payoff. Those dropouts also serve to buy another 16 bars of the same repetitive riff.

The chorus by no means has the corner on the market where payoff is concerned. Take Pink Floyd's "Money." There really is no chorus on this song, and what would normally act as the chorus is more of a turnaround to get us back into the hooky verse. It's a great turnaround, but the biggest payoff comes from the reverberant, climactic guitar solo, which then drops down to a bone-dry track, only to climax once again. Even the return to the original groove acts as an enormous payoff. Each guitar solo section sets up the next, in order to maximize payoff and push us forward through the song. But it's the changes in reflectivity and density that serve to enhance the payoff through contrast.

This doesn't mean you have to use every available dynamic all the time. There are many great productions that don't make use of mix dynamics. Take Daft Punk's "Get Lucky" Featuring Pharrell Williams and Nile Rodgers. The retro groove never changes from the verse, to the prechorus, to the chorus. In terms of the mix, the track is nearly static. It's the song that offers us the dynamic, as the vocals on the prechorus accelerate in their rhythmic structure and pace of delivery. That prechorus sets off the chorus, which then slides back into the verse without ever changing the groove. That works as forward motion without contrast (which is pretty slick). It seems the only real production dynamic is the breakdown to the funky guitar followed by the introduction of electronic instrumentation over the same retro groove.

I mean, if you think about it, if every song was a wild ride of explosive dynamics, this would be boring in its own right. Some songs are designed to keep us in a certain headspace. As long as the track and vocal draws you in and keeps your attention as the listener, the forward motion exists. You can enhance that forward motion with contrast when it's appropriate, but don't go out of your way to create a dynamic that's not necessary. You always want to follow the song and production.

A payoff only exists based on the contrast of what comes before it. You can derive this contrast first from the song and then enhance it through the production (and therefore the mix).

Refining and Enhancing

If you've mixed as you go—as I recommend—what remains is mostly refinement and enhancement. The further along you are in the mixing process, the finer your adjustments become.

As you refine, your attention to detail increases, and your perception becomes more acute. By the end of a mix, you should be able to hear even the most minute internal balance differences—down to 1/10th of a dB. At the very least, you'll think you can hear differences that small.

I'm convinced I can hear an internal balance change of 1/10th of a dB when I'm toward the end of a mix. Whether I actually can is irrelevant, and I've never bothered to test my sensitivity at that stage—partially because I'm too tired to care, but mostly because it really doesn't matter. There's no way anyone can hear a tenth of a dB difference outside of a hypersensitive state. You most certainly won't hear it on a consumer system. So, if you find yourself making adjustments that tiny—and I've done it— you're probably hypersensitive and likely wasting your time.

Which brings us to the question: how small of an internal balance change is reasonable? That depends on how refined your mix is. By the time I'm finishing a mix, a half-dB reduction in the vocal can be the difference between the singer sitting just on top of the track or slightly in it. That's a major perceptual shift for such a small move—and it can dramatically affect how the listener feels about the performance.

Conversely, at the beginning of a mix, a half-dB change won't even register. The track is in too rough a state for you to hear the true impact of such a subtle adjustment, and you're not even warmed up yet.

Paradoxically, as your mix becomes more refined, the scope of your adjustments often broadens. At the start, you're zoomed in—tweaking the snare, adjusting a guitar phrase, nudging a vocal line. But toward the end of the process, the changes you make tend to affect entire sections: "The drums need to come up overall." "The guitars need to come down." "All the chorus vocals need to come up." That's because all your internal balances are now working as a unified whole. At this stage of the

mix, it becomes more about how these broader structures interact across sections than in the moment.

As you get deeper into the refinement process, your focus
should naturally shift from how your balances affect the mix at
a given moment to how they shape the journey through the
song. The tiny details only matter in how they serve the big picture. Once the basic frame and overall tone of the production is
in place, your job becomes to maximize forward motion, emotional impact, and payoff.

Does the section land? Does the vocal lift in the right places?
Is the payoff paying off? Does the production keep pushing me
forward? Is there good contrast? All your refinements should
serve these kinds of questions. They move you out of the headspace of sound and into the headspace of reaction. Once that
becomes your primary concern, you're making the right refinements.

If you evaluate your mix based on how you *feel*, then you'll
always know when you're done. If you listen down from the top
and find yourself singing, moving, and unable to focus on what's
wrong—your mix is doing everything that it should. If you keep
forgetting you're evaluating and get swept up in the music,
that's a reaction. Cause that in yourself, and you'll cause it in
others.

That's the goal.

Proportionality in Balance

You have the absolute power to direct the listener's focus
with your balance decisions. And while that power comes from
proportion, the best mixes are rarely proportional. In fact, the
pursuit of perfect balance is often what kills them.

An overly balanced production lacks contrast, fails to offer
the listener a clear focal point, and ultimately reduces forward
motion. Given that, a perfectly proportional production does a

poor job of manipulating the listener's emotions. An overly balanced mix would be the exact opposite of a great mix, and this is a common mistake in a production. It's like a disease.

I've actually been thanked on more than one occasion for my "unbalanced mixes." I don't know for certain, but I think that would insult most mixers. I can assure you it's meant as a compliment and taken as such. There's nothing more boring than a perfectly balanced mix.

The difference between a mix with bold balance decisions and an overly proportional mix is the difference between a mix where everything seems loud and a mix where everything sounds soft.

If parts in your mix seem to jump out at you and command attention without distracting from the vocal, you've got a killer mix on your hands. If everything just sounds soft, you have a flat, limp, unexciting mix.

Don't be afraid of bold balance decisions. They will help to set your mix apart.

Mixing Vocals

There are times I'll produce a vocal with copious and obvious compression. There are other times that I want the compression completely invisible. Much of that has to do with the genre or song, although trends might have some influence. Obvious vocal compression was all the rage in the mid-nineties. Currently, it's the obvious tuning artifacts and distortion that are popular. Like everything, that will change.

When you've been through enough trends, you treat them for what they are. Or at least you should. They are moments in time where technology is used in an unintended manner to produce a new trend. Once one artist uses it in a hit song, then everyone jumps on the bandwagon. That makes trendiness a useful module to implement in your productions. Following a production trend is a great way to bring in something modern and familiar to your production, especially if your record falls outside of what is trending musically.

The precise nature of the desired vocal tone is often dictated by the genre and placement within the track. You can dip an aggressive vocal into a production and have it cut through like a knife. You can also put a big warm vocal boldly over the track, but that requires space in your arrangement and a low end that can support it. Otherwise, you'll dwarf the track. People don't dance to a little pitter patter of rhythm in the background behind a stupidly loud vocal.

You have two competing forces that operate in tandem to provide the listener enjoyment—rhythm and melody. The only way to get them to work together is to give them both their due. Your rhythmic elements cause the listener to move, and your melodic elements cause them to sing. And if you have no rhythmic structure in your production? Then you have the rubato melodic meanderings of a poet. A melody doesn't even exist without a rhythmic structure.

There's no way around it; you want the listener to move appropriately to the track and you want them to sing. If you get the balance wrong between the track and the vocal, you will kill one of those reactions. That said, you're far better off placing a vocal too loud than trying to duck it into a track.

If you want to keep the vocal loud and the track strong, then your vocal must sit perfectly in the mix from top to bottom. Compressors and limiters are the first step toward accomplishing this—vocal rides through automation are the second. The more aggressive you are with the compressor, the less vocal rides you'll need to automate. Aggressive compression on a vocal brings out breaths, sibilance, lip smacks, foot shuffling, rustling, and any other noise the mic happened to pick up during the recording process. Sometimes all that noise is perfectly acceptable—desirable, even—in which case you can be as aggressive as you like with your compressors. Should you choose to implement a few compressors in series, you will also reduce the need for automation.

The bottom line is the vocal sells the song, and you don't do yourself any favors by making it difficult to hear. Place it loud and proud, and keep it focused with compression and automation. And if you leave lots of space in the middle for it, you'll derive strength from the sides too.

Finishing Your Mix

I've been toward the end of mixes that were seemingly a total disaster, in which just one or two key moves completely focused the track. I know it sounds weird, but a finished mix can completely sneak up on you, although admittedly, the completion of a mix is typically a little less random than that.

I pointed this out earlier, but it's worth repeating. I know I'm near the end of a mix when I can't stop singing and moving. I mean, if I can make myself sing after many long hours of working on the song, it must be a good mix.

There are other indicators as well. If I can't seem to make adjustments to the mix without rejecting them outright, I know I'm getting close. It's almost as if you get a mix to near completion, and everything locks up on you.

If every move you make seems to completely destroy the integrity of the mix, you're probably done. At some point you just have to admit you can't improve it any longer. When you reach that point, it's about time to pull out your mastering tools.

Mastering Your Own Projects

There's an order of magnitude difference between mastering a mix you still have control over and mastering a printed 2-track stereo file. A Mastering Engineer (ME) only has access to your bounce, and the tools they choose have everything to do with that lack of control.

For example, if you send a track to an ME where the KIK and snare transients are overbearing, one of the best tools in their kit is a clipper. They'll use it to muscle your balances—in this case, to tame the KIK and snare. And sure, a clipper can help deliver a louder track, but that's only because the balances were out of whack to begin with.

If a simple balance move isn't enough, you can apply more aggressive processing to the individual channels—KIK and snare in this case—to bring them into compliance without introducing distortion outside your sound design choices. You don't need to strap a clipper across your entire mix when you still have internal control.

I'm all for distortion as a sound design choice. That's intentional. It serves a purpose. It's the *added* distortion that's the problem—an artifact of aggressive processing, usually in pursuit of loudness. If you love the result and the distortion doesn't bother you, that's a viable strategy. If not, then you need to seriously weigh the cost-to-benefit ratio of your processing.

These days, I hear about people inserting clippers on their drum bus. I've experimented plenty with clippers—both during mixing and mastering. I've never once felt they improved my mix. But then again, when my balances are off, it's by design.

You can use anything you like. You won't get an argument from me. I'm not handing down rules. "Never use a clipper" is just as ridiculous as "always use a clipper." And yet, you'll see people touting a clipper as a must-have on every production.

In reality, it's a brute-force tool—something you use to muscle balances when you no longer have mix control. If you want distortion on your KIK and snare, do it while you're mixing. Don't wait until the final stage.

Many people insist that you should master the finished mix in a separate session. I bought into that idea for years— mostly because that's how it was always done. Eventually, I found myself constantly bouncing back and forth. I'd apply a mastering chain, hear a problem, go back to the mix session, adjust a balance, re-bounce, re-import—around and around I'd go. It was an illogically inefficient way to work.

When the technology and the process change, so should the strategy. Once my computer could handle the processing, it made way more sense to apply the mastering chain directly on the mix session itself.

You can work in an archaic way because that's how it was done—or you can strategize based on how you *actually* work. I recommend the latter.

Loudness

There are countless people convinced that loudness offers a value added to their mix, but that is easily proven untrue. If you master the same song twice—once at -7 LUFS and again at -14 LUFS—and then level match them, you can randomly cut between the two and the edits will go by seamlessly as it plays back. I even made a YouTube video proving this called *Let's Talk LUFS*. The -7 LUFS mix had obvious added distortion (which is a degradation, not a value added), and even then, most people wouldn't notice the switches. That's because loudness is not about what happens now. It's about what happens over the course of time. Loudness is all about setting your mix's overall dynamics.

That's why LUFS are measured as integrated loudness. It doesn't matter how loud one section is—what matters is the loudness of the track as a whole. Streaming platforms use integrated LUFS because it gives us a picture of the overall dynamic.

Just as a sheer matter of logic, if we measure loudness as the integrated dynamic range of the entire track (and we do), then a louder track will have less variance in level between sections than a more dynamic one. If you have a 24-bar breakdown section that drops way down in level, that will have a significant influence on the measured LUFS of your track.

While everything you do in your mix will affect your overall loudness, most MEs, and many mixers, maximize their loudness with a brickwall limiter on their mix bus.

In broad terms, -10 LUFS is often a reasonable loudness for many modern productions, as it doesn't tend to bring in obvious distortion artifacts. Once you get to -7 LUFS and louder, the added distortion is difficult to avoid. Meanwhile, many house and electronica producers put their records out at -5 LUFS.

House producers are absolutely convinced DJs won't play their records unless they deliver them that loud—which is kind of funny, since music with dynamics bumps harder on the dance floor.

So, how loud should you make your record?

First, you need to understand the tradeoff. The louder you want your record, the more you have to sacrifice your low end to get there. This is true in terms of both measurable and apparent loudness. When you remove low end, you remove what makes a record big and warm. Brickwall limiters don't make your record bump harder. Compressors do that.

Brickwall limiters merely make your mixes denser and even out the dynamics between sections. The density makes it so that you can turn your mix way down and still hear everything. The dynamic reduction makes it so that all sections of your song can be heard at low levels. Which brings us to the pertinent question: Does loudness offer you an advantage?

If you deliver your mastered mix to most major streaming platforms at -14 LUFS and someone else delivers theirs at -5 LUFS, the streaming platforms will apply 9 dB of negative gain to the much louder -5 LUFS mix. Now both mixes will measure at -14 LUFS, and the large preponderance of listeners won't notice any difference in loudness because of the default normalization setting.

Many people imagine that their much louder track will grab the listener's attention. Or that the more dynamic song will be ignored. In reality, it's more likely that the really loud song will be turned down, much like oppressively loud commercials. Meanwhile, the dynamic song will be turned up.

Do you want your record turned up? Or do you want it turned down? Which of those is a positive act? I can assure you, the song the listener prefers will have nothing to do with the loudness, and everything to do with the song itself. Loudness doesn't make the record better. That said, I don't think excessive loudness will kill a record either.

Which brings us back to the question at hand: How loud should you make your record?

There is no hard LUFS value that I could offer you, because there is no universal value that would be appropriate for every record. If you're making house music and you're convinced the DJ mafia won't play your record if it doesn't conform to a -5 LUFS measurement, then you should make your record -5 LUFS. If you're making a hard rock record and you're absolutely convinced people will skip your record if it's not as loud as the last one, then you should make your record as loud as you possibly can. The reality is, if the song and production are great, no matter what loudness you choose, it will have no bearing on your record's success.

Conversely, if you want your record to sound dynamic and wildly exciting in the confines of an isolated listening room, then even Apple's recommended -16 LUFS could prove too loud. Of course, there's always the middle ground.

I don't ever shoot for a specific LUFS value because the loudness really depends on the nature of the music. I won't be able to get a high LUFS measurement from a 3-minute song with an uber-dynamic one-minute breakdown, not unless I level the breakdown to more evenly match the rest of the track. The mix itself has everything to do with how loud you can make it.

I also find that mixes are more exciting when I give them a nice dynamic lift and then bring that dynamic into compliance with the brickwall limiter. Although the volume dynamic is surely reduced, the contrast dynamic remains. That said, if you make a mix in an overly dynamic manner, and then you add a brickwall limiter to try and make it super loud, you're working against yourself.

All of this takes practice. It took many years of mixing for me to have a sense of the dynamic that would translate best outside the quiet studio.

Most records that I mix and/or master end up somewhere between -9 and -11 LUFS. I don't set my LUFS by a value. I set it by ear and then measure the value after I'm done. I also don't tend to work on super aggressive genres, and as such, that's the range where I typically land. I find it offers the best compromise for the way music is heard today. If that somehow changes, then you should change with it.

Brickwall Limiter Revisited

There are a number of ways to help with your overall loudness. Compressors, clippers, and even saturators (used aggressively) can, and will, reduce the dynamic range of a mix. But brickwall limiters are our most effective tools for the job.

I've used many brickwall limiters over the years. Each have their own sound. Out of all the limiters I've used, I prefer the FabFilter Pro-L2, by far. It's remarkably transparent even when used aggressively. It comes with a variety of useful presets, an integrated loudness meter, available dither, and best of all, oversampling. If you know nothing about using a limiter, you can get great results with just the presets.

You can hit a quality brickwall limiter like the FabFilter L2 with quite a bit of level before you're bringing in added distortion, but that also depends on how well balanced your mix is. When applying brickwall limiting to your mix, you may want to adjust your levels based on how the limiter changes your balances. An aggressive brickwall limiter will tend to bring up the center information.

While it's true that the line for audible clipping lives at 0 dBFS, you want to leave a small buffer so as to avoid common playback issues. Consumer playback DACs can sometimes overshoot when decoding signal near 0 dBFS, which can result in clipping distortion. Streaming platforms transcode your audio to a compressed format (like MP3), which can introduce peak level changes that cause clipping. Streaming sites recommend you set your output level from the brickwall limiter to -1 dBFS. I prefer to set the output level to -0.3 dBFS, but I also apply oversampling with the brickwall limiter, which greatly reduces the possibility of intersample peaks in the conversion process. The oversampling allows the brickwall limiter to more accurately detect true peaks, which would otherwise be missed at standard sampling rates. If your brickwall limiter doesn't offer oversampling, then it's safer to set your output level to -1 dBFS.

Oversampling

In digital audio, we work with samples—tiny snapshots of sound taken at regular intervals. But when we process audio, like applying a limiter or a compressor, those processes can create artifacts.

This is where oversampling comes in. It temporarily increases the sample rate, essentially creating more snapshots between the existing ones. This lets the processing tools work with far greater precision, avoiding nasty side effects like aliasing, where unwanted noise folds back into the audible range.

Once the processing is done, the audio is downsampled back to the original rate. Think of it as doing surgery with a magnifying glass and then stepping back to admire the clean results. The more oversampling you use—2x, 8x, even 32x—the finer the detail, but there's a tradeoff: higher CPU load. So, while oversampling is great for maintaining clarity and avoiding artifacts, it's important to find the sweet spot that works best for your session without crashing your computer in the process.

Frankly, it's remarkable just how much clarity oversampling offers, especially at the brickwall limiter stage. It's what I love most about the FabFilter L2.

Oversampling is not something that you need to apply on every part that you process. You might not even notice the benefits on individual parts within the totality of a mix, and it could get rather labor intensive for your computer. The advantage you gain from oversampling any given part is minimal. The advantage you gain when oversampling the brickwall limiter on the entire mix is significant, and worth implementing.

Dither

Dither is used in digital audio to minimize the distortion that occurs when reducing the bit-depth of a digital signal (e.g., from 24-bit to 16-bit). It works by adding a very small amount of low-level random noise to the audio signal before the bit-depth reduction process. This prevents the digital rounding errors, known as quantization distortion, from creating audible artifacts, particularly in quiet passages of music.

Digital audio stores sound as numerical values, and bit-depth determines how many possible values can be used to represent the audio's amplitude. For example: A 16-bit signal has 65,536 possible values. A 24-bit signal has over 16,000,000 possible values.

When reducing bit-depth, the extra values that can't fit into the smaller bit-depth are rounded off, which can introduce distortion.

Dither introduces low-level noise before the bit-depth reduction process. This randomizes the rounding errors, making them less predictable and less likely to produce harsh or tonal distortion.

WHEN TO USE DITHER

The time to apply dither is when exporting from a higher bit-depth (e.g., 24-bit) to a lower one (e.g., 16-bit for CD). Dither should be the last process applied in your signal chain after all other processing (e.g., EQ, compression, limiting). You can apply dither from many brickwall limiters or as part of your DAW's bounce options.

All of that said, after all of that technical explanation, I will admit that I almost never apply dither anymore.

This is where audio engineers begin to swoon and will surely question my sanity. But the louder your record is, the less necessary dither becomes. Given how loud records are today, and given how many people use clippers to get there, I fail to grasp the benefit of dither.

If you're making a super dynamic record and exporting to a lower bit-depth, then you should use dither. If you're making a relatively loud record, you can apply it or not, and nobody will ever be the wiser. Not even the people who insist you need to use dither.

True Peak Limiting

True peak or not true peak, that is the question.

Some limiters are true peak limiters, and some are sample peak limiters (the FabFilter L2 offers both). The debates over which is better can get fierce when you consider how subtle the differences actually are. No Music Fan would ever know which you chose, and I find the arguments to go way too far in the weeds for me to engage.

I personally turn True Peak off. Sample peak limiting sounds more natural to me, but once again, I use the oversampling, which prevents problems with intersample peaks. I encourage you to fire up your favorite AI and ask it about True Peak, because after you read the arguments pro and con, you'll wonder why you even wasted your time.

EQ Shaping

Once the mix is done, it can often benefit from some EQ. This is where mastering your own record can become a bit tricky. You can easily apply loudness and adjust your balances to the limiter, because you're merely matching balances that you already naturally prefer. But how do you apply EQ to a record you've been listening to for many hours over the course of days—or even weeks? Presumably, you've designed your record to sound the way you want it. Why should you now magically know what EQ to apply to it?

The purpose of EQ is to compensate for your room and to help the record translate in other environments. So, if you don't really know how your room is affecting the translation, then applying EQ can be nothing more than guesswork.

There are AI plugin packages available that can apply EQ for you, like the iZotope Ozone suite, but I rarely agree with the AI's suggestion on my own mixes. The suggested EQ is also wholly dependent on what part of the track you feed it. And as if that's not bad enough, each subsequent version of the Ozone plugin seems to get more aggressive in its recommendations—especially with the top end. The Ozone AI will also add other processors that affect the overall EQ curve of your track.

Apple's Logic now comes with a built-in mastering AI that evaluates the entirety of the track, but I don't find those recommendations to be any more accurate. So, how then do you determine what EQ and processing your record needs?

If your room is an acoustic disaster, it might be worth investing in an AI package to help you master your records. At the very least, you'll get a better idea of your low-end issues. But where it comes to translation outside of a compromised room, you need to actually listen to your record in other environments and make your determinations that way.

Ultimately, you want to be in a position where you can trust your mix room and know how it translates. But until that time, you really have no choice but to check it in outside environments—and that can be exceptionally difficult and confusing, because you're so used to how the record sounds in your room.

Many EQs, like the FabFilter Pro-Q 3 and 4, allow you to EQ the sides or the center of your mix. This is useful when you're mastering a 2-track bounce of a completed mix, because it allows an ME to adjust sides that are out of balance. But if you already know that your sides need adjustment, it makes more sense to fix that in the mix.

If you find yourself making radical EQ adjustments while mastering your mix, then either the mix isn't ready for mastering—or you're doing way too much.

Intelligent EQ

The original intelligent mastering EQ was Gullfoss, developed by Sound Theory. Gullfoss analyzes the audio signal and applies precise adjustments to enhance clarity, detail, and balance. It dynamically boosts or attenuates frequencies to ensure the audio sounds more natural and cohesive. You apply Gullfoss to your stereo mix or master bus to improve overall clarity, reduce masking, and bring out hidden details.

I've been using Gullfoss for a few years now. It's definitely an interesting tool—one that I find myself using about half the time. It does add clarity to the mix, but it can also introduce brightness, which isn't always a good thing.

Frankly, it's a very useful tool that can likely help a lot of people who are new to mastering their own records. It's not fully automated, so you still have to set it by ear. But as a tool, intelligent EQs will only become more ubiquitous over time.

Aggressive Processors

There are all sorts of tools you can use as part of the mastering process. There are multiband compressors, clippers (which we've already discussed), saturators, stereo imaging tools, noise reduction tools, transient shapers, and tape simulators—none of which I would recommend you use on a mix you still have control over.

All of these tools are designed to fix problems with a finished stereo mix. Clippers fix balance issues that could have been adjusted in the mix itself. Saturators apply distortion for purposes of sound design—decisions that should have already been made. Stereo imaging tools add width through phase manipulation, which is an exceptionally weak way to derive width. Your transients should already be presented as you hear them. And there isn't a tape simulator on the planet that actually sounds like tape.

Every one of those tools becomes unnecessary on a well-balanced, well-designed mix with a present midrange.

A well-balanced mix in terms of frequency (not necessarily in terms of mix balances) can take any kind of processing and it won't fall apart. It can take broad EQ adjustments. It can take compression. It can take lots of limiter gain.

So, if you can't make your mix balanced and present during the mixing process, how on earth will you do it during the mastering process? If you're doing it all yourself, then the two stages become one integrated process. And while you want to reserve your loudness for the end, that's because—beyond a few initial minor balance adjustments—the limiter doesn't change the fundamental sound of your mix. So why exhaust yourself listening all day through a limiter when it has no real bearing on the sound?

You know, if your whole mix is just a little closed down, and a 1 dB boost of an 8 kHz shelf opens things up nicely, then that's an efficient way to fix a common problem. Not everything has to be done at the channels or the busses themselves. You can apply global processing across your mix if it quickly fixes an issue. That makes sense.

But why would you want to apply all sorts of aggressive processing that will dramatically alter your overall sound design, when you didn't feel compelled to treat your mix that way in the first place? What happened between the moment you felt your mix was finished and the moment you wanted to alter it dramatically—this time with stereo processors on the whole mix?

Aggressive processing tools do not automatically add value to a mix or to its overall sound design. Here you've gone out of your way to make a mix that causes a reaction—you've diligently and artistically applied your distortion throughout the process—you now wish to summon tools that will aggressively alter all that hard work? For what purpose?

My point is this: don't confuse what an aggressive ME might do to a bounced mix with how you might process your own mix. The ME has limited control and can only alter balances with aggressive tools. You have full control.

What you lose by mastering your own record is the consultation. So, if you need consultation, you might hire an ME to help you deliver your finished record. If you don't need consultation, then trust yourself and the decisions you've made throughout the process—and don't seek to mangle your hard work for little possible gain.

The mixing and mastering processes become a single process when performed by one person. If you're mastering your own record right in the mix session itself (which is how I do it), then it doesn't make a lot of sense to add all sorts of aggressive sound-manipulation tools as a substitute for merely adjusting the mix itself.

Gain Staging for Mastering

The order in which you set your processors will significantly affect your results. There really are no rules to that order—except for one: the brickwall limiter must come last in your chain. You set your final output level from the limiter, and any processing that occurs after it will affect that level, which could result in clipping.

We talked about this already, but it bears repeating here. If your Stereo Output fader exists *after* the inserts (as it does in Logic), then you need to keep that fader at unity at all times—otherwise it will affect the output level from your limiter. We want the brickwall limiter to determine the final output level. Nothing else. So, keep it last in the chain, and don't touch that fader.

As for everything else, that's largely a matter of preference, though there are some reasonable strategies. I like to compress my mix on the ALL BUS and then put the rest of my chain on the Stereo Output. This way, the fader on the ALL BUS channel adjusts my output level from the compressor *to* the mix bus. If I put the compressor as the first insert on the mix bus, then my ALL BUS fader adjusts the level going into the compressor—which I don't want. Once I have my compression set, I want it to stay that way.

Just make sure you don't set up your gain staging such that you're working against yourself.

Versions

Once you've completed your project and it's ready to be released, you'll want to generate some alternate versions of your production—*including stems*, which are stereo submixes of your mix.

When mixing in the analog domain, it's normal to print the mix and a number of alternates the moment you're done with it—mostly because you have to break down the setup and start the next mix. In a DAW, you typically don't bounce your alternate versions until all the mixes are complete. Whether you're working in the analog or digital domain, once the project is complete, you should bounce alternate versions of the mix, so you have them.

While you may be able to recall the mix precisely today, that won't necessarily be the case in a year—in fact, it probably won't be. The moment you perform a software update, your past mix sessions may no longer recall accurately. Even if you don't need the alternates now, you might sometime down the line.

There was a time when we would print alternate vocal-up and vocal-down versions of the mix, but that really isn't necessary anymore unless you're mixing in the analog domain. Those alternates were printed to avoid recalls for vocal level tweaks.

The usual alternates are as follows: Instrumental (mix minus all vocals), TV Mix (instrumental minus lead vocals only), a cappella (vocals only), and stems.

All alternate mixes should be bounced with effects. You can use solo to accomplish this, but the safest way to make your alternates is with the mute button. For example, to make an instrumental, mute all the vocal channels (including their busses). This way, your effects still apply to the other instruments, but not on the vocals since they're cut.

TV Mix

The TV mix has no lead vocal. Harmonies stay intact, and double tracks are optional. The purpose of the mix is for those occasions when the singer must perform to a track, which is common for TV performances—hence the name. You can also call this the "karaoke" mix. Hey, if your production makes it into karaoke machines, that means it was a huge success. Good for you.

Instrumental

The instrumental has no vocals whatsoever. This track can be quite useful for editing purposes, particularly if you wish to prepare a radio edit after the fact. If an edit needs to be performed at a vocal overlap, the instrumental can be used in conjunction with the a cappella to make it seamless. In some genres, like hip-hop, the instrumental is often included with the single as a bonus track. You want to apply your loudness to an instrumental set for release, and you want to leave the limiter off for edits.

A cappella

The a cappella is a vocals-only mix and can be quite handy for edits and remixes. Oftentimes I'll make two a cappella versions: Lead Vocals Only and Background Vocals Only. Both versions include their respective effects.

Stems

Stems are stereo submixes that combine as your mix when set at unity gain. Stems are an absolute necessity for songwriters today, as they're required for those seeking sync opportunities for movies and television. Sync is critical to their exposure.

Contrary to popular belief, stems are not multitrack audio files. I don't know how on earth the term *stems* were appropriated like this, but stereo submixes have been called stems for the entirety of my career. *Stems* is what directors call them, and if you send them your multitrack files, you'll reveal yourself as an amateur. And yes, I realize Logic now calls your multitrack files stems, which only serves to further entrench the misappropriated version of the term—but that doesn't change the fact that when stems are requested for sync purposes, it's stereo submixes that are expected.

The purpose of stems is to provide the re-recording engineers who mix for movies and TV some modicum of control over your mix. At first blush, that might cause you to recoil. *They're going to change my mix?* Well, yes—but not because there's a problem with the mix.

Movies include dialogue and Foley, and your song is part of the overall audio fabric tied to a visual medium. Just as you need control over the individual parts in your arrangement, the re-recording engineer needs control over all the audio, as it's subservient to the needs of the movie itself. For example, if dialogue comes in over the music, the engineer might lower the vocals in the song. This way, the music stays up, and the vocals don't compete with the dialogue.

Stems are bounced as stereo files and include effects. Here's a list of some typical stems:

- Bass
- Drums and Perc
- Guitars
- Keys
- Background Vox
- Lead Vox

There may be times you choose to combine the keys and guitars. Other times, you may have horns, strings, or other instrumentation in need of stems. Do what makes the most sense for the production but try to limit the stems to eight stereo pairs whenever possible.

Mixing and Mastering Plugins

In the *Home Producer* chapter, I told you that stock plugins are good enough to get you started. And they are. But when it comes to our most commonly used processing plugins, there is one suite that I recommend over any other—and that's the Fab-Filter Pro Series. These are, hands down, the best suite of professional processing tools you can buy. You can purchase them individually or pick up one of their various bundles. Students get 50% off.

I use lots of processing plugins from many developers on my mixes. Some plugins do things others don't, and I pull those out when they suit the situation. But at a baseline, the FabFilter package is my most dependable and versatile toolset, and I find it indispensable. I'm really not going out on a limb here—the package is virtually ubiquitous in mixing and mastering circles.

Since FabFilter was so kind as to sponsor this work, I'd like to present to you their FabFilter Pro Series:

Pro-Q3 and Q4 Equalizers (EQ): Features dynamic EQ, linear phase modes, mid/side processing, dynamic processing, and a spectrum analyzer. Offers precision EQ for mixing and mastering. Great GUI. Great sound. I find the dynamic EQ functionality nothing short of essential for dealing with problem frequencies that don't remain static. The Pro-Q4 includes distortion algorithms for a more analog tone.

Pro-C2 Compressor: Features multiple compression styles (clean, vintage, vocal), sidechain, and lookahead. Transparent or characterful compression for individual tracks, busses, or mastering. This is a super versatile compressor—useful for anyone at any level. This is by far my favorite compressor these days.

Pro-L2 Brickwall Limiter: Features multiple limiting algorithms, oversampling, True Peak limiting, and detailed metering. Loudness control and peak limiting in mastering.

Pro-DS De-Esser: Features intelligent sibilance detection and wideband or split-band processing, reducing sibilance in vocals or harshness in high frequencies. This is one of the more effective de-essers on the market.

Pro-MB Multiband Compressor: Up to six bands, dynamic range control, and mid/side processing. Offers precision dynamic control across different frequency ranges.

Pro-G Gate/Expander: Features Flexible gating and expansion with sidechain and MIDI triggering. Useful for noise reduction, creative gating, or dynamic control.

Pro-R Reverb: Features natural, musical reverb with advanced decay shaping and EQ. Add depth and space to vocals, instruments, or mixes. This has become one of my favorite reverbs because it's algorithmic and easy to program.

Saturn 2 Saturation/Distortion: Features multi-band saturation, modulation, and a variety of distortion styles. Add warmth, grit, or character to tracks. I have many flavors of distortion in my arsenal, all that offer their own sound. The Saturn is an important part of that collection.

Timeless 3 Delay: Features tape delay with modulation, filters, and creative effects. Echo, delay, and time-based effects with modulation options. Super easy to program for simple delay effects, but you can also get insanely creative with it.

Volcano 3 Filter: Features multi-mode filters, modulation, and creative filtering effects. Offers sweeps, resonances, and intricate filter-based sound design. This is a great tool for motion effects.

Practice Makes Perfect

Where it comes to mixing and mastering, there is no bypassing practice. Nobody wants to hear that, but it took me four years of practice before I was even *good*. And I was learning in a proper 24-track recording studio with mentors. It took me another two years of mixing nearly every day in Los Angeles before I was delivering great mixes with consistency.

Anyone can make a great mix. Few can deliver a great mix with consistency. And those who can have been mixing exclusively for years.

The good news is there's no shortage of songs. It's not like you get just one shot at it. You will work on or write hundreds upon hundreds of songs. Possibly thousands. You have time to develop all of your skills. The best way to do that is to make as many records as possible. But you have to finish them.

There's a lot of young producers who get hung up on perfection, which can prevent them from finishing records. I saw a poll in a mixing group, and that was by far the number one issue people faced when it came to finishing songs. I get it. You hear professional records, and you wonder how on earth you can get that sound—or make a song like that—and it can be a bit deflating.

You don't need to attain perfection on every mix of every production of every song. Even if you were to manage to accidentally attain perfection for a moment, you probably went past that days ago, because you're not in a position to recognize it. In fact, you should try the opposite of perfection, which could only be "not perfection." Try to purposely attain "not perfection." Just as an exercise. Especially if finishing songs is a problem for you.

It's absolutely critical that you finish your records. You learn your most powerful lessons when you do, and you experience the complete process too. If you don't finish records, you'll only excel at starting them.

Finished records also allow you to evaluate your progress—especially when you give yourself some distance. When you listen back to a record a week after it's done, it sounds different. The more time that passes, the more your perception shifts. When you listen to it a month later, you notice things you didn't before. And after a year? Now you have the distance necessary to truly understand what you've made.

Distance allows us to forget our internal fights and biases. It allows us to hear the record outside of our involvement. In the early stages of your journey, you'll understand and appreciate your improvement. In the early stages of your journey, you'll understand and appreciate your improvement. As you become great, you'll get confirmation of that. Hopefully, anyway.

The point of this is to say, nobody makes great early records. Few write great early songs. None are good at mixing or mastering. There's a lot to learn and it takes time to learn it. So, be patient. Just keep finishing records. You'll get there.

CHAPTER EIGHT

The Politics of a Band Entity

Bands are complex entities that require you to engage in politics. It's like being in a marriage with several people instead of just two, and everyone's feelings need to be taken into account. That said, a band is also a business—and as with any business, everyone wants their piece of the pie.

It's a rare band that operates purely as a democracy—so rare, I've never seen one. It's the songwriters who hold the most sway, because without songs, there's nothing for anyone to play. And when there's one person driving both the songwriting and the overall presentation of the band, I refer to that person as the *Child of Brain*. If the project is their brainchild, then they are Child of Brain. They're the leader—and the person you'll work with most closely to achieve your goals.

How much power the Child of Brain wields is almost directly proportional to how many songs they write for the band. The more songs they contribute, the more influence they hold within the structure of the group. There's a good reason for this: the songwriter is the one person in the band who can't really be replaced—not without significantly altering the band's identity. Cover bands notwithstanding, the band exists because of the songs, and whoever writes the songs has the most say.

Occasionally, you'll come across a band with multiple songwriters, and that changes the dynamic—though often in predictable ways. The power structure will almost always mirror the songwriting relationships. For instance, two songwriters who write as a partnership will typically share leadership equally. A band with four separate songwriters will often function as a democracy in business matters, but rotate creative authority based on who wrote any given track.

Some bands work out songs together and share credit equally among the members. Although rare, it's by far the healthiest business structure for a band. Everyone gets paid equally, which helps prevent a non-songwriting player from insisting that their two shitty songs make the album. Clearly, that's a scenario best avoided. A frank business discussion with the band can help address that dynamic before it becomes a problem. Otherwise, you might find yourself recording and prioritizing less important songs just to accommodate a somewhat business-savvy band member.

There are only three major music revenue streams when it comes to bands: record sales, live performance (which includes merchandise), and publishing. For all intents and purposes, record sales no longer exist—they've been mostly replaced by Streams.

Since the record itself won't bring in significant revenue, it's often used as a loss leader for ticket sales. Live performance monies can be a lucrative revenue stream, and the band typically shares equally in these revenues. Touring is the crux of the band's business, but it carries a rather large overhead. As a result, many bands require tour support—which is a nice way of saying they need a subsidy from a label. As the band becomes more popular, its need for support begins to drop.

Publishing is the Mother of All Revenue Streams. It's where the big money is in this business—and without sales, it's the only stream that can still generate "mailbox money." A hit song—one that's spun relentlessly on radio, streamed on the Internet, licensed for commercials and movies, played in clubs, and successfully covered by others—can generate revenue for decades. While live revenues require the band to physically tour in order to earn, the successful songwriter will continue to make money long after the band entity itself has disbanded.

Given these realities, any band member who isn't a songwriter will only make money on the band's efforts when they're on tour. Once the non-writers come to this realization, they often attempt to write songs—and will likely insist on getting some of those songs on the album. If a player gets two songs out of ten, they'll receive one-fifth of the writer's royalties for the album. The problem with this logic? People don't really listen to albums anymore. They listen to songs through playlists. Which tends to preclude the non-writing member from making any money on their shitty bullshit song. The listener doesn't even discover it—unless they happen to play the entire album.

If you find yourself in a situation where the worst songwriter in the band is demanding song representation on the album, you'll either need to capitulate and record those songs—or finesse the issue. If you simply ignore the problem and steamroll over the band by refusing to record them, you risk blowing up the entire project.

Since it's in the band's best interest to put out as many great songs as possible, the most effective solution is for the songwriter(s) to give the band a stake in the publishing royalties—enough of a share that everyone has a financial incentive to choose songs based on quality first and foremost.

It's impossible to come up with a fair percentage for the band to receive without understanding the band's contributions. Even then I would be reticent to offer any hard numbers. If the songwriter typically comes into rehearsal with a completed song in which they spoon-feed parts to the band members, then the band is not particularly integral to the process beyond performing the songs. Given that scenario, a nominal percentage of the publishing would be downright generous, and likely uncalled for.

If the songwriter usually brings in half-baked ideas, and the band develops the song as an entity, then there's a strong argument for sharing some of the songwriting royalties. Technically, only those involved in the lyric and melody are the songwriters. But if the band entity is integral to shaping the song, it makes sense for the songwriter to reward the band through profit-sharing revenues.

Politically, it would be foolish for you, as the producer, to suggest this sort of business arrangement in an open forum. This conversation should happen directly with the songwriter and should be framed entirely in business terms, not moral ones. Your case should be based on the band's contributions, the realities of the business, and the importance of keeping the band happy. If the band is the vehicle through which the songwriter can best release their songs, then the band carries significant value. All you want to do is present the dilemma—and let the songwriter figure out the incentives from there.

This is not a discussion you should initiate unless it's clearly becoming a problem. You don't want to fuck with a band that's content with its business arrangements, even if you think they're unfair. Poking at a stable situation could blow things up, and the band will renegotiate its terms if and when it becomes necessary. The real issue arises when your involvement is perceived as raising the stakes. That's when songwriting royalties can turn into a political landmine—and one worth monitoring closely.

Sharing Credit

Bands and artists alike frequently ask to share production credit. I've done this in the past, and I don't recommend it.

In this book, I've laid out exactly what producing is. In concise terms, it's a leadership role rooted in morale management and creative vision—and an organizational role rooted in resource management. Regardless of what you bring to the party in terms of song enhancements, creative contributions, arrangement, parts, and the overall presentation of the band, they still get all the credit. They're the band. It's their album, their music. That's everything. They need to take credit as producer too? I think not.

From the band's perspective, they are a major part of "producing" their album—and in a sense, they're right. They wrote the songs and demoed them up in a way that attracted you. But the credit is *Produced by*—and in all but rare cases, that task is handled by one person: you.

Sharing your producer credit is as ludicrous as sharing credit for being in the band. Believe me, if you do your job right, by the time you finish the project, they'll consider you part of the band anyway. Of course, that feeling will fade quickly as they spend months on the road, and you move on to produce other projects.

The one time you might consider sharing producer credit is if you're asked to function as an Engineer Producer for a long-established band with multiple releases. Even then, you should resist unless it's the difference between winning and losing the gig. Just remember: any time you draw a line in the sand, you risk losing the job.

This entire book is one big argument against sharing credit. Don't be afraid to shoot down such a request outright. A young band will rarely push beyond an initial ask—especially if you lay

570   Mixerman's Ultimate Guide to PRODUCING Records, Music & Songs

out your reasons clearly, firmly, and without apology. Consider a request to share credit as the most important early test of your leadership and communication skills. Pass that test, and the band will accept you as the leader of the project.

Even if you're working with an artist and cowriting with them, that doesn't automatically entitle them to co-producer credit. They're still the artist. They still need a producer. Don't give away that credit too readily.

How to Rule

I think I've made this pretty clear throughout the book but let there be no doubt: producing is not a dictatorship. It's the band's or the artist's album. They're the ones who need to be proud of the finished product. They're the ones with their pictures on the cover, not you. The band is who ends up most branded by the results. You work on many albums over the course of your career, and your brand will be based largely on your most successful works.

That said, you're not there to cater to their every whim; you're there as an expert—a leader who understands how to make successful music. You're beholden to a budget and you share in profits if the album does well. Your expertise on how to accomplish the best album possible for the band is what puts you in this position. Therefore, you're not there to serve purely at the pleasure of the band. You're there to lead them through the creative process—with structure. If you consistently yield creatively to the will of the band against your stated vision, you are no longer making the album you promised. A yes man has no value to a band, or any other creative entity, for that matter.

How the hell do you reconcile the idea that you are hired by the band with the idea that you must maintain some control over the creative process?

Very carefully.

Ultimately, it all comes down to the setup. There's a reason why I say you should be wholly honest at all times—it sets the tone for open and honest communication. There's a reason why I suggest you not only have a vision, but that you sell the band on your vision, because it puts you in the leadership position. There's a reason why I suggest you wait until after preproduction before you even begin to talk contracts. It gives you the opportunity to get the band wholly on board with your vision— which gives you leverage. You're the one with the vision and the plan, and once the band buys into that completely, the only way they get to hear your completed vision is to buy into your leadership.

That doesn't mean there won't be disagreements. It doesn't mean your client won't make attempts to pull you and the project off vision. It doesn't mean you won't have a problem band member hell-bent on putting a wrench in the works.

All of those things can and will happen on occasion, no matter how clear you are in your communication. But if you were honest and forthright in your vision, if you laid out the plan— both musical and logistical—there can't be much argument against sticking with the agreed upon plan. The entire presentation system as I've laid out for you is meant to force the band to stick with you until the very end, and when one band member revolts temporarily, the others will keep them in check.

Given the nature of producing, and despite the fact that you work for the band, there will be times when you must stand your ground. The temporary mutiny of a single irritant is nothing more than a test of your resolve. Stand firm. An attempt by the Child of Brain to involve you in a three-hour Science Experiment during the tracking session is a test of your focus. Stand firm and keep the session on track. If the singer is a terrible guitar player, yet insists on laying down guitar doubles, it's an internal power play. Stand firm. Of course, since you're working with a band, it's rare that you will have to "stand firm" without the support of others. You can and must use this support to your advantage.

Whenever you work with a group on a creative project, alliances will constantly shift. It is unusual for cliques to remain unified and unchanging throughout the process. When the band is evenly split, you become the tiebreaker. When the band is split unevenly in your favor, you can leverage the support necessary to push through your agenda. When the band is split out of your favor, you need only sway one or two band members to your side.

From the shrewd position of pure political calculation, you can use divide-and-conquer techniques to get your way all day long. The problem is that sort of leadership is divisive in nature—hence the term "*divide* and conquer." This would seem to make you the anti-producer. When you're short on time, you may have to use these kinds of political calculations just to keep the session moving forward. But overall, you want to engage in consensus building; otherwise alliances could become firmly entrenched.

Compromise is a part of all record-making. When you deal with a large team of people who have varying opinions, there must be some give and take from everyone involved. Again, as the leader, you set the tone.

Every person on the team will compromise throughout the course of the project. The art of compromise from a leadership position is to agree when a decision makes no difference, to offer other viable alternatives when it does make a difference, and to stand firm when all reasonable alternatives have been exhausted. If your Child of Brain has an idea they wish to attempt, why would you want to shoot it down? You don't want the band shooting down your crazy ideas. So don't shoot down theirs.

You must lead by example. You'll be seen as nothing short of a hypocrite if you don't hear out ideas. At the same time, if your Child of Brain's ideas come fast and furious and completely lack focus, you can't possibly entertain them all. You have a re-sponsibility to keep the session on track, and you have the authority to keep the session focused.

You must also take into consideration the level of passion exhibited in any given protest. A drummer who is adamantly against a drum fill will likely trump the rest of the band that loves the fill, seeing as they're the ones who played it. The drummer who describes themselves as "not particularly fond" of a fill has essentially admitted that they will yield to the con-sensus of the group. That said, if fixing the fill is as easy as grabbing one from another take, or a quick edit, then why not just solve the issue for the drummer? Unless the drum fill is somehow critical to the production as-is (and that's possible), then why not help make the drummer more comfortable? This would fall under "choose your battles."

Acquiescing at a time that doesn't require it will give you significant political capital later on. It sends the message that you're not going to stand firm unless it really matters to the production. It also sends the message that you want everyone in the band to be happy with their record. These are good messages to send.

As much as the Child of Brain has more weight, the band has some power too. The full band against you and the Child of Brain puts you in a tough spot politically. To go against the entire band can cause feelings of resentment. Often the band will acquiesce to the Child of Brain, but not always. If the band members are standing firm, you would be foolish to act as anything other than arbitrator. Placing your thumb on the scale in favor of a single person in the band is ill-advised unless the issue has to do di-rectly with their own personal performance. A guitar player who is unhappy with their part trumps the rest of the band in regard to those parts. A Child of Brain who is unhappy with the guitar parts must negotiate that with the guitar player and producer.

You should avoid voting positions that are not in your favor. Producing can't be done well by committee, so don't put yourself in a position where you only get one vote out of many. Issues will come up, and if most of the band is unhappy, you really have no choice but to find an alternative. If that doesn't work, then you should probably defer the problem.

One of the more compelling reasons to cozy up to the Child of Brain in the first place is to help you navigate the politics of the band. It's not so you can give yourself permission to treat everyone else like second-class citizens. Band members are just as aware of the natural pecking order as you are. Given this, you should go out of your way to give them a sense of importance. If the entire band isn't performing at their best, your production will suffer.

The Art of Presentation

Your best weapon against a political crisis is presentation. How you pitch an idea often matters more than the idea itself. Sometimes, a bold, unexpected suggestion is just the jolt a session needs—especially if you're trying to reassert control or if the band is particularly open and malleable. Other times, it's better to ease the room into a new idea, especially when there's resistance in the air.

The beauty of ideas is that they spark other ideas. When I know exactly what I'm trying to accomplish, I'll often present a concept with full confidence and little explanation—I'm simply lighting the next fuse. But when I'm unsure, and hoping the band can help shape or refine the direction, I'll present that same idea more tentatively, inviting feedback and collaboration.

A large part of your job as producer is sales. Before you ever step into a studio, you're selling yourself, your enthusiasm, your vision, and your value. That sales job doesn't end once the red light goes on. Any time you face resistance, you'll need to sell your ideas—and your most effective tool for doing so is demonstration.

The entire process of making a record should be one demonstration after another—all of them leading toward your vision. Don't waste time debating abstract concepts that can be tested in real time. If there's disagreement over direction, try it. Build it. Listen to it. Evaluate it. If your way really is better, it'll become obvious. But if someone else has a strong idea, shutting it down without investigation is shortsighted.

You never want to brush off your band's concerns with vague promises. If you've told them they'll always know where they are in the record, you can't turn around and say, "It'll all work out later." If there's a problem, acknowledge it—even if you're not ready to solve it yet. Deferment is fine; dismissal is not. And whatever you do, don't tell your band you'll "fix it in the mix" (even if it's true). If you can fix it in the mix, chances are, you can fix it right now.

Festering concerns kill morale. Communication keeps it alive. If you're struggling with a track, let the band in on it. They're not just your clients—they're your partners in this. And they might just have the solution you need.

Deferring Decisions

As we've already established, it's generally best to avoid deferring decisions when producing a record. Politically, however, there are times when it's necessary to table a discussion. Whether you're dealing with a split band too entrenched in their positions to negotiate, or an emotionally charged Child of Brain, deferment can be a useful tool. There's no point in allowing a debate between two sides incapable of hearing each other. Use time to your advantage.

The passage of time allows emotions to settle, which makes compromise more likely. You can also use success as emotional leverage to reopen dialogue and solve difficult problems. Success tends to emulsify hardened positions and serves as proof of what can happen when everyone works together. Of course, whatever you do, don't return to your problem track on the heels of another disaster.

Deferment also gives the band time to live with the track in its controversial state. If you give them a rough mix as it stands, chances are they'll listen to it a number of times before you revisit it. Often, a controversial part grows on people—and if it doesn't, you'll likely be offered all sorts of solutions when you return to the track. This goes for you as a producer too. If you're unsure about a part, live with it before you shoot it down entirely. And if deferment doesn't resolve the issue, you always have the power of veto.

The Power of Veto

Technically, you don't really have veto power unless the band is willing to give it to you. And even if they do, it's in limited supply. The extent of your veto power can only be measured by how much political capital you've accrued—and that capital may be needed elsewhere. Treat your veto as if you have but one. Frankly, that's probably about right.

You have all sorts of tools to sway a band, starting with demonstration and continuing with your ability to persuade. But if you find yourself at a crossroads—where your act wants to do something you view as detrimental—your veto becomes your last resort. Even then, you need some numbers to back you up. You can't rightly exercise a veto if you're going against the will of everyone on the team. You'll need at least some support from within the band.

If you make light of your veto power, you might be able to buy yourself a few soft vetoes. The mere mention of one—expressed jokingly—can soften positions, if only to avoid seeing it actually happen. That said, don't wield it as an overt threat. Use it to keep people in a mindset of compromise—and only pull it out when absolutely necessary and when you've built the political capital to support it.

Frankly, the veto is a risky play—one that could alienate your act from liking their own record. Treat the hard veto as a measure of last resort.

Setting the Mood

Humor is one of your best weapons when it comes to running a session. Making a record is serious business, sure—but the goal is to make it fun. And why not? If you can keep your band in a good mood and make the process enjoyable, they'll be far less likely to get bogged down in inconsequential bullshit. Creative disagreements are rare when everyone's enjoying themselves, and as the leader, if you can take their mind off the stakes, you'll make your life considerably easier.

Your bedside manner is important to the vibe of a session. No matter how lousy your mood, it's critical to put on a game face for your band. They rely on you to keep the mood up—and they're watching you for any signs of trouble.

Prioritization

Whenever you record more songs than will make the album, you must be prepared to cut your losses based on the song prioritization list. If you allow your band to divert your attention to a low-priority track early on, you could end up mismanaging your time. There's no way to predict with perfect accuracy which tracks will be problematic and which will fall into place effortlessly. You don't want to find yourself in a position where a lack of discipline on your part either forces you to dump an important song or diminishes the overall quality of the project. A priority list is useless if you're not actually going to use it.

That said, there are times when it makes sense to pivot to a low-priority track—especially if it offers some kind of relief for the session. A goofy song can lighten a dismal mood, in which case you could argue that it's momentarily the highest-priority track. Time and morale management are the fulcrum for keeping your session on an even keel. Lower-priority songs can serve as a break from the grind—and those are often the tracks that end up surprising everyone.

Let Them Play

One of the most meaningful ways you can empower a band is by letting them actually play.

Today, a producer isn't limited by track count, and a mistake doesn't even need to be replayed by the musician. A technician can manipulate it, move it, tune it, time it, stretch it—even alter the tone beyond recognition—without ever getting up from their chair. What was once a musician-driven process, where all the performance power lay in the hands of the players, has become a technician-driven process, where a significant share of that power now rests with the producer.

Given the power available in the DAW, producing a band takes discipline. I'm a nut about getting the musicians to play their parts. And while players often find this approach amusing at first, by the time we're done, that amusement has turned into appreciation. Why? Because the band feels like it's their record. They feel like they *played* their record. And even though there might be some edits—a nip or tuck here or there—it doesn't cheapen the hard work of developing and performing their music. Nor should it. The confidence you instill by insisting they perform should not be underestimated.

There's a difference between performing music and playing notes. Performing moves people. You can't perform snippets. That's not music—that's a snippet. It carries no emotional impact for the listener. So, if you're producing a band, you must be willing to record their *music*—and that means capturing their *performances.*

For your band to perform, there has to be a plan—a vision, worked out ahead of the recording session. The creative process is fraught with possibilities. As sure as you might be of your intentions, there will be times when a part or idea takes the record in a wholly unexpected direction. That can be disorienting—especially if it clearly falls outside your original concept. Sometimes those left turns are brilliant and require no debate at all. Other times, they'll leave you stuck on the fence, unsure of which way to jump. You may even fall in love with a part that makes you feel downright uncomfortable.

If you set that part aside and move forward with the production, you'll most likely strand it. As much as I insist you stick to your vision, an exciting and compelling left turn deserves to be explored. The best way to evaluate a part is to build upon it until you're sure of it. And the moment you realize you've taken a wrong turn, get rid of the part—and anything that came as a result.

Left turns can be positive developments, but they require moderation. If you're easily distracted by ideas that veer far outside your original plan, you'll not only go over budget—you'll lose your way. The setup of the record happens in preproduction. The foundation is laid during tracking. The making of the record occurs in the overdub phase. And if you work with discipline and purpose, you'll have your record the moment you complete the last overdub.

Once you can get to that place—where your results match your vision—you're building productions that will move people and stand the test of time. Best of all, you'll be proud of your results, because you'll have built a production with intent, based on the music and the reaction it causes.

That's great producing right there.

Conclusion

Why is it that we expect our visual artists to be wholly unique, but when it comes to music, so many of us go out of our way to conform to what everyone else is doing? That is the universal and perpetual conundrum of the music business. Be different—but don't be *too* different, and make sure you follow all of the current trends so that your music sounds like everything else—never mind the impossibility of the goal.

I'm not suggesting you shouldn't follow production trends. I'm saying you should strive to be unique, whether you follow trends or not. Uniqueness and trendiness are not mutually exclusive. Even if you avoided all trends, your music would still be more familiar than unique.

As far as I'm concerned, there are entire genres of music that should be pronounced dead. What other diagnosis could we come up with when creativity cedes all ground to similarity? How else could we describe genres that have been placed in a veritable box—a coffin, as it were—to the point that even the slightest deviation from standards can somehow disqualify it from the genre?

Oh, I wouldn't dare offer specifics. That would only alienate a great many people who couldn't fathom such an ignorant statement. *Obviously he doesn't know anything about the genre!*—my critics would say. Who needs critics? Nobody.

Music is art. It's also largely ubiquitous and free. You can't go anywhere without hearing music. And sure, perhaps you shell out $15 of your hard-earned money every month to Big Streaming, but I would call that a rather nominal charge considering what you get. You can listen to just about any music at any time without any limits or commercial interruptions. Or you could buy an album this month. From the perspective of the consumer, that's a big win. From the perspective of the artist or producer, it's a problem.

It becomes a constant battle to stand out in a world where over 100,000 records are released every single day. That's the same number of records that were released in *all* of 1989. And that stunning volume of material will only increase in the coming years. Once producers are able to harness the power of AI to generate music faster and more efficiently, daily releases will grow exponentially.

Then how will you be heard?

You can scoff, of course, and dismiss AI as uninventive and derivative and incapable of creating anything human-like—which isn't true by any stretch of the imagination. Or you could hold dear to the notion that AI is stealing from humanity. But I'm not sure you can claim both are true at the same time.

Can something uninventive and derivative really be "stolen" when it has already been recycled countless times? If the music lacks originality, who exactly was it stolen from? Humanity? Really? So, on the one hand AI can't make anything original or human-like, but on the other it's stealing from humanity? Pick one.

The truth is, 99% of what we do is a rehash of what we've heard before. Probably more. Were you to produce a record that was truly original—one that didn't rely on any of the many patterns that make up the music we know and love—nobody would understand it. Musical advancement is constant and incremental. Everything we write and produce is built on the art that came before us.

When we make music, we take with impunity from everything we've heard in our lifetimes. That is the fundamental truth of music as an artform. It's all derivative to some extent. If it weren't, it wouldn't work.

Once you understand this underlying principle, building a production becomes similar to patching a modular synthesizer. You start with simple building blocks—an oscillator, a filter, an envelope. On their own, they don't do much. But once you connect them together—an oscillator into a filter, modulated by an LFO, shaped by an envelope—you create a bigger building block: a bass patch, a lead, a texture. And once you've built that bigger structure, you don't think about the individual parts anymore. It becomes its own new building block—a Module—which you can plug into future productions without having to reconstruct it from scratch. That's how record-making works too. You combine small Modules into larger creative ones, and over time, you pull from those bigger Modules to more efficiently build your production. As a result, the longer you write songs or produce records, the more simplified the processes become.

There is no creativity born from whole cloth. How could there be? If you asked me to "make something," I would have no idea where to begin. But if you asked me to make a song, now I have a starting point—and my creativity can be effectively unleashed within the confines of that existing structure.

Conceptually building a production with Modules allows us to work quickly and efficiently within those boundaries of structure and familiarity, drawing from everything we've done and heard in the past.

Module number one—the Song Module. It's a sonic medium. Special reproduction equipment is required by both the creator and the consumer. We have limits of audible frequency range.

Technical limits. Spatial limits. We have harmonic and rhythmic limits, which provide us with musical structure. We're only on the first Module, and we've already been placed in a creative box.

The Song Module is constructed of smaller modules—like the Harmony Module. Some historians claim Bach used every possible chord progression in his lifetime. Truth or hyperbole, it's undeniable that countless songs share identical progressions.

You can try to get creative with harmony, but there's not much you can come up with that hasn't been done in some form or another by someone. As you write songs, you are continually adding to your collection of immediately accessible Harmony Modules, which you combine to make the chord structure of the song.

Next up, the Melodic Phrase Module. Melodies are tied to harmonic structure, and that naturally restricts our available melodic options to some degree. Just as there's no such thing as an original chord progression, there's no such thing as a new melodic phrase. But when we combine several melodic phrases, we construct a larger Melody Module, which is far more likely to come off as original.

Then, of course, we have the Lyric Module, which falls in line with The Song Form Modules: Intro, Verse, prechorus, chorus, bridge, outro, tag—all of them plug and play.

The Feeling Module. Want to evoke a triumphant feeling in the bridge? Then your Harmony, Melody, and Lyric Modules must combine to create that emotional payoff. Those, in turn, plug directly into your Bridge Module, which sits inside the larger Song Module.

Next up, our Production Modules.

Let's say we're Producing a song. Do we want to present this record raw or polished? Edgy or sweet? Trendy or classic? Harmonic or dissident? Upbeat or solemn? Some Modules are binary, others variable, and we use them specifically to mirror the emotion of the song.

Perhaps we want a polished programmed sound using a MIDI beat. Four to the Floor Module? Nah. Let's use our KIKs on 1 and 3, snares on 2 and 4 Module. These then plug in to our Rhythm Module. Up tempo? Ballad? Drums driven? Funky? Swing? Time signature? Which decisions work best with the Song Module?

Hi-hat pattern in the verse? Ride in the chorus? Contrast module. Rhythm Modules.

Perhaps the programmed ride is too stiff. We choose a loop for the ride pattern—a topper—which sounds considerably more natural than the sample. Organic Module. Plugged into the chorus, the Organic Module pulls us from a fully canned sound across the entirety of the production to something that presents a bit more natural and less programmed.

Next we add 808 KIKs to function as a bass part. We apply saturation distortion on the 808s to bring out the fourth octave from the fundamental—a commonly heard technique that provides us a nice trendy element to the track. Trendiness Module. Distortion Module. Perhaps even Audibility Module.

A well-known guitar sample playing a lick in the verse? Familiarity Module. A counter melodic string part in the prechorus? Forward Motion Module. Big double guitars playing sustaining power chords in the chorus? Contrast module. Width module. Payoff Module. Distortion Module.

Let's high-pass filter our vocal on the verse. This offers the Artist some distance from an edgy lyric. Intimacy Module (which is variable in nature since there are degrees of intimacy that can be applied). We then add stacked harmonies and full voice doubled vocals on the chorus, smothered in reverb for a bigger than life presentation. Contrast Module. Intimacy Module.

A musical drop before the chorus; a delay tap on the vocal out of the chorus; a rhythmic acceleration at the prechorus; a snare fill before the bridge; a breakdown—Forward Motion Module. Refinement Module. Polish Module. Contrast Module.

Some of you might read all of that and find it a somewhat cynical way to create musical production. To which I would argue, it's not a "way" of doing things. It's actually how our brains innately compartmentalize micro-decisions into larger buckets based on their core purpose—to cause an emotional reaction and push the listener forward through the song. That's true of both Production Modules and Song Modules. It's just we construct our Production Modules based on the song.

This is why Songwriting is considered a craft. Because crafts have structure, and you become great at a craft when you have systems that allow you to create effective works quickly and efficiently. It's the Music *Business*, after all, which is a numbers game.

The more records you make, the more chance you have at success. If you're not in business, then you needn't adhere to any structure nor concern yourself with efficiency. There are no stakes. But when you *are* in business, you have to create music that resonates with a lot of people—and that takes more intention than inspiration.

The longer you make records, the more you pull from your experience. Patterns emerge. Effective production and songwriting techniques are used repeatedly and purposely. There are only so many techniques available to us. We can't just throw them each out because they've been done before. We'd be out of Modules before breakfast.

I bring all of this to your attention, because music creation is about to change dramatically. The bar for entry is already at a historical low and about to get lower. In the foreseeable future, anyone—and I mean *anyone*—will be able to create fully viable songs and productions with the help of AI. We are on the precipice of a new tool that can simplify processes down to Modules through prompt.

For instance:

"AI, I want an acoustic guitar in the verse. Melancholy. Finger picking style. Played with the sensibilities of a virtuoso player."

"AI, scratch that. Give me an acoustic guitar in the verse. Strumming. Upbeat. Raw. Tough. Gritty. Played with reckless abandon and without a lot of skill."

Or how about this?

"AI, I want a part in the verse that promotes a feeling of melancholy, both in tone and chord structure."

Once we can direct AI this way—by describing parts or even the feeling we want to elicit—we'll strip away many of the innate creative restrictions we face today. You don't play guitar? Now you do.

I'll leave a deeper discussion of my views on AI for the next edition of this book, largely because we still have quite a ways to go before it's a viable, controllable production tool. But I can tell you with absolute certainty, whether you like it or not, it's coming. And AI will use precisely the same musical decision-making Modules that I've described here—only considerably faster and with far greater aplomb.

Of course, new technology always brings unintended consequences. Whereas we once needed expensive studios to produce reproducible music, now a laptop will do. That's great. But we also once needed a Distributor with connections to radio and retail. Now, we have access to billions of listeners through Streaming.

We call that "exposure" which is really just a means for companies to control costs. It's a grift. *If a billion people listen to your song you'll be rich! So put it up there and see if you can garner a billion streams!* Never mind the impossibility of doing that without a major label backing you.

One could record music at home and release it into the world for nobody to hear in 1980 too. That's not new. What's changed is the volume. The supply of great music long ago far exceeded demand—certainly as it relates to your capacity to listen to it all.

Our existing technology allows any independent artist the ability to make music and get it to market—both of which are ostensibly positive advancements. But that accessibility has only made it more difficult to break through the cacophony.

All of this to point out it's more important than ever that you stand out. Which is nearly impossible within such a restrictive structure. And yet, every week, we hear songs that do indeed— stand out.

I've given you all sorts of methods, insights, and strategies throughout this book—most of which you can and should be willing to reject in the name of creativity. But if you really want to make stand out music, that isn't derivative and uninventive, but still familiar? Then you need to get creative and stop trying to conform to a sonic standardization that doesn't actually exist.

Forget about what everyone else is doing. Forget about whether your production "sounds" as good as someone else's. Songs become hits. Productions don't.

Forget about whether you're using the microphone that everyone online seems to use. Forget about whether you're using a famous model of compressor that you've never even heard in its analog form. Forget about whether you're using your tools the way a "pro" would. Forget about *sound*.

Nobody will ever know what you did or what tools you've used to implement your sonic artistic decisions. They won't know if you used dither or whether you recorded at 96kHz or used a linear phase EQ. They won't know if you made technical mistakes. And the only people who might criticize you for those things are other record-makers—often with less experience than you. In fact, I'd advise you *never* seek opinions from other similarly positioned music makers. They're too biased, and they listen for all the wrong things.

All that matters is you make music that moves people—that causes them to react. Fans will have no idea why they like your song, but I can guarantee it will have nothing to do with the sound of it. 2% of the market cares about sound. This is why there has never been a successful Surround system for music. Not even Atmos will become mainstream in music, no matter how much Apple tries to muscle the market.

How successful you are at causing a reaction to your music comes down to your decisions, which is why I see them as Modules. The more intent you put behind those decisions, the happier you'll be with your results.

There is no sonic or musical decision that you can make that hasn't been made before. It's how you combine and balance your Decision Modules that creates a new and unique work.

If you listen to 10 random songs from different genres, they will all sound completely different from each other. Some will be bright. Others will be dark. Some will be sparse. Others dense. Some will sound programmed, others organic. So, don't get bogged down on conforming to some phantom sonic gold standard. The conformity is already built in to the process of making music. Focus on what makes you and your music unique, and capitalize on that.

Enjoy, Mixerman

I need your review!

If you purchased your book from Amazon I would ask you kindly to leave a review there as a verified buyer. User generated reviews bring visibility to my book on Amazon, which is critical to its success.

If you purchased the book elsewhere, please leave me a review at that marketplace.

It doesn't have to be a long review. In fact, you can just rate it if you like. Or you can describe how you feel about the book in just a word or two or three. But whatever you do—please review.

Finding Mixerman

I still primarily work as a mixer and producer, and accept projects from independent artists all over the world. If you would like to inquire with me about my record-making services, you can reach me at mixerman@mixerman.net. Or you can go to my website, https://mixerman.net and send me a note through my contact portal. While you're there, check out my blog entries, and be sure to join my email list.

Visit me on the net:

Blog:	*mixerman.net/blogcast*
Mailing list:	*mixerman.net*
Facebook:	*facebook.com/mixerman*
YouTube:	*@MixermanPublishes*
Instagram:	*_mixerman_*

www.ingramcontent.com/pod-product-compliance
Lightning Source LLC
Chambersburg PA
CBHW022041020426
42335CB00012B/494